NEGOTIATING STATE AND NON-STATE LAW

The Challenge of Global and Local Legal Pluralism

Trends in legal philosophy, international law, transnational law, law and religion, and political science all point toward the increasing role played by non-state law in both public and private ordering. Numerous organizations, institutions, associations, and groups have emerged alongside the nation-state, each purporting to provide its members with rules and norms to govern their conduct and organize their affairs. The nation-state increasingly finds itself sandwiched, so to speak, between two broad and contrasting categories of non-state law. The first category – law above the state – captures a wide range of legal systems that function across the territorial borders of nation-states. The second category – law below the state – includes various forms of local customary, religious, and indigenous law. Indeed, as these forms of non-state law persist and proliferate alongside the nation-state, the relationship between state and non-state law becomes more complex, multifaceted, and tense. This volume addresses this relationship between the nation-state and these various forms of non-state law, considering whether and to what extent state and non-state law can coexist and how each form of law seeks to influence, as well as transform, the other.

Michael A. Helfand is an associate professor at the Pepperdine University School of Law, as well as the associate director of the Diane and Guilford Glazer Institute for Jewish Studies. Helfand is an expert on religious law and religious liberty, focusing on how U.S. law treats religious law, custom, and practice. A frequent author and lecturer, he has published in numerous law journals, including the *Yale Law Journal*, the *New York University Law Review*, and the *Duke Law Journal*, as well as in various public audience publications, including the *Los Angeles Times* and the *National Law Journal*. He received his J.D. from Yale Law School in 2007 and his Ph.D. from Yale University in 2009.

The purpose of the American Society of International Law (ASIL) Studies in International Legal Theory series is to clarify and improve the theoretical foundations of international law. Too often the progressive development and implementation of international law have foundered on confusion about first principles. This series raises the level of public and scholarly discussion about the structure and purposes of the world legal order and how best to achieve global justice through law.

This series grows out of the International Legal Theory project of the ASIL. The ASIL Studies in International Legal Theory series deepens this conversation by publishing scholarly monographs and edited volumes of essays considering subjects in international legal theory.

Volumes in the Series

Negotiating State and Non-State Law

THE CHALLENGE OF GLOBAL AND LOCAL LEGAL PLURALISM

Edited by

MICHAEL A. HELFAND

Pepperdine University School of Law

CAMBRIDGE
UNIVERSITY PRESS

32 Avenue of the Americas, New York, NY 10013-2473, USA

Cambridge University Press is part of the University of Cambridge.

It furthers the University's mission by disseminating knowledge in the pursuit of education, learning, and research at the highest international levels of excellence.

www.cambridge.org
Information on this title: www.cambridge.org/9781107083769

© Cambridge University Press 2015

First published 2015

A catalog record for this publication is available from the British Library.

Library of Congress Cataloging in Publication Data
Negotiating state and non-state law : the challenge of global and local
legal pluralism / Michael Helfand, Pepperdine University School of Law.
   pages cm. – (ASIL studies in international legal theory)
Includes bibliographical references and index.
1. Legal polycentricity.   2. Customary law.   3. Religious law and legislation.
I. Helfand, Michael A., 1979– editor.
K236.N44   2015
340.9–dc23   2014037993

ISBN 978-1-107-08376-9 Hardback

Contents

List of Contributors

Aqeel Al-Dahhan is an Assistant Professor of Law at the University of Basra College of Law.

Wasfi H. Al-Sharaa is an Assistant Professor of Law at the University of Basra College of Law.

Haider Ala Hamoudi is an Associate Professor of Law at the University of Pittsburgh School of Law.

Daphne Barak-Erez is a Justice of the Supreme Court of Israel and was formerly Professor of Law at Tel Aviv University, Israel.

Paul Schiff Berman is the Vice Provost for Online Education and Academic Innovation and Manatt/Ahn Professor of Law at the George Washington University.

Harlan Grant Cohen is an Associate Professor of Law at the University of Georgia School of Law.

Michael A. Helfand is an Associate Professor of Law at Pepperdine University School of Law and Associate Director of the Diane and Guilford Glazer Institute for Jewish Studies at Pepperdine University.

Sally Engle Merry is the Silver Professor of Anthropology at New York University.

Ralf Michaels is the Arthur Larson Professor of Law at Duke University School of Law.

Joel A. Nichols is the Associate Dean for Academic Affairs and Professor of Law at the University of St. Thomas School of Law (Minnesota) and Senior Fellow at the Emory University Center for the Study of Law and Religion.

Oren Perez is a Professor of Law at Bar-Ilan University, Israel.

Helen Quane is an Associate Professor at the College of Law, Swansea University, United Kingdom.

Nomi Maya Stolzenberg is the Nathan and Lilly Shapell Chair in Law at the USC Gould School of Law.

Peer Zumbansen is the Professor of Transnational Law at the Dickson Poon School of Law, King's College London, and Director of the Dickson Poon Transnational Law Institute.

Introduction

Michael A. Helfand

"Law is everywhere."[1] Law governs all facets of the human condition, providing rules and principles that are intended to coordinate all spheres of human interaction. Although we typically associate law with the law of the nation-state, the growing recognition of law's ubiquity has led to an explosion of interest in a vast range of legal systems outside the nation-state. Thus, we have seen in recent years increasing interest in various forms of *non-state* law – from transnational law to international law and from religious law to indigenous law. In each of these areas, scholars have studied the internal workings of these legal systems, demonstrating how they at times coexist and at other times conflict with the law of the nation-state.

To be sure, scholarly focus on this dynamic is not new; it has long been at the core of academic interest in *legal pluralism* – a term whose meaning has itself been contested – but covers a wide range of scholarship that identifies, explores, and interrogates the relationship between overlapping legal systems.[2] Over the years, scholars have approached legal pluralism from a variety of vantage points. Starting in the 1970s, anthropologists explored the topic as part of their research into legal systems in colonial and postcolonial

---

[1] *See, e.g.*, Aharon Barak, The Judge in a Democracy 179, 309 (2006); Owen Fiss, *Law is Everywhere*, 117 Yale L.J. 257 (2007); Werner Menski, *Indian Secular Pluralism and Its Relevance for Europe*, *in* Legal Practice and Cultural Diversity 46 (Ralph Grillo et al eds., 2009).

[2] Sally Engle Merry, *Legal Pluralism*, 22 L. & Soc'y Rev. 869, 879 (1988) ("Legal pluralism not only posits the existence of multiple legal spheres, but develops hypotheses concerning the relationship between them."); Oren Perez, *Legal Pluralism*, *in* The Oxford Encyclopedia of American Political and Legal History (Donald T. Critchlow & Philip R. VanderMeer eds., 2013). For some helpful discussions of the evolution of legal pluralism, see also Paul Schiff Berman, *The New Legal Pluralism*, 5 Ann. Rev. L. Soc. Sci. 226 (2009); Brian Z. Tamanaha, *Understanding Legal Pluralism: Past to Present, Local to Global*, 30 Sydney L. Rev. 375, 375 (2008); Ralf Michaels, *Global Legal Pluralism*, 5 Ann. Rev. L. Soc. Sci. 243 (2009).

societies.[3] In the 1980s, scholars began drawing on the concept of legal pluralism to consider overlapping legal systems in noncolonized societies as part of an effort to "reconceptualiz[e] the law/society relation."[4] In recent years, there has been renewed scholarly interest in legal pluralism as a framework for evaluating the rapid trend of globalization, especially with respect to developments in transnational and international law.[5] But notwithstanding these divergent approaches and objectives, legal pluralists generally embrace two core commitments: first, that law is not solely the province of the nation-state,[6] and second, that legal systems frequently overlap such that two or more legal systems coexist in the same social field.[7]

However, even with the perceived success of the legal pluralist agenda, problems still remain. Most formidably, the so-called ubiquity of law raises a fundamental problem: What do mean by "law"?[8] Does finding law in everything undermine our ability to speak of law as an intelligible category?

Now, the "what is law" question is a philosophical Mount Everest of sorts – trying to provide an answer is remarkably treacherous with few claiming to have succeeded. And yet, even with persisting philosophical debates over the definition of law, scholarly consensus has continued to coalesce around the central tenets of legal pluralism. Thus, even as scholars disagree over some applications of the term "law," one would be hard pressed to find many scholars still claiming that the nation-state is the exclusive source of law.[9] Such a

---

[3] *See, e.g.*, LEOPOLD POSPISIL, THE ANTHROPOLOGY OF LAW: A COMPARATIVE THEORY (1971).

[4] Sally Engle Merry, *Legal Pluralism*, 22 L. & SOC'Y REV. 869, 869 (1988); *see also* Gunther Teubner, *The Two Faces of Janus: Rethinking Legal Pluralism*, 12 CARDOZO L. REV. 1443 (1992); Boaventura de Sousa Santos, *Law: A Map of Misreading: Towards a Postmodern Conception of Law*, 14 J.L. & SOC'Y 279 (1987).

[5] *See generally* PAUL SCHIFF BERMAN, GLOBAL LEGAL PLURALISM: A JURISPRUDENCE OF LAW BEYOND BORDERS (2012); *see also* sources cited *infra* note 23.

[6] *See, e.g.*, Marc Galanter, *Justice in Many Rooms: Courts, Private Orderings, and Indigenous Law*, 19 J. LEGAL PLURALISM & UNOFFICIAL L. 1 (1981).

[7] *See, e.g.*, John Griffiths, *What is Legal Pluralism?*, 24 J. LEGAL PLURALISM 1, 2 (1986) (describing legal pluralism as a "state of affairs, for any social field, in which behavior pursuant to more than one legal orders occurs"); *see also* Sally Falk Moore, *Law and Social Change: The Semi-Autonomous Social Field as an Appropriate Subject of Study*, 7 L. & SOC' REV. 719 (1978).

[8] A number of scholars have noted this fundamental question at the heart of the legal pluralism project. *See, e.g.*, Brian Z. Tamanaha, *A Non-Essentialist Version of Legal Pluralism*, 27 J.L. & SOC'Y 296 (2000); Sally Engle Merry, *Legal Pluralism*, 22 L. & SOC'Y REV. 869, 878 (1988); Gunther Teubner, *Global Bukowina: Legal Pluralism in the World Society*, in GLOBAL LAW WITHOUT A STATE 3, 14–15 (Gunther Teubner ed., 1997); Marc Galanter, *Justice in Many Rooms: Courts, Private Ordering, and Indigenous Law*, 19 J. LEGAL PLURALISM 1, 18 (1981).

[9] In an important series of articles, Ralf Michaels has highlighted that notwithstanding the growing enthusiasm for legal pluralism, the concept continues to entrench the importance of the nation-state to our concept of legality – a dynamic that he argues will continue until legal pluralism finds a way to move "beyond the state." *See* Ralf Michaels, *The Re-State-Ment of Non-State Law: The State, Choice of Law, and the Challenge from Global Legal Pluralism*,

claim – popular among philosophers of past generations[10] – has retained limited resonance within current discourse. And once the nation-state is no longer understood as the exclusive source of law, the existence of multiple legal systems follows.[11] Indeed, with multiple legal systems inhabiting our world, the possibility of coexisting legal systems looms large. In fact, the increasing acceptance of the two core commitments has led some to comment that "we are all legal pluralists."[12]

Of course, the fact that scholarly consensus has – to varying degrees – embraced legal pluralism does not mean that everybody is happy about it. Since 2010, over half the state legislatures in the United States have considered so-called "anti-foreign law" bills – which generally prohibit state courts from considering religious, foreign, and international law in their decisions – with nearly 20 percent of states actually passing such bills in one form or another.[13]

---

51 WAYNE L. REV. 1209 (2005); Ralf Michaels, *The Mirage of Non-State Governance*, 2010 UTAH L. REV. 31; Ralf Michaels, *Global Legal Pluralism*, 5 ANN. REV. L. SOC. SCI. 243 (2009).

10 *See, e.g.*, THOMAS HOBBES, LEVIATHAN 186 (C. B. MacPherson ed., 1968); JOHN AUSTIN, THE PROVINCE OF JURISPRUDENCE DETERMINED (Wilfred E. Rumble ed. 1995).

11 I use the term "legal system" here in the non-technical sense. For my discussion of the distinction between law and legal system, see Chapter 10.

12 *See, e.g.*, Harm Schepel, *Rules of Recognition: A Legal Constructivist Approach to Transnational Private Regulation, in* REGULATORY HYBRIDIZATION IN THE TRANSNATIONAL SPHERE 198 (Poul F. Kjaer, Paulius Jurčys & Ren Yatsunami eds., 2013).

13 These states include Arizona (ARIZ. REV. STAT. ANN. §§ 12-3102 to -3103 (West, Westlaw through Apr. 20, 2014, legislation) (applying only to individuals, not businesses)); Florida (2014 FLA. LAWS ch. 2014-10, *available at* http://laws.flrules.org/2014/10); Kansas (KAN. STAT. ANN. §§ 60-5101 to -5108 (West, Westlaw through July 1, 2014, legislation) (not applicable to any contract in which a business agrees to subject itself to foreign law)); Louisiana (LA. REV. STAT. ANN. § 9:6001 (West, Westlaw through 2013 Legis. Sess.)); North Carolina (N.C. GEN. STAT. ANN. §§ 1-87.12 to -87.20 (West, Westlaw through 2013 Legis. Sess.) (restricting application of such law in family law matters and providing guidance when contracts specify choice of foreign law)); Oklahoma (OKLA. STAT. ANN. tit. 12, § 20 (West, Westlaw through 2d Reg. Sess. of 54th Legis. (2014)) (not applicable to any contract in which a business binds itself)); South Dakota (S.D. CODIFIED LAWS § 19-8-7 (West, Westlaw through 2013 Legis. Sess.) (providing "No court, administrative agency, or other governmental agency may enforce any provisions of any religious code.")); Tennessee (TENN. CODE ANN. §§ 20-15-101 to -106 (West, Westlaw through Apr. 8, 2014, legislation) (applying only to individuals, not businesses)); and Washington (WASH. REV. CODE ANN. § 2.28.165 (West, Westlaw through June 12, 2014, legislation) (restricting the use of foreign laws in therapeutic and specialty courts)). Most recently, Alabama Constitutional Amendments, proposed by Act 2013-269, appeared on the Nov. 4, 2014, ballot and was passed by the Alabama voters. Ballot Statement for Statewide Amendment 1, ALABAMA LEGISLATURE, *available at* http://www.legislature.state.al.us/statewide_ballot_measures/BALLOT_STATEMENT_FOR_STATEWIDE_AMENDMENT_1.pdf, and *Alabama 2014 General Election: Results for Statewide, Congressional, Legislative Races*, ASSOCIATED PRESS, last updated Nov. 5, 2014, 12:45 PM, *available at* http://www.al.com/news/index.ssf/2014/11/alabama_2014_election_results.html (identifying that State Amendment 1 – Foreign Laws – Ballot Issue passed with 72 percent of the vote). Accordingly, the Amendment will be added to the Alabama Constitution. Greg Garrison, *Amendment Banning "Foreign Law" in Alabama Courts Passes; Will*

Much of the support for these bills stems from a fear of Islamic law, leading these proposed bills to be dubbed "anti-Sharia" bills.[14]

But beyond the fear of Islamic law, these bills also prohibit courts from considering all forms of non-state law, indicating a general rejection of any law that is not U.S. law.[15] In so doing, the widespread consideration – and growing embrace – of these bills represents heightened skepticism of non-state law in the United States. Indeed, this desire to avoid foreign law may already have filtered into the U.S. judicial system. According to recent articles by Donald Childress and Christopher Whytock, federal district courts in the United States dismiss transnational forum non conveniens cases approximately 50 percent of the time;[16] and this number rose to 63 percent when a foreign plaintiff was involved.[17] As Childress notes, these staggering numbers may very well indicate that federal district court judges are "dismissing suits on forum non conveniens grounds to avoid cases involving the application of foreign law."[18]

But such desperate attempts to protect the law of the nations-state – and reject other "foreign" legal systems – only further highlight the fact that "legal pluralism is everywhere,"[19] and that our experience of legality is undeniably multifaceted and multifarious, overlapping and conflicting. Thus, in the words of Brian Tamanaha, "There is, in every social arena one examines, a seeming

Be Added to Alabama Constitution (last updated Nov. 4, 2014, 11:40 PM), *available at* http://www.al.com/news/index.ssf/2014/11/amendment_banning_foreign_law.html.

 See generally Kimberly Railey, *More States Move to Ban Foreign Law in Courts*, USA TODAY, Aug. 4, 2013, *available at* http://www.usatoday.com/story/news/nation/2013/08/04/states-ban-foreign-law/2602511/; FAIZA PATEL, MATTHEW DUSS & AMOS TOH, BRENNAN CTR. FOR JUSTICE, *Foreign Law Bans: Legal Uncertainties and Practical Problems* (May 2013), *available at* http://www.brennancenter.org/sites/default/files/publications/ForeignLawBans.pdf; *see also* Bill Cotterell, *Florida Legislature Forbids Use of Foreign Law in State Court*, REUTERS, Apr. 30, 2014, *available at* http://www.reuters.com/article/2014/04/30/us-usa-florida-sharialaw-idUSBREA3T14H20140430.

[14] *See generally* Asma Uddin & Dave Pantzer, *A First Amendment Analysis of Anti-Sharia Initiatives*, 10 FIRST AMEND. L. REV. 363 (2012).

[15] *See* MARTHA F. DAVIS & JOHANNA KALB, AM. CONST. SOC'Y FOR L. & POL'Y, OKLAHOMA STATE QUESTION 755 AND AN ANALYSIS OF ANTI-INTERNATIONAL LAW INITIATIVES 4, *available at* http://www.acslaw.org/sites/default/files/davis_and_kalb_anti-international_law.pdf (noting that "[s]ome commentators couch their objections to courts' consideration of international or foreign material in the language of sovereignty.").

[16] Christopher A. Whytock, Politics and the Rule of Law in Transnational Judicial Governance: The Case of Forum Non Conveniens 15 (Feb. 28, 2007) (unpublished manuscript), *available at* http://papers.ssrn.com/sol3/papers.cfm?abstract_id=969033.

[17] Donald Earl Childress, III, *Rethinking Legal Globalization: The Case of Transnational Personal Jurisdiction*, 54 WM. & MARY L. REV. 1489, 1536–37 (2013).

[18] Donald Earl Childress, III, *When Erie Goes International*, 105 NW. U. L. REV. 1531, 1562 (2011); *see also* Christopher A. Whytock, *Myth of Mess? International Choice of Law in Action*, 84 N.Y.U. L. REV. 719, 721 (2009) (arguing that there exist "strong biases favoring domestic over foreign law").

[19] Brian Z. Tamanaha, *Understanding Legal Pluralism: Past to Present, Local to Global*, 30 SYDNEY L. REV. 375, 375 (2008).

multiplicity of legal orders, from the lowest local level to the most expansive global level."[20] And, as expressed by Paul Schiff Berman, the existence of these plural legal orders stems from the fact that "[w]e live in a world of multiple, overlapping normative communities"[21] and "[l]aw is constantly constructed through the contest of these various norm-generating communities."[22]

If the core insights of legal pluralism accurately describe the social spheres we inhabit, then the nation-state can no longer be seen as the sole provider of law. Instead, non-state law continues to emerge alongside the state, further contributing to our pluralistic experience of legality. Although the totality of non-state law often defies description, it can be subdivided into two broad categories: law above the state and law below the state.

The first category – law above the state – captures a wide range of legal systems that function across the territorial borders of nation-state. These include a various international and transnational legal institutions, including examples such as the European Court of Human Rights, human rights nongovernmental organizations, transnational regulatory institutions, and the International Centre for Settlement of Investment Disputes, just to name a few.[23]

The second category – law below the state – includes various forms of local customary, religious, and indigenous law,[24] including religious arbitration tribunals,[25] tightly knitted trade associations,[26] tribal courts,[27] and

---

[20] *Id.*

[21] Paul Schiff Berman, *The New Legal Pluralism*, 5 Ann. Rev. L. Soc. Sci. 226 (2009).

[22] Paul Schiff Berman, *Global Legal Pluralism*, 80 S. Cal. L. Rev. 1156, 1157–58 (2007).

[23] *See, e.g.*, William Twining, *Normative and Legal Pluralism: A Global Perspective*, 20 Duke J. Comp. & Int'l L. 473 (2010); Berman, *Global Legal Pluralism*, *supra* note 22, at 1157–58 (2007); Peer Zumbansen, *Transnational Legal Pluralism*, 1 Transnat'l Legal Theory 141 (2010); Roger Cotterrell, *Transnational Communities and the Concept of Law*, 21 Ratio Juris 1 (2008); Oren Perez, *Normative Creativity and Global Legal Pluralism: Reflections on the Democratic Critique of Transnational Law*, 10 Ind. J. Global Legal Stud. 25 (2003); Gunther Teubner, *Global Bukowina: Legal Pluralism in the World Society*, *in* Global Law Without a State 3, 14–15 (Gunther Teubner ed., 1997).

[24] *See, e.g.*, Gypsy Law: Romani Legal Traditions and Culture (Walter O. Weyrauch ed., 2001); Nomi Maya Stolzenberg & David N. Myers, *Community, Constitution and Culture: The Case of the Jewish Kehilah*, 25 U. Mich. J.L. Reform 633 (1992).

[25] Michael A. Helfand, *Religious Arbitration and the New Multiculturalism: Negotiating Conflicting Legal Orders*, 86 N.Y.U. L. Rev. 1231 (2011); Adam S. Hofri-Winogradow, *A Plurality of Discontent: Legal Pluralism, Religious Adjudication and the State*, 26 J.L. & Religion 101 (2010).

[26] Lisa Bernstein, *Opting Out of the Legal System: Extralegal Contractual Relations in the Diamond Industry*, 21 J. Legal Stud. 115 (1992); Barak D. Richman, *How Community Institutions Create Economic Advantage: Jewish Diamond Merchants in New York*, 31 L. & Soc. Inquiry 383 (2006).

[27] *See, e.g.*, Karl N. Llewellyn & E. Adamson Hoebel, The Cheyenne Way: Conflict and Case Law in Primitive Jurisprudence (1941).

neighborhood-dispute resolution norms.[28] These institutions generally function as local pockets of legality, providing and enforcing their own system of rules within the borders of the nation-state.

Accordingly, as the multiplicity of legal systems continues to proliferate, the nation-state finds itself sandwiched, so to speak, between two broad categories of non-state law. And although the dynamics among these three levels of law differ in important ways, many of the questions about this increasingly plural legal space converge. It is to this series of questions to which this volume is dedicated:

(1) To what extent can state and non-state law peacefully coexist?
(2) What is the nature of the relationship between state and non-state law?
(3) To what extent do these relationships lead to the transformation and development of both state and non-state law?
(4) Through what mechanisms do state and non-state law seek to influence each other's development?

To explore these and related questions, the present volume is divided into three sections.

PART I: NEGOTIATING STATE AND NON-STATE LAW: THE LEGAL PLURALIST PROJECT

The first section considers some of the fundamental questions for the legal pluralist project and explores shared themes of global and local legal pluralism. First, Paul Schiff Berman considers the relationship between his own vision of global legal pluralism and liberalism, arguing that legal pluralism is neither irreconcilable with nor reducible to liberalism. Berman argues that liberalism too often focuses on only non-state law when it comes into conflict with state law, limiting the purview of its inquiry to whether and to what extent the state should tolerate non-state law. Adopting the perspective of liberalism – that is, focusing on non-state law through only the prism of state law – neglects the potential for procedural and institutional innovation that can enhance the relationship between state and non-state law. Thus, concludes Berman, the project of global legal pluralism is to identify and

---

[28] Robert C. Ellickson, *Of Coase and Cattle: Dispute Resolution Among Neighbors in Shasta County*, 38 STAN. L. REV. 623 (1986).

capitalize on opportunities to improve the relationship between state and non-state law by recognizing that a legal pluralist framework provides both a superior lens for understanding the plural nature of law and by improving our ability to navigate the complex interactions between overlapping legal communities.

Second, Ralf Michaels uses the recent decision of a district court in Cologne, Germany – which ruled that circumcision of male children constitutes an illegal bodily injury – as a frame to interrogate how we should define the category of "non-state law." In searching for a definition of non-state law, Michaels discusses and critiques attempts in legal philosophy, legal anthropology, and systems theory, to find a definition for non-state law that is both universally applicable and nonhegemonial. Michaels' own proposal, using an analogy to private international law, includes a twofold structure for the definition of law. First, each system determines for itself whether it regards its norms as legal norms. Second, although this self-determination provides an opportunity for autonomous definition, it does not bind other legal systems as each state retains the right to recognize – or not recognize – other systems as legal systems. Such an account of non-state law incorporates the empiricism of legal anthropology – each system defines for itself whether it is, in fact, a legal system – but at the same time each legal system retains the opportunity to impose its own rule of recognition that differentiates between what it deems law and what it deems non-law. In this way, Michaels aims to decentralize the concept of a legal system, rejecting the possibility of providing a uniform definition of the term.

Third, Sally Engle Merry presents her vision of spatial legal pluralism, which – by building on global legal pluralism among other models – seeks to contextualize the nation-state within the global and local legal regimes that exist both above and below the nation-state. Doing so provides a thicker account of law's pluralism, identifying how questions of law are intimately connected to questions of space and place. In turn, a focus on the spatial dimensions of law breaks down the sense of law's uniformity and contiguity, highlighting how other factors can sometimes circumscribe legal systems and at other times expand legal systems in ways that cut across physical borders.

Together, the three chapters in this section provide a broader frame for the subsequent chapters that consider the relationship between the nation-state and non-state law both above the state as well as below the state. In so doing, they consider new approaches to what we mean by non-state law, how non-state law interacts with the liberal nation-state, and the various spaces in which these interactions occur.

PART II: NEGOTIATING STATE LAW AND INTERNATIONAL/TRANSNATIONAL LAW

The second section of this volume considers these questions of legal pluralism and non-state law in the context of international and transnational law – that is, law above the nation-state.

Peer Zumbansen explores the perceived legitimacy deficit of transnational private regulatory governance and its impact on the definition and purpose of law in an increasingly interconnected world. For Zumbansen, the growth of transnational governance requires that we shift our concept of law away from something inextricably linked to the nation-state and toward a more process-based understanding of law. This shift has enormous consequences for the way in which a political critique of the stakes in regulatory governance must now occur; without the backdrop of states and established ways – both institutionally and normatively – of identifying "right" and "left" positions, we need to develop a more bottom-up, learning approach to understand the workings of "transnational law in context." Thus, Zumbansen encourages us to embrace a methodological transnationalism where we refocus our attention on the actors, norms, and processes that typify law and use those categories to discern the evolving role of law for the emerging system of transnational private governance.

Oren Perez and Daphne Barak-Erez also contend with the perceived legitimacy deficit in transnational law, focusing specifically on these challenges in the context of global administrative law. As they note, various international agencies have growing and multifaceted influence over the domestic regulatory process on a wide range of issues, including trade, financial regulation, public health, and the environment. Perez and Barak-Erez identify significant problems with this transnational administrative scheme: It is often driven by a capitalist ethos that does not sufficiently account for other important values; it creates confusion when it comes to accountability by exposing domestic decision makers to competing sets of expectations and norms; and it creates a lack of democratic justification for many administrative regimes. In response to these concerns, Perez and Barak-Erez argue that global and domestic regulatory institutions must create new mechanisms that promote joint deliberation and consultation in the production and enforcement of norms within the growing transnational regulatory networks. Such an approach steers a middle course between two alternative extremes – sovereign exceptionalism and global constitutionalism – by focusing on the potential for democratic innovativeness at the micro level of administrative praxis. In turn, such innovation holds out the hope of making the emerging global administrative framework more democratic, accountable, and pluralistic.

Next, Helen Quane analyzes the relationship between international law and the nation-state, arguing that the nation-state can serve as the medium through which international law can both promote as well as reform various forms of non-state law within the nation-state's borders. By imposing requirements on nation-states, international law has the potential for a twofold impact on various forms of non-state law within religious and indigenous communities: International law can exert considerable influence on the nation-state's recognition of religious and indigenous law; international law can also influence the development of religious and indigenous law by requiring the nation-state, for example, assist in the elimination of discrimination against women. Accordingly, not only does non-state law impact the law of the nation-state, but the various forms of non-state law are themselves also in a conversation, with the nation-state serving as a go-between – a dynamic that holds out the potential to promote reform.

This section concludes with Harlan Cohen's exploration of precedent's surprisingly central role in international law notwithstanding the fact that, in principle, international law precedents are supposed to lack any doctrinal force. To explain this puzzle, Cohen argues that law is primarily a "practice" – thus, we need to think less about the way in which states "make" international law and more about how the community of legal practitioners actually "do" law. By focusing on the community of legal practitioners, as opposed to the nation-state, Cohen suggests that we can better account for the resilience of precedent in international law. This resilience is of particular importance given some of the conventional reasons why nation-states have resisted the doctrinal relevance of precedent; limiting the legal impact of precedent ensured that the nation-state did not cede total authority over legal meaning, leaving room to challenge the decision of an international body in subsequent cases. In this way, tying precedent to a community of practitioners provides insight into how the practice of international law has dislodged, to some extent, the centrality of the nation-state.

In sum, these four chapters highlight the relationship between the nation-state and non-state law above the nation-state. In a number of ways, the migration of law away from the nation-state and toward both international and transnational law has posed some significant challenges. It has raised worries about the legitimacy of law above the nation-state, leaving the nation-state to reconsider its place within this global legal environment. And yet at the same time state and non-state law can also work together to solve key challenges, providing opportunities to improve the relationship between the nation-state and communities that live within its borders.

PART III: NEGOTIATING STATE LAW AND RELIGIOUS/INDIGENOUS LAW

The final section of this volume explores similar themes in the context of the relationship between the nation-state and both religious and indigenous law – that is, non-state law below the nation-state. It begins with Joel Nichols's prognosis of current tensions between religious law and state law over marriage and divorce. When it comes to these issues in the United States, religious laws and values have become increasingly marginalized; examples include the waning influence of conservative Protestant Christians, as evidenced by the recent same-sex marriage trends, as well as the spread of anti-Sharia laws in the United States, which have wrongly and unnecessarily stigmatized Islamic law. In this context, Nichols considers the role religious law can play when it comes to family, dismissing arguments that either have the state leaving marriage and divorce exclusively to religion or having the state embrace a particular religious worldview when it comes to family law questions. Instead, Nichols argues that the state should grant more – albeit not unlimited – solicitude to the private contractual choices made by couples, enabling them to incorporate religious law into their family arrangements via prenuptial or arbitration agreements. Although the state might instinctively resist such incursions into its authority, Nichols contends that enforcing the private choices of religious couples can provide the state with increasing opportunities to influence religious law and protect vulnerable parties in the family law context.

In the next chapter, Haider Ala Hamoudi, Wasfi H. Al-Sharaa, and Aqeel Al-Dahhan present a model of cooperative legal pluralism through a case study of the current relationship between Shi'i tribes and the Iraqi judicial system as well as Iraqi law enforcement. Hamoudi, Al-Sharaa, and Al-Dahhan contrast this model with what they note is the dominant narrative in the legal pluralist literature – one of legal competition and conflict. While still retaining some of those themes, Hamoudi, Al-Sharaa, and Al-Dahhan highlight ways in which Shi'i tribes and Iraqi law enforcement show restraint in resolving conflicts, working toward optimal outcomes instead of seeking to exercise maximum influence. Thus, in detailing various forms of power sharing in this context, Hamoudi, Al-Sharaa, and Al-Dahhan outline an alternative cooperative pluralist paradigm, identifying in the process both the benefits of and challenges for such a framework.

Finally, my own contribution to this volume considers the recent wave of anti-Sharia and anti-international law initiatives in the United States within the context of a larger philosophical debate over the relationship between law and sovereignty. In so doing, it unpacks an often-unrecognized distinction in the work of H.L.A. Hart – the distinction between law and legal system – to better diagnose the points of conflict and contestation between state and non-state law. In particular, I highlight how many forms of religious law lack what Hart termed "secondary rules" – rules of recognition, change, and adjudication – rendering them, to again use Hart's distinction, mere "law" as opposed to a coordinated "legal system." And because the law of some religious communities lack the secondary rules to coordinate their judicial efforts, such communities often face significant obstacles when trying to effectively navigate conflicts between their own law and the law of the nation-state. Therefore, this dynamic can at times leave the nation-state in a better position to negotiate these conflicts; and given this advantage, I argue that instead of adopting laws that attempt to expel religious law from its judicial system, the nation-state would be better served leveraging its position by developing methods to promote coordination between state and non-state law to address the unique dilemmas experienced by individuals who understand themselves as subject to the demands of multiple forms of law.

In total, the chapters in this section focus on the unique relationship between state law and non-state law below the nation-state. In so doing, they address the theme of coordination between state and non-state law, identifying the importance of – and opportunities for – a more collaborative framework for mediating the interactions among the law of the nation-state and communities that follow various form of religious and indigenous law.

✻ ✻ ✻ ✻

The goal of this volume is not only to consider some of the larger questions for the legal pluralist framework, but also to consider the concrete implications of this framework in terms of law above the nation-state, such as international and transnational law, as well as in terms of law below the nation-state – such as religious and indigenous law. Pulling together these concrete applications of the pluralist framework can help identify the contours of the relationship between state and non-state law, highlighting the mechanisms for mutual influence, change, and cooperation. Indeed, as this relationship continues to evolve globally and locally, the lessons we learn from the local challenges of legal pluralism might very well help inform future decisions from the global challenges and vice versa. It is to this task that we now turn.

PART I

Negotiating State and Non-State Law: The Legal Pluralist Project

1

Non-State Lawmaking through the Lens of Global Legal Pluralism

*Paul Schiff Berman**

If you are interested in non-state lawmaking, you are, almost by definition, drawn to legal pluralism (and its more recent variant, *global* legal pluralism) as an interpretive lens. This is because while liberal legal theorists generally presume that state-based law wipes out all competing normative systems, pluralists challenge the centrality of the state. Whether considering canon law, indigenous law, or the law of ethnic groups, pluralists have long refused to accept that the state is the only relevant actor on the stage of law. As such, those most interested in charting the influence and power of non-state lawmaking have looked to legal pluralism as a possible solution to the problem of traditional liberal legality's state-centrism. And global legal pluralism adds transnational and international normative assertions into the mix, again challenging the presumed autonomy of state law.

But when considering non-state actors and non-state lawmaking of various forms, what does a pluralist perspective actually add to the classic liberal approach? After all, liberalism is not unalterably opposed to non-state norms, and even those who focus only on the central legal authority of the liberal state think it important that the state sometimes defer to such norms. Indeed, one of the core notions of liberalism is that government should not take sides in debates about competing visions of the good, and therefore space is allowed for non-state normative commitments. So long as a non-state normative community does not infringe unduly on the rights of others, liberalism allows those communities a tremendous amount of freedom and scope. For their part most

* Vice Provost for Online Education and Academic Innovation and Manatt/Ahn Professor of Law, The George Washington University. This chapter draws upon (and includes material derived from) Paul Schiff Berman, GLOBAL LEGAL PLURALISM: A JURISPRUDENCE OF LAW BEYOND BORDERS (2012) and Paul Schiff Berman, *Towards a Jurisprudence of Hybridity*, 2010 UTAH L. REV. 11. Special thanks to Jamie Noonan for excellent research assistance in the final stages of preparation for this chapter.

pluralists do not deny the importance of the state, nor even the fact that the state often has greater coercive power at its disposal and therefore is better able to enforce its norms than non-state entities. After all, recognizing non-state lawmaking as important does not in and of itself mean that all sources of law are equally powerful or influential.

So, on the surface it appears that legal pluralism and legal liberalism effectively merge into one. The merged statement reads something like this: "The state is the most powerful lawmaker; it allows scope for non-state norms when it chooses to, and it often does choose to defer because non-state norms have a strong emotional pull and should be accorded deference as long as those norms don't get out of hand." And if that's all legal pluralism is adding, then the voluminous legal pluralism scholarship does not appear to have altered the basic liberal legal framework very much. This is a view most recently expounded by Dennis Patterson and Alexis Galán in their review[1] of my book, *Global Legal Pluralism: A Jurisprudence of Law Beyond Borders.*[2]

Interestingly, this critique of legal pluralism – that it is not a radical reshaping of the landscape but simply liberalism in another guise – is precisely the opposite of the criticism global legal pluralists usually receive. Typically, the worry is that a pluralist framework will give too *much* space for plural norms. Sovereigntists tend to object to the idea that nation-states should ever take into account international, transnational, or non-state norms. Meanwhile, international law triumphalists chafe at the idea that international norms should ever be subordinated to local practices that may be less liberal or less rights-protecting. But both positions are principally concerned that global legal pluralism will result in too much fragmentation and too much deference to what are viewed as illegitimate norms.

In contrast, Patterson and Galán view legal pluralism (or at least the proceduralist version of legal pluralism I have advocated) as completely consonant with liberalism and therefore essentially conventional and not pluralist enough to provide a true alternative vision. Accordingly, I am in some sense happy to welcome this critique because it offers a response to those who claim pluralism is too extreme and destabilizing. After all, a position cannot easily be

---

[1] Alexis Galán & Dennis Patterson, *The Limits of Normative Legal Pluralism: Review of Paul Schiff Berman, Global Legal Pluralism: A Jurisprudence of Law Beyond Borders*, 11 INT'L J. CONST. L. 783 (2013). For my response to Patterson and Galán, see Paul Schiff Berman, *How Legal Pluralism Is and Is Not Distinct from Liberalism: A Response to Patterson and Galán*, 11 INT'L J. CONST. L. 801 (2013).

[2] PAUL SCHIFF BERMAN, GLOBAL LEGAL PLURALISM: A JURISPRUDENCE OF LAW BEYOND BORDERS (2012).

simultaneously too radical and not radical enough. Thus, I am tempted to simply embrace the criticism, allow for the fact that pluralism is less radical than some imagine, and end the discussion there.

And yet I think there's more to it than that. Although pluralism need not be conceptualized as *inconsistent* with liberalism, it is also not precisely the *same* as liberalism. Accordingly, in this chapter, I hope to suggest that legal pluralism is in fact significantly different from the classic liberal vision in at least two important ways, one descriptive and one normative.

First, as a descriptive matter (and it is important to recognize that legal pluralism was historically a descriptive project) legal pluralists are far more likely than traditional liberals even to *notice* the pluralism of legal and quasi-legal norms that exist apart from the state. A liberal institutionalist will tend to focus on state-based formal entities exclusively and will therefore analyze non-state normative communities only when such communities assert rights in forums created by those state-based entities or when those communities propagate norms that seem to present major conflicts with the state. As a result, the low-level, day-to-day interaction of non-state normative communities will tend to disappear from view. Moreover, when non-state norms do arise, the question is often framed only in terms of how much the state should defer to or tolerate the non-state community, not as a true conflict of normative systems. Thus, the state-centric view will tend to miss much that legal pluralism uncovers and will bias the analytical framework from the start.

Second, as legal pluralism has developed a more normative bite, it has been used to justify procedural mechanisms, institutional designs, and discursive practices aimed at developing habits of mind in decision makers that will encourage those decision makers to use restraint in insisting jurispathically on their own norms to the exclusion of the norms of other communities. Thus, the key normative question from a pluralist perspective is not simply: Here are my norms, now how much should I tolerate others? Instead, this sort of proceduralist pluralism will favor hybrid institutional designs and practices that will embed such principles of toleration and accommodation into day-to-day operations. These designs and practices may well be consonant with liberalism, but, as I will suggest, they result in a very different set of institutional arrangements, inquiries, and jurisprudential tropes.

Thus, in the end, I believe global legal pluralism offers a fundamentally different analytical framework – both descriptively and normatively – from liberalism. And although it may be that a pluralist perspective can fit comfortably within a liberal philosophical stance (that depends on how far the pluralist impulse is pushed in particular cases), I think a pluralist perspective is likely to lead to both a more nuanced descriptive understanding of the world and a more desirable legal and political framework for addressing the hybridity that surrounds us every day.

PLURALISM'S DESCRIPTIVE PROJECT

Pluralism starts with an entirely different set of inquiries from liberalism, and it is therefore not surprising that, purely as a descriptive matter, pluralism would forge a distinctive understanding of the social field of law. After all, liberalism begins fundamentally with the state: how it is formed, how it is justified, and the philosophical underpinnings for its operations. Non-state actors are surely important to this inquiry in that they clash with the liberal state, and of course the state, under liberalism, should often reach positions of accommodation with these non-state actors. But what is being described is fundamentally the state and how *it* views the non-state.

In contrast, pluralism assumes that the inquiry is the entire range of legalities that course through the everyday experience of people on the ground. This means that the lived reality of communities and day-to-day perceptions of legitimacy and efficacy are far more important than philosophical models. Moreover, a pluralist perspective is far more likely to see individuals and groups, rather than just the state, as having agency and therefore playing crucial roles in navigating the interaction of normative systems and using those systems strategically.

For example, in the classic colonial interaction, a quasi-liberal, state-based legality was layered on top of an indigenous legal system. A liberal theorist would focus on the newly imposed system and on how it either accommodated or refused to accommodate local communities. In contrast, pluralists would observe that the colonial system did not wipe out the indigenous system altogether and then focus on the interaction of these legal systems and the ways in which local actors used both systems strategically to gain leverage.

This is only one of many possible examples. But the point is that where liberalism sees only state legal systems and the challenges they face, pluralists will see interactions among legal systems. And *global* legal pluralism insists that a simple model that looks only to territorial delineations among official nation-states is now simply untenable (if it was ever useful to begin with). Thankfully, debates about globalization have moved beyond the polarizing question of whether the nation-state is dying or not. But one does not need to believe in the death of the nation-state to recognize that nation-states must work within a framework of multiple overlapping jurisdictional assertions by state, international, and non-state communities. Each of these types of overlapping jurisdictional assertions creates a potentially hybrid legal space that is not easily eliminated.

With regard to conflicts between and among states, the growth of global communications technologies, the rise of multinational corporate entities with no significant territorial center of gravity, and the mobility of capital and people across borders mean that many jurisdictions will feel effects of activities around the globe, leading inevitably to multiple assertions of legal authority over the same act, without regard to territorial location. Nation-states must also often share legal authority with one or more international and regional courts, tribunals, or regulatory entities. And, of course, non-state legal (or quasi-legal) norms add to the hybridity. Given increased migration and global communication, it is not surprising that people feel ties to, and act on the basis of, affiliations with multiple communities in addition to their territorial ones. Such communities may be ethnic, religious, or epistemic; transnational, subnational, or international; and the norms asserted by such communities frequently challenge state-based authority. Obviously, canon law and other religious community norms have long operated in significant overlap with state law. And in the Middle East and elsewhere, conflicts between a personal law tied to religion and a territorial law tied to the nation-state continue to pose constitutional and other challenges. Bonds of ethnicity can also create significant normative communities. Finally, we see communities of transnational bankers and accountants developing their own regulatory regimes governing trade finance or accounting standards, as well as the use of modern forms of lex mercatoria to govern business relations.

Just as important, pluralists are much less likely to insist on positivist definitions of law and will therefore be willing to see law even in the absence of coercive power. This is especially significant in the global arena where statements of legal norms may be highly effective even in the absence of such formal enforcement power. For example, liberal sovereigntists sometimes insist that international, transnational, and non-state legal norms have no independent valence and that instead states simply pursue their own interests. In contrast, pluralists unpack the idea of a state interest, recognizing that conceptions of proper policy do not simply arise in a vacuum. Rather, they are developed by human beings operating with various sets of assumptions, ideas about justice, conceptions of global strategy, and beliefs about morality. These assumptions, ideas, and cognitive categories are themselves shaped in part by what sociolegal scholars have long termed legal consciousness. Accordingly, the legal norms that are "in the air" at any given moment of history – including international, transnational, and non-state legal norms – may well affect how both policy makers and ordinary citizens think about the state's interests.

Thus, legal pluralism provides a richer account of how law actually operates, both domestically and internationally, than the positivist vision of sovereigntism. We imbibe legal norms and cognitive categories even when we are not consciously aware of the norm in question. We are persuaded by legal norms even when those norms are not literally enforceable. We act in accordance with law because doing so has become habitual, not necessarily because we seek to avoid sanction. We conceive of our interrelations with others in terms of law because our long-term interests require that we do so, even when our short-term interests might seem to counsel otherwise. And the existence of a legal norm alters the constitutive terms of our relationships with others as well as the costs of noncompliance. All of these factors may be overcome in some circumstances. Indeed, people sometimes violate domestic law just as states sometimes violate non-state law. But in neither case does that mean that the law in question has no significant constraining force. And only by thinking more broadly about changes in legal consciousness and the complicated social, political, and psychological factors that enter into the conceptualization of state interests can we begin to understand how non-state law operates.

In addition, instead of treating the state as a unitary "personality" with a single set of interests, pluralists recognize that the real world is far messier, with a vast number of constituencies both within the governmental bureaucracy and outside it. This cacophony of voices is important because many of these voices, when advocating policy positions, can use the moral authority or persuasive power of international, transnational, and non-state norms for leverage. These norms therefore become a tool of empowerment for particular actors. And given that any state policy decision is inevitably the result of a contest among various bureaucratic power centers, all of which are themselves influenced by outside pressure groups, lobbyists, NGOs, and the like, a more complex understanding of the global legal arena would need to explore ways in which plural legal norms empower specific interests both within and without the state policy-making apparatus and provide arguments and leverage that they might not otherwise have had.

For example, although the well-known efforts of Spanish Judge Baltasar Garzón to try former Chilean leader Augusto Pinochet[3] were not literally

---

3 Judge Garzón issued an arrest order based on allegations of kidnappings, torture, and planned disappearances of Chilean citizens and citizens of other countries. Spanish Request to Arrest General Pinochet, Oct. 16, 1998, *reprinted in* THE PINOCHET PAPERS: THE CASE OF AUGUSTO PINOCHET IN SPAIN AND BRITAIN 57, 57–59 (Reed Brody & Michael Ratner eds., 2000) [hereinafter THE PINOCHET PAPERS]. *See also* Anne Swardson, *Pinochet Case Tries Spanish Legal Establishment*, WASH. POST, Oct. 22, 1998, at A27 ("As Chilean president from 1973 to 1990, Garzón's arrest order said, Pinochet was 'the leader of an international organization

"successful" because Pinochet was never extradited to Spain,[4] they strengthened the hands of human rights advocates within Chile itself and provided the impetus for a movement that led to a Chilean Supreme Court decision stripping Pinochet of his lifetime immunity.[5] Likewise, Spanish efforts to prosecute members of the Argentine military bolstered reformers within the Argentine government, most notably then–President Néstor Kirchner. Judge Garzón sought extradition from Argentina of dozens of Argentines for human rights abuses committed under the Argentine military government in the 1970s[6] and successfully extradited from Mexico one former Argentine Navy lieutenant who was accused of murdering hundreds of people.[7] In the wake of Garzón's actions, sovereigntist observers complained that such transnational

created... to conceive, develop and execute the systematic planning of illegal detentions [kidnappings], torture, forced relocations, assassinations and/or disappearances of numerous persons, including Argentines, Spaniards, Britons, Americans, Chileans and other nationalities.'"). On October 30, 1998, the Spanish National Court ruled unanimously that Spanish courts had jurisdiction over the matter based both on the principle of universal jurisdiction (that crimes against humanity can be tried anywhere at any time) and the passive personality principle of jurisdiction (that courts may try cases if their nationals are victims of crime, regardless of where the crime was committed). Order of the Criminal Chamber of the Spanish *Audiencia Nacional* affirming Spain's Jurisdiction, Nov. 5, 1998, *reprinted in* THE PINOCHET PAPERS, *supra* at 95, 95–107. The Office of the Special [the book says the Office of the Public Prosecutor] Prosecutor alleged that Spaniards living in Chile were among those killed under Pinochet's rule. *Id.* at 106.

4 Pinochet was physically in Great Britain. The British House of Lords ultimately ruled that Pinochet was not entitled to head-of-state immunity for acts of torture and could be extradited to Spain. R v. Bow St. Metro. Stipendiary Magistrate, *Ex parte* Pinochet Ugarte (No. 3), [2000] 1 A.C. 147 (H.L.) 204–05 (holding that the International Convention Against Torture, incorporated into United Kingdom law in 1988, prevented Pinochet from claiming head-of-state immunity after 1988, because the universal jurisdiction contemplated by the Convention is inconsistent with immunity for former heads of state). Nevertheless, the British government refused to extradite, citing Pinochet's failing health. *See* Statement of Secretary of State Jack Straw in the House of Commons, Mar. 2, 2000, *in* THE PINOCHET PAPERS, *supra* note 3, at 481, 482 ("[I]n the light of th[e] medical evidence... I... conclude[d] that no purpose would be served by continuing the Spanish extradition request."). Pinochet was eventually returned to Chile.

5 *See Chile's Top Court Strips Pinochet of Immunity*, N.Y. TIMES, Aug. 27, 2004, at A3 ("Chile's Supreme Court stripped the former dictator Augusto Pinochet of immunity from prosecution in a notorious human rights case on Thursday, raising hopes of victims that he may finally face trial for abuses during his 17-year rule.").

6 *See* Larry Rohter, *Argentine Congress Likely to Void "Dirty War" Amnesties*, N.Y. TIMES, Aug. 21, 2003, at A3 (recounting Garzón's extradition request).

7 Emma Daly, *Spanish Judge Sends Argentine to Prison on Genocide Charge*, N.Y. TIMES, June 30, 2003, at A3 ("In an unusual act of international judicial cooperation, and a victory for the Spanish Judge Baltasar Garzón, Mexico's Supreme Court ruled this month that the former officer, Ricardo Miguel Cavallo, could be extradited to Spain for crimes reportedly committed in a third country, Argentina.").

prosecutions were illegitimate because Argentina had previously conferred amnesty on those who had been involved in the period of military rule and therefore any prosecution would infringe on Argentina's sovereign "choice" to grant amnesty.[8]

But the amnesty decision was not simply a unitary choice made by some unified "state" of Argentina; it was a politically contested act that remained controversial within the country.[9] And the Spanish extradition request itself gave President Kirchner more leverage in his tug-of-war with the legal establishment over the amnesty laws. Just a month after Garzón's request, both houses of the Argentine Congress voted by large majorities to annul the laws.[10] Meanwhile the Spanish government decided that it would not make the formal extradition request to Argentina that Garzón sought, but it did so based primarily on the fact that Argentina had begun to scrap its amnesty laws, and the accused would therefore be subject to domestic human rights prosecution.[11] President Kirchner, therefore, could use Spain's announcement to increase pressure on the Argentine Supreme Court to officially overturn the amnesty laws.[12]

Finally, on June 14, 2005, the Argentine Supreme Court did in fact strike down the amnesty laws, thus clearing the way for domestic human rights prosecutions.[13] Not only was the pressure exerted by Spain instrumental in these efforts, but also it is significant that the Argentine Court cited as legal

---

[8] *See* David B. Rivkin, Jr. & Lee A. Casey, *Crimes Outside the World's Jurisdiction*, N.Y. TIMES, July 22, 2003, at A19 (noting that Argentina had granted amnesty to Cavallo and arguing that "Judge Garzón is essentially ignoring Argentina's own history and desires").

[9] The Argentine army, for example, made known its desire for amnesty for human rights abuses through several revolts in the late 1980s. The Argentine Congress granted amnesty after one such uprising in 1987. *See* Joseph B. Treaster, *Argentine President Orders Troops To End Revolt*, N.Y. TIMES, Dec. 4, 1988, § 1, at 3 (describing an army revolt in Buenos Aires).

[10] *Argentina's Day of Reckoning*, CHI. TRIB., Apr. 24, 2004, at C26.

[11] Elizabeth Nash, *Garzón Blocked Over "Dirty War" Extraditions*, THE INDEPENDENT (London), Aug. 30, 2003, at 14; *see also* Al Goodman, *Spain Blocks Trials of Argentines*, CNN.COM, Aug. 29, 2003, http://www.cnn.com/2003/WORLD/europe/08/29/spanish.argentina/index.html (quoting the Spanish attorney for the victims saying that the Spanish government's decision sends a "powerful message" to Argentina's Supreme Court to overturn the amnesty laws).

[12] *See* Héctor Tobar, *Judge Orders Officers Freed: The Argentine Military Men Accused of Rights Abuses in the '70s and '80s May Still Face Trials*, L.A. TIMES, Sept. 2, 2003, at A3 ("President Nestor Kirchner used Spain's announcement to increase pressure on the Argentine Supreme Court to overturn the amnesty laws that prohibit trying the men here.").

[13] Corte Suprema de Justicia de la Nación [CSJN] [National Supreme Court of Justice], 14/6/2005, "Simón, Julio Héctor y otros s/ privación ilegítima de la libertad," causa No. 17.768, S.1767.XXXVIII (Arg.). *See also* Press Release, Human Rights Watch, Argentina: Amnesty Laws Struck Down (June 15, 2005), *available at* http://http://www.hrw.org/news/2005/06/14/ argentina-amnesty-laws-struck-down.

precedent a 2001 decision of the Inter-American Court of Human Rights striking down a similar amnesty provision in Peru as incompatible with the American Convention on Human Rights and hence without legal effect.[14] So, in the end, the "sovereign" state of Argentina made political and legal choices to repeal the amnesty laws just as it had previously made choices to create them. But in this change of heart we can see the degree to which international and transnational legal pronouncements, even if they are without any literal constraining effect, may significantly alter the domestic political terrain.

Likewise, official international institutions, such as the United Nations, can also pressure local bureaucracies by creating international commissions of inquiry concerning alleged atrocities, or by threatening prosecutions in international courts. Such declarations can empower reformers within local bureaucracies, who can then argue for institutional changes as a way of staving off international interference. For example, in the aftermath of the violence in East Timor that followed its vote for independence, there were grave concerns that the Indonesian government would not pursue human rights investigations of the military personnel allegedly responsible for the violence.[15] Thus, an International Commission of Inquiry was established, and U.N. officials warned that an international court might be necessary.[16] As with Chile and Argentina, such actions strengthened the hand of reformers within Indonesia, such as then–Attorney General Marzuki Darusman. With the specter of international action hanging over Indonesia, Darusman made several statements arguing that, for nationalist reasons, a hard-hitting Indonesian investigation was necessary to forestall an international takeover of the process.[17] Not surprisingly, when this international pressure dissipated after the terrorist attacks of September 11, 2001, so did the momentum to provide real accountability

---

[14] Corte Suprema de Justicia de la Nación [CSJN] [National Supreme Court of Justice], 14/6/2005, "Simón, Julio Héctor y otros s/ privación ilegítima de la libertad," causa No. 17.768, S.1767.XXXVIII (Arg.). *See also* Argentina: Amnesty Laws Struck Down, *supra* note 13.

[15] *See, e.g.*, Laura A. Dickinson, *The Dance of Complementarity: Relationships Among Domestic, International, and Transnational Accountability Mechanisms in East Timor and Indonesia, in* ACCOUNTABILITY FOR ATROCITIES. NATIONAL AND INTERNATIONAL RESPONSES 319, 358–61 (Jane E. Stromseth ed., 2003) (discussing ways in which international pressure on Indonesia in the period just after East Timor gained its independence strengthened the hand of reformers within the Indonesian government to push for robust domestic accountability mechanisms for atrocities committed during the period leading up to the independence vote).

[16] *Id.* at 358–59.

[17] *See id.* at 360 (documenting the response of the Indonesian government, which appointed an investigative team, identified priority cases, named suspects, and collected evidence).

in Indonesia for the atrocities committed.[18] Thus, we can again see that international legal activity (or the lack thereof) alters the domestic terrain.

Finally, there can be little doubt that local actors, outside official government bureaucracies or judicial institutions, can at times leverage international, transnational, and non-state legal norms to press causes within their countries.[19] For example, as late as 1994, women in Hong Kong were unable to inherit land.[20] That year a group of rural indigenous women joined forces with urban women's groups to demand legal change. As detailed by Sally Engle Merry and Rachel E. Stern, "[t]he indigenous women slowly shifted from seeing their stories as individual kinship violations to broader examples of discrimination."[21] Ultimately, the women learned to protest these unjust customary laws in the language of international human rights and gender equality.[22] Having done so, they were successful at getting the inheritance rules overturned.[23] And though we might regret the fact that these women were forced to "translate" their grievances into an internationally recognized language in order to be heard, the success of the movement in accessing political power surely attests to the strength and importance of the international law discourse.

This same story has been replicated numerous times around the world. Assisted by a global network of NGOs and activists, indigenous movements use international norms to influence local political or judicial actors. For example, in June 2005 communities from across the Niger Delta filed a case in the Federal High Court of Nigeria against several oil companies to stop the practice of "gas flaring," which poses severe health risks and contributes to greenhouse

---

[18] *See id.* at 364–66 (discussing the shifting priorities of the Bush administration following the 9/11 attacks and tracing the impact of outside pressure in efforts to hold individuals accountable for the violence in East Timor).

[19] Of course, such local actors do not only "use" international law as "given" to them, but also, through their social movements, shape the international legal norms themselves. For an argument that human rights discourse has been fundamentally shaped by Third World resistance to development, see generally BALAKRISHNAN RAJAGOPAL, INTERNATIONAL LAW FROM BELOW: DEVELOPMENT, SOCIAL MOVEMENTS, AND THIRD WORLD RESISTANCE (2003).

[20] Sally Engle Merry & Rachel E. Stern, *The Female Inheritance Movement in Hong Kong: Theorizing the Local/Global Interface*, 46 CURRENT ANTHROPOLOGY 387, 387 (2005).

[21] *Id.* at 399.

[22] *See id.* at 390 (explaining the evolution of the Anti-Discrimination Female Indigenous Residents Committee from a group that perceived the prohibition of female inheritance as a personal wrong perpetrated by relatives to a group arguing that the male-only inheritance laws failed to comply with international agreements, such as the Convention on the Elimination of Discrimination Against Women and the International Covenant on Civil and Political Rights).

[23] *Id.* at 394.

gas emissions.[24] Though nominally brought under the Nigerian Constitution, the complaint explicitly referenced the African Charter on Human and People's Rights and argued for a right to a "clean, poison-free, pollution free and healthy environment."[25] Other environmental groups have sought to place sites on UNESCO's World Heritage Committee list of protected sites so that they can then pressure their local governments to take steps to limit environmental damage to the sites.[26] Consumer groups organize worldwide boycotts on the rhetorical strength of rights discourse.[27] Meanwhile, many African countries, responding in part to pressure from international human rights activists, have enacted laws forbidding the practice known as female genital cutting.[28] And of course, it isn't only social movements that use the language and institutions of international law to access domestic power. Transnational corporations have deployed the rhetoric of international free trade law and have used bodies such

[24] Gbemre v. Shell Petroleum Dev. Co. Nig., Suit No. FHC/B/CS/153/2005. On November 14, 2005, the Federal High Court of Nigeria in Benin City ruled that Royal Dutch Shell, Chevron, Exxon Mobil, and other oil companies must end natural gas flaring in Nigeria, claiming that the practice was a waste and violated the local communities' constitutional rights to life and dignity. A copy of the judicial order is available at http://lasulawsenvironmental.blogspot.com/2012/04/nigeria-gbemre-v-shell-petroleum_8079.html.

[25] *Id.*

[26] For example, the countries of Belize, Nepal, and Peru recently petitioned the World Heritage Committee to place the Belize Barrier Reef, Mount Everest, and Huarascan National Park on its list of World Heritage in Danger Sites, because of threats to the sites due to global climate change. *See* Press Release, Climate Justice, UNESCO Danger-Listing Petitions Presented (Nov. 17, 2004), *available at* http://www.climatelaw.org/media/2004Nov17/. "Danger-listing" is a legal mechanism under the Convention for the Protection of the World Cultural and Natural Heritage, Nov. 16, 1972, 27 U.S.T. 37, which requires State Parties to the Convention to take action to transmit World Heritage Sites to future generations.

[27] *See* Paul Schiff Berman, *The Globalization of Jurisdiction*, 151 U. Pa. L. Rev. 311, 480–82 (2002) (discussing such efforts). As The Economist has observed, "a multinational's failure to look like a good global citizen is increasingly expensive in a world where consumers and pressure groups can be quickly mobilised behind a cause." *Multinationals and Their Morals*, The Economist (London), Dec. 2, 1995, at 18, 20. For discussion of how noncompliance with entrenched international law norms may result in lost economic opportunities for subnational units, crucial to economic prosperity in a globalized economy, see Peter J. Spiro, *Globalization and the (Foreign Affairs) Constitution*, 63 Ohio St. L.J. 649, 672–73 (2002), in which he outlines ways that consumers, nongovernmental organizations, and states can pressure corporations to boycott investment and development in regions that fail to follow standards of international law.

[28] Leigh A. Trueblood, *Female Genital Mutilation: A Discussion of International Human Rights Instruments, Cultural Sovereignty and Dominance Theory*, 28 Denv. J. Int'l L. & Pol'y 437, 464–65 (2000) (describing how the efforts of international organizations, NGOs, and other groups have led many countries, including Cameroon, Egypt, Kenya, Sudan, Burkina Faso, and Ivory Coast, to pass legislation against female genital cutting).

as the NAFTA tribunals or the World Trade Organization to avoid being subject to domestic regulation.[29] And even lower domestic courts within the European Union have more readily embraced the jurisprudence of the European Court of Justice, perhaps in part as a way to leverage power that had previously been retained by national high courts.[30]

Whether or not one thinks the proliferation and deployment of non-state norms in domestic political and legal debates is a good thing, it is difficult to deny the reality. Thus, the interaction between state and non-state cannot simply be reduced to a vision of the state pursuing a single set of interests either completely constrained or completely unconstrained by non-state norms. Rather, as part of the multivalent, messy process by which various state constituencies vie to have their preferred policies adopted, international, transnational, and non-state norms can be a powerful tool. These norms provide a set of moral, rhetorical, and strategic arguments that may empower constituencies that might not otherwise have a voice, or they may be used by already powerful forces to protect their own interests. In any event, only by going beyond the simplistic model of the unitary state pursuing a single set of interests can we see the power of international, transnational, and non-state law coursing below the surface.

In short, legal pluralism offers a more complicated descriptive account of the interaction of normative systems, the strategic maneuverings of individuals and groups in deploying these multiple systems to pursue their interests, and the subtle processes by which even norms without coercive power can change legal consciousness and have impact over time. These nuances are often elided in the traditional liberal legal analysis.

PLURALISM'S NORMATIVE PROJECT

As noted at the outset, in recent years legal pluralism has moved beyond its traditional realm of sociolegal thick description and embraced a more ambitious normative project. Here, the goal is not simply to catalog interaction among legal systems but to argue that procedural mechanisms, institutional designs, and discursive practices that foster such interactions may sometimes be preferable to more traditional liberal legal hierarchies. From a pluralist

---

[29] *See, e.g.*, Benjamin W. Putnam, Note, *The Cross-Border Trucking Dispute: Finding a Way Out of the Conflict Between NAFTA and U.S. Environmental Law*, 82 Tex. L. Rev. 1287, 1307–08 (2004) (describing cases in which regulated entities cite NAFTA to avoid the requirements of domestic environmental laws).

[30] *See* Karen J. Alter, Establishing the Supremacy of European Law: The Making of an International Rule of Law in Europe (2001).

perspective, such hybrid arrangements are preferable for four reasons. First, they acknowledge the reality that people hold multiple community affiliations, rather than dissolving that multiplicity into either universality or separatism. Second, they encourage decision makers to take a restrained approach to their own potentially jurispathic power, always asking whether deference to other norms might potentially be possible. Third, providing space for multiple communities may actually result in better substantive decisions because there is more opportunity for variations and experimentation.[31] Fourth, broader participation may make it more likely that various communities will at least acquiesce in the ultimate decision, even if they do not agree with the result. Such mechanisms, institutions, and practices can help mediate conflicts by recognizing that multiple communities may legitimately wish to assert their norms over a given act or actor, by seeking ways of reconciling competing norms, and by deferring to alternative approaches if possible. And even when a decision maker cannot defer to an alternative norm (because some assertions of norms are repressive, violent, and/or profoundly illiberal), procedures for managing pluralism can at least require an explanation of why deference is impossible.

The normative pluralist framework recognizes that conflict is unavoidable and so, instead of trying to erase conflict, it seeks to manage that conflict through procedural mechanisms, institutions, and practices that might at least draw the participants to the conflict into a shared social space. This approach draws on Ludwig Wittgenstein's idea that agreements are reached principally through participation in common forms of life, rather than agreement on substance.[32] Or, as the political theorist Chantal Mouffe has put it, we need to transform "enemies" – who have no common symbolic space – into

---

[31] In focusing on the pluralist opportunities inherent in jurisdictional redundancy, I echo the insights of Robert Cover. Robert M. Cover, *The Uses of Jurisdictional Redundancy: Interest, Ideology, and Innovation*, 22 Wm. & Mary L. Rev. 639 (1981). Although his essay was focused particularly on the variety of "official" law pronouncers in the U.S. federal system, Cover celebrated the benefits that accrue from having multiple overlapping jurisdictional assertions. Such benefits included greater possibility for error correction, a more robust field for norm articulation, and a larger space for creative innovation. And though Cover acknowledged that it might seem perverse "to seek out a messy and indeterminate end to conflicts which may be tied neatly together by a single authoritative verdict," he nevertheless argued that we should "embrace" a system "that permits tensions and conflicts of the social order" to be played out in the jurisdictional structure of the system. *Id.* at 682. Thus, Cover's pluralism, though here focused on U.S. federalism, can be said to include the creative possibilities inherent in multiple overlapping jurisdictions asserted by both state and non-state entities in whatever context they arise.

[32] Ludwig Wittgenstein, Philosophical Investigations pt. I, § 241 (G.E.M. Anscombe trans., 3d ed. 1958).

"adversaries."[33] Adversaries, according to Mouffe, are "friendly enemies": friends because they "share a common symbolic space but also enemies because they want to organize this common symbolic space in a different way."[34] Ideally, law can function as the sort of common symbolic space that Mouffe envisions and can therefore play a constructive role in transforming enemies into adversaries. As philosopher Stuart Hampshire has argued, because normative agreement is impossible, "fairness and justice in procedures" are the only virtues that offer even the possibility for broader sharing.[35] Accordingly, the key is to create spaces for such broader sharing, spaces for turning enemies into adversaries, without insisting on normative agreement.[36]

Finally – and of great significance to those interested in non-state lawmaking – procedural mechanisms, institutions, and practices for managing pluralism ideally encourage decision makers to wrestle explicitly with questions of multiple community affiliation and the effects of activities across territorial borders, rather than shunting aside normative difference. As a result, a pluralist framework invites questions that otherwise might not be asked: How are communities appropriately defined in today's world? To what degree do people act on the basis of affiliations with non-state or supranational communities? How should the various norm-generating communities in the global system interact so as to provide opportunities for contestation and expression of difference? Such questions must be considered carefully in order to develop mechanisms that will take seriously the multifaceted interactions of such communities.

This normative legal pluralism is again not necessarily inconsistent with liberalism, but at the same time it does result in a significantly different emphasis and set of institutional arrangements from the standard version of liberal institutional tolerance. For example, consider a governing council of decision makers popularly elected by citizens of a community. Assume that every council member happens to be a member of the same majority ethnic, racial, or religious group within that broader community. If the election were conducted fairly and the governing body does not unduly infringe minority rights in its substantive decisions, then under most theories of liberalism there

---

[33] Chantal Mouffe, The Democratic Paradox 13 (2000).

[34] *Id.*

[35] Stuart Hampshire, Justice Is Conflict 53 (2000).

[36] *Cf.* Jeremy Waldron, *Tribalism and the Myth of the Framework: Some Popperian Thoughts on the Politics of Cultural Recognition, in* Karl Popper: Critical Appraisals 203, 221 (Philip Catton & Graham Macdonald eds., 2004) ("Humans are enormously curious about each other's ideas and reasons, and, when they want to be, they are resourceful in listening to and trying to learn from one another across what appear to be barriers of cultural comprehensibility, often far beyond what philosophers and theorists of culture give them credit for.").

is at least some justification for saying that this is a legitimate arrangement. If one embraces the vision of legal pluralism I pursue, however, one might reach the conclusion that even if this rule solely by members of the dominant group is *legitimate*, it is likely not *preferable*. This is because the procedural pluralist approach adds in a preference for greater dialogue among multiple communities to improve the quality of decision making, to build habits of mind that inculcate tolerance, and to make it more likely that the losing party will acquiesce in whatever substantive decisions are ultimately reached. Accordingly, following a more pluralist approach, one might decide to set aside certain seats on the governing council for the minority group. Either of these arrangements is likely compatible with liberalism; however, the pluralist perspective adds an additional set of considerations to weigh in the institutional design decision.

Thus, where liberal institutionalists might simply tolerate minority viewpoints, a commitment to pluralist arrangements might lead to institutional designs that require hybrid participation. For example, hybrid courts might require judges or jurors to hail from different communities or from different religious or ethnic backgrounds.[37] Such hybrid courts have been employed in transitional justice settings in Kosovo, East Timor, Sierra Leone, and Cambodia. In these courts, domestic judges – ideally drawn from the multiple political, racial, or ethnic groups involved in the larger geopolitical conflict – sit alongside international judges, and domestic and international lawyers also work together to prosecute the cases.[38] The design of hybrid courts goes beyond mere liberal toleration and builds pluralism into the very structures of the institutional arrangements.

Pluralist mechanisms can also create structural feedback loops, where institutional decision makers are forced to consider the approaches of other communities. For example, the oft-discussed "margin of appreciation" doctrine[39] of the European Court of Human Rights (ECHR) is a structural inquiry that does not simply focus on whether a practice should be tolerated within the overarching order of universalist human rights regimes. Instead, the ECHR asserts a norm, but then domestic polities have room to maneuver in implementing ECHR decisions so as to accommodate local variation. Such a doctrine disciplines the ECHR and forces it to consider, as a structural matter, the alternative norms of other communities.

---

[37] *See, e.g.*, Laura A. Dickinson, *The Promise of Hybrid Courts*, 97 Am. J. Int'l. L. 295 (2003).

[38] *See id.*

[39] A particularly useful, succinct summary can be found in Lawrence R. Helfer & Anne-Marie Slaughter, *Toward a Theory of Effective Supranational Adjudication*, 107 Yale L.J. 273, 316–17 (1997).

Likewise, the Canadian Constitution explicitly contemplates a dialectical interaction between national courts and provincial legislatures concerning constitutional interpretation. Section 33's so-called "notwithstanding clause" permits Parliament or a provincial legislature to authorize the operation of a law for a five-year period, even after it has been declared invalid by a court.[40] As with the ECHR example, this provision potentially has a disciplining effect on the court and encourages a more nuanced iterative process in working out constitutional norms. It is true of course that the notwithstanding clause, though often invoked rhetorically, has only rarely actually been used by provincial governments to continue a judicially invalidated law.[41] Yet, this relative infrequency of use may not be evidence of a failed constitutional innovation. Instead, it may indicate just the opposite: that the various institutional actors have sufficiently internalized this mechanism for managing hybridity such that the precipice is rarely reached.[42]

A third example of structurally embedded, habitual deference is subsidiarity. Unlike sovereignty, a subsidiarity regime does not pose an outright bar to governance at the "higher" level of authority. But it does not offer a blank check either. The idea is to foster careful and repeated *consideration* of other potential lawmaking communities. Thus, "[a]t its core the principle of subsidiarity requires any infringements of the autonomy of the local level by means of preemptive norms enacted on the higher level to be justified by good reasons."[43] Fundamentally, subsidiarity doctrines always force decision

---

[40] *See* Canadian Charter of Rights and Freedoms, Part I of the Constitution Act, 1982, *being* Schedule B to the Canada Act, 1982, c. 11, § 33 (U.K.).

[41] For example, the Quebec Parliament overrode the Canadian Supreme Court's invalidation of provisions of a language law. *See* Ford v. Attorney General of Quebec, [1988] 2 S.C.R. 712 (Can.). However, outside of Quebec, the notwithstanding clause has never been used to overturn a judicial decision. *See* James Allan & Grant Huscroft, *Constitutional Rights Coming Home to Roost? Rights Internationalism in American Courts*, 43 SAN DIEGO L. REV. 1, 21 (2006). In addition, according to one account, the clause has been disavowed by successive Prime Ministers because "[i]ts use has come to be seen as undermining the Charter, in part because judicial decisions interpreting the Charter have come to be seen as synonymous with the Charter itself." *Id.* at 20.

[42] On the other hand, it is possible that "the notwithstanding clause frees Canadian courts to be *less* deferential to elected legislatures than they otherwise would have been in the absence of such a clause, because it allows judges to act on the basis that their decisions are not final." Allan & Huscroft, *supra* note 41, at 21–22. In any event, the important point for this chapter is that the clause is structured as a mechanism for managing the hybridity of multiple communities within a federal system. For an account supporting the approach of the notwithstanding clause from the perspective of political theory, see JENNIFER NEDELSKY, LAW'S RELATIONS: A RELATIONAL THEORY OF SELF, AUTONOMY, AND LAW 247 (2011).

[43] Mattias Kumm, *Democratic Constitutionalism Encounters International Law: Terms of Engagement, in* THE MIGRATION OF CONSTITUTIONAL IDEAS 256, 264 (Sujit Choudhry ed., 2006).

makers to ask whether there is another authority better positioned to decide an issue.

Although these sorts of approaches are often applied within a preexisting liberal state order, the point is that they create structural interactions among communities and therefore might be used effectively with regard to non-state community norms as well. Such a flexible approach might allow communities more leeway in trying to make statements of rights work within a particularized community context. Moreover, while not necessarily in opposition to liberalism, these institutional arrangements instantiate a set of concerns about structural interactions that is distinct from liberalism.

Finally, a pluralist approach would also focus less on whether a state institution tolerates a non-state community from a position of inherent superiority and instead conceptualize the conflict between state and non-state lawmaking as a true conflict-of-laws problem. Because non-state lawmaking is not usually conceived of as law, we do not usually think of clashes between state and non-state law through the prism of conflict-of-laws jurisprudence. But we could. By way of example, consider two classic U.S. constitutional cases that are usually framed as issues of religious or ethnic toleration, but which can usefully be analyzed in terms of choice of law.

First, in *Bob Jones University* v. *United States*, the Internal Revenue Service had interpreted Section 501(c)(3) of the Internal Revenue Code, which gives tax-exempt status to qualifying charitable institutions, to apply to schools only if such schools have a "racially nondiscriminatory policy as to students."[44] Accordingly, the IRS denied tax exemption to Bob Jones University, which had not admitted blacks at all until 1971 and had admitted them thereafter but had forbidden interracial dating, interracial marriage, the espousal of violation of these prohibitions, and membership in groups that advocated interracial marriage. Crucial to the case was the fact that the University grounded its rule not on racial attitudes, but on Biblical scripture. The school therefore considered the exclusion of interracial dating to be a principal tenet of its religious community. Nevertheless, although the text of section 501(c)(3) did not speak to racial discrimination at all, the U.S. Supreme Court upheld the IRS determination, finding the Service's interpretation of the Code provision to be permissible.

Robert Cover, in his article *Nomos and Narrative*, has famously criticized the reasoning of the *Bob Jones* decision, even while agreeing with the Court's result. According to Cover, the Court assumed "a position that places nothing at risk and from which the Court makes no interpretive gesture at all, save

---

[44] 461 U.S. 574, 579 (1983).

the quintessential gesture to the jurisdictional canons: the statement that an exercise of political authority was not unconstitutional."[45] In particular, Cover argued that, by grounding its decision on an interpretation of the Internal Revenue Code, the Court had side-stepped the crucial constitutional question of whether Congress could grant tax exemptions to schools that discriminated on the basis of race. This was a problem for Cover because he believed that if a state legal authority were going to "kill off" the competing normative commitment of an alternative community, it should do so based on a profound normative commitment of its own.[46] By avoiding the constitutional question, Cover complained, the Court had disserved both the religious community – whose normative commitments would be placed at the mercy of mere administrative judgments – and racial minorities – who "deserved a constitutional commitment to avoiding public subsidization of racism."[47]

In contrast, had the clash between the university's religious rule and the IRS code, or between the religious rule and the U.S. Constitution, been viewed as a choice-of-law decision, two aspects of the case would have been clarified. First, the Court would have analyzed and defined the relevant community affiliations at stake. Second, the Court would have been forced to grapple with the strength of its commitment to the principle of nondiscrimination, just as Cover urged. As a result, instead of simply asserting federal law, a conflicts analysis encourages negotiation among the different norms advanced by different communities.

A more pluralist vision of conflict of laws recognizes that people and groups hold multiple community affiliations and takes those affiliations seriously. Thus, when a non-state legal practice is largely internal and primarily reflects individuals' affiliation with the non-state community, the practice should be given more leeway than when the state itself is part of the relevant affiliation. In this case, the issue at stake was a tax exemption, a quintessentially state matter. Indeed, Bob Jones University was asking for a particular benefit for charitable organizations that was contained in the U.S. tax code. Therefore, for these purposes the place of the university within the nation-state was the most salient tie, making application of the federal law more justifiable. In contrast, as we shall see, other non-state normative commitments do not implicate the nation-state so directly.

Moreover, even if the relevant community ties were largely with the religious community itself, certain norms might be held so strongly by the nation-state

---

[45] Robert M. Cover, *The Supreme Court, 1982 Term – Foreword: Nomos and Narrative*, 97 HARV. L. REV. 4, 66 (1983) [hereinafter Cover, *Nomos and Narrative*].

[46] *See id.* at 52–60.

[47] *Id.* at 67.

community that such norms would be applied *regardless* of the community affiliation. In choice-of-law analysis, this is usually called the public policy exception, and it allows courts to refuse to apply foreign law that would otherwise apply, if those legal norms are sufficiently repugnant. But application of the public policy exception is rare, both as a normative and descriptive matter. Thus, if a court asserts such an exception, it must justify the use of public policy grounds by reference to precisely the sorts of deeply held commitments that Cover envisioned. In the *Bob Jones* case, for example, it might be that the nation-state's deep commitment to eradicating racial discrimination would independently justify overriding the religious norms, regardless of the community affiliation analysis.

Accordingly, a conflicts approach would not simply throw the claim of protected religious insularity to the mercy of political or bureaucratic judgments. Taking the ban on interracial dating seriously as law and performing a choice-of-law analysis would create the obligation to engage in crucial balancing of the strength of the commitments at stake. And although the community affiliation and public policy exception analyses *in this case* might justify application of state law, that will not always be true.

Consider, by way of contrast, *Employment Division, Department of Human Resources of Oregon v. Smith*, in which the U.S. Supreme Court refused to extend First Amendment protection to the religious use of peyote by a tribal community.[48] Here, unlike the tax exemption at issue in *Bob Jones*, the tribe was not negotiating its relationship with the state; rather the use of peyote was part of a purely internal religious practice open primarily (or exclusively) to members of that community. Thus, a choice-of-law analysis based on community affiliation might well result in deference to the non-state norm. Moreover, the normative commitment to drug enforcement is perhaps better characterized as a governance choice than as an inexorable normative command. As such, the public policy exception is arguably less appropriate in this context than when addressing racial discrimination and a constitutional commitment to its eradication. Applying these principles, a choice-of-law analysis might well have permitted the religious practice in *Smith*.

In the end, however, I am less concerned with the outcome in particular cases than with the analytical framework employed. Conceiving of these clashes between religious and state law in conflicts terms reorients the inquiry in a way that takes more seriously the non-state community assertion. As a result, courts must wrestle both with the nature of the multiple community affiliations potentially at issue and with the need to articulate truly strong

---

[48] 494 U.S. 872 (1990).

normative justifications for not deferring to the non-state norm. Both consequences make the choice-of-law decision a constructive terrain of engagement among multiple normative systems, rather than an arm of state government automatically and without reflection imposing its normative vision on all within its coercive power.

Of course, this vision is not unproblematic. Two related objections immediately present themselves. First, a choice-of-law rule that tends to defer to non-state norms when they implicate only internal community affiliation might be seen to rest on the often-criticized distinction between public and private action. Indeed, the idea of deference in this context might come to look like the classic state deference to family privacy or autonomy.[49] And just as family privacy was often invoked to shield domestic violence and gender hierarchy, so too may deference to "internal" community norms become deference to fundamentally illiberal norms.

Second, as in the family context, we may make a mistake by assuming that the non-state community at issue is monolithic. Indeed, it may be that some members of the relevant community would prefer to have the state norm applied to their situation. As Judith Resnik has noted, Cover's vision of multiple norm-generating communities did not address the problem of conflict "within [such] communities about their own practices and authoritative interpretations."[50] Yet, such "contestation from within"[51] (which is likely to occur along the fault lines of power hierarchies within the community) is an almost inevitable part of community norm creation. Thus, the choice-of-law question becomes, in part, a question of whose voices within a community are heard by which speakers of nation-state power.

As to the concern that too much deference to "private" norms within a community will overly empower illiberal groups, it is important to remember that, because of the public policy exception, these norms, if sufficiently abhorrent, need not be applied by the state authority. After all, a lynch mob may also be a statement of community norms, but it need not for that reason necessarily be embraced. The object of a choice-of-law analysis is not to blindly follow non-state community norms, but to insure that if a state asserts its own norms it does so self-consciously. Indeed, simply identifying the state's jurispathic power does not necessarily mean that we must reject all exercises

---

[49] *See, e.g.*, Frances E. Olsen, *The Myth of State Intervention in the Family*, 18 U. MICH. J.L. REFORM 835, 836–37 (1985).

[50] Judith Resnik, *Living Their Legal Commitments: Paideic Communities, Courts, and Robert Cover (An Essay on Racial Segregation at Bob Jones University, Patrilineal Membership Rules, Veiling, and Jurisgenerative Practices)*, 17 YALE J.L. & HUMAN. 17, 27 (2005).

[51] *Id.*

of that power.[52] Even Cover recognized the utility of a state court's speaking in "imperial mode."[53] He noted that when judges kill off competing law by asserting that "this one is the law," they may do violence to the competing visions, but they also enable peace both because too much law is too chaotic to sustain and because some laws are simply too noxious to be applied.[54] The point then is simply to make sure that the imposition of imperial, jurispathic law is not done blindly or arrogantly, but with intentionality and a respect for the other sources of lawmaking that are being displaced.[55] A conflicts analysis at least opens space for such self-consciousness and care.

More difficult is the problem of how to respond to Resnik's arguments about inevitable conflicts within a non-state community concerning the content of that community's norms. Certainly the existence of significant disagreement within the community might be factored into the decision of whether to apply the non-state norm. Thus, if some substantial portion of the non-state community were clamoring for the application of state law, such clamoring might blunt somewhat the need to defer to the non-state norm.

More important, in thinking about how to address disputes within a non-state community, we must distinguish between two types of challenge. One concerns the proper understanding of what the content of the community's law actually is and the other concerns what that law ought to be. For example, in *Santa Clara Pueblo v. Martinez*, a woman who was a member of an Indian tribe challenged her tribe's refusal to consider her children to be tribal members.[56] She did so, however, not based on an argument that the tribe had improperly interpreted its own community law (which based the child's tribal membership on the father's status not the mother's). Instead, she argued that the tribe's law was inconsistent with a federal equal protection statute. Thus, the case did not present a contestation about the content of the community's norms; it merely raised a choice-of-law issue about whether the tribal law or the federal statute should govern. And however difficult the resolution of that choice-of-law question might be, it does not raise the conundrum of how to determine the appropriate content of the non-state norms in the first place.

Finally, in those relatively infrequent situations when the actual content of the non-state norm is at issue, courts can seek evidence to determine that

---

[52] *See id.* at 25.

[53] Cover, *Nomos and Narrative, supra* note 45, at 13–14.

[54] *Id.* at 53.

[55] *See* Resnik, *supra* note 50, at 25 ("[Cover] wanted the state's actors . . . to be uncomfortable in their knowledge of their own power, respectful of the legitimacy of competing legal systems, and aware of the possibility that multiple meanings and divergent practices ought sometimes to be tolerated, even if painfully so.").

[56] 436 U.S. 49 (1978).

community's governing norm. Historical documentation, anthropological testimony, and evidence of ongoing practice might all be relevant. And again, to the extent that there are concerns that the non-state norm is the product of hierarchy, those concerns can be factored into the choice-of-law inquiry itself; they do not render it impossible to determine the content of the norm.

One might think that this approach is not pluralist enough. After all, in this scenario it is still the state choosing whether or not to allow space for the non-state norm. Accordingly, all this may simply look like liberal constitutionalism under another name. But leveling such criticism is to misunderstand the pluralist project I have in mind. An embrace of principles of pluralism doesn't erase all power dynamics with the wave of a magic wand. Accordingly, the fact that it is the U.S. Supreme Court deciding how much to defer is largely a reflection of the simple fact that in this example the state has literal power through its police force, and so its judgment matters. In other scenarios, one could imagine conflicts between two state or non-state entities that are more symmetric in their enforcement power (or lack thereof). Regardless, it will always be one community that is being asked to make an exception to its norms because of deference to another community, and very little turns, it seems to me, on which community is being asked to make the decision. The point is the *approach* that the decision making community takes.

In a similar vein, Patterson and Galán criticize a suggestion in my book that liberal communities might try to open limited space for Sharia courts to operate in their midst, so long as those courts do not trench upon fundamental values of the liberal community. Patterson and Galán claim that it is not really pluralism unless I go all the way and advocate that liberal communities allow Sharia courts to operate *regardless* of whether or not they violate fundamental values of the liberal community. This strikes me as absurd. Just because one embraces insights from legal pluralism, after all, does not mean that the values of pluralism must necessarily and always trump any other values a community might hold. It simply cannot be that legal pluralism is only a true normative position if it is pursued to the exclusion of all other values, interests, and commitments. Thus, I find it entirely unproblematic that the normative version of legal pluralism I am advocating is consistent with liberalism.

But just because it is consistent with liberalism does not make it precisely the same inquiry. As the *Bob Jones* decision and Cover's critique suggest, different procedural tropes, institutional designs, and discursive practices prompt different types of inquiries. The important point, from a pluralist perspective, is to devise structures that create habits of mind in decision makers where they will be more likely to consider multiple communities and multiple sources of law. These habits of mind become embedded in day-to-day practice, and eventually become simply the "way things are." Accordingly, over time, nor-mative legal pluralism builds into the landscape a set of inquiries that explicitly acknowledge and take seriously the claims of non-state lawmaking. And this acknowledgment is not mere toleration but the respect habitually accorded other lawmaking entities. Such respect does not mean that the norms of other lawmaking entities are always followed, but they are included in the inquiry, and if deference is impossible, the decision maker will at least need to justify such lack of deference. In the end, this is likely to result in a very different form of legal treatment accorded to non-state lawmaking than under traditional liberal institutionalism.

The same sort of conflicts framework can be applied in cases with a transnational or international dimension. For example, consider *Telnikoff* v. *Matusevitch*,[57] a case decided by the Maryland Court of Appeals. This was a libel action between two British citizens concerning writings that appeared in a British newspaper.[58] After a complicated sequence of proceedings in the United Kingdom, a jury ruled for the plaintiff and ordered damages. However, Matusevitch moved to Maryland and subsequently sought a declaratory order that the British libel judgment could not be enforced in the United States, pursuant to the First Amendment.[59] The Maryland court ultimately ruled that, because British libel law violates the speech-protective First Amendment stan-dards laid out by the U.S. Supreme Court in *New York Times Co.* v. *Sullivan*[60] and its progeny, the British judgment violated Maryland public policy and could not be enforced.[61]

Using a pluralist framework might well lead to a different result because a pluralist vision of judgment recognition requires judges to see themselves as part of an international network of normative communities and the par-ties before them as potentially affiliated with multiple such communities, both state and non-state. Those various communities might legitimately seek to impose their norms on such affiliated parties. Thus, when faced with an enforcement decision regarding a foreign judgment, courts would not nec-essarily assume that their own local public policies trump the dictates of the foreign judgment. Instead, courts must undertake a nuanced inquiry con-cerning whether the affiliations of the parties render the original judgment legitimate. Although the local policies of the forum country are not irrelevant,

---

[57] 702 A.2d 230 (Md. 1997).
[58] *Id.*
[59] *Id.*
[60] 376 U.S. 254 (1964).
[61] *Telnikoff*, 702 A.2d at 249.

those policies should be weighed against the overall interest in creating an interlocking system of international adjudication.

In the *Telnikoff* case, there is in fact no reason to think the U.S. Constitution is necessarily implicated in an enforcement action. First, it is debatable whether the simple enforcement of a judgment creates the requisite state action to generate constitutional concerns.[62] Second, with regard to interstate harmony, a refusal to enforce the British libel judgment effectively imposes U.S. First Amendment norms on the United Kingdom. Such parochialism is cause for concern. Third, although it is true that constitutional norms could conceivably create sufficient public policy reasons to refuse to enforce a judgment, the libel dispute in *Telnikoff* did not in any way implicate U.S. public policy because neither party had any particular affiliation with the United States at the time of the events at issue.

Thus, even if U.S. constitutional values or public policy considerations might *sometimes* require a court to refuse to enforce a judgment, there is no basis (at least using a pluralist frame) for a categorical rule preventing

---

[62] In *Shelley v. Kraemer*, 334 U.S. 1 (1948), the U.S. Supreme Court ruled that the Equal Protection Clause precluded a court from enforcing a private, racially restrictive covenant. In so doing, the Court determined that, although the covenant itself was entered into by private actors who were not subject to the commands of the Fourteenth Amendment, the action by the courts in enforcing the covenant was sufficient state action to trigger constitutional scrutiny. *See id.* at 14. *Shelley*, therefore, appears to block judicial enforcement of a private agreement (or a foreign order) that would be unconstitutional. Indeed, courts, in refusing to enforce foreign "unconstitutional" judgments, have explicitly relied on *Shelley*. *See, e.g.*, Yahoo!, Inc. v. La Ligue Contre Le Racisme et L'Antisemitisme, 169 F. Supp. 2d 1181, 1189 (N.D. Cal. 2001), *rev'd on other grounds*, 433 F.3d 1199 (9th Cir. 2006). However, since the time *Shelley* was issued, courts and commentators have backed away from the sweeping ramifications of *Shelley*. This is because, under *Shelley*'s reasoning, any private contract that is being enforced by a police officer or court would be transformed into state action. *See* Laurence H. Tribe, American Constitutional Law 1697 (2d ed. 1988) (arguing that *Shelley*'s approach, "consistently applied, would require individuals to conform their private agreements to constitutional standards whenever, as almost always, the individuals might later seek the security of potential judicial enforcement."). Although generations of legal realists and critical legal studies scholars have articulated similarly sweeping conceptions of state action, see Paul Schiff Berman, *Cyberspace and the State Action Debate: The Cultural Value of Applying Constitutional Norms to "Private" Regulation*, 71 U. Colo. L. Rev. 1263, 1279–81 (2000) (surveying these critiques), courts have largely resisted *Shelley* and have limited its holding only to the context of racially restrictive covenants. Indeed, even in cases implicating the First Amendment, "with virtually no exceptions, courts have concluded that the judicial enforcement of private agreements inhibiting speech does not trigger constitutional review, despite the fact that identical legislative limitations on speech would have." *See* Mark D. Rosen, *Exporting the Constitution*, 53 Emory L.J. 171, 192–95 (2004) (collecting cases). Thus, it is not clear how robust *Shelley* still is and whether it would truly pose a constitutional bar in an action to enforce a foreign judgment. For further discussion of *Shelly* and its implications for judgment recognition, see Rosen, *supra* at 186–209.

enforcement, and little reason to refuse to enforce a foreign judgment absent significant ties between the dispute and the United States. Instead, courts should take seriously the values that would be effectuated by enforcing the foreign judgment, weigh the importance of such values against the relative importance of the local public policy or constitutional norm, and then consider the degree to which the parties have affiliated themselves with the forum. Only then can courts take into account the multistate character of the dispute and the flexible nature of community affiliation in a multivariate world. Again, while this approach is not necessarily inconsistent with liberalism, it adds a very different set of variables and considerations into the mix.

CONCLUSION

Although there is nothing inherently illiberal about a jurisprudential or institutional framework based on global legal pluralism, we must be careful not to equate liberalism and pluralism as interpretive lenses. This is particularly important when considering non-state lawmaking of various forms. In this context, global legal pluralism is likely to have two advantages over a liberal framework, one descriptive, one normative.

First, starting from a pluralist perspective means that we will be much more likely to recognize the very existence of non-state lawmaking communities as well as the individual agency that comes from strategic actors navigating the interaction among those communities and the institutions they support. Thus, while liberalism simply assumes state centralism and looks only to how the state responds to non-state communities, a pluralist framework starts from a premise of interaction, dynamic change, and strategic deployment of law by multiple actors.

Second, as a normative matter, global legal pluralism yields a jurisprudence and set of institutional design features that seek to maximize structural interaction among multiple normative communities. These structural interactions become embedded in jurisprudential doctrines and discursive practices that harden into habits of mind that are distinctively different from the liberal frame. Instead of the state simply encountering the external (or internal) Other and deciding whether to tolerate its norms, pluralist structures require decision makers to take seriously the claims of other lawmaking entities, think in terms of deference, respect, and inclusion, work toward hybrid participation, and justify any exclusion or nonadherence in terms other than the assumed supremacy of the state.

In short, non-state lawmaking looks very different from a framework that starts with global legal pluralism as compared to liberalism. And though there is nothing inherent in the pluralist framework to alarm committed liberals, adopting such a framework provides both a richer understanding of the rise of non-state lawmaking and a better roadmap for negotiating among plural lawmaking communities than the view from traditional liberal theory. Interpretive lenses construct reality over time, and the lens of legal pluralism offers distinct advantages in navigating the hybrid legal spaces that are our day-to-day reality.

2

What Is Non-State Law?

A Primer*

Ralf Michaels[1]

INTRODUCTION

Is this law?

"This is my covenant, which ye shall keep, between me and you and thy seed after thee; Every man child among you shall be circumcised. And ye shall circumcise the flesh of your foreskin; and it shall be a token of the covenant betwixt me and you. And he that is eight days old shall be circumcised among you, every man child in your generations, he that is born in the house, or bought with money of any stranger, which is not of thy seed. He that is born in thy house, and he that is bought with thy money, must needs be circumcised: and my covenant shall be in your flesh for an everlasting covenant. And the uncircumcised man child whose flesh of his foreskin is not circumcised, that soul shall be cut off from his people; he hath broken my covenant."[2]

This is not a rule of German law. Consequently, the district court Cologne felt justified to ignore it (or rather, the comparable rule in Islamic law)[3] when it ruled that the circumcision of newborn boys constitutes an illegal bodily injury.[4] The decision caused great outrage especially among members of

---

* A slightly different German version has been published as *Was ist Recht jenseits des Staates? Eine Einführung, in* TRANSNATIONALES RECHT – STAND UND PERSPEKTIVEN 39 (Gralf-Peter Calliess ed., 2014). Thanks to Diana Schawlowski for drafting a first translation of that chapter.

[1] Arthur Larson Professor of Law, Duke University School of Law.

[2] *Genesis* 17, 10–14 (King James version).

[3] The specific case dealt with a Muslim child. The Q'uran does not require circumcision, and circumcision is not, other than in Jewish law, viewed as constitutive. *See, e.g.,* DAVID L. GOLLAHER, CIRCUMCISION: A HISTORY OF THE WORLD'S MOST CONTROVERSIAL SURGERY 44–52 (2001).

[4] Landgericht Köln, 151 Ns 169/11, 7 May 2012, 2012 *Neue Juristische Wochenschrift* 2128 = 67 JURISTENZEITUNG 805 (2012) with note by *Rox*, summarized in English by Michael Bohlander, 2 OX. J.L. & RELIGION 217 (2013). For a semi-official presentation, including translated excerpts, see Jan F. Orth, *Explaining the Cologne Circumcision Decision*, 77 J. CRIM. L. 497 (2013).

religious communities that require circumcision, such as Jews and Muslims, but also with others. "Do you still want us Jews?" asked the chairwoman of the Central Council of Jews in Germany.[5] She pointed out that, if the district court's decision was upheld, Jews would not be able to comply simultaneously with both the mandates of German law and those of their religion. In response to such criticism, the legislators added the new § 1631d to the German Civil Code, which allows parents to decide whether to circumcise their sons while imposing certain requirements on the execution of circumcision.[6] This law emulates a similar Swedish law[7] as well as a German decree of the Agency for Sanitary Matters from 1843, which triggered the so-called circumcision debate at the time.[8]

At first sight, we are dealing with a balancing of different legal rights granted by the constitution.[9] On one side is the child's right to his bodily integrity; on the other side we find the parents' right to decide on the education of their children and the freedom to exercise their (and their child's) religion, according to which circumcision is essential to the newborn's entrance into

See also Angelika Günzel, *Nationalization of Religious Parental Education? The German Circumcision Case*, 2 OXFORD J.L. & RELIGION 206 (2013); Gerhard Robbers, *Recent Legal Developments in Germany: Infant Circumcision and Church Tax*, 15 ECCLESIASTICAL L.J. 69 (2013).

[5] *Jewish Leader Lays into Germany: "Do You Still Want Us Jews?"* Spiegel Online International, Sept. 5, 2012, *available at* http://www.spiegel.de/international/germany/german-jewish-leader-attacks-germany-over-circumcision-debate-a-854070.html.

[6] Gesetz über den Umfang der Personensorge bei einer Beschneidung des männlichen Kindes [Law on the Scope of Personal Custody regarding the circumcision of male children], Dec. 20, 2012, BGBL. I at 2749; *cf.* Stephan Rixen, *Das Gesetz über den Umfang der Personensorge bei einer Beschneidung des männlichen Kindes*, 2013 NEUE JURISTISCHE WOCHENSCHRIFT 257; for critique, see, for example, Josef Isensee, *Grundrechtliche Konsequenz wider geheiligte Tradition – Der Streit um die Beschneidung*, 68 JURISTENZEITSCHRIFT 317 (2013); DIE BESCHNEIDUNG VON JUNGEN – EIN TRAURIGES VERMÄCHTNIS (Mathias Franz ed., 2014). More broadly on the German debate, see Diana Aurenque & Urban Wiesing, *German Law on Circumcision and Its Debate: How an Ethical and Legal Issue Turned Political*, BIOETHICS (Dec. 23, 2013), doi: 10.1111/bioe.12077.

[7] Lag om omskärelse av pojkar, SFS 2001:449; *cf.* Johanna Schiratzki, *Banning God's Law in the Name of the Holy Body – The Nordic Position on Ritual Male Circumcision*, 5 THE FAMILY IN LAW 35, 37–39 (2011), *available at* http://din-online.info/pdf/fam5-3.pdf; Kimberley A. Greenfield, *Cutting Away Religious Freedom: The Global and National Debate Surrounding Male Circumcision*, 15 RUTGERS J.L. & RELIGION 353, 361–63 (2013).

[8] *See* ROBERT LIBERLES, RELIGIOUS CONFLICT IN SOCIAL CONTEXT: THE RESURGENCE OF ORTHODOX JUDAISM IN FRANKFURT AM MAIN, 1838–1877 (1985); ROBIN JUDD, CONTESTED RITUALS: CIRCUMCISION, KOSHER BUTCHERING, AND JEWISH POLITICAL LIFE IN GERMANY, 1843–1933, at 21–57 (2007).

[9] Werner Beulke/Annika Dießner, *ein kleiner Schnitt für einen Menschen, aber ein großes Thema für die Menschheit – Warum das Urteil des LG Köln zur religiös motivierten Beschneidung von Knaben nicht überzeugt*, 7 ZEITSCHRIFT FÜR INTERNATIONALE STRAFRECHTSDOGMATIK 338, 343–45 (2012).

the religion. Such rights must be balanced against each other. In some cases, the parents' right to determine their children's care and religion prevail; in others, this authority must give way to other rights. But these are all legal rights of German law. So, what is the connection to non-state law?

In this case, the legislator ultimately regarded the religious justification for circumcision as irrelevant: "This law does not require courts to inquire into religiously motivated circumcision," it was noted during the presentation of the draft law.[10] Believers, however, regard religious mandates as law. "This is my covenant, which ye shall keep, between me and you and thy seed after thee; Every man child among you shall be circumcised." This is not merely the formulation of a ritual. Rather, God spells out a command: You shall circumcise; and a sanction for its violation: his soul shall be cut off from his people. It is thus evidently a norm. Now, there are many norms: decency norms, moral norms, religious norms. Not all norms are legal rules. The question remains: Is the command formulated by God in this case law?

Dieter Graumann, President of the Central Council of Jews in Germany, thinks yes.[11] The requirement of circumcision is a principle of the Halakhah, Jewish law, and as such legally binding for each Jew. My quotation stems from the First Book of Moses,[12] but the positions on the Jewish law of circumcision are numerous.[13] Holm Putzke, Professor in Passau, says no, at least implicitly: If one leaves decisions about circumcision uncontrolled to the realm of religion, one finds oneself in a "space without law."[14]

And whether the circumcision requirement is law, is – so it seems – important. If it is not law, one can demand that Jews and Muslims in Germany comply first with German law. The exercise of their religion is then clearly

---

[10] Press Release, German Ministry of Justice, Beschneidung bleibt künftig möglich (Oct 10, 2012), *available at* http://www.bmj.de/SharedDocs/Archiv/DE/Pressemitteilungen/2012/20121010_Beschneidung_bleibt_kuenftig_moeglich.html?nn=1514722; *see also* BT-Drucks. 17/11295, p. 16.

[11] Press Release, Central Council of Jews in Germany, On the Decision of the District Court of Cologne Concerning Circumcision of Boys (June 26, 2012), *available at* http://www.zentralratdjuden.de/en/article/3706.on-the-decision-of-the-district-court-of-cologne-concerning-circumcision-of-boys.html ("Circumcision of newborn boys is an inherent part of the Jewish religion and has been practiced worldwide for centuries. This religious right is respected in every country in the world.").

[12] *See supra* note 2.

[13] J.M. Glass, *Religious Circumcision: A Jewish View*, 83 Brit. J. Urology Int'l 17 (1999); J. David Bleich, *Circumcision: The Current Controversy*, 33 Tradition 45 (1999); J. David Bleich, Judaism and Healing: Halakhic Perspectives 48–51 (2002).

[14] Holm Putzke, *Die strafrechtliche Relevanz der Beschneidung von Knaben. Zugleich ein Beitrag über die Grenzen der Einwilligung in Fällen der Personensorge*, in Strafrecht zwischen System und Telos: Festschrift für Rolf Dietrich Herzberg zum siebzigsten Geburtstag 669, 701 (Putzke et al. eds., 2008). For Putzke's critique of the decision in English, see Reinhard Merkel & Holm Putzke, *After Cologne: Male Circumcision and the Law. Parental Right, Religious Liberty or Criminal Assault?*, 39 J. Med. Ethics 444 (2013).

subject to the limitations imposed by German law. And one can demand that Jews and Muslims adapt their rituals to comply with German law – or, if this is not possible, that they abolish these rituals or leave the country. If, however, the circumcision requirement is a principle of Jewish law, and this law is enforceable in Germany, this case is more complex. We see two legal systems clashing and it is not a priori clear, which must prevail.

This potential clash illustrates the most important issue with which legal scholars must deal today: global legal pluralism.[15] A vast array of normative systems exists in the world today. These normative systems at times complement each other, overlap, compete with each other, influence each other, or clash with each other. For a long time, we have not been prepared for these developments. We have envisioned law as a collection of rules, which must be made compatible with each other within a system – the system of state law. Such approach is only slightly helpful given the fragmentation of law today. We are thus in need of new theories to understand law today. This means that we must first understand what exactly we can define as law.

TYPES OF LAW

When we speak about law today, we typically mean state law. If this were the end of the inquiry, the answer would be easy: A religious rule is not a rule mandated by the state and therefore, not law. But of course, numerous rules exist that are clearly legal rules even though they are not mandated by the state.

Law below, above, and beside the State

First, there is law *below* the state. In Germany, for instance, there are not only federal law and the law of the individual *Länder*, but also municipal law, the law of individual cities. A comparable situation exists in the United States with its federal system.

But there is also law *above* the state, that is, supranational law. This means, the law of the European Union, on the one hand, and public international law on the other. Public international law is, traditionally, the law regulating relations between states, such as, for instance, when a state may defend against a military attack or how a state must treat foreign ambassadors. In recent times, public international law has been expanded to define the rights of individuals

---

[15] Ralf Michaels, *Global Legal Pluralism*, 5 ANN. REV. L. & SOC. SCI. 243 (2009); Paul Schiff Berman, GLOBAL LEGAL PLURALISM: A JURISPRUDENCE OF LAW BEYOND BORDERS (2012); Anne Griffiths, *Reviewing Legal Pluralism*, *in* LAW AND SOCIAL THEORY 269 (Reza Banakar & Max Travers eds., 2d ed. 2013).

as well, especially in human rights law.[16] A part of public international law is based on treaties between individual states. Another part consists of customary law. Yet another part is the so-called ius cogens – those rules regarded as so important that states are not even allowed to derogate from them through treaties.

Lastly, there is law *beside* the state. In fact, there is not only one, "the" state, but many states that recognize each other as states. Each state has its own law, and these laws stand next to each other and must be distinguished from one another in individual cases.

These laws are not directly state law. Nonetheless, they do not represent a real challenge to the state because they can all be traced back to the state.

This is most evidently true for law *below* the state. The fact that this is law can be shown by means of the Constitution. The Constitution regulates the legislative competence of the *Länder* and the independence of the municipalities. The *Länder* in turn have laws that enable certain regional bodies to legislate. All effective laws in Germany can be traced back, just like the steps of a pyramid, directly or indirectly, to the constitution. We speak, based on the theory of Austrian legal philosopher Hans Kelsen, of the *Stufenbau* of the legal system.[17]

Law *above* the state can also be traced back to the state.[18] Treaty law is law precisely because states agreed to it as contracting parties. Customary law is law because states customarily abide by it. Only ius cogens is somewhat problematic; I will return to it later.

What about law *beside* the state, that is, the law of other states? This can also become relevant in our home state. For instance, when a German court is faced with the question of the validity of a marriage that was concluded in Italy, it will apply Italian law, not German law. It does so not, however, because Italy has competence to legislate for Germany in this case. Instead,

---

[16] Kate Partlett, The Individual in the International Legal System: Continuity and Change in International Law (2011).

[17] Hans Kelsen, Pure Theory of Law (1967) (where *Stufenbau* is translated as 'hierarchical structure'). *Cf* Adolf Merkl, *Prolegomena einer Theorie des rechtlichen Stufenbaus, in* Gesellschaft, Staat und Recht: Untersuchungen zur reinen Rechtslehre: Festschrift Hans Kelsen zum 50. Geburtstag gewidmet 252 (Alfred Verdross ed., 1931), *reprinted in* Die Wiener rechtstheoretische Schule, Band II, S. 1311 (Hans Klecatsky, René Marcic & Herbert Schambeck eds., 1968); Stanley Paulson, *How Merkl's* Stufenbaulehre *Informs Kelsen's Concept of Law*, 21 Revus – J. Const. Theory & Phil. of L. 29 (2013), *available at* http://revus.revues.org/2727.

[18] And perhaps even be integrated into Kelsen's *Stufenbau*. Theo Öhlinger, Unity of the Legal System or Legal Pluralism: The Stufenbau Doctrine in Present-Day Europe, in National Constitutions in the Era of Integration 163 (A. Jyränki ed., 1999); Gerhard Baumgartner, *Der Rang des Gemeinschaftsrechts im Stufenbau der Rechtsordnung*, 8 Journal für Rechtspolitik 84 (2000).

it applies Italian law because a rule of German (or European Union) law, a so-called private international law rule, determines that the law of the place of marriage shall be applicable. Therefore, even the application of Italian law in Germany originates in German law.[19]

Non-State Law

Jewish law did not appear in any of these categories. Such law is not *above*, not *under* and not *beside* the state. It is thus, at least in principle, non-state law.

Types

A great number of non-state laws exist.[20] First, there is the group of religious laws – for instance, as we have seen, Jewish and Islamic law[21] – but also Protestant and Catholic Church law. Such law can be state law if a state declares it to be official law.[22] This is the case in Saudi Arabia where Islamic law is declared to be official law in the constitution[23] – and of course, in the Vatican for Catholic Church law.[24] More commonly, however, religious law is non-state, transnational law – oftentimes with regional variations – is valid for believers all over the world.

Another type of non-state law is so-called customary law or folk laws. Customary law exists in modern state law as well, but what is meant here is something else. After the downfall of the Roman Empire, most of the legal

---

[19] *Cf.* MICHAEL BOGDAN, PRIVATE INTERNATIONAL LAW AS COMPONENT OF THE LAW OF THE FORUM (2012).

[20] Marc Hertogh, *What is Non-State Law? Mapping the Other Hemisphere of the Legal World, in* INTERNATIONAL GOVERNANCE AND LAW: STATE REGULATION AND NON-STATE LAW 11 (Hanneke van Schooten & Jonathan Verschuuren eds., 2008).

[21] AN INTRODUCTION TO THE HISTORY AND SOURCES OF JEWISH LAW (N.S. Hecht et al. eds, 1996); JOSEPH SCHACHT, AN INTRODUCTION TO ISLAMIC LAW (1964); N.J. COULSON, A HISTORY OF ISLAMIC LAW (2011).

[22] *E.g.*, Kilian Bälz, *"Die Islamisierung" des Rechts in Ägypten und Libyen: Islamische Rechtsetzung im Nationalstaat*, 62 RABELSZ 437 (1998); Sherman A. Jackson, *Islamic Reform between Islamic Law and the Nation-State, in* THE OXFORD HANDBOOK OF ISLAM AND POLITICS 42 (John L. Esposito & Emad El-Din Shahin eds., 2013).

[23] FRANK E. VOGEL, ISLAMIC LAW AND THE LEGAL SYSTEM OF SAUDÍ: STUDIES OF SAUDI ARABIA (2000).

[24] However, much Vatican law is quite similar to Italian law. Giuseppe DallaTorre, *L'ordinamento giudiziario, in* OTTANTA ANNI DELLO STATO DELLA CITTÀ DEL VATICANO 135 (Barbara Jatta ed., 2009); *see also* Nicola Picardi, *Nell'ottantesimo anniversario della giurisdizione vaticana, in* I STUDI IN ONORE DI GIOVANNI GIACOBBE 145 (Giuseppe Dalla Torre ed., 2010); Giuseppe DallaTorre, *Aspetti della Giustizia Vaticana*, 18 STATO, CHIESE E PLURALISMO CONFESSIONALE (2013), *available at* http://riviste.unimi.it/index.php/statoechiese/article/view/2988.

systems were tribal laws in Europe as well.[25] In large parts of Africa and Polynesia, this was true until colonization – and, in part, even after colonization, as the colonial powers allowed the tribes to retain a certain degree of autonomy.[26]

Another and completely different example is the self-created business law, the so-called lex mercatoria. The story goes that merchants in the Middle Ages created their own law that was binding all over Europe while being independent of local cities and courts.[27] Most of this story is fabricated.[28] But this myth has been used as inspiration for a new lex mercatoria: The globalized business community, it is asserted, is creating its own law – through standard contracts and trade usages, but also through rules written down by non governmental organizations such as the International Chamber of Commerce.[29]

This lex mercatoria serves as a model for a number of other non-state laws of globalization. A *lex digitalis* or *informatica* is said to describe the private law of the Internet.[30] A *lex sportiva* describes the self-created rules of international sport and its federations such as UEFA and FIFA and its courts, such as the Court of Arbitration for Sports.[31] *Lex constructionis* describes the standards for large construction projects;[32] *lex financiaria* is the privately created law of the international financial markets,[33] *lex maritima* is the largely privately created sea trade law.[34] One might almost think that a non-state law can be found simply by giving it a Latin name.

---

[25] 1 Karl Kroeschell, Deutsche Rechtsgeschichte 21–34 (13th ed. 2008).

[26] *See* Werner Menski, Comparative Law in a Global Context – The Legal Systems of Asia and Africa (2006).

[27] Most recently, Bruce L. Benson, *The Law Merchant's Story: How Romantic Is It?*, in Law, Economics and Evolutionary Theory 68 (Peer Zumbansen & Gralf-Peter Calliess eds., 2011).

[28] Emily Kadens, *The Myth of the Customary Law Merchant*, 90 Tex. L. Rev. 1153 (2012).

[29] Klaus Peter Berger, The Creeping Codification of the New Lex Mercatoria (2010); I Jan Hendrik Dalhuisen, Dalhuisen on Transnational Comparative, Commercial, Financial and Trade Law, Introduction: The New Lex Mercatoria and Its Sources (2010).

[30] Aron Mefford, *Lex Informatica: Foundations of Law on the Internet*, 5 Ind. J. Global Legal Stud. 211 (1997); Joel Reidenberg, *Lex Informatica: The Formulation of Information Policy Rules Through Technology*, 78 Tex. L. Rev. 553 (1998).

[31] Lex Sportiva: What is Sports Law? (Robert C.R. Siekmann & Janwillem Soek eds., 2012).

[32] Charles Molineau, *Moving Toward a Lex Mercatoria – A Lex Constructionis*, 14 J. Int'l Arb. 55 (1997); *see also* Hans Lindahl, Fault Lines of Globalization: Legal Order and the Politics of A-Legality 59–64 (2013).

[33] Annelise Riles, Collateral Knowledge: Legal Reasoning in the Global Financial Markets (2011).

[34] William Tetley, *The General Maritime Law – The Lex Maritima*, 20 Syracuse J. Int'l. L. & Com. 105 (1004); Andreas Maurer, Lex Maritima: Grundzüge eines transnationalen Seehandelsrechts (2012).

Characteristics

Thus far an incomplete overview. Some of these legal systems are based on written texts – such as the Bible, or the UNIDROIT Principles of International Commercial Contracts, a non-state codification of contract law.[35] Other laws are not based on texts, such as African customary laws – attempts to codify these in the twentieth century are today widely regarded as having failed.[36] Some of these legal systems have their own judicial bodies – such as the Court of Arbitration for Sports for the *lex sportiva*, or the Ecclesiatical Courts for the Catholic Church law. Others do not administer justice centrally. Islamic Law, for instance, is largely administered through legal opinions, the so-called *fatwa*. Some of these legal systems apply only to the members of a certain community, such as the community of believers, or the community of tribe members. Others apply to each person participating in a certain system, without a real community necessarily being created through this participation. For instance, the group of all merchants is hardly a community; if this were the case, it would likely be an illegal cartel.

As we can see by now, non-state law is in fact not a real category. These legal systems have almost nothing in common except that, precisely, they are non-state law. It is therefore not clear that we can treat them all alike.

Legal Nature

Indeed, we have to ask the same question with regard to these legal systems that we already asked at the beginning: Are they law or not? For a long time, since the rise of legal positivism, we have recognized only state law as law. This would mean that all these legal systems are not law.[37]

An overly simple response to this proposition would be this: For a long time, all law was non-state law because law predates the state.[38] The state, in the modern sense of the word, dates back only to the sixteenth century.[39] Before that, certain orders existed but they were fundamentally different. In addition, prestate systems as well as the premodern state did not claim a monopoly over

---

[35] On such texts, see NILS JANSEN, THE MAKING OF LEGAL AUTHORITY – NON-LEGISLATIVE CODIFICATION IN HISTORICAL AND COMPARATIVE PERSPECTIVE (2010).

[36] Kaarlo Tuori, *Legal Pluralism and Modernization: American Law Professors in Ethiopia and the Downfall of the Restatements of African Customary Law*, 62 J. LEGAL PLURALISM 43 (2010).

[37] Simon Roberts, *After Government? On Representing Law Without the State*, 68 MOD. L. REV. 1 (2005).

[38] HAROLD BERMAN, LAW AND REVOLUTION: THE FORMATION OF THE WESTERN LEGAL TRADITION (1983).

[39] MARTIN VAN CREVELD, THE RISE AND DECLINE OF THE STATE (1999).

legislation. It was always clear that states, or rulers, could legislate. However, such legislation occurred over centuries largely through sporadic special laws, and in no case comprehensively. This was initially true even for the modern state. It was not until the eighteenth and nineteenth centuries that European states began to formulate their entire private law in the form of codes; no earlier than the twentieth century, the idea prevailed that the common law created by courts could be traced back to the state's legislative monopoly.[40]

But this simple answer is too simple. The idea that for a world *without* states, all law is non-state law does not tell us much about a world *with* states.[41] A contemporary concept of law must grapple with contemporary circumstances and this means also with the state's legislative monopoly. The question is thus not, Can Jewish law be law in any era? Rather the question is, Is it law today?

IS THIS LAW? THREE DEBATES

The question what is law has always been at the center of legal theory. I am presenting elements from three debates – philosophical, anthropological, and theoretical – before I submit my own proposition.

Philosophy of Law

Philosophy of law is first among the disciplines that ask "What is law?" Philosophers of law have asked for centuries how the state differs from a gang of thieves,[42] though they have been mostly interested in the law of the state than the law of the gang of thieves. A large part of modern philosophy of law deals with the relationship between positive law on the one hand and justice or morality or natural law on the other, and especially with the question about the extent to which positive state law has to comply with general principles that transcend the state. This would be relevant in practice, for example, for the question of whether Nazi SS officers or East German border guards can rely on the defense that the killings they committed were justified by the law of the Third Reich or the German Democratic Republic respectively, even though these killings were evidently immoral.[43]

---

[40] *See* BEYOND THE STATE – RETHINKING PRIVATE LAW (Nils Jansen & Ralf Michaels eds., 2008).

[41] Ralf Michaels, *The Mirage of Non-State Governance*, 2010 UTAH L. REV. 31.

[42] Augustine, De Civitate Dei, Liber IV.

[43] For the German debate and cases, see Robert Alexy, *A Defence of Radbruch's Formula, in* RECRAFTING THE RULE OF LAW: THE LIMITS OF LEGAL ORDER 15 (David Dyzenhaus ed., 1999).

This contrast between positive state law and supranational natural law is not helpful in answering our question. This is because Jewish law, for instance, is neither positive state law nor an expression of a supranational, universal system of norms. It is rather the system of laws of a defined community.

Social Efficacy

Robert Alexy, a legal philosopher at the University of Kiel, identifies three criteria necessary to qualify a system of norms as law: authoritative issuance, social efficacy, and correctness of content.[44] This second criterion appears to be of special importance for our question. Eugen Ehrlich, a famous legal sociologist, explained, for instance, that the law that was in fact effective at the borders of the Austro-Hungarian Empire differed significantly from the law made in Vienna, and that it must be regarded as the actual law of the Empire.[45] Scholars who want to prove that lex mercatoria is law rely on arguments such as Ehrlich's.[46] They claim that the norms that merchants adhere to in practice is what constitutes real law, or *law in action*, because it is efficacious, unlike law on the books, which has only formal character.

This alone would, however, be a false conclusion. Alexy (who does not discuss non-state law) says that a state rule that is never adhered to cannot be law. The converse argument, however, does not follow from this. Hence, a non-state rule is not automatically law merely because it is widely adhered to and enforced. Many moral, decency, and religious rules are adhered to by great numbers of people. But we cannot call them law merely for this reason.

Rule of Recognition

The famous British legal philosopher H.L.A. Hart formulated an answer to this conundrum. He proposed that the commands of a sovereign are not law merely because he can enforce them. What is necessary is that his subjects recognize his order as law; hence, they legitimate this order as law through a so-called rule of recognition. Hart admittedly applied this thought especially to state law and in part to public international law. For him, non-state law could

---

44 ROBERT ALEXY, THE ARGUMENT FROM INJUSTICE: A REPLY TO LEGAL POSITIVISM (2002).

45 EUGEN EHRLICH, FUNDAMENTAL PRINCIPLES OF THE SOCIOLOGY OF LAW (1936); on Ehrlich see also MANFRED REHBINDER, DIE BEGRÜNDUNG DER RECHTSSOZIOLOGIE DURCH EUGEN EHRLICH (1986); LIVING LAW: RECONSIDERING EUGEN EHRLICH (Marc Hertogh ed., 2009).

46 Gunther Teubner, *Global Bukowina – Legal Pluralism in the World Society*, in GLOBAL LAW WITHOUT A STATE (Gunther Teubner ed., 1996). For a critique of Teubner's use of Ehrlich, see David Nelken, *An E-mail from Global Bukowina*, 3 INT'L J.L IN CONTEXT 189 (2007).

become part of a legal system only once state law recognized it as such.[47] This means, for instance for Jewish law, that it is only law once state law invokes it as such. This happens in countries that apply religious law based on their constitution. For instance in India, Hindu law is in force for Hindus and Islamic law is in force for Muslims.

It is not certain, however, that such a rule of recognition can be applied to a sovereign only. Indeed, attempts have been made to apply Hart's model to non-state law. John Gardner, another legal philosopher from Oxford, maintains that customary law can be law, as long as there are only officials who administer this law.[48] Without institutionalization, therefore, there shall be no law.

Canon law would consequently be recognized as law without any problems, as the Catholic Church has a great number of officials. Islamic law is a more difficult case. Although there are Islamic law experts and even officials, every individual believer is called upon to interpret and develop the law. Lex mercatoria, as well, is not clearly law under this approach. The most important enforcers of lex mercatoria, its own arbitral courts, are precisely not officials; they are merely appointed by private parties. This suggests a weakness of the approach. Ultimately, the model for non-state law is, in this case, state law. It does not need to be exactly like state law, but it must conform in essence.

Sociology and Anthropology of Law

In Oxford, the definition of non-state law may be predominantly an intellectual pastime over a glass of port. For sociologists and anthropologists of law, in contrast, it is on the daily agenda. It was anthropologists and ethnologists of law who, in the context of colonization, found societies that had something that looked like law, even though it was very different from the law of a modern nation state. It was sociologists of law, like Ehrlich who was previously mentioned, who found that customary law – or, socially constructed law – was very important even in our Western societies.

Legal Pluralism

For the colonies, just like for us, the problem arose that more than one law claimed validity. In the colonies, these laws were the law of the colonizer and the previously valid law of the indigenous peoples. It is precisely for this situation that the term legal pluralism has been made useful. Legal pluralism

---

[47] H.L.A. Hart, The Concept of Law 45 (2d ed. 1994).
[48] John Gardner, Law as a Leap of Faith 289 (2012).

has been famously defined as "a situation in which two or more legal systems coexist in the same social field."[49] Only one of these legal systems is the law of the state.

Colonialism is, of course, not a very attractive model. In colonialism, the non-state law of the indigenous peoples is law only to the extent it is recognized as such by the state and is subordinated to state law. In this form, legal pluralism still exists in many countries, for example, in India, Israel, and South Africa. In these cases, the dominance of the state is not challenged. This is referred to, based on an essay by John Griffiths from 1986, as weak legal pluralism, which in fact is not really legal pluralism at all.[50] Griffiths distinguishes a so-called strong legal pluralism, which is marked by the absence of a hierarchy between state and non-state law. Both legal systems coexist, are sometimes mutually constitutive, and, if not, have an imprecise but in any case, very complex relationship to each other. What is important for Griffiths is to challenge the monopoly of the state. He writes polemically that the monopoly of the state is a myth, while legal pluralism is reality. And he rejects attempts to make the legal character of non-state legal systems dependent on their recognition by the state. He refutes these arguments because they cast doubt on the autonomy of non-state law.

The Concept of Legal Pluralism

This indeed leads to another problem. If norms do not become law because the state acknowledges them as such, another criterion is needed. Legal sociologists, in particular, have tried to identify such a term based on certain basic functions of law. For instance, they see the function of law in the resolution of disputes; to the extent a non-state legal system serves to resolve disputes, therefore, it must be acknowledged as law. Or they ascertain it is the main function of law to create a social order; this can also happen through non-state norms. And so forth.

Such attempts, however, are doomed to fail. I see at least three problems. First, today we are no longer convinced that institutions such as law necessarily fulfill certain functions – an idea posited by the functionalists of the last century. Instead, we view law as fulfilling a vast array of functions, or alternatively, at times, as simply not fulfilling any function at all. (There is such a thing as dysfunctional law.) Second, two institutions that fulfill the same function are not identical; they are merely functionally equivalent. I can exclude strangers

---

[49] Sally E. Merry, *Legal Pluralism*, 22 Law & Soc'y Rev. 869, 870 (1988).
[50] John Griffiths, *What Is Legal Pluralism?*, 24 J. Legal Pluralism 1 (1986).

from my backyard through legal rules, especially through property laws, as well as by building a fence. This, however, does not make the fence law.[51] As John Gardner puts it, "law is not, 'whatever resolves disputes' but a special way of resolving disputes."[52] Third – and this is perhaps the most important argument – this method validates state law as benchmark: Non-state norms become law to the extent they are consistent with state law. A concept of law that is independent from the state cannot be achieved in this way.

Problems similar to this have led many scholars to abandon the search for a definition of law. Brian Tamanaha, for example, suggests that we should regard as law whatever members of a community regard as law.[53] Others go even further. They propose a complete renouncement of the concept of law and instead a focus solely on norms.[54] Even John Griffiths, who was authoritative for the idea of legal pluralism twenty-five years ago, now wants to replace the concept of legal pluralism with normative pluralism.[55] For this perspective, the question whether Jewish law is law or not is therefore irrelevant for its description.

SYSTEMS THEORY

So far, it seems, we have not made a lot of headway. The concept of legal philosophy is traditionally bound to the state and too little focused on phenomena outside the state. Legal anthropology, on the other hand, deals with these phenomena by completely renouncing the concept of law. It therefore abandons the ability to describe appropriately that which is specific to law.

An attempt to combine and thereby transcend these two approaches can be found in systems theory. Niklas Luhmann, a sociologist at the University of Bielefeld, proposed to define law, as a subsystem of society, not only through its function but also through the code with which it is discussed. According to him, law is a discourse, more precisely the discourse that follows the binary code legal/illegal.[56] This approach to law as discourse does not need to be

---

[51] *But see, e.g.,* LARRY LESSIG, CODE AND OTHER LAWS OF CYBERSPACE (1999).

[52] GARDNER, *supra* note 48, at 293.

[53] Brian Tamanaha, *A Non-Essentialist Version of Legal Pluralism*, 27 J.L & SOC'Y 296 (2000).

[54] *See, e.g.,* William Twining, *Normative and Legal Pluralism: A Global Perspective*, 20 DUKE J. COMP. & INT'L L. 473 (2010).

[55] John Griffiths, *The Idea of Sociology of Law and Its Relation to Law and to Sociology*, *in* 8 LAW AND SOCIOLOGY – CURRENT LEGAL ISSUES 49, 63–64. (Michael Freeman ed., 2006).

[56] *E.g.,* Niklas Luhmann, *Operational Closure and Structural Coupling: The Differentiation of the Legal System*, 13 CARDOZO L. REV. 1419 (1991–1992).

attached to the state. Gunther Teubner has used this approach to design what he termed "private law without the state."[57] According to Teubner, the new lex mercatoria, for instance, is an entire legal regime developed on the basis of contract. This legal regime follows the code legal/illegal without having to rely on the state. Other scholars have expanded the application of this discourse-oriented approach to other areas of law.[58] Jewish law, in particular, has been recognized as an attractive object of study.[59]

This approach is promising. It combines the empirical approach of legal anthropology to start with phenomena observed in society, with the theoretical approach of legal philosophy to enable a general concept of law. This is, however, easier in theory than in practice. The primacy of the code legal/illegal, for instance, is often stated rather than empirically determined. This is true even for Teubner's groundbreaking approach, in which the new lex mercatoria is designed more as a hypothetical construct than as an empirical fact.[60] It is also questionable how universal this binary code is in fact. Islamic law, for instance, distinguishes not between two, but between five assessments: obligatory, recommended, neutral, abominable, and sinful. This rationality cannot be classified within the binary legal/illegal.[61]

Another point is important at this stage. Teubner claims that this is one of the few cases in which legal theory produces binding results for legal doctrine. Given that lex mercatoria uses the code legal/illegal, Teubner asserts it is law and must therefore be acknowledged as such by state law.[62] Dieter Graumann should be glad to hear this. Holm Putzke, on the other hand, would ask from where this duty to acknowledge arises – and he would be right. A group can hardly force another to acknowledge their norms merely by using a certain form of discourse.

---

[57] Teubner, *supra* note 46.

[58] GRALF-PETER CALLIESS & PEER ZUMBANSEN, ROUGH CONSENSUS AND RUNNING CODE: A THEORY OF TRANSNATIONAL PRIVATE LAW (2010); MAURER, *supra* note 34.

[59] JUSTUS VON DANIELS, RELIGIÖSES RECHT ALS REFERENZ – JÜDISCHES RECHT IM RECHTSWIS-SENSCHAFTLICHEN VERGLEICH (2009); TALMUDISCHE TRADITION UND MODERNE RECHTSTHE-ORIE – KONTEXTE UND PERSPEKTIVEN EINER BEGEGNUNG (Karl H. Ladeur & Ino Augsberg eds., 2012). For critical assessments of using Jewish law, see Suzanne Last Stone, *In Pursuit of the Countertext: The Turn to the Jewish Legal Model in Contemporary American Legal Theory*, 106 HARV. L. REV. 813 (1993).

[60] Ralf Michaels, *The True Lex Mercatoria: Law Beyond the State*, 14 IND. J. GLOBAL LEGAL STUD. 447, 452–60 (2007).

[61] Nonetheless, one of Teubner's students applied his approach to Islamic law. Kilian Bälz, *Shari'a and Qanun in Egyptian Law: A Systems Theory Approach to Legal Pluralism*, 2 Y.B. ISLAMIC & MIDDLE EASTERN L. 37 (1995).

[62] Teubner, *supra* note 46, at 9 ("The debate on [lex mercatoria] is one of the rare cases in which practical legal decision making becomes directly dependent upon legal theory.").

TOWARD A RELATIONAL CONCEPT OF LAW

Systems theory has thus also failed to provide an answer to the question whether the judge in Cologne should acknowledge Jewish law as law. Ultimately, systems theorists face the same dilemma as legal philosophers and anthropologists. One option is to find a universally valid definition of law. In this case, one would have to justify why this definition is the right one, as opposed to another. In particular, it would be necessary to determine whether one is merely expanding the application of a concept from state law to non-state phenomena instead of in fact finding a truly universal definition. The other option is to leave it up to each group to determine what it wants to acknowledge as law. Then, however, the question arises why this self-determination must be binding for others.

I believe that this dialectic between the claims of universality and relativism itself can be fruitful for a definition of law.[63] I want to explain this by taking a detour. This detour leads us to private international law or, as it is called in the United States, conflict of laws. This is the legal discipline that determines in which cases a court must apply a foreign law.

Private international law has, at least traditionally, a curious structure. On the one hand, it is a sort of metalaw, a law above all laws, because it defines the borders between various laws. On the other hand, the rules of private international law themselves are not situated above the state but belong precisely to state law. This means that each state has its own private international law which determines when that state's own law and when another state's law must be applied. For instance, both Germany and Italy determine for themselves whether German or Italian law must be applied to a particular case pursuant to their own private international law rules, and, depending on the circumstances, the outcomes may be different.

It is the case that today's private international law generally allows the application of only the law of other states. It does not acknowledge non-state law, such as Jewish law, as law.[64] The reason for this, however, lies not in the nature of private international law – structurally, it could call for the application for non-state law, and some private international laws do so. Private international law derives the question, what is acknowledged as law – that is, what can be determined as applicable law – not from legal philosophy or anthropology. Rather, it answers this question itself and for itself. The concept of law itself becomes a legal concept.

---

[63] *Cf.* Michaels, *supra* note 15, at 250, 256.
[64] Ralf Michaels, *The Re-State-Ment of Non-State Law: The State, Choice of Law, and the Challenge from Global Legal Pluralism*, 51 Wayne L. Rev. 1209 (2005).

Finally, it is also the case that non-state legal systems have their own conflicts rules. It is not only state law that determines under which circumstances a non-state law shall be applied. Rather, non-state law also determines under which circumstances state law must be applied – provided that non-state law acknowledges state law as law. Non-state law, as well, determines for itself what it recognizes as law.

The concept of law that I want to propose, on this basis, basically consists of two elements.

First, each system determines whether it regards itself as law or not. In particular, members of non-state communities can also define their own norms as law. This may be effected through a *rule of recognition* or through the usage of certain terms (Luhmann's Code). If, therefore, a Jewish community designates its norms as law, it is free to do so. Therewith, I adopt in this first step the demand particularly of legal anthropology to rely on the legal normative phenomenon itself and not to impose an abstract concept on it.

This self-determination – autonomy in the true sense of the word – does not have a binding effect for other legal systems. This leads me to the second element. In relation to other systems – such as that of the state – law, such as Jewish law, only becomes law insofar as the state recognizes it as such. For the applicability and binding nature of law, this is the standard procedure of private international law: foreign law is applicable and binding in the state only to the extent it is designated as such by private international law. I want to expand this thought to the definition of law itself: whether the law of Y is law for X is a matter of its recognition by X.

This is not a completely unfamiliar though process. Rather, an example exists in public international law. In public international law, a new state does not become a state merely because it fulfills certain objective criteria, at least not pursuant to constitutive theory, but because the community of states acknowledges it as such.[65]

Insofar, the state is autonomous. However, it does not have – and this is the answer to the criticism of legal anthropology – the ultimate deciding power. This is because the state can decide if Jewish law is law for itself only. It cannot bind other states. Moreover, and this is an important point, the same consideration applies vice versa. Jewish law as well can decide independently whether it will recognize state law as law.

---

[65] *E.g.*, Lassa Oppenheim, International Law § 71 (1955). *See also* Stephen Talmon, *The Constitutive Versus the Declaratory Doctrine of Recognition: Tertium Non Datur?*, 75 Brit. Y.B. Int'l L. 101–81 (2004).

The law of globalization is thus not a uniform system. It is certainly not a *Stufenbau* like state law, with a single highest norm or a single rule of recognition.[66] At the same time it is not a coming together of normative orders on an equal level. Whether these orders are equal is precisely not determined by a central authority but by each individual order, effectively in a decentralized manner. The complexity of fragmented law, which I have just hinted at, is better described as a plurality of recognition relationships.

I believe that this approach overcomes three problems. The first one is the dilemma between the universality and the relativity of the concept of law. My concept of law is both universal and relative at the same time. Each law determines for itself universally what it considers to be law, and what not. It claims this determination not only for itself, as it would under a strict relativism, but also for foreign laws. But this autonomous determination is in itself only relative, as each legal order can make this determination validly only for itself. I call the concept relational: a normative order is law in relation to another legal order.

The second problem is whether we can find a concept of law independent from the state. My concept of law is inspired by private international law and to the extent that private international law is traditionally state law, it is also inspired by state law. But private international law is a necessary element of each normative order: Each order must necessarily define its limitations and also to what extent it will allow foreign law. The starting point is thus not state law but merely the idea of a legal system.

The third problem is the one pointed out by Griffiths. The quality of a law as law should not be dependent on its acknowledgment by the state. For my concept of law, recognition indeed plays a role. But I universalize this recognition requirement and apply it as well to the recognition of the state by other legal systems. Griffith's main complaint went against the idea that the state occupies a superior position; in my concept, it occupies no such place.

What does this mean finally for the argument between Dieter Graumann and Holm Putzke about whether Jewish law is law or not? The answer: both are right. Graumann is right: the Halakhah is law, because it is accepted as law by the Jews. But Putzke is also right: It is up to the state to determine what it acknowledges as law.

The fact that states today recognize only state law as law is grounded in tradition. The state uses private international law to defend its lawgiving monopoly. We can see this in the criticism of the English Archbishop's proposal to

---

[66] Un Jong Pak, *Kelsen's Pure Theory of Law from the Perspective of Globalization*, 9 J. KOREAN L. 147 (2009).

recognize Islamic law in England.[67] We can see this in the decision of the European Court of Human Rights to uphold the ban of the Turkish Welfare Party, which demanded that Islamic law apply alongside state law.[68] And we see it in the arguments on circumcision in Germany, which is too often seen as a conflict between law and religion, between law and parents' freedom to decide on the education of their children, and not as a conflict between German law and Jewish law.

To criticize this, it is not enough to insist that religious law is law. Ultimately, the formal character as law is not essential. What is essential is that the state sees itself as one of many legal systems in the world and designs its relation to these systems in an optimal way, just as these other systems must order their relations in an optimal way. How the state goes about this is up to the state. Whether it is wise to deny recognition to religious law is a separate question.

[67] Robin Griffith-Jones, *The "Unavoidable" Adoption of Shari'a Law – The Generation of a Media Storm, in* ISLAM AND ENGLISH LAW: RIGHTS, RESPONSIBILITIES AND THE PLACE OF SHARI'A 9 (Robin Griffith-Jones ed., 2013).

[68] Refah Partisi (The Welfare Party) and others v. Turkey, Eur. Ct. H.R. 41340/98. My own analysis of the decision is in Ralf Michaels, *On Liberalism and Legal Pluralism, in* TRANSNATIONAL LAW – RETHINKING LAW AND LEGAL THINKING 122 (Miguel Maduro et al. eds., 2014).

3

International Law and Sociolegal Scholarship

*Toward a Spatial Global Legal Pluralism**

Sally Engle Merry[1]

At a recent conference on international law at UConn law school, I was intrigued by a talk on the bottom-up production of international law. Janet Koven Levit, whose article is published in the *Yale Journal of International Law*, argued that she was describing a process quite different from that normally told by international law scholars.[2] The common approach to understanding international law is to tell a top-down story of states' treaty-based commitments or an intergovernmental organization formed by treaty. Insofar as there is a discussion of process, it focuses on diplomats in luxurious sites fine-tuning the language of a treaty. Yet, there are also forms of international lawmaking happening as practitioners figure out how to handle problems on a day-to-day basis. As they do so, they create and interpret rules, producing their own informal rules and practices. These ultimately become as much law as those based on top-down treaties. Levit says that there are many situations in which practice-based ways of doing things gradually become law.[3] In the terminology of international law, "soft law" becomes "hard law." Soft law refers to a wide range of international instruments, communications, informal agreements, memoranda of understanding, codes of conduct, or "gentlemen's agreements," whereas hard law comprises international rules and norms that are at least technically binding.[4]

---

* This chapter was originally published in 2007 as Sally Engle Merry, *International Law and Sociolegal Scholarship: Toward a Spatial Global Legal Pluralism*, in 41 STUDIES IN LAW, POLITICS, AND SOCIETY 149–68 (Austin Sarat ed., 2007) (special issue – Law and Society Reconsidered) (all rights of reproduction in any form reserved ISSN: 1059–4337/doi:10.1016/S1059-4337(07)00006–3).

[1] Silver Professor of Anthropology at New York University.

[2] Janet Koven Levit, *A Bottom-Up Approach to International Lawmaking: The Tale of Three Trade Finance Instruments*, 30 YALE J. INT'L L. 125, 126 (2005).

[3] *Id.*

[4] *Id.* at 127.

                    Sally Engle Merry

Levit looks at three little-known institutions in the world of international trade finance, one of which is the International Union of Credit and Investment Insurers (Berne Union), a nongovernmental organization that regulates export credit insurance policies for its members, both public and private export credit insurers.[5] Some of the rules developed by this organization have been adopted by formal international lawmaking institutions, transforming them into hard law. Yet, she notes that these rules have never been written about because the Berne Union rules have been accessible only to members.[6] Indeed, she had a great deal of difficulty getting access to the organization, which resisted her inquiries. As the conference attendees discussed why there was compliance with the technical rules that this group developed, she noted that the members form a close-knit group. Although this group comes from several different nations, members are from the same social class and routinely play golf and socialize together.

I found this a fascinating example of a process of lawmaking eminently suitable to sociolegal analysis. It sounded like a close-knit group using informal social control. Exclusion would be financially as well as socially costly. This demonstrated for me the value of sociolegal research on international law. The Berne Union seemed ripe for this kind of study. Here is law made by a transnational group of public and private actors that shape the way transnational finance takes place. Furthermore, the idea that small groups of practitioners develop ways of doing things to make the system work and that these rules and practices are then appropriated by more formal institutions describes a process well known to anthropologists that study village law and its relationship to state law.

International law offers contemporary sociolegal scholars an opportunity to provide a sociological and cultural analysis of how international law works. This is a moment, as Levit notes, for the study of international law to move beyond a defensive insistence that international law is real law, with clear codes and formal institutions. It is a time to recognize the multiplicity of sources of law and practices that constitute it. Sociolegal studies took this approach to analyzing state law, showing that understanding it required looking at social organization, cultural meanings, and context as well as rules and formal institutions. Law and society scholarship insisted that law is constituted in multiple ways and that the practices that shape the way law operates take place not only in courts but also in lawyers' offices, district court clerks' rooms, mediation centers, and government offices where regulations are negotiated.

---

[5] *Id.*

[6] *Id.* at 128.

Despite the excellent legal scholarship on international law processes, however, there has been relatively little sociolegal scholarship in this domain.[7] One consequence of the absence of sociological focus on international law is a lack of attention to three critical domains of sociolegal analysis: the relations of power among legal actors and legal regimes, processes of meaning making and legal consciousness, and the impact of various structures of social relationships on informal social processes such as shaming and social pressure. There are some exceptions: for example, Paul Schiff Berman recently showed how theoretical frameworks from sociolegal scholarship such as legal consciousness, the study of governments and NGOs, and legal pluralism can contribute to analyzing to a variety of issues in the study of international law.[8]

Although the concept of global legal pluralism has been proposed as an analytic framework for international law, it has not always been used with the theoretical depth of sociologically informed legal pluralism. This means considering the power relations among legal spheres, the extent to which any legal sphere expresses local normative standards, and social interactions among spheres. The concept can be used in a simplistic way to argue that there are multiple forms of law that exist side by side without examining the differences among them in the ways they exercise power and authority, their links to each other, and the various levels of moral and social support that they enjoy. This chapter suggests a framework of spatial legal pluralism that incorporates of power, meaning, and social relationships into a legal pluralist framework along with an analysis of spatial relationships.

The sociolegal study of international law is important because international law is increasingly imbricated in domestic law – the law of the nation-state. International regulations, agreements, human rights conventions, and other forms of law are increasingly merging with domestic law. It is no longer possible to study domestic law in isolation from these influences. International legal regimes like human rights shape domestic law, as do international tribunals such as those in Bosnia and Rwanda. Foreign aid is increasingly linked to instituting rule of law programs.[9]

---

[7] *But see* Terrence C. Halliday & Pavel Osinsky, *Globalization of Law*, 32 ANN. REV. SOC. 447 (2006); Benedict Kingsbury, *The International Legal Order*, in OXFORD HANDBOOK OF LEGAL STUDIES 271–91 (Peter Cane & Mark V. Tushnet eds., 2003).

[8] Paul Schiff Berman, *From International Law to Law and Globalization*, 43 COLUM. J. TRANSNAT'L L. 485–556 (2005).

[9] Thomas Carothers, *The Rule-of-Law Revival*, in PROMOTING THE RULE OF LAW ABROAD: IN SEARCH OF KNOWLEDGE 3–15 (Thomas Carothers ed., 2006); Frank Upham, *Mythmaking in the Rule-of-Law Orthodoxy*, in PROMOTING THE RULE OF LAW ABROAD: IN SEARCH OF KNOWLEDGE 75–105 (Thomas Carothers ed., 2006); Peer Zumbansen, *Transnational Law and*

A sociolegal approach to international law begins from a recognition of the plurality of law. As Roger Cotterrell observes, the law and society relationship requires a rethinking of society under postmodern conditions.[10] Communities shape the law that governs them and gives the law its authority and legitimacy. When communities are fragmented, fluid, and changing, linked through networks rather than territories and subject to movement of people and ideas, the law that they produce and that governs them becomes more plural. Imagining a stable system of law connected to a nation-state is no longer adequate. This fluidity and plurality of law is particularly characteristic of international law, with its competing forms of ordering and grounding in a highly mobile and fragmented set of social relationships.

The study of international law requires following the people who move transnationally as well as tracking the movement of legal ideas and practices. Communities of expertise made up of lawyers, judges, and business elites as well as social scientists move along these circuits. These communities of expertise, which include social science approaches, travel from the metropole to former colonies and back. Concepts such as culture, race, gender, and legal pluralism move through these global and neocolonial circuits as well. Translators play critical intermediary roles in circulating ideas from metropoles to more remote regions.[11] Thus, research on international law demands attention to the spatial distribution of actors and institutions as well multi-sited ethnography.[12]

The pioneering research of Yves Dezalay and Bryant Garth, which traces the global circulation of "notables" between educational institutions and law firms in North America and governments and international agencies in Latin America, is one example of this approach to sociolegal research on international law.[13] But it is only a beginning. Clearly more analysis is needed, including work that is more attentive to the role of social movements and nonelite actors than their Bourdieuian approach tends to be. Rajagopal's study of international law shows how international legal institutions have long been shaped by protest movements from Third World countries.[14] Santos's and

Societal Memory, in LAW AND THE POLITICS OF RECONCILIATION 129–46 (Scott Veitch ed., 2007).

[10] ROGER COTTERRELL, LAW, CULTURE AND SOCIETY: LEGAL IDEAS IN THE MIRROR OF SOCIAL THEORY (2006).

[11] Sally Engle Merry, *Transnational Human Rights and Local Activism: Mapping the Middle*, 108 AM. ANTHROPOLOGIST 38–52 (2006).

[12] GEORGE E. MARCUS, ETHNOGRAPHY THROUGH THICK AND THIN (1998).

[13] YVES DEZALAY & BRYANT G. GARTH, THE INTERNATIONALIZATION OF PALACE WARS: LAWYERS, ECONOMISTS, AND THE CONTEST TO TRANSFORM LATIN AMERICAN STATES (2002).

[14] BALAKRISHNAN RAJAGOPAL, INTERNATIONAL LAW FROM BELOW: DEVELOPMENT, SOCIAL MOVEMENTS, AND THIRD WORLD RESISTANCE (2003).

Rodriquez's work on the mobilization of law from below, which they refer to as "subaltern cosmopolitan legality," emphasizes the importance of transnational law to grassroots social movements.[15] Sidney Tarrow's analysis of social movements focuses less on the role of law but foregrounds the importance of the diffusion of cultural conceptions of rights and social justice, linking the analysis of social movements with changes in legal consciousness.[16]

Research on international law also demands attention to the new legal institutions that have been formed. This includes tribunals that endeavor to provide justice by prosecuting criminally those who have violated major human rights principles. These institutions include the formal tribunals established at the end of the Rwanda and Yugoslavia conflict and the International Criminal Court as well as more informal village tribunals in Rwanda. Although these are new institutions, each incorporates in complicated ways laws, procedures, and practices from various previously existing national and local systems of law. These institutions are contributing to the creation of a new legal order, but they are also deeply constrained in their authority and practice by the system of sovereignty that underlies all transnational endeavors. They act both to hold leaders accountable and to create histories of periods of conflict and violence.[17]

APPROACHES TO INTERNATIONAL LAW

This essay will consider three theories developed by international law scholars to analyze the international legal terrain and the strengths of each as well as issues they fail to address sufficiently in the dimensions of power, meaning, and social relationships: bottom-up lawmaking, transnational legal processes, and global legal pluralism. The idea of bottom-up lawmaking, already discussed, has the strength of beginning from the everyday practices by which problems are solved that lead eventually to the creation of a body of law. However, the

---

[15] Boaventura de Sousa Santos & César A. Rodríguez-Garavito, *Law, Politics, and the Subaltern in Counter-Hegemonic Globalization, in* LAW AND GLOBALIZATION FROM BELOW: TOWARDS A COSMOPOLITAN LEGALITY 1–27 (César A Rodríguez Garavito & Boaventura de Sousa Santos eds., 2005). *See also* César A. Rodríguez-Garavito, *Nike's Law: The Anti-Sweatshop Movement, Transnational Corporations, and the Struggle over International Labor Rights in the Americas, in* LAW AND GLOBALIZATION FROM BELOW: TOWARDS A COSMOPOLITAN LEGALITY 66–91 (César A Rodríguez Garavito & Boaventura de Sousa Santos eds., 2005).

[16] SIDNEY G. TARROW, POWER IN MOVEMENTS: SOCIAL MOVEMENTS AND CONTENTIOUS POLITICS (2d ed. 1998).

[17] *See* RUTI G. TEITEL, TRANSITIONAL JUSTICE (2000); Richard A. Wilson, *Reconciliation and Revenge in Post-Apartheid South Africa: Rethinking Legal Pluralism and Human Rights,* 41 CURRENT ANTHROPOLOGY 75–98 (2000); RICHARD A. WILSON, THE POLITICS OF TRUTH AND RECONCILIATION IN SOUTH AFRICA: LEGITIMIZING THE POST-APARTHEID STATE (2001); Richard A. Wilson, *Judging History: The Historical Record of the International Criminal Tribunal for the Former Yugoslavia,* 27 HUM. RTS. Q. 908–42 (2005); John Hagan & Ron Levi, *Crimes of War and the Force of Law,* 83 SOC. FORCES 1499–1534 (2005).

phrase bottom-up suggests that this is a grassroots movement, although it is typically cosmopolitan elites who generate the informal rules that become established over time. Explicit attention to the power relationships underlying this process would help to clarify what "bottom-up" means. As Judith Resnick points out, the terms "soft law" and "hard law" are themselves problematic, incorporating gender ideologies and suggesting that some international laws are enforced firmly, which is rarely the case in practice.[18]

The transnational legal process approach argues that compliance with international law depends on normative change produced by social interactions among international legal actors. It is closely related to the work on international advocacy networks and coalitions in international relations that argue that these activities produce normative change over time. Transnational legal process joins both international and domestic law, public and private actors, state and non-state actors, and the dynamic production of new rules through interaction, interpretation, and practice that then shape further interactions and induce state compliance.[19] Even if nations are simply pursuing their interests, they internalize shared norms through interaction. Inside countries, interaction and discussion further internalization of norms into domestic social and political processes.[20]

This model addresses the question of why nations obey international law. Abram and Antonia Chayes propose a "managerial model," arguing that nations obey international law because of management by national actors pursing a cooperative model of compliance through interactive processes of justification, discourse, and persuasion.[21] States are motivated to comply not because of fear of sanction but fear of loss of reputation. Compliance occurs through an iterative process of discourse among the parties, the treaties, and the wider public. Harold Hongju Koh builds on both the Chayes's managerial model and Thomas Franck's fairness model as ways to explain compliance, but finds them lacking in that both claim that compliance depends on voluntary choice. Instead, he advocates the idea of "transnational legal process":

> the complex process of institutional interaction whereby global norms are not just debated and interpreted, but ultimately internalized by domestic legal systems. Both the managerial and the fairness accounts fail to describe the pathways whereby a "managerial" discourse or "fair" international rule

---

[18] Personal communication with Judith Resnick, Arthur Liman Professor of Law at Yale Law School.

[19] Harold Hongju Koh, *Transnational Legal Process*, 75 Neb. L. Rev. 181, 184 (1996).

[20] *Id.* at 204.

[21] Abram Chayes & Antonia Handler Chayes, The New Sovereignty: Compliance with International Regulatory Agreements (1995). *See also* Harold Hongju Koh, *Why Do Nations Obey International Law?*, 106 Yale L.J. 2599, 2635–37 (1997).

penetrates into a domestic legal system, thus becoming part of that nation's internal value set.[22]

His primary concern is norm internalization, which he sees as key to compliance. Koh argues that there is an evolutionary process whereby repeated compliance gradually becomes habitual obedience, and that it is this process of interaction, interpretation, and internalization of international norms into domestic legal systems that explains why nations follow international law rather than conforming only when it is convenient.[23] The practices and norms become internalized and therefore shape future behavior.

Anne-Marie Slaughter has similarly examined the processes by which international law operates in practice, focusing on the role of liberal states.[24] All these theories place norm change at the center, because compliance ultimately depends on commitment to norms, whether on the basis of perceived interest, voluntary choice, or internalization. Koh offers a case study of the 1985 effort by Reagan and others in the U.S. government to redefine the antiballistic missile treaty to enable the Star Wars program to develop.[25] He notes that a variety of committed actors, political leaders, and NGOs, mobilized against the change. In 1993, along with a shift in the presidency, came an end to this effort. He argues that this outcome was the product not only of rules and interests, but also of the ongoing interactions among actors over time along with their normative commitments.

Studies of transnational advocacy networks in international relations, particularly by Keck and Sikkink and Khagram, Riker and Sikkink similarly emphasize the centrality of normative change to the spread and effects of human rights.[26] Some versions postulate a "norm cascade" when the process of adopting new international norms such as human rights becomes widespread in a country.

However, this body of scholarship focuses on states, institutions, and social movements rather than on the legal consciousness of ordinary citizens. These scholars recognize that the power of human rights depends on extensive local normative change, but they do not explore how and when actors change

---

[22] Koh, *supra* note 20.

[23] *Id.* at 2602–03.

[24] ANNE-MARIE SLAUGHTER, A NEW WORLD ORDER (2004). *See also* Oona A. Hathaway, *Do Human Rights Treaties Make a Difference?*, 111 YALE L.J. 1935–2042 (2002).

[25] Koh, *supra* note 18.

[26] MARGARET E. KECK & KATHRYN SIKKINK, ACTIVISTS BEYOND BORDERS: ADVOCACY NETWORKS IN INTERNATIONAL POLITICS (1998); RESTRUCTURING WORLD POLITICS: TRANSRATIONAL SOCIAL MOVEMENTS, NETWORKS AND NORMS (Sanjeev Khagram, James V. Riker & Kathryn Sikkink eds., 2002); *See also* THE POWER OF HUMAN RIGHTS: INTERNATIONAL NORMS AND DOMESTIC CHANGE (Thomas Risse-Kappen, Steve C. Ropp & Kathryn Sikkink eds., 1999).

their normative understandings and subjectivities to incorporate a notion of rights. Thus, although this approach incorporates a sophisticated analysis of social interactions, it pays relatively little attention to processes of meaning making and individual consciousness. Anthropological work on meaning and subjectivity and law and society research on legal consciousness both offer a deeper understanding of how, where, and under what conditions norm change takes place.[27]

Nor does this work theorize the effects of inequalities in power on processes of norm change and compliance. For example, although shaming is a critical normative process that is central to the way international law operates, it is more effective against weaker countries than stronger ones. Moreover, it is more effective when supplemented by political and economic pressure. When a group of rebels pulled off a coup against the elected government of Fiji in 2000, for example, the country faced serious economic and political sanctions. They were suspended from the Commonwealth, Australian tourists cancelled trips and then boycotted the islands, and Australian longshoremen's unions refused to unload ships from Fiji, among other consequences. For a small, economically dependent country like Fiji, these economic pressures were major concerns, in addition to the shaming. In 2006, the military executed another coup, throwing out the elected prime minister and driving out its Australian-born police chief. Australia again threatened to suspend its membership in the Commonwealth and to implement defense and travel bans against the Fijian military and any government it set up.[28] The international community also threatened to suspend financial and technical assistance.[29]

Clearly, large and powerful countries are less vulnerable to such economic pressures than small and economically dependent ones. For example, both China and the U.S. have resisted human rights surveillance of their domestic activities, showing that more powerful countries are less vulnerable to social pressure. Thus, the way transnational legal processes operate depends greatly on inequalities in power among nation-states.

A third approach to international law developed by legal scholars is global legal pluralism. This model focuses on the multiplicity of international and

---

[27] *See* SALLY ENGLE MERRY, GETTING JUSTICE AND GETTING EVEN: LEGAL CONSCIOUSNESS AMONG WORKING-CLASS AMERICANS (1990); MICHAEL W. MCCANN, RIGHTS AT WORK: PAY EQUITY REFORM AND THE POLITICS OF LEGAL MOBILIZATION (1994); PATRICIA EWICK & SUSAN S. SILBEY, THE COMMON PLACE OF LAW: STORIES FROM EVERYDAY LIFE (1998); Mark Goodale, *Legal Ethnography in an Era of Globalization: The Arrival of Western Human Rights Discourse to Rural Bolivia, in* PRACTICING ETHNOGRAPHY IN LAW: NEW DIALOGUES, ENDURING METHODS 50–72 (June Starr & Mark Goodale eds., 2002); LAURA BETH NIELSEN, LICENSE TO HARASS: LAW, HIERARCHY, AND OFFENSIVE PUBLIC SPEECH (2004).

[28] *See Aussies Cut Aid Plans for Fiji,* FIJI TIMES, Dec. 22, 2006, at 3.

[29] *See id.; France Cuts Army Ties,* FIJI TIMES, Dec. 23, 2006, at 2.

national laws, legal institutions, and forms of dispute resolution and the inter-actions among them. Although the transnational legal process approach tells a story of increasing coherence and interconnections among laws as a result of these interactions, global legal pluralism focuses on the diversity and incom-patibility of the systems. For some, this plurality provides myriad opportunities for social movements that use some forms of law and resist others whereas for others, it represents chaos and a weak international judicial order. For exam-ple, in Rajagopal's study of the Narmada dam dispute in India, he describes how international actors and organizations, human rights laws, and the Indian Supreme Court were all involved in determining the outcome of the con-flict over the building of a dam on the Narmada River.[30] This multiplicity of actors and normative systems provided greater space for mobilization and legal resistance than would a more coherent and integrated system.

Global legal pluralism builds on sociolegal and legal anthropological stud-ies of situations of multiple regimes of law and applies it to international law. The concept, as used within anthropological scholarship, is used to describe the multiple forms law takes in different communities and the nature of the interactions among them. Legally plural situations have differing but coex-isting conceptions of permissible actions, valid transactions, and ideas and procedures for dealing with conflict in the same social field.[31] Some pre-date colonialism. Colonialism has layered new systems over existing ones. On occasion, colonial law recognized earlier systems of law, such as the British colonial incorporation of Hindu, Muslim, and Christian personal law into the administration of the Indian empire. The systems often have incompatible standards and procedures, and it is not unusual for individuals to engage in forum shopping among them.[32]

Although some of the first work on legal pluralism imagined that relatively separate legal systems coexist, as they did in the dual legal systems common to British colonialism, Sally Falk Moore's notion of the "semi-autonomous social field" argued that such legal subgroups existed in industrial societies as

---

[30] Balakrishnan Rajagopal, *The Role of Law in Counter-Hegemonic Globalization and Global Legal Pluralism: Lessons from the Narmada Valley Struggle in India*, 18 LEIDEN J. INT'L L. 345–87 (2005).

[31] Franz von Benda-Beckmann, *Who's Afraid of Legal Pluralism?*, 47 J. LEGAL PLURALISM & UNOFFICIAL L. 37–82 (2002); Keebet von Benda-Beckmann, *Transnational Dimensions of Legal Pluralism, in* BEGEGNUNG UND KONFLIKT – EINE KULTURANTHROPOLOGISCHE BESTANDSAUF-NAME 33–48 (Wolfgang Fikentscher ed., 2001).

[32] Keebet von Benda-Beckmann, *Forum Shopping and Shopping Forums: Dispute Processing in a Minangkabau Village in West Sumatra*, 19 J. LEGAL PLURALISM 117–59 (1981); KEEBET VON BENDA-BECKMANN, THE BROKEN STAIRWAYS TO CONSENSUS: VILLAGE JUSTICE AND STATE COURTS IN MINANGKABAU (1984).

well.[33] Rather than seeing plural legal systems as circumscribed and bounded, she argued that they are semiautonomous, operating within other social fields but not entirely governed by them.

But what constitutes a legal field? This question has caused major debates about the status of informal, non-state forms of normative ordering. Should these be called law? Although some legal pluralists argue that a series of legal fields coexist, ranging from the informal regulations of family and neighborhood life to forms of private governance in institutions such as universities and state law, others counter that not all these forms of ordering should be called law.[34] Brian Tamanaha made this argument forcefully and has since moderated his position.[35] There are certainly differences among forms of ordering, particularly between informal forms of social ordering and state law. Indeed, much of the history of the anthropology of law has focused on this problem: Can informal social ordering practices such as reciprocity and other binding obligations be called law, as Malinowski argued,[36] or should the term be reserved for forms of ordering that represent a socially legitimate exercise of force, as E. Adamson Hoebel argued.[37] Although the question of defining what law is remains unsettled in anthropology, from a pragmatic perspective using a very broad conception that includes all forms of ordering has proved unhelpful, because it fails to distinguish those forms of law that exercise state power from those that do not. Moreover, various forms of order operate with quite different forms of authority and legitimacy. Whether they are referred to as law, lumping them together blurs these important distinctions.

Paul Schiff Berman suggests that legal pluralism offers a valuable framework for conflict-of-laws scholars in arenas as diverse as religions practices and Internet jurisdiction.[38] Thinking of such clashes as conflicts among

---

[33] Sally Falk Moore, *The Semi-Autonomous Social Field, in* Law as Process: An Anthropological Approach (1978).

[34] Martin Chanock, Law, Custom, and Social Order: The Colonial Experience in Malawi and Zambia (1985); Emmanuel Melissaris, *The More the Merrier? A New Take on Legal Pluralism*, 13 Soc. & Legal Stud. 57–79 (2004).

[35] Brian Z. Tamanaha, *The Folly of the Social-Scientific Concept of Legal Pluralism*, 20 J.L. & Soc'y 192–217 (1993); Brian Z. Tamanaha, *A Non-Essentialist Version of Legal Pluralism*, 27 J.L. & Soc'y 296–321 (2000).

[36] Bronislaw Malinowski, Crime and Custom in Savage Society (1926).

[37] Edward Adamson Hoebel, The Law of Primitive Man (Harv. U. Press 2006) (1954).

[38] Paul Schiff Berman, *The Globalization of Jurisdiction*, 151 U. Pa. L. Rev. 311 (2002); Paul Schiff Berman, *Towards a Cosmopolitan Vision of Conflict of Laws: Redefining Governmental Interests in a Global Era*, 153 U. Pa. L. Rev. 1819 (2005); Berman, *supra* note 7; Paul Schiff Berman, *Conflict of Laws and the Challenge of Legal Pluralism*, Annual Meeting of the Association for the Study of Law, Culture & the Humanities, Syracuse Univ. (March 2006). *See also* Oren Perez, *Normative Creativity and Global Legal Pluralism: Reflections on the Democratic*

various legal regimes has several benefits, he thinks. It leads scholars to trace the shape of communities that hold particular views, even when they cross national boundaries. It forces state-sanctioned courts to take account of non-state normative commitments and treat them as law. It encourages respect for foreign judgments and laws. He argues that this framework provides a way for state-sanctioned courts to recognize the multiple sources of law and claims to authority so characteristic of modern society, including that of states, international bodies, or non-state entities.[39] Finally, he advocates viewing these conflicts as a good thing, a way of celebrating difference, rather than as a step on the path to convergence and harmony among the world's legal regimes. Instead of focusing on the emergence of "world law" as nation-state legal regimes converge, he advocates conflicts as a way of emphasizing the important differences among people.

Where Rajagopal and Berman see possibilities of creativity and resistance in the plurality of international law, others see global legal pluralism as a problem: a source of chaos and an assault on legitimacy. For international lawyers committed to a vision of increasing global coherence and order, the inconsistencies in the rulings of different tribunals and fora, the lack of a clear hierarchy, and the ambiguity of authority pose a serious problem. The multiplicity of tribunals with varying mandates and decisions weaken the force of international law. Martti Koskenniemi and Päivi Leino describe the dismay over the fragmentation of international law expressed by leaders of the International Court of Justice, distressed at the proliferation of special tribunals not under their authority.[40] This fragmentation reflects the different interest groups engaged in constructing international law.[41]

But as scholars of global legal pluralism, Koskenniemi and Leino see this proliferation of tribunals with overlapping jurisdictions and differing normative orders as a product of political pressures, not technical errors in the edifice of international law.[42] For example, they argue that human rights and economic values represent two competing universal logics, conventionally seen as quite different. The WTO and World Bank are engaged in promoting a regime of free trade, whereas human rights bodies are seeking to develop universalistic

---

Critique of Transnational Law, 10 IND. J. GLOBAL LEGAL STUD. 25–64 (2003); BOAVENTURA DE SOUSA SANTOS, TOWARD A NEW COMMON SENSE: LAW, SCIENCE AND POLITICS IN THE PARADIGMATIC TRANSITION (1995).

[39] Berman, *Conflict of Laws, supra* note 37, at 7.

[40] Martti Koskenniemi & Päivi Leino, *Fragmentation of International Law? Postmodern Anxieties*, 15 LEIDEN J. INT'L L. 553–79 (2002).

[41] *Id.* at 553–78.

[42] *Id.* at 561.

standards with a political orientation. In some ways, these two orders are separate in terms of ideology and institutional grounding. Yet, Koskenniemi and Leino argue that they are coming together as human rights bodies increasingly focused on economic rights, and the World Bank and other economic actors appropriate the language of human rights to describe their projects. This enables the World Bank to define them in ways compatible with their own ideologies, and at the same time acquire their legitimacy. Thus, political pressures have driven them together. However, Koskenniemi and Leino note that the risk is that as human rights become broader, they move toward indeterminacy.[43]

The global legal pluralist model attends to both social interactions and to differences in the power of various legal regimes. Although it does not address questions of meaning and consciousness, it assumes that each legal regime bears with it a set of ideas about justice, rights, and process. Where it is portrayed in a static framework without sufficient attention to the interactions among systems and the way they are arranged in terms of relative power, the model fails to describe the nature of international legal processes adequately. However, a sociologically and culturally sophisticated version of global legal pluralism promises an effective analytic framework for understanding international law. But it needs to incorporate spatial considerations as well.

SPATIAL LEGAL PLURALISM

These three models of international law – bottom-up lawmaking, horizontal interactions leading to norm internalization, and global legal pluralism – all describe some dimensions of the practice of international law. If we add questions of space to global legal pluralism, it produces an even more useful way to theorize this complex legal field. Thinking in terms of law's geography foregrounds connections through spatial arrangements and leaves open questions about the nature of the overlaps and boundaries among systems. Spatial legal pluralism provides a way to conceptualize the state, with its domestic law and preeminent concerns about borders, as embedded within a global regime of law stretching across national lines. It also makes possible the analysis of forms of law that are not geographically circumscribed but move in a transnational way, jumping across borders and taking root in several separate and physically unconnected spaces. The legal systems of Native American tribes in the United States, for example, represent pockets within the state legal system.[44] It provides a way around the global/local model, with its hierarchies and verticality.

---

[43] *Id.* at 569–70.

[44] *See* Thomas Biolsi, *Bringing the Law Back In: Legal Rights and the Regulation of Indian-White Relations on Rosebud Reservation*, 36 CURRENT ANTHROPOLOGY 543, 562 (1995).

Recent scholarship on a critical geography of law examines the connections among law, space, and power, recognizing that law constitutes not only identities and groups but also spaces and boundaries.[45] As a project of critical analysis, this body of scholarship joins questions of meaning, discourse, and normativity with questions of power, but does so with a "spatial turn," examining how the social meanings of spaces are shaped by power relationships and materialize those relationships.[46] Within anthropology, there is also substantial work on space and place that emphasizes the way places take on social and cultural meanings and significance.[47]

Social phenomenon usually has spatial dimensions, although these often escape theorization. For example, certain spaces may be defined as open only to particular races, while excluding others. Here, race and its spatialization reinforce each other, as the meanings of race are defined by spatial exclusions.[48] Similarly, the distinctions made in some societies between male public space and female private space, which leads to restrictions on women's movements expressed through purdah, the need for women to get male permission to leave the home and travel, and the importance of women who move into male space to cover themselves and dress modestly, are all ways that unequal power relationships are expressed through the demarcations of space. Insofar as these demarcations have a legal basis, as they did under the Jim Crow system in the American South and they do in some conservative Islamic countries, there is an inextricable link between the way law regulates persons and the way it regulates space.

The spatialized dimensions of law's power are likely to become naturalized and rendered invisible both in everyday social life and in sociolegal analyses.[49] As Blomley, Delaney and Ford observe, "much of social space represents a materialization of power, and much of law consists in highly significant and specialized descriptions and prescriptions of this same power."[50] Although much of legal regulation defines spaces, from zoning regulations to immigration laws, its spatial grounding tends to escape analytic attention. Greater attention to the spatial dimension of law reveals not only its pervasiveness but also the extent to which it is overlapping, multiple, and inconsistent even in the same place.

---

[45] The Legal Geographies Reader: Law, Power, and Space (Nicholas K. Blomley, David Delaney & Richard T. Ford eds., 2001).

[46] *Id.* at xvii.

[47] *See* The Anthropology of Space and Place: Locating Culture (Setha M. Low & Denise Lawrence-Zúñiga eds., 2003).

[48] The Legal Geographies Reader, *supra* note 44, at xvi.

[49] *Id.*

[50] *Id.* at xix.

Not only is law's power expressed through its demarcation of spaces, but the social meanings of spaces are defined by law. Borders, sovereign nations, and local communities are all spatial entities constructed by law. Indeed, Blomley, Delaney and Ford ask if law and space are in some ways identical, as in the example of the state, which is both a territorial and a legal entity at the same time. Transnational spaces are particularly interesting because they are simultaneously defined as part of local communities, as the U.N. is part of New York City, but also they are constructing legal regimes that are global in reach and significance. The sociolegal analysis of international law raises questions of space with particular urgency. Where does it exist, how does it regulate, and how does it regulate differently in different spaces? There are a few transnationally regulated spaces that are not regulated by other systems of law at the same time, raising questions about the intersections among these multiple forms of law.

A spatial version of legal pluralism emphasizes how law is different in different kinds of spaces such as urban, rural, global cities, isolated places and that there are connections among and across these spatial fields. It offers a way to think about the connections of legal regimes by examining the places they overlap, the boundaries and arenas of conflict, and the holes where no law governs. Unlike managerial approaches that assume that norm consensus emerges over time, a spatial approach suggests that normative and institutional differences may persist in separate spaces. Or they may coexist in the same space, remaining distinct but influencing each other. Unlike global legal pluralism models that see this multiplicity of legal orders as a problem, this approach recognizes that such contestations are inevitable and possibly productive.

Thinking of these interactions through the metaphor of geography highlights the dynamics of borders and contiguity, places where there is intersection and movement across, engagement and redefinition at the edges, the possibility of negotiation and adaptation. It also suggests that there are spheres of closure and refusal, where barriers are erected and the influence of other legal orders and conceptions is resisted. It suggests a complicated set of relationships among legal regimes and actors, international, regional, and domestic. For example, Tobias Kelly's study of law in the West Bank shows how changes in the legal demarcation of space shifts the mobility of Palestinian residents as it redefines their identities.[51] Although they stay in one place, the law that governs them changes.

Spatial relations are very important to the constitution of social groups. Isin notes that "as groups realize themselves in space, they engage in strategies

---

[51] Tobias Kelly, *Returning Home? Law, Violence, and Displacement among West Bank Palestinians*, 27 PoLAR: Pol. & Legal Anthropology Rev. 95–112 (2004).

by inventing various technologies that alter configurations and properties of space so as to fragment, weaken, destabilize, constrain, immobilize, segregate, incarcerate, or disperse other groups as much as possible while increasing their own solidarities."[52] The Berne Union is, after all, in Berne, and it is here that the members meet and perhaps where they play golf together (although they do not want to say so). Clearly, place matters.

The well-worn global/local dichotomy does imply spatiality, but not with any specificity. The local is any small place, whereas the global is everywhere and therefore nowhere. Dezalay and Garth emphasize the circulation of elites from North American economics departments and law schools to top governmental positions in Latin America and international agencies.[53] They rely on Bourdieu's concept of the law as a social field but do not theorize the spatial dimensions of that field. As Isin notes, although Bourdieu uses a spatial metaphor to describe "a network, or a configuration, of objective relations between positions," he does not investigate fields spatially but instead assumes that social space can be mapped more or less well onto physical space. Isin counters that social and physical spaces are in fact quite distinct in their constitution of groups.[54] My study of human rights and gender violence traced the circulation of ideas that violence against women was a human rights violation, a process linked to periodic conferences and meetings and the movement of individuals and knowledge across space.[55]

This model opens up the analysis of holes or gaps in state law: Regions where state law does not reach and other forms of ordering take precedence. The tribal regions of Pakistan have long held this status. Janet Roitman's analysis of the Chad Basin in West Africa, a region of border crossing, smuggling, and organized criminal activity, is also a hole in state law, a place where legal regulation is local but not national, defined by border crossings rather than by a single state law.[56] Clearly, people who are legal in one place become illegal in another and subject to deportation if they move, so that who they are depends on where they are.[57]

---

[52] Engin F. Isin, Being Political: Genealogies of Citizenship 49 (2002).

[53] Dezalay & Garth, *supra* note 12.

[54] Isin, *supra* note 51, at 42.

[55] Sally Engle Merry, Human Rights and Gender Violence: Translating International Law into Local Justice (2006).

[56] Janet Roitman, *The Garrison-Entrepesôt: A Mode of Governing in the Chad Basin, in* Global Assemblages: Technology, Politics, and Ethics as Anthropological Problems 417–37 (Aihwa Ong & Stephen J. Collier eds., 2005).

[57] *See* Susan Bibler Coutin, Legalizing Moves: Salvadoran Immigrants' Struggle for U.S. Residency (2000); Barbara Yngvesson & Susan Bibler Coutin, *Backed by Papers: Undoing Persons, Histories, and Return*, 33 Am. Ethnologist 177–91 (2008).

The spatial metaphor provides a way to focus on regional regimes of international governance. There are regional human rights conventions and courts in the Americas and in Europe and one that is developing in Africa, for example. Some regions are organized into dominant powers and weaker ones, with the stronger ones taking the lead in establishing contacts with global regimes and housing the major regional organizations and governance systems. India plays this role in South Asia and Fiji in the Pacific. To call international law "global" suggests that it envelops the world equally. However, its regional influence is quite varied, depending on the form of government of a country or the strength of regional institutions. It may be stronger in the richer states of the global North than the poorer states in the global South. On the other hand, states of the global South are less able to set the terms of debate and often less free to ignore it.

The legal situation of Hong Kong provides a useful example of spatial legal pluralism. Hong Kong is a place with a complex and layered system of law that connects it geographically with a variety of other places depending on which layer of law is considered. It is tied to the Commonwealth through British colonial law, to China through its customary law, to the global community of states that have ratified the International Covenant on Civil and Political Rights (ICCPR), the basis of its 1991 Basic Law. Each of these fields of law has its own geography, its own shape and reach, and incorporates different sections of the world in legal similarity. Each draws different kinds of connections and boundaries. Chinese customary law links the New Territories with Han communities in China, British colonial law with the British empire, mercantile law with trading partners, Chinese law with the People's Republic of China, and the human rights law of ICCPR with approximately 150 other signatories including the United States and Canada.

Urban Hong Kong was governed by British colonial law since the nineteenth century, creating linkages between it and other former British colonies. When the British took over the rural New Territories near Hong Kong from China in 1899, they agreed to maintain its system of Chinese customary law. As the city worried about the handover to China in 1997, it passed a Basic Law based on the ICCPR in 1991. Since 1997, Hong Kong has been a Semi-Autonomous Region within China, under the oversight of a Standing Committee of the National People's Congress of China. Finally, Hong Kong shares mercantile regulations and treaties with many other parts of the world and is a desirable trading location because of its reliance on British law.

In its 2005 report from Hong Kong to the Human Rights Committee, the monitoring body for the ICCPR, China's regulation of Hong Kong came under international scrutiny. The Human Rights Committee asked for information on the Standing Committee's reinterpretation of the Basic Law in terms of its impact on the principle of universal suffrage in the elections of the Chief Executive and Legislative Council in 2007 and 2008.[58] The committee asked how this interpretation is consistent with the Standing Committee's obligation to respect civil and political rights in the Hong Kong Semi-Autonomous Region.[59] When I observed this hearing in New York in early 2006, the committee was critical of the Standing Committee's failure to abide by the terms of the Basic Law and sought to protect Hong Kong's autonomy from China, as specified in this law. Its intervention was part of a process that links Hong Kong to other ratifying states.

A dramatic confrontation over rules for women to inherit property in the early 1990s vividly illustrated the importance of taking a spatial approach to legal pluralism.[60] Although urban Hong Kong women could inherit property, when they moved to the New Towns built in the formerly rural areas, they unknowingly fell into the space of Chinese customary law. The urban women moved, but their law did not. The architects of these towns failed to petition to change the law, so that suddenly a large number of urbanites living in high rises in the New Territories discovered, in the early 1990s, that they had moved into the territory of a different legal regime of inheritance. The protest movement demanded equal inheritance rights for rural women as well as urban ones, thus demanding a shift in the law regulating the territory as a whole and not just for the urbanites who had moved there. Just as immigrants discover that their legal status changes as they cross borders, these urban women found out that being in a different place changed their rights and privileges. Thinking of legal pluralism in terms of space thus opens up the analysis of movement and location in understanding how legal regimes intersect.

Another example foregrounds the role of the city as a distinct legal space with its own relationship to international law. In the United States, progressive initiatives are increasingly coming from states and cities rather than the federal government. For example, CEDAW was passed in San Francisco in 2004 by a coalition: a human rights group called WILD for Human Rights; the

---

[58] "Annex C" to Legislative Council Panel on Home Affairs, Hearing of the United Nations Human Rights Committee on the Second Report of the Hong Kong Special Administrative Region in Light of the International Covenant on Civil and Political Rights, *Human Rights Comm., List of Issues to be Taken up in Connection with the Consideration of the Second Periodic Report of Hong Kong Special Administrative Region of the People's Republic of China*, CCPR/C/HKG/Q/2 (Nov. 15, 1999), *available at* http://www.legco.gov.hk/yr05-06/english/panels/ha/papers/ha0310cb2-1291-1e.pdf.

[59] *Id.* at "Annex C," p. 1.

[60] *See* Sally Engle Merry & Rachel E. Stern, *The Female Inheritance Movement in Hong Kong: Theorizing the Local/Global Interface*, 46 CURRENT ANTHROPOLOGY 387–409 (2005).

Western office of Amnesty International USA; the San Francisco Commission on the Status of Women, originally part of the city's Human Rights Commission but established as chartered department in 1994; and the Women's Foundation of California, a foundation that funds programs for women and girls in California.[61] In the interest of developing an intersectionality approach, they added references to the convention on racism, CERD, to the convention on women, CEDAW. These groups are now trying to pass ICCPR and ICESCR as city ordinances. A similar initiative in New York City is working on a combined, intersectional CEDAW/CERD ordinance. There are also efforts in Boston, including plans to train state legislators in human rights in Massachusetts. These examples show how a geography of law framework can foreground such initiatives at the city level that seek to join urban space with international law, bypassing the nation-state.

An important feature of spatial legal pluralism is the way pockets of legal regimes jump to new regions through transplants, global legal institutions, ratification of human rights treaties, the creation of special tribunals, and myriad other processes. One of the most important is that of vernacularization, through which global legal ideas become reinterpreted in local terms.[62] These regimes are all rooted in place rather than disembodied, but often in pockets rather than in a single contiguous territory. Their jurisdictions are often overlapping or pocked with openings where they do not apply. Rebel sections of states in civil war, territories subject to distinctive legal regimes such as Native American reservations, sections of cities subject to different rules such as embassies, all represent spatial pockets of distinct legal fields or holes within state legal fields. People move from places where they can live legally to those where they are illegal. Not only do groups change the legal regimes that govern them as they cross borders from places where they are citizens to those where they are aliens, but even those who stay in one place may find the legal nature of the place they occupy changing.

CONCLUSION

In conclusion, these examples show the value of a sociolegal analysis of international law that incorporates attention to power, intersections among systems, social networks, meaning and subjectivity, and space. Ideas of spatial legal pluralism provide one framework for thinking about these intersections. This approach does not posit sharp distinctions between international and domestic

---

[61] Interview with Diana Yoon by WILD for Human Rights (May 2006).
[62] *See* MERRY, *supra* note 54; Merry, *supra* note 10.

law. It recognizes transnational forms of law and gaps or holes in legal orders. It recognizes the multiplicity of law, countering the narrative of progress and increasing coherence of some international law scholars. It provides a framework for examining the varieties of legal consciousness, including differences in the awareness of and commitment to various forms of law, rather than examining only a progressive incorporation of norms. And adding the spatial dimension to the analysis of international law emphasizes overlaps, openings, gaps, and borders. This model builds on all three approaches discussed here, bottom-up lawmaking, transnational legal processes, and global legal pluralism, but it emphasizes power, meaning, social interaction, and the spatial dimensions of legal fields.

References

Berman, Paul Schiff. "The Globalization of Jurisdiction." *University of Pennsylvania Law Review* 151 (2002):311.

Berman, Paul Schiff. "Towards a Cosmopolitan Vision of Conflict of Laws: Redefining Governmental Interests in a Global Era." *University of Pennsylvania Law Review* 153 (2005):1819.

Berman, Paul Schiff. "From International Law to Law and Globalization." *Columbia Journal of Transnational Law* 43 (2005):485–556.

Berman, Paul Schiff (2006). Conflict of Laws and the Challenge of Legal Pluralism (draft).

Biolsi, Thomas. "Bringing the Law Back In: Legal Rights and the Regulation of Indian-White Relations on Rosebud Reservation." *Current Anthropology* 36 (1995):562.

Blomley, Nickolas, David Delaney and Richard T. Ford, eds. *The Legal Geographies Reader: Law, Power, and Space*. Oxford, UK: Blackwell Publishing, 2001.

Carothers, Thomas. "The Rule-of-Law Revival." In *Promoting the Rule of Law Abroad: In Search of Knowledge*, edited by Thomas Carothers, 3–15. Washington, DC: Carnegie Endowment for International Peace, 2006.

Chanock, Martin. *Law, Custom, and Social Order: The Colonial Experience in Malawi and Zambia*. Cambridge, UK: Cambridge University Press, 1985.

Chayes, Abram and Antonia Handler Chayes. *The New Sovereignty: Compliance with International Regulatory Agreement*. Cambridge, MA: Harvard University Press, 1995.

Comaroff, Jean and John, L. Comaroff. *Of Revelation and Revolution: Christianity, Colonialism, and Consciousness in South Africa (Vol. I)*. Chicago: University of Chicago Press, 1991

Comaroff, John L. and Jean Comaroff. *Of Revelation and Revolution: The Dialectics of Modernity on a South African Frontier (Vol. II)*. Chicago: University of Chicago Press, 1997.

Cotterrell, R. *Law, Culture and Society: Legal Ideas in the Mirror of Social Theory*. Aldershot, UK: Ashgate, 2006.

Coutin, S. *Legalizing Moves: Salvadoran Immigrants' Struggle for US Residency*. Ann Arbor, MI: University of Michigan Press, 2000.

Dezalay, Y. and B. Garth. *The Internationalization of Palace Wars: Lawyers, Economists, and the Contest to Transform Latin American States*. Chicago: University of Chicago Press, 2002.

Ewick, P. and S. Silbey. *The Common Place of Law: Stories from Everyday Life*. Chicago: University of Chicago Press, 1998.

Goodale, M. "Legal Ethnography in an Era of Globalization: The Arrival of Western Human Rights Discourse to Rural Bolivia." In *Practicing Ethnography in Law: New Dialogues, Enduring Methods*, edited by J. Starr and M. Goodale, 50–72. New York: Palgrave Macmillan, 2002.

Hagan, J. and R. Levi. "Crimes of War and the Force of Law." *Social Forces* 83 (2005):1499–1534.

Halliday, T. C. and P. Osinsky. "Globalization of Law." *Annual Review of Sociology* 32 (2006):447–70.

Hathaway, O. "Do Human Rights Treaties Make a Difference?" *Yale Law Journal* 111 (2002):1935–2042.

Hoebel, E. A. *"The Law of Primitive Man."* Reissued 2006, Harvard University Press, 1954.

Isin, E. F. *Being Political: Genealogies of Citizenship*. Minneapolis, MN: University of Minnesota Press, 2002.

Keck, M. E. and K. Sikkink. *Activists Beyond Borders: Advocacy Networks in International Politics*. Ithaca: Cornell University Press, 1998.

Kelly, T. "Returning Home? Law, Violence, and Displacement Among West Bank Palestinians." *Political and Legal Anthropology Review* 27 (2004):95–112.

Khagram, S., J. V. Riker and K. Sikkink, eds. *Restructuring World Politics: Transnational Social Movements, Networks, and Norms*. Minneapolis, MN: University of Minnesota Press, 2002.

Kingsbury, B. "The International Legal Order." In *The Oxford Handbook of Legal Studies*, edited by P. Cane and M. Tushnet, 271–291. Oxford: Oxford University Press, 2003.

Koh, H. H. "Transnational Legal Process." *Nebraska Law Review* 75 (1996):181.

Koh, H. H. "Why Do Nations Obey International Law?" *Yale Law Journal* 106 (1997):2599–2659.

Koh, H. H. "How Is International Human Rights Law Enforced?" *Indiana Law Journal* 74 (1999):1397.

Koh, H. H. "On American Exceptionalism." *Stanford Law Review* 55 (2003):1479–1527.

Koskenniemi, M. and P. Leino. "Fragmentation of International Law? Postmodern Anxieties." *Leiden Journal of International Law* 15 (2002):553–79.

Levit, J. K. "A Bottom-Up Approach to International Lawmaking: The Tale of Three Trade Finance Instruments." *Yale Journal of International Law* 30 (2005):125–209.

Low, S. M. and D. Lawrence-Zuniga, eds. *The Anthropology of Space and Place: Locating Culture*. Oxford and Malden, MA: Blackwell Publishing, 2003.

Malinowski, B. *Crime and Custom in Savage Society*. Littlefield Adams, 1926.

Marcus, G. *Ethnography Through Thick and Thin*. Princeton, NJ: Princeton University Press, 1998.

McCann, M. *Rights at Work: Pay Equity Reform and the Politics of Legal Mobilization*. Chicago: University of Chicago Press, 1994.

Melissaris, E. "The More the Merrier? A New Take on Legal Pluralism." *Social and Legal Studies* 13 (2004):57–79.

Merry, S. E. *Getting Justice and Getting Even: Legal Consciousness Among Working-Class Americans.* Chicago: University of Chicago Press, 1990.

Merry, S. E. *Human Rights and Gender Violence: Translating International Law into Local Justice.* Chicago: University of Chicago Press, 2006.

Merry, S. E. "Transnational Human Rights and Local Activism: Mapping the Middle." *American Anthropologist* 108 (2006):38–52.

Merry, S. E. and R. Stern. "The Female Inheritance Movement in Hong Kong: Theorizing the Local/Global Interface." *Current Anthropology* 46 (2005):387–409.

Moore, S. F. "The Semi-Autonomous Social Feld." In *Law as Process: An Anthropological Approach.* New York: Routledge, 1978.

Nielsen, L. B. *License to Harass: Law, Hierarchy, and Offensive Public Speech.* Princeton, NJ: Princeton University Press, 2004.

Perez, O. "Normative Creativity and Global Legal Pluralism: Reflections on the Democratic Critique of Transnational Law." *Indiana Journal of Global Legal Studies* 10 (2003):25–64.

Rajagopal, B. *International Law from Below: Development, Social Movements, and Third World Resistance.* Cambridge, UK: Cambridge University Press, 2003.

Rajagopal, B. "The Role of Law in Counter-Hegemonic Globalization and Global Legal Pluralism: Lessons from the Narmada Valley Struggle in India." *Leiden Journal of International Law* 18 (2005):345–87.

Risse, T., S. C. Ropp and K. Sikkink, eds. *The Power of Human Rights: International Norms and Domestic Change.* Cambridge, UK: Cambridge University Press, 1999.

Rodriguez-Garavito, C. A. "Nike's Law: The Anti-Sweatshop Movement, Transnational Corporations, and the Struggle over International Labor Rights in the Americas." In *Law and Globalization from Below: Towards a Cosmopolitan Legality,* edited by B. de S. Santos and C. A. Rodriguez-Garavito, 66–91. Cambridge, UK: Cambridge University Press, 2005.

Roitman, J. "The Garrison-Entrepôt: A mode of Governing in the Chad Basin." In *Global Assemblages: Technology, Politics, and Ethics as Anthropological Problems,* edited by A. Ong and S. J. Collier, 417–37. Blackwell, 2005.

Santos, B. de S. *Toward a New Common Sense: Law, Science and Politics in the Paradigmatic Transition.* New York: Routledge, 1995.

Santos, B. de S. and C. A. Rodriguez-Garavito. "Law, Politics, and the Subaltern in Counter-Hegemonic Globalization." In *Law and Globalization from Below: Towards a Cosmopolitan Legality,* edited by B. de S. Santos and C. A. Rodriguez-Garavito, 1–27. Cambridge, UK: Cambridge University Press, 2005.

Slaughter, A.-M. *A New World Order.* Princeton, NJ: Princeton University Press, 2004.

Tamanaha, B. Z. "The Folly of the Social-Scientific Concept of Legal Pluralism." *Journal of Law and Society* 20 (1993):192–217.

Tamanaha, B. Z. "A Non-Essentialist Version of Legal Pluralism." *Journal of Law and Society* 27 (2000):296–321.

Tarrow, S. *Power in Movements: Social Movements and Contentious Politics.* 2d ed. Cambridge, UK: Cambridge University Press, 1998.

Teitel, R. *Transitional Justice.* Oxford: Oxford University Press, 2000.

Upham, F. "Mythmaking in the Rule-of-Law Orthodoxy." In *Promoting the Rule of Law Abroad: In Search of Knowledge*, edited by T. Carothers, 75–105. Washington, DC: Carnegie Endowment for International Peace, 2006.

von Benda-Beckmann, Franz. "Who's Afraid of Legal Pluralism?" *Journal of Legal Pluralism & Unofficial Law* 47 (2002):37–82.

von Benda-Beckmann, Keebet. "Forum Shopping and Shopping Forums: Dispute Processing in a Minangkabau Village in West Sumatra." *Journal of Legal Pluralism* 19 (1981):117–59.

von Benda-Beckmann, Keebet. *The Broken Stairways to Consensus: Village Justice and State Courts in Minangkabau*. Dordrecht: ForisPublications, 1984.

von Benda-Beckmann, Keebet. "Transnational Dimensions of Legal Pluralism." In *Begegnung und Konflikt – eine kulturanthropologische Bestandsaufname*, edited by W. Fikentscher, 33–48. Muenchen: Verlagder BayerischenAkademieder Wissenschaften. C.H. Beck Verlag, 2001.

Wilson, R. A. "Reconciliation and Revenge in Post-Apartheid South Africa: Rethinking Legal Pluralism and Human Rights." *Current Anthropology* 41 (2000):75–98.

Wilson, R. A. *The Politics of Truth and Reconciliation in South Africa: Legitimizing the Post-Apartheid State*. Cambridge, UK: Cambridge University Press, 2001.

Wilson, R. A. "Judging History: The Historical Record of the international Criminal Tribunal for the Former Yugoslavia." *Human Rights Quarterly* 27 (2005):908–42.

Yngvesson, B. and S. B. Coutin. "Backed by Papers: Undoing Persons, Histories, and Return." *American Ethnologist* 33 (2006):177–91.

Zumbansen, P. "Transnational Law and Societal Memory." In *Law and the Politics of Reconciliation*, edited by S. Veitch, 129–46. Aldershot, England: Ashgate, 2007.

PART II

Negotiating State Law and International/Transnational Law

4

The Constitutional Itch

Transnational Private Regulatory Governance and the Woes of Legitimacy

Peer Zumbansen[1]

As transnational commercial lawyers have long known, border crossing, globe-spanning economic activities and business practices prompt legal responses that extend the public–private interplay and legal pluralism of the nation-state to – literally – unchartered territory.[2] In the transnational space of exchange and trade of the modern age, law evolves through the interplay of "transnational lift-off and juridical touchdown,"[3] constantly re-drawing the boundaries between private agency and public authority. As for lawyers, these contemplate

[1] Professor of law, Director, Transnational Law Institute, The Dickson Poon School of Law, King's College London; 2013–2014, Senior Research Scholar, University of Michigan, School of Law; and 2014, Visiting Professor, Yale Law School; 2004-2014, Canada Research Chair, Osgoode Hall Law School, Toronto. This chapter is part of an ongoing research project investigating the tensions between the global proliferation of private regulatory arrangements and a growing concern regarding the protection of public interests in this constellation. The following pages are based on my presentation at the American Society of International Law – ASIL – International Legal Theory Interest Group Symposium, "The Rise of Non-State Law," Tillar House, Washington, DC, in May 2013. I am grateful to Professor Michael Helfand for the invitation and for the organization of a very stimulating and diverse symposium. My paper builds on earlier presentations at Indiana University, Maurer School of Law at, Osgoode Hall Law School, the European University Institute, at McGill University, Faculty of Law, and the Law School of Graduate Studies, Nagoya University, Japan. I am indebted to Yuki Asano, Larry Backer, Paul Berman, Takeshi Fujitani, Sally Merry, Christiana Ochoa, Alessandro Somma, Colin Scott, and Dai Yokomizo for generous comments and feedback. Special thanks to Michael Helfand for putting an inspiring conference together at Tiller House and for his excellent comments on this paper. Finally, I am grateful for the permission to draw in very small parts on my essay, "The Ins and Outs of Transnational Private Regulatory Governance," published in the German Law Journal in December 2012.

[2] Clive M. Schmitthoff, *International Business Law: A New Law Merchant*, 2 CURRENT L. & SOC. PROBS. 129 (1961); Roy Goode, *Usage and Its Reception in Transnational Commercial Law*, 46 INT'L & COMP. L.Q. 1 (1997); Ross Cranston, *Theorizing Transnational Commercial Law*, 42 TEX. INT'L L.J. 597 (2007).

[3] Robert Wai, *Transnational Liftoff and Juridical Touchdown: The Regulatory Function of Private International Law in an Era of Globalization*, 40 COLUM. J. TRANSNAT'L L. 209 (2002).

whether or to what degree segments of this transnational regulatory regime – the mysterious and mesmerizing lex mercatoria – should properly be called law.[4] And whereas from the perspective of sociology and geography the evolving landscape challenges conceptions of location and boundaries,[5] for political science the focus must be on the element of authority.[6] In other words, the urgent political question of transnational governance regards control, the emblem of power. As the sites and trajectories of transnational governance continue to span more and more regulatory areas, the combined question of who's in charge and to whose benefit has to move into the center of an interdisciplinary engagement. Law's history of interdisciplinarity situates it well for a productive contribution to this enterprise, which is one that must go beyond lip service to the need for thinking about law and globalization from an interdisciplinary perspective; crucially, it is the normative challenge of transnational governance that prompts a reflection on its stakes, interests, and aspirations. Law's engagement with the spatialization of transnational governance regimes under postnational[7] conditions must address the normative challenge political philosophers and political scientists have long been addressing.[8] The question raised in this chapter is how law and, more specifically, developments in private law theory address the normative challenges of transnational private regulatory governance. The larger issue behind this question concerns private law's contribution to a legal theory of global governance, with the contention – from a historical perspective – that private law has always played a central

---

[4] Berthold Goldman, *Frontières du droit et "lex mercatoria,"* 13 ARCHIVES DE LA PHILOSOPHIE DE DROIT 177 (1964); Klaus-Peter Berger, *Transnational Commercial Law in the Age of Globalization*, 42 CENTRO DI STUDI E RICERCHE DI DIRITTO COMPARATO E STRANIERO 1 (2001).

[5] Saskia Sassen, *The Places and Spaces of the Global: An Expanded Analytic Terrain, in* GLOBALIZATION THEORY: APPROACHES AND CONTROVERSIES 79–105 (David Held & Andrew McGrew eds., 2007); David Harvey, *The Sociological and Geographical Imaginations*, 18 INT'L J. POL., CULTURE & SOC'Y 211 (2005).

[6] See the analysis by NICOLE ROUGHAN, AUTHORITIES (2012), as well as by Larry Catá Backer, *Governance without Government – An Overview, in* BEYOND TERRITORIALITY: TRANSNATIONAL LEGAL AUTHORITY IN AN AGE OF GLOBALIZATION (Gunther Handl, Joachim Zekoll & Peer Zumbansen eds., 2012).

[7] DAVID HELD, DEMOCRACY AND THE GLOBAL ORDER (1995); JÜRGEN HABERMAS, THE POSTNATIONAL CONSTELLATION (2001).

[8] *See, e.g.*, ATHENA CLAIR CUTLER, GLOBAL CAPITALISM AND LIBERAL MYTHS: DISPUTE SETTLEMENT IN PRIVATE INTERNATIONAL TRADE RELATIONS 24, 377–97 (1995); David Levi-Faur, *The Global Diffusion of Regulatory Capitalism*, 598 ANNALS AM. ACAD. POL. & SOC. SCI. 12–29 (2005); John Gerard Ruggie, *Reconstituting the Global Public Domain – Issues, Actors, and Practices*, 10 EUR. J. INT'L REL. 499 (2004); and the contributions to RULING THE WORLD? CONSTITUTIONALISM, INTERNATIONAL LAW, AND GLOBAL GOVERNANCE (Jeffrey L. Dunoff & Joel P. Trachtman eds., 2009).

role in social regulation.[9] The chapter will provide a brief account of what I refer to as "the Global Governance condition" and the particular challenges emanating therefrom for the development of political agency and for law's imagination against the background of competing accounts of functionalism and normativism. Thereafter follows a discussion of the particular role played by private law in this context in navigating public and private interests and the (futile?) aspirations for a political critique, whereas the next section contextualizes the public–private law dynamics studied earlier against the background of the high degrees of functional and sectorial specialization that characterize transnationalization processes and the significant challenges these pose for any effort of designing overarching and inclusive models or concepts of postnational justice. The concluding section interrogates the prospects of an interdisciplinary and normative engagement with the pressing political regulatory challenges that arise from law's transnationalization.

THE GLOBAL GOVERNANCE CONDITION: QUESTIONING THE STANDARD ACCOUNT

As in Shakespeare's plays, it is only when a third party arrives, knocks on the door and enters the scene that the actors on stage are bound to see more clearly what it is they are in fact struggling with. Public law's catch-up game with transnational private regulatory governance over the past decades is illustrative in that regard.[10] Whether the focus is on food safety[11] or intellectual property rights attached to foods[12]; on accounting standards[13]; on

---

[9] *See, e.g.*, Max Weber, On Law in Economy and Society (Max Rheinstein ed., Edward Shils trans., Simon Schuster 2d ed. 1967) (1925); Karl Renner, The Institutions of Private Law and Their Social Functions (Routledge and Kegan Paul 1949) (orig. German 1929).

[10] *See, e.g.*, Steven Bernstein & Benjamin Cashore, *Can Non-state Global Governance Be Legitimate? An Analytical Framework* 1 Reg. & Governance 347 (2007); Armin von Bogdandy, Philipp Dann & Matthias Goldmann, *Developing the Publicness of Public International Law*, 9 German L.J. 1375 (2008), as well as the comprehensive case studies included in the same issue.

[11] Donal K. Casey & James S. Lawless, *The Parable of the Poisoned Pork: Network Governance and the 2008 Irish Pork Dioxin Contamination*, 5 Reg. & Governance 333 (2011); Dayna Nadine Scott, *Nature/Culture Clash: The Transnational Trade in GMOs* (Global Law Working Paper Series 2005), *available at* http://www.academia.edu/1043249/Nature_Culture_Clash_The_Transnational_Trade_Dispute_over_GMOs.

[12] Matthew J. Rippon, *Traditional Foods, Territorial Boundaries and the TRIPS Agreement: The Case of the Melton Mowbray Pork Pie*, 16 J. World Intellectual Prop. 262 (2013).

[13] Bernhard Grossfeld, *Comparative Corporate Governance: Generally Accepted Accounting Principles v. International Accounting Standards*, 28 N.C. J. Int'l L. & Com. Reg. 847 (2003); Yuri Biondi & Tomo Suzuki, *Socio-Economic Impacts of International Accounting Standards: An Introduction*, 5 Socio-Economic Review 585 (2007).

forestry[14] or marine stewardship[15]; on the taming of multinational corporations[16] or the promotion of human rights principles[17] as well as social, labor,[18] and environmental[19] standards in the context of trade agreements[20] and finance arrangements,[21] each field raises pertinent questions as to the possibilities of influencing the evolving governance structures with a view to protecting public interests and social, environmental, and cultural values. Most certainly, the complexity of these challenges drives the general state of alert, in which policy makers, scholars, activists, community groups, and NGOs have been for a long time, being engaged in political awareness building and analysis, policy development, agenda formulating, and resistance.[22] Whereas for the West the globalization challenge continues to be analyzed against the background of an alleged erosion of state sovereignty,[23] the analysis offered by scholars

[14] Philipp Pattberg, *What Role for Private Rule-Making in Global Environmental Governance? Analysing the Forest Stewardship Council*, 5 INT'L ENVTL. AGREEMENTS 175 (2005); Errol Meidinger, *The Administrative Law of Global Private-Public Regulation: The Case of Forestry*, 17 EUR. J. INT'L L. 47 (2006).

[15] Stefano Ponte, *The Marine Stewardship Council (MSC) and the Making of a Market for "Sustainable Fish,"* 12 J. AGRARIAN CHANGE 300 (2012). See also the main website for the Marine Stewardship Council, http://www.msc.org/.

[16] Lynn Bennie, Patrick Bernhagen & Neil J. Mitchell, *The Logic of Transnational Action: The Good Corporation and the Global Compact*, 55 POL. STUD. 733 (2007); Phillip I. Blumberg, *Asserting Human Rights Against Multinational Corporations under United States Law: Conceptual and Procedural Problems*, 50 AM. J. COMP. L. 493 (2002); JOHN GERARD RUGGIE, JUST BUSINESS. MULTINATIONAL CORPORATIONS AND HUMAN RIGHTS (2013).

[17] See the excellent discussion and analysis in ANDREW G. LANG, WORLD TRADE LAW AFTER NEOLIBERALISM: RE-IMAGINING THE GLOBAL ECONOMIC ORDER 23–60 (2011).

[18] Stephen Joseph Powell & Trisha Low, *Beyond Labor Rights: Which Core Human Rights Must Regional Trade Agreements Protect?*, 12 RICH. J. GLOBAL L. & BUS. 91 (2012).

[19] David Vogel, *Trading Up and Governing Across: Transnational Governance and Environmental Protection*, 4 J. EUR. PUB. POL'Y 556 (1997); Surya P. Subedi, *Balancing International Trade with Environmental Protection: International Legal Aspects of Eco-Labels*, 25 BROOK. J. INT'L L. 373 (1999); Kathryn Gordon, Joachim Pohl & Marie Bouchard, *Investment Treaty Law, Sustainable Development and Responsible Business Conduct: A Fact Finding Survey* (OECD Working Papers on International Investment, OECD Investment Division, Working Paper No. 2014/01), *available at* http://www.oecd.org/investment/2014RBCMinisterial-TreatyRBC.pdf.

[20] Janet Dine, *Democratization: The Contribution of Fair Trade and Ethical Trading Movements*, 15 IND. J. GLOBAL LEGAL STUD. 177 (2008); Lorand Bartels, *Trade and Human Rights*, in OXFORD HANDBOOK OF INTERNATIONAL TRADE LAW 571–96 (Daniel Bethlehem et al. eds., 2009).

[21] BENJAMIN J. RICHARDSON, SOCIALLY RESPONSIBLE INVESTMENT LAW: REGULATING THE UNSEEN POLLUTERS (2008). *See also* http://www.ussif.org/.

[22] César Rodríguez-Garavito, *Ethnicity.gov: Global Governance, Indigenous Peoples, and the Right to Prior Consultation in Social Minefields*, 18 IND. J. GLOBAL LEGAL STUD. 263 (2011); Kgomotso H. Moahi, *Globalization, Knowledge Economy and the Implication for Indigenous Knowledge*, 7 INT'L J. INFO. ETHICS 1 (2007).

[23] Louis Henkin, *That "S" Word: Sovereignty, and Globalization, and Human Rights, Et Cetera*, 68 FORDHAM L. REV. 1 (1999); Dinah Shelton, *Globalization and the Erosion of Sovereignty:*

focusing on indigenous peoples[24] as well as on constitutional developments in the "Global South"[25] points to the significant asymmetries and omissions in this "postnational" narrative.[26]

It is against this background that the original stage setting for our analysis will likely have to be revisited in a fundamental way. It is within a *Western, post*nation state scenario that the question about the role of private law in an ever faster proliferating realm of "private" transnational regulatory governance unfolds against the growing concerns with the precariousness of safeguarding public interest representation (so-called input-legitimacy[27]) on a global level. From the Global South perspective, the red thread of the narrative that traces the rise of the nation-state from the Middle Ages through nationalization and constitutionalization processes and two world wars toward the consolidation of an international political order of sovereign and equal nation states[28] is in fact much more porous, ripped, and stitched together throughout time, revealing a host of contestations, alternative paths, and roads not taken.[29] We can hardly overestimate the significance of the tensions in this constellation, which arise between the standard Western account of the nation-state and its claim to political sovereignty and economic competition on the one

---

Protecting Human Rights in a Globalized World, 25 B.C. INT'L & COMP. L. REV. 273 (2002); ERIC A. POSNER, THE PERILS OF GLOBAL LEGALISM (2009).

[24] Gaetano Pentassuglia, *Towards a Jurisprudential Articulation of Indigenous Land Rights*, 22 EUR. J. INT'L L. 165 (2011); Lillian Aponte Miranda, *The Role of International Law in Intrastate Natural Resource Allocation: Sovereignty, Human Rights, and Peoples-Based Development*, 45 VAND. J. TRANSNAT'L L. 785 (2012). For an insightful perspective on the emerging European discourse, see Timo Koivurova, *Jurisprudence of the European Court of Human Rights Regarding Indigenous Peoples: Retrospect and Prospects*, in THE INTERPRETATION AND APPLICATION OF THE EUROPEAN CONVENTION OF HUMAN RIGHTS: LEGAL AND PRACTICAL IMPLICATIONS 217–57 (Malgosia Fitzmaurice & Panos Merkouris eds., 2013).

[25] See the case studies on India, Colombia, and South Africa in CONSTITUTIONALISM OF THE GLOBAL SOUTH (Daniel Bonilla ed., 2012).

[26] ACHILLE MBEMBE, ON THE POSTCOLONY (2001); ACHILLE MBEMBE, KRITIK DER SCHWARZEN VERNUNFT (2014); B.S. Chimni, *Third World Approaches to International Law: A Manifesto*, 8 INT'L COMMUNITY L. REV. 3 (2006); Obiora Chinedu Okafor, *Critical Third World Approaches to International Law (TWAIL): Theory, Methodology, or Both?*, 10 INT'L COMMUNITY L. REV. 371 (2008). See also SUNDHYA PAHUJA, DECOLONISING INTERNATIONAL LAW. DEVELOPMENT, ECONOMIC GROWTH AND THE POLITICS OF UNIVERSALITY (2011).

[27] Fritz W. Scharpf, *The Viability of Advanced Welfare States in the International Economy: Vulnerabilities and Options*, 8 EUR. REV. 399 (2008).

[28] WILHELM G. GREWE, THE EPOCHS OF INTERNATIONAL LAW (Michael Byers trans., 2000).

[29] See the excellent analysis by ANTONY ANGHIE, IMPERIALISM, SOVEREIGNTY AND THE MAKING OF INTERNATIONAL LAW (2005). See, more recently, the fine investigation by Sundhya Pahuja, *Laws of Encounter: A Jurisdictional Account of International Law*, 1 LONDON REV. INT'L L. 63 (2013).

hand, and the challenging of that account through evidence of the omission, suppression, violence, and asymmetry that really shaped the evolution of the international order, on the other.[30] It is one of the greatest challenges in global governance research in general, and in legal theory in particular, to find a suitable, adequate way to address the relationship between "societal" and "political" ordering, between market and state, private and public, against the background of such contested framework narratives. But, although such context-sensitive work has been done for a while already in the realm of human rights theory in the context of a critical engagement with "comparative legal traditions"[31] and "cultures,"[32] promising evidence in the area of private regulatory governance, or in private law more generally, is still lagging behind. As private lawyers strive to underscore a normative foundation for their field, they point to private law's efforts in resisting the continuously forceful, neoliberal thrust of the prevailing *international* economic order.[33] Meanwhile, scholars who associate themselves with different strands of systems theory, regulation theory, or critical theory focus on the *messy-ness* of the inchoate and highly decentralized landscape of transnational *private* regulatory governance,[34] rendering the boundaries between a public and a private law approach to economic globalization more ambiguous. In contrast then, the institutional and constitutionalist investigations by political scientists[35] focus

[30] José-Manuel Barreto, *Decolonial Strategies and Dialogue in the Human Rights Field: A Manifesto*, 3 Transnat'l Legal Theory 1 (2012); *see also* Anne Orford, *Muscular Humanitarianism: Reading the Narratives of the New Interventionism*, 10 Eur. J. Int'l L. 679 (2003).

[31] H. Patrick Glenn, *Comparative Legal Families and Comparative Legal Traditions*, *in* Oxford Handbook of Comparative Law 431–40 (Mathias Reimann & Reinhard Zimmermann eds., 2006).

[32] Upendra Baxi, *The Colonialist Heritage*, *in* Comparative Legal Studies: Traditions and Transitions 46–75 (Pierre Legrand & Roderick Munday eds., 2003); Upendra Baxi, The Future of Human Rights (2002); William Twining, Human Rights, Southern Voices: Francis Deng, Abdullahi An-Na'im, Yash Ghai and Upendra Baxi (2009).

[33] Jürgen Basedow, *The State's Private Law and the Economy: Commercial Law as an Amalgam of Public and Private Rule-Making*, 56 Am. J. Comp. L. 703 (2008). For a critical perspective, see James Thuo Gathii, *Third World Approaches to International Economic Governance*, *in* International Law and the Future 255–67 (Richard A. Falk, Balakrishnan Rajagopal & Jacqueline Stevens eds., 2008), and Lang, World Trade Law after Neoliberalism, *supra* note 16.

[34] For an excellent discussion, see the symposium introduction in *The Challenge of Transnational Private Regulation: Conceptual and Constitutional Debates*, 38 J.L. & Soc'y 1–188 (Colin Scott, Fabrizio Cafaggi & Linda Senden eds., special issue 2011). For an earlier assessment, see Oren Perez, *Normative Creativity and Global Legal Pluralism: Reflections on the Democratic Critique of Transnational Law*, 10 Ind. J. Global Legal Stud. 25 (2003). *See also* Gralf-Peter Calliess & Peer Zumbansen, Rough Consensus and Running Code: A Theory of Transnational Private Law (2010), in particular, chapters 2 and 5.

[35] Ruggie, *Reconstituting the Global Public Domain*, *supra* note 6.

on questions of *agency*, *interests*, and *accountability*, and such studies find their echoes, above all, in *public* and *public international law* scholarship.[36] By contrast, private law and private law theory are, for the most part, still the missing voices here,[37] although the field has a rich tradition in critically investigating the regulatory challenges that arise from a state's political apparatus responding to rapid societal and economic change.[38] Furthermore, it seems obvious how the task to decipher the hybrid regulatory code of transnational governance would require a substantial contribution from scholars working in these traditions.[39]

I want to argue that the reinvigoration of private law within the political science and public law dominated discourses on global governance must occur against a background of a comprehensively reconceptualized framework of how we – and others – are speaking about globalization and the law in the first place. This reconceptualization is prompted by the significant challenges that scholars using postcolonial and third-world approaches to international law have been formulating in response to the otherwise canonic and typical account of the Westphalian rise of the Western nation-state, its transformation in the twentieth century, and the erosion of the nation-states' regulatory sovereignty in an increasingly globalized world of the twenty-first century.[40] The postcolonial challenge in legal and political theory makes more than clear today that a reinvigoration of private law's abilities to "pierce the legal veil"

---

[36] *See* Benedict Kingsbury, Nico Krisch & Richard B. Stewart, *The Emergence of Global Administrative Law*, 68 L. & CONTEMP. PROBS. 15 (2005).

[37] There are exceptions. *See, e.g.,* Robert Wai, *Transnational Private Law and Private Ordering in Contested Global Society*, 46 HARV. INT'L L.J. 471 (2005), and Daniela Caruso, *Private Law and State-Making in the Age of Globalization*, 39 N.Y.U. J. INT'L L. & POL. 1 (2006).

[38] *See, e.g.,* Karl N. Llewellyn, *What Price Contract? – An Essay in Perspective*, 40 YALE L.J. 704 (1930), and the recent assessment by Hanoch Dagan, *The Realist Conception of Law*, 57 U. TORONTO L.J. 607 (2007).

[39] *See, e.g.,* Gunther Teubner, *Global Private Regimes: Neo-spontaneous Law and Dual Constitution of Autonomous Sectors in World Society?, in* GLOBALIZATION AND PUBLIC GOVERNANCE 71–87 (Karl-Heinz Ladeur ed., 2004). *See also* Peer C. Zumbansen, *Law and Legal Pluralism: Hybridity in Transnational Governance, in* REGULATORY HYBRIDIZATION IN THE TRANSNATIONAL SPHERE 49–70 (Paulius Jurcys, Poul F. Kjaer & Ren Yatsunami eds., 2013). From a public and constitutional law perspective, see Christoph Engel, *Hybrid Governance Across National Jurisdictions as a Challenge to Constitutional Law*, 2 EUR. BUS. ORG. L. REV. 569 (2001), preprints aus der Max-Planck-Projektgruppe Recht der Gemeinschaftsgüter Bonn 2001/8, *available at* http://www.coll.mpg.de/pdf_dat/2001_08online.pdf; Karl-Heinz Ladeur, *Globalization and Public Governance – A Contradiction?, in* PUBLIC GOVERNANCE IN THE AGE OF GLOBALIZATION 1 (Karl-Heinz Ladeur ed., 2004); and Henry Farrell, *Hybrid Institutions and the Law*, 23 ZEITSCHRIFT FÜR RECHTSSOZIOLOGIE 25 (2002).

[40] *See, e.g.,* James Thuo Gathii, *TWAIL: A Brief History of Its Origins, Its Decentralized Network, and a Tentative Bibliography*, 3 TRADE, L. & DEV. 26 (2011).

in an attempt to render visible the social and economic inequalities that pervade the realities underneath the floorboards of rules and principles in legal argument[41] can no longer take the troubled regulatory history of the Western welfare state as its obvious starting point and as its all determining frame of reference. The next order of the day must be to ironicize,[42] to relativize[43] and to provincialize[44] the ever so sophisticated analysis of the decline of the regulatory (Western welfare) state in the 1970s and 1980s[45] to more adequately interrogate the public–private divide – a pillar in the standard Western account of law's historical development[46] – against the background of the present transnational context. Such a project, however, would go beyond what can even remotely be attempted in the confines of these brief remarks. Meanwhile, it helps to better understand the confined nature of most of the conversations about the legitimacy deficit in (private) global governance, if we substantively widen our scope of analysis.[47] In other words, it will no longer be enough to engage in efforts of patching the legitimacy deficits of transnational private regulatory governance solely against the background of a (Western) welfare state with the dramatic erosions of its regulatory powers. Instead, in the years ahead we will need to critically engage with the phenomenon of private regulatory power against the background of a far-reaching, postcolonial critique of the universalist accounts of the rise of the Westphalian international order (of

[41] Robert L. Hale, *Coercion and Distribution in a Supposedly Non-Coercive State*, 38 POL. SCI. Q. 470 (1923); David M. Trubek, *Toward a Social Theory of Law: An Essay on the Study of Law and Development*, (1972) 82 YALE L.J. 1 (1972); Duncan Kennedy, *Form and Substance in Private Law Adjudication*, 89 HARV. L. REV. 1685 (1976); Peer Zumbansen, *Introduction: Private Ordering in a Globalizing World: Still Searching for the Basis of Contract*, 14 IND. J. GLOBAL LEGAL STUD. 181 (2007).

[42] Kerry Rittich, *Functionalism and Formalism: Their Latest Incarnations in Contemporary Development and Governance Debates*, 55 U. TORONTO L.J. 853, 868 (2005). *See also* Peer Zumbansen, *Law After the Welfare State: Formalism, Functionalism and the Ironic Turn of Reflexive Law*, 56 AM. J. COMP. L. 769 (2008).

[43] EVE DARIAN-SMITH, LAWS AND SOCIETIES IN GLOBAL CONTEXTS. CONTEMPORARY APPROACHES (2013).

[44] DIPESH CHAKRABARTY, PROVINCIALIZING EUROPE. POSTCOLONIAL THOUGHT AND HISTORICAL DIFFERENCE (2d ed. 2007).

[45] See the contributions in DILEMMAS OF LAW IN THE WELFARE STATE (Gunther Teubner ed., 1986).

[46] *See* Carol Harlow, *"Public" and "Private" Law: Definition without Distinction*, 43 MOD. L. REV. 241 (1980); Duncan Kennedy, *The Stages of the Decline of the Public/Private Distinction*, (1982) 130 U. PA. L. REV. 1349 (1982), and A. Claire Cutler, *Artifice, Ideology and Paradox: the Public/Private Distinction in International Law*, 4 REV. INT'L POL. ECON. 261 (1997).

[47] An area where this North–South dialogue has been taking place for quite some time, however, is international investment law. *See, e.g.,* MUTHUCUMARASWAMY SORNARAJAH, THE INTERNATIONAL LAW ON FOREIGN INVESTMENT (3d ed. 2010), and SURYA P. SUBEDI, INTERNATIONAL INVESTMENT LAW: RECONCILING POLICY AND PRINCIPLE (2012).

sovereign nation states) and of their subsequent demise through "privatization (Europeanization) and globalization."[48]

THE ASPIRATIONAL, NAVIGATIONAL ROLE OF LAWYERS IN THE TRANSNATIONAL SPACE

For the time being, the engagement with the legitimacy deficit of a proliferating, neoliberal global order has been based on the rise-and-fall narrative of the Westphalian order and its subsequent transformation into fragmented international legal regimes and hybrid, public–private governance arrangements.[49] The explanation offered for the precarious stance of public values in the emergence of a market-driven sphere of global private self-regulation has had its origin in the alleged exhaustion of the nation state's regulatory capacity – with globalization merely accentuating and amplifying the state's inherent adaptation problems to complex social arrangements and financial pressures.[50] In light of overwhelming, spatial regulatory challenges such as climate change, security, migration, poverty, and hunger, legal theorists began translating the otherwise recently learned lessons from the death of the "regulatory state"[51] and the rise of its successor[52] into an evolving theory of global governance, which aspires to generate a multidisciplinary account of the challenges of globalization for political and legal theory. Although scholarly contributions to that endeavor fill the metaphorical shelves of ever faster expanding online library resources,[53] we can – for the purposes of our present inquiry – distinguish between two broad strands in legal scholarship on this question, which turn out to largely correspond to alternatives in the underlying social-political

---

[48] For such a standard narrative, see Ralf Michaels & Nils Jansen, *Private Law Beyond the State? Europeanization, Globalization, Privatization*, 55 Am. J. Comp. L. 843 (2007).

[49] Jan Klabbers, *Of Round Pegs and Square Holes: International Law and the Private Sector*, in Regulatory Hybridization in the Transnational Sphere 29–48 (Paulius Jurcys, Poul F. Kjaer & Ren Yatsunami eds., 2013).

[50] Jürgen Habermas, *The New Obscurity: The Crisis of the Welfare State and the Exhaustion of Utopian Energies*, in Jürgen Habermas, The New Conservatism. Cultural Criticism and the Historians' Debate: Studies in Contemporary German Thought 48–70 (Shierry Weber Nicholsen, ed. & trans., 1989).

[51] Gunther Teubner, *Regulatory Law: Chronicle of a Death Foretold*, 1 Soc. & Legal Stud 451 (1992).

[52] Colin Scott, *Regulation in the Age of Governance: The Rise of the Post Regulatory State*, in The Politics of Regulation: Institutions and Regulatory Reforms for the Age of Governance 145–74 (Jacint Jordana & David Levi-Faur eds., 2004).

[53] N. Krishnan & C. K. Das, *Globalization and Challenges in Library Management in the 21st Century: An Appraisal of the University Library Systems in India and the USA*, in Challenges in Library Management System 381–85 (2012).

theory. The rough demarcation, then, emerges as between what we may call "functionalist" and "normative" approaches to the analysis of law's role in a globalized world. While scholars sympathizing with the former approach seem more ready and willing to accept a high degree of world society's functional differentiation into specialized, self-regulating fields of activity (and corresponding rationality[54]), scholars who endorse a normative stance have tended to highlight the dramatic risks of the loss of coherence and legitimacy in a fragmented global order.[55]

Regardless of the side on which scholars see themselves in this dispute, each group finds itself struggling over at least a working definition of law in this global context. Again, the juxtaposition would follow well-known lines: while one group (the "normative" one) adhered to a model of law, which would be defined through an institutionalized framework to produce, enforce, and adjudicate binding norms,[56] the other group – in a functionalist vein – would understand law, above all, as a process of stabilizing expectations.[57] Meanwhile, complementing and complicating these accounts, we find two contentions about the nature of law, which shift the definitorial perspective toward an assessment of the long-term effects of legal governance. Here, we find, on the one hand, assertions whereby law primarily serves purposes of emancipation and should thus be associated with ideas of hope, liberation, "voice"), while law's character, as defined on the other hand, is governed by its function as oppressor, silencer and violent actor.

Now, the dramatic and sobering experience of those engaged in the functionalist-normative debate over law's role in global governance has been that these distinctions do not matter that much at the end of the day. From the perspective of ever faster evolving regimes of transnational private regulatory norms and standard setting – seen as potentially responding to a decline of

---

[54] Gunther Teubner, *"Global Bukowina": Legal Pluralism in the World Society, in* GLOBAL LAW WITHOUT A STATE 3–28 (Gunther Teubner ed., 1997); Gunther Teubner, *Societal Constitutionalism: Alternatives to State-Centred Constitutional Theory?, in* CONSTITUTIONALISM AND TRANSNATIONAL GOVERNANCE 3–28 (Christian Joerges, Inger-Johanne Sand & Gunther Teubner eds., 2004); Andreas Fischer-Lescano & Gunther Teubner, *Regime-Collisions: The Vain Search for Legal Unity in the Fragmentation of Global Law,* 25 MICH. J. INT'L L. 999 (2004).

[55] See the contributions to INTERNATIONAL JUDICIAL LAWMAKING ON PUBLIC AUTHORITY AND DEMOCRATIC LEGITIMATION IN GLOBAL GOVERNANCE (Armin von Bogdandy & Ingo Venzke eds., 2012).

[56] Armin von Bogdandy, Philipp Dann & Matthias Goldmann, *Developing the Publicness of Public International Law,* 9 GERMAN L.J. 1375 (2008).

[57] NIKLAS LUHMANN, A SOCIOLOGICAL THEORY OF LAW (1985); Gunther Teubner, *How the Law Thinks: Toward a Constructivist Epistemology of Law,* 23 L. & SOC'Y REV. 727 (1989).

state regulatory capacity by filling public goods gaps[58] – it became more and more clear, that the second definitional approach of law's globalized nature might in fact be the most appropriate: Law in a global context comes in many forms, shapes, and sizes but its main function can be seen as consisting of stabilizing the expectations of its stakeholders.[59] That, however, renders the original starting point of an ambiguous, complementary state of public and private law perspectives on global governance ever more poignant. Recognizing that the "public" rescue of private regulatory arrangements would have to occur in a context that we find increasingly difficult to assess on the basis of an all-encompassing, uncontested normative foundation such as a universalist human rights account, the bright line distinction between public and private continues to fade. In a fragmented global sphere, which is marked above all by existential contestations of normative stances, there appears to be little room for a one-size-fits-all theory of global justice. Instead, in a gesture of denial, we may either resort to quasirevisionist, post-Westphalian accounts of state sovereignty[60], which entirely ignore the postcolonial and indigenous contestation of the international legal order narrative or we can throw ourselves into the godless and centerless realm of global functional differentiation, in which the stakes of a transnational merchant community[61] compete with the moral stakes raised by indigenous, epistemic, and other situational communities. In that constellation, even a renewed interest in "power"[62] is not likely to solve the differentiation conundrum we are faced with per se, but will have to take the diverse accounts of what constitutes societal, institutional, and structural power as a necessary starting point. The differentiation of human interactions and

---

[58] Colin Scott, *Beyond Taxonomies of Private Authority in Transnational Regulation*, 13 GERMAN L.J. 1329 (2012). See also the standard work by NILS BRUNSSON & BENGT JACOBSSON, A WORLD OF STANDARDS (2000).

[59] For an elaboration of the nature of stakeholders in global norm-setting in the form of "affected communities," see Roger Cotterrell, *Transnational Communities and the Concept of Law*, 21 RATIO JURIS 1 (2008), and Roger Cotterrell, *Spectres of Transnationalism: Changing Terrains of Sociology of Law*, 36 J.L. & SOC'Y 481 (2009).

[60] JACK L. GOLDSMITH AND ERIC A. POSNER, THE LIMITS OF INTERNATIONAL LAW (2005); ANDREW T. GUZMAN, HOW INTERNATIONAL LAW WORKS: A RATIONAL CHOICE THEORY (2008); *supra* note 22.

[61] EMMANUEL GAILLARD, LEGAL THEORY OF INTERNATIONAL ARBITRATION (2010); Teubner, "*Global Bukowina*", *supra* note 53.

[62] See Roger Cotterrell, *What is Transnational Law?*, 37 L. & SOC. INQUIRY 500, esp. 513–14 (2012); *see also* Roger Cotterrell, *Rethinking "Embeddedness": Law, Economy, Community*, 40 J.L. & SOC'Y 49 (2013), which critically revisits the usefulness of "community" as an distinct organizational entity and shifts the emphasis toward "*social relations of community* of various contrasting types." *Id.* at 55 (emphasis added).

epistemes[63] has rendered the normative landscape unpenetrable and unintelligible for any attempt to provide an exclusive, coherent account of who's "up," "down," "right," or "wrong."

That said, where can we situate today the ever more pressing anxieties about the legitimacy deficits of transnational private regulatory governance? It appears as if we are back to where we started from, with the only difference now being, that we realize that it is not just a simple choice between a functionalist and a normative theory of global regulatory governance. Instead, we see that the former gives expression to the undeniable degree of societal differentiation on a global scale, whereas the latter points to the complementing efforts to submit these processes to a critical engagement. Although proponents of the systems theory account of societal differentiation would contend that such critical engagement is impossible as there is no general outside vantage point from which such interrogation would be possible,[64] critical (legal, political) scholars (must) insist on a way in, behind, and underneath this facade.[65]

Surely, and in light of the previously described tensions, the main character of transnational legal governance must be defined as *functionalist*, in that law (along with various forms of "soft" law, norms, codes, standards, recommendations, and guidelines) responds and adapts to the regulatory–organizational challenges of complex fields of global interaction. Echoing the changing roles that lawyers have assumed in the context of transformed and globalized state functions in the twentieth century, transnational lawyers today must be at once litigators, policy makers, legislators, and norm entrepreneurs, activists, and community organizers.[66] The nature, roles, and functions of the transnational lawyer evolve in relation to the functional differentiation of their areas of engagement. With the rise of expert knowledge, the scrutiny

---

[63] NIKLAS LUHMANN, POLITICAL THEORY IN THE WELFARE STATE (John Bednarz, Jr., trans., Walter de Gruyter 1990) (1981), and BRUNO LATOUR, WE HAVE NEVER BEEN MODERN (Catherine Porter trans., 1993).

[64] Niklas Luhmann, *Quod omnes tangit: Remarks on Jürgen Habermas' Legal Theory, in* HABERMAS ON LAW AND DEMOCRACY: CRITICAL EXCHANGES 157–73 (Michael Rosenfeld & Andrew Arato eds., 1998).

[65] ROBERTO MANGOBEIRA UNGER, THE CRITICAL LEGAL STUDIES MOVEMENT (1986); David Kennedy, *Law and the Political Economy of the World*, 26 LEIDEN J. INT'L L. 7 (2013).

[66] Sue Bryant & Jean Koh Peters, *Five Habits for Cross-Cultural Lawyering, in* RACE, CULTURE, PSYCHOLOGY, AND LAW ch. 4 (Kimberly H. Barrett & William H. George eds., 2004); LAWYERS IN PRACTICE: ETHICAL DECISION MAKING IN CONTEXT (Leslie C. Levin & Lynn Mather eds., 2012); Bryant G. Garth, *Introduction: Taking New Legal Realism to Transnational Issues and Institutions*, 31 L. & SOC. INQUIRY 939 (2006).

of competing opinions and epistemes, law, and legal consultancy fuses into a complex, multitiered enterprise of regulatory governance. And while the normative challenges arising from these developments accrue, the questions of how to adequately address them grow in complexity.[67] Lawyers, stepping out of their traditional roles of serving a client's interests and/or promoting the public interest, find themselves engaged in navigating ethnographies of competing stakes and interests,[68] mapping and identifying competences and authorities, formulating policy and identifying appropriate levels of regulation, contributing to the formulation and creation of adequate norms, and maintaining, overall, a highly functional, particularized outlook and focus. Lawyers as regulatory actors, then, operate in newly expanding frameworks, which evolve around the transformation, disaggregation,[69] and transnationalization of municipal institutional safeguards and representation processes.[70] Among those, we find international organizations, regulatory networks and regimes, hybrid governance institutions and shifting interest coalitions such as the "G 20." This is in addition to grassroots movements, community organizations, and social movements,[71] as well as information and community-building fora for new voices, new movements, and actors such as the World Social Forum[72] that bring core political concerns around representation and affectedness, participation, and accountability into sharp relief.[73] If a straightforward, institutionally and normatively coherent public (rescue) response to the legitimacy woes of transnational private regulatory governance were possible, then how would such a response look like, in view of the diversified institutional and organizational landscape we just depicted? From which vantage point

---

[67] Colin Scott, Professor of EU Regulation and Governance, Inaugural Lecture at University College Dublin, School of Law: Regulating Everything (Feb. 26, 2008), *available at* http://www.ucd.ie/geary/static/publications/workingpapers/gearywp200824.pdf.

[68] David A. Westbrook, *Theorizing the Diffusion of Law: Conceptual Difficulties, Unstable Imaginations, and the Effort to Think Gracefully Nevertheless*, 47 Harv. Int'l L.J. 489 (2006).

[69] Anne-Marie Slaughter, *Disaggregated Sovereignty: Towards the Public Accountability of Global Government Networks*, 39 Gov't & Opposition 159 (2004).

[70] Sabino Cassese, *New Paths for Administrative Law: A Manifesto*, 10 Int'l J. Const. L. 603 (2012); Alfred C. Aman, Jr., The Democracy Deficit: Taming Globalization Through Law Reform (2004)

[71] Balakrishnan Rajagopal, *International Law and Social Movements: Challenges of Theorizing Resistance*, 41 Colum. J. Transnat'l L. 397 (2003).

[72] Boaventura de Sousa Santos, *The World Social Forum and the Global Left*, 36 Pol. & Soc'y 247 (2008); José Corrêa Leite & Carolina Gil, The World Social Forum: Strategies for Resistance (Traci Romine trans., 2005).

[73] Regina Kreide, *The Ambivalence of Juridification. On Legitimate Governance in the International Context*, 2 Global Just.: Theory Prac. Rhetoric 18 (2009).

should we begin to look for answers to the question of *who's in* and *who's out?* Attempts to formulate responses are made from within a host of disciplinary, conceptual imaginations, including *Global Administrative Law*,[74] *Global Constitutionalism*[75] and *Cosmopolitanism*,[76] *Regulatory Capitalism*[77] as well as *Transnational Governance*.[78] Offering rich accounts of the institutional and normative conundrum presented by law's entanglement with globalization, this scholarship can no longer easily be categorized as either descriptive or prescriptive, an observation that seems to confirm our previous contention that it is unlikely to find a quick fix for the increasingly detailed accounts of regulatory differentiation and ever more pressing normative questions.

PRIVATE LAW'S ROLE IN THE TRANSNATIONAL SPACE:
COMPLICITY OR RESISTANCE?

So, what can be done? The continuing proliferation of transnational private regulatory governance raises dramatic challenges to conceptions of legal authority, legitimacy, and public regulation of economic activity. The pace at which these developments occur is set by a coalescence of multiple regime changes, predominantly in commercial law areas,[79] but also in the field of

---

[74] Benedict Kingsbury, *The Concept of 'Law' in Global Administrative Law*, 20 EUR. J. INT'L L. 23 (2003). For a critical engagement, see Carol Harlow, *Global Administrative Law: The Quest for Principles and Values*, 17 EUR. J. INT'L L. 187 (2006).

[75] Jeffrey L. Dunoff & J. P. Trachtman, *A Functional Approach to Global Constitutionalism*, in RULING THE WORLD? CONSTITUTIONALISM, INTERNATIONAL LAW, AND GLOBAL GOVERNANCE 3–35 (Jeffrey L. Dunoff & Joel P. Trachtman eds., 2009); Christine E.J. Schwöbel, *The Appeal of the Project of Global Constitutionalism for Public International Lawyers*, 13 GERMAN L.J. 1 (2012).

[76] David Held, *Cosmopolitanism*, in Stanford Encyclopedia of Philosophy (Feb. 23, 2002, revised July 1, 2013), *available at* http://plato.stanford.edu/entries/cosmopolitanism. *See also* Alec Stone Sweet, *Constitutionalism, Legal Pluralism, and International Regimes*, 16 IND. J. GLOBAL LEGAL STUD. 621 (2009).

[77] JOHN BRAITHWAITE, REGULATORY CAPITALISM. HOW IT WORKS, IDEAS FOR MAKING IT WORK BETTER (2008); Levi-Faur, *supra* note 7.

[78] See the contributions to HANDBOOK OF TRANSNATIONAL GOVERNANCE. INSTITUTIONS AND INNOVATIONS (Thomas Hale & David Held eds., 2011).

[79] Thomas Schultz, *Does Online Dispute Resolution Need Governmental Intervention? The Case for Architectures of Control and Trust*, 71 N.C. J.L. & TECH. 71 (2004); Gralf-Peter Calliess, *Transnational Civil Regimes: Economic Globalization and the Evolution of Commercial Law*, in CONTRACTUAL CERTAINTY IN INTERNATIONAL TRADE. EMPIRICAL STUDIES AND THEORETICAL DEBATES ON INSTITUTIONAL SUPPORT FOR GLOBAL ECONOMIC EXCHANGES 215–38 (Volkmar Gessner ed., 2009).

Internet governance,[80] corporate law,[81] and labor law,[82] where the rise to prominence of private actors has become a defining feature of the evolving transnational regulatory landscape. One of the most belabored fields, the transnational law merchant or, lex mercatoria, for some time had assumed the status of a poster child, as it represented a laboratory for the exploration of private contractual governance in a context, in which the assertion of public or private authority had itself become contentious.[83] But, the ambiguity surrounding many forms of today's contractual governance in the transnational arena echoes that of the far-reaching transformation of public regulatory governance, which has been characteristic of Western welfare states over the last few decades. What is particularly remarkable, however, is the way in which the depictions of private instruments and public interests in the postwelfare-state regulatory environment have given rise to a rise in importance of social norms, self-regulation, and a general antistate affect in the assessment of judicial enforcement or administration of contractual arrangements.[84] As noted, with regard to the deep contestations of established narratives of modernization, progress and universalization, a central challenge resulting from case studies such as the transnational law merchant is from which perspective we ought to adequately study and assess the justifications that are being offered for a *contractual governance* model, which prioritizes and seeks to insulate private

---

[80] UNDERSTANDING THE WEB: SOCIAL, POLITICAL, AND ECONOMIC DIMENSIONS OF THE INTERNET (Alan B. Albarran & David H. Goff eds., 2000); Christoph Engel, *The Role of Law in the Governance of the* Internet, 20 INT'L REV. L., COMPUTERS & TECH. 201 (2006).

[81] Amir N. Licht, *The Mother of all Path-Dependencies: Towards a Cross-Cultural Theory of Corporate Governance Systems*, 26 DEL. J. CORP. L. 147 (2001); Carston Gerner-Beuerle, *Determinants of Corporate Governance Codes*, (LSE Legal Studes Working Paper No. 5/2014), *available at* http://ssrn.com/abstract=2346673.

[82] Katherine van Wezel Stone, *Labour in the Global Economy: Four Approaches to Transnational Labour Regulation*, in INTERNATIONAL REGULATORY COMPETITION AND COORDINATION. PERSPECTIVES ON ECONOMIC REGULATION IN EUROPE AND THE UNITED STATES 445–77 (Joseph McCahery, William W. Bratton, Sol Picciotto & Colin Scott eds., 1996); Harry Arthurs, *Reinventing Labor Law for the Global Economy: The Benjamin Aaron Lecture*, 22 BERKELEY J. EMP. & LAB. L. 271 (2001).

[83] Gralf-Peter Calliess, *Lex Mercatoria: A Reflexive Law Guide to an Autonomous Legal System*, 2 GERMAN L.J. 17 (2001), *available at* http://www.germanlawjournal.com/article.php?id=109; A. CLAIRE CUTLER, PRIVATE POWER AND GLOBAL AUTHORITY: TRANSNATIONAL MERCHANT LAW IN THE GLOBAL ECONOMY (2003).

[84] Representative is law and economics' rather ahistorical "discovery" of "social norms." ERIC A. POSNER, LAW AND SOCIAL NORMS (2000). Robert C. Ellickson, *Law and Economics Discovers Social Norms*, 27 J. LEGAL STUD. 537 (1998). Stewart Macaulay, *Relational Contracts Floating on a Sea of Custom? Thoughts About the Ideas of Ian Macneil and Lisa Bernstein*, 94 Nw. U. L. REV. 775 (2000).

arrangements from their embeddedness in regulated market contexts, on both the national and transnational level.

It seems obvious by now, that by focusing on the law/nonlaw nature of the lex mercatoria[85] we fall short of grasping the more important question, namely, why this distinction matters and what the *stakes* are of searching for a solution in this context. To be sure, striving to either ascertain or to reject the legal nature of the predominantly self-made norms of the lex mercatoria redirects attention to the setting and context in which legal norms are created, enforced, and adjudicated. From a traditional perspective, such questions have regularly been raised with reference to dimensions of legality, on the one hand, and legitimacy, on the other.[86] In response, I contend that what appears to be emerging from the here suggested rise in importance of private as well as hybrid actors engaged in transnational norm production, standards, guidelines, codes and best practices, however, is a new concept of context. Whereas much of legal theory and philosophy, especially in the analytical tradition, chose to scrutinize the nature of law and legal ordering without taking a greater interest in the context or environment, in which legal ordering as well as social conflicts occur, legal pluralist accounts of law challenge such an approach in a fundamental way. Once the reference framework, illustrated by assertions of the "rule of law," "legal unity," "normative hierarchy," or the "separation of powers" becomes questionable in a global setting, law's relation to its outside, its context, as it were, moves into the center of analysis. From that perspective, the legal pluralist critique of the monist model of legal ordering[87] can productively inform the analysis of transnational law. The law–state nexus, which has for so long been one of the centrally underlying assumptions at least in Western, Northern legal epistemology, becomes relativized to the degree that regulation through law becomes decentred (J. Black). This decentering of state-originating law into highly specialized fields of norm production had long marked the transformation of the welfare state and is further propelled and amplified by the transnationalization of

---

[85] See the altogether unproductive dispute between Teubner, *"Global Bukowina" supra* note 53, at 3–28, and Albrecht Cordes, *The Search for a Medieval Lex Mercatoria*, Oxford U. Comp. L.F. 5 (2003), http://ouclf.iuscomp.org/articles/cordes.shtml.

[86] Karsten Schmidt, *Lex mercatoria: Allheilmittel? Rätsel? Chimäre?, in* Globalisierung und Recht: Beiträge Japans und Deutschlands zu einer internationalen Rechtsordnung im 21. Jahrhundert 153–74 (Junichi Murakami, Hans-Peter Marutschke & Karl Riesenhuber eds., 2007).

[87] Peter Fitzpatrick, *Law and Societies*, 22 Osgoode Hall L.J. 115 (1984); Roderick A. MacDonald, *Whose Access? Which Justice?*, 7 Canadian J.L & Soc'y 175 (1992); Boaventura de Sousa Santos, Toward a New Legal Common Sense: Law, Globalization, and Emancipation (2002).

law.[88] These developments, as long as they were conceived to be taking place within a more or less institutionalized nation state setting prompted legal sociologists to question law's and lawyers' grasp of the reality in which legal decisions were being made, norms produced and their effectiveness measured.[89] The legal sociological contribution to a fundamental critique of law can hardly be overstated, and the current interdisciplinary engagement with transnational law and regulatory governance must be seen as a continuation of these approaches.[90]

As a result, the context in which the analysis of law, its foundations and its effectiveness take place is a context that cannot simply be seen[91] or taken for granted when contemplating the legal nature of regulatory norms. Instead, *context* has become a factor that forms a crucial part of our assessment of the legal nature of the norms and their processes of creation and implementation under consideration. For example, a simple distinction between a national and a global context of law does not go far enough in addressing the correlation between a theory of law and a theory of the context in which law is embedded. Precisely because processes of globalization or transnationalization have decentered, relativized, and provincialized the prior assumed role of the state in the production of legal norms, we need to scrutinize the new environment in which norms are being created and their nature ascertained.

Such a shift of perspective has far-reaching consequences for legal theory and for the philosophy of law but also for legal doctrine, in that many of the routinely assumed institutional frameworks for references to public or private law, for example, constitutional and administrative law on the one hand, contract, labor, or corporate law on the other, can be seen in a new light. With the prevailing unavailability of a world government, or a global constitution, lawyers find themselves not only in an unavoidable, but also a necessary conversation with other disciplines. Such conversations concern the nature and structure of a sphere, which continues to be depicted through labels that hide rather than reveal the disciplinary grounding of the analytical assessment.

---

[88] Peer C. Zumbansen, *Transnational Legal Pluralism*, 1 TRANSNAT'L LEGAL THEORY 141 (2010), *available at* http://ssrn.com/abstract=1542907.

[89] Roger Cotterrell, *Why Must Legal Ideas Be Interpreted Sociologically?*, 25 J.L & SOC'Y 171 (1998).

[90] David Nelken, *Transnational Legal Processes and the (Re)construction of the "Social": The Case of Human Trafficking*, in EXPLORING THE "SOCIO" OF SOCIO-LEGAL STUDIES 137–56 (Dermot Feenan ed., 2013); Prabha Kotiswaran, *Do Feminists Need an Economic Sociology of Law?*, 40 J.L. & SOC'Y 115 (2013).

[91] That, however, is the contention of Ralf Michaels, *Globalization and Law: Law Beyond the State*, in LAW AND SOCIAL THEORY 287–303 (Reza Banakar & Max Travers eds., 2d ed. 2013), *available at* http://scholarship.law.duke.edu/faculty_scholarship/2862.

References to global governance, world society, or global constitutionalism abound, but their definitional scope remains unsatisfying. At the same time, the promise of such conceptual labels should be seen as lying in the *opening up of perspectives* that they generate. Global governance, arguably, is a term with a predominantly operational function within a political science framework, but it is by no means limited to the categories and concepts of that discipline. Instead, global governance cuts across disciplinary boundaries in that it pushes established frameworks (politics), distinctions (public/private), instruments (elections) and concepts (sovereignty) to extreme limits, at which point it becomes obvious how this strain on the architecture of one discipline is echoed and similarly resounds in other disciplines as they are dealing with pressures of globalization. From this perspective, global governance becomes a formula with which we can depict changes internal to respective disciplinary frameworks, and through which we can verbalize the coalescing and overlapping of different disciplinary perspectives in a collaborative effort to make sense of the transformations associated with globalization.

What then, however, can or should be the role of law? In this chapter we identified the dominant definition to be a functionalist one, a definition which holds law to be concerned, above all, with the stabilization of (highly heterogeneous) expectations of various stakeholders. At the same time, it is possible then to generalize the place of such defined law in the context of globalization. I contend that under conditions of globalization, law assumes the role of providing for a particular *perspective* on regulatory governance. The latter is no longer fully consumed under the heading of law, but must instead be deconstructed through different disciplinary lenses, only one of which is law. In light of the *functionalist* rule of law framework on the global level that we identified earlier, say, with respect to the regulation of global financial markets[92] or the protection of social rights,[93] the simultaneously increasing proliferation of *private* agency in the creation of governing norms and their dissemination[94] causes a considerable constitutional itch. It comes as no surprise, then, that from a host of disciplinary, descriptive, and prescriptive perspectives, the prospects of a legal framework for global governance have become a major concern. Ranging from law to sociology, political science and, geography to political philosophy, law's disembeddedness from the nation-state

---

[92] *See, e.g.*, Michael S. Barr & Geoffrey P. Miller, *Global Administrative Law: The View from Basel*, 17 Eur. J. Int'l L. 15 (2006).

[93] Simon Deakin, *Social Rights in a Globalized Economy*, *in* Labour Rights as Human Rights 25–60 (Philip Alston ed., 2005).

[94] *See, e.g.*, Tim Büthe & Walter Mattli, The New Global Rulers: The Privatization of Regulation in the World Economy (2012).

prompts inquiries into the possibilities of reembedding law or, alternatively, transposing and translating nation-state-tested frameworks and categories of legal regulation into the global governance context.[95] Whatever might be the outcome in the short term or long term, law's "empire" has come under considerable pressure by having to reassess its role and its bearing in a complex regulatory and normative environment.

LAW AND SOCIETY: A VIEW FROM EVERYWHERE OR NOWHERE?

Just to be sure, the ongoing disputes over law's global role, including its institutional and normative dimensions – although these may be contested as nonuniversalist – occur in the context of deep-running divides between competing theories of society and social organization. And, it is against that background that the so far offered observations with regard to the contested legal nature of transnational private regulatory governance are only stand-ins or echoes of much larger concerns within the fundamental transformation of legal regulation today. As we saw, the contentions concerning, for example, lex mercatoria's autonomy and the legal nature of its norms then illustrate the pressure that the continuing societal differentiation and an increasingly fragmented regulatory transnational fabric creates for legal doctrine, terminology, and concepts. This suggests, then, that questions such as those pertaining to the legal versus nonlegal nature of norms, which are clearly central not only to lex mercatoria but also to the phenomena of transnational private regulatory governance more generally, are pointers to the more pressing and previously alluded to need to fundamentally rethink and reimagine the relationship between law and society in light of a loosening state-law nexus. From this perspective, it becomes a necessity for legal scholars to consider theories of society when making statements about the quality and function of legal norms.

Importantly, such questions are not in any way new to law and legal scholars. Over time, the need to adapt law, its theory, doctrine, and instruments to ever-changing societal conditions has only grown. And, however contested law's place and contribution to such changes became, such investigations regularly unfold with a view to the ambivalent, constantly changing relations between law and the state. Regarding the latter, depictions of the role of the state shifted between ruler and protector, mediator and facilitator, long before state transformation would become a topic of studying the impact of globalization on

---

[95] Sabine Frerichs, *From Credit to Crisis: Max Weber, Karl Polanyi, and the Other Side of the Coin*, 40 J.L. & Soc'y 7 (2013).

law.[96] For an emerging transnational legal theory, then, it will be decisive to learn how to engage with the lessons of the nation-state as well as with the increasing calls for their provincialization and relativization. An engagement with the regulatory experiences of the Western rule of law and welfare state of the twentieth century remains crucial in light of the fact that the nation state provided the institutional, but also the discursive context in which law's role was negotiated, contested and continually redefined. The content and reach of such lessons, however, depends on the degree to which it is possible to simultaneously reflect on the underlying theory of society. As previously noted, we need to distinguish between the institutional and normative stakes of a state/society model,[97] on the one hand, and those concepts that challenge the hierarchy model of "state and society" by emphasizing the dynamics of coevolving rationality systems (such as the economy, politics, religion, art, or law) in the context of a functionally differentiated (world) society, on the other. Such a distinction remains significant as it helps us to see more clearly the degree to which much of the current Western legal response to globalization has so far been shaped by a narrow account of state formation and subsequent changes. Although this challenge lurks beneath the contemporary preoccupation with the perceived gap between a functionally minded mode of transnational regulatory governance and normative contentions of justice, this is not always easy to recognize and even more difficult to address. The reasons for this contraction in view can be found in law's struggle with the overwhelming evidence of functionally differentiated societal activities.[98] Whereas in the context of the nation state law was primarily tasked with stabilizing both institutional and normative expectations,[99] its role in a differentiated world society appears to be undermined and relativized. Central to this shift is a reorientation of the function foremost ascribed to law: Rather than stabilizing *normative* expectations, the law can now be seen as having to stabilize, above all, *cognitive* expectations. In other words, when no societal system can claim normative

---

[96] Philip Abrams, *Notes on the Difficulty of Studying the State*, 1 J. Hist. Soc. 58 (1988); Michel-Rolph Trouillot, *The Anthropology of the State in the Age of Globalization: Close Encounters of the Deceptive Kind*, 42 Current Anthropology 125 (2001).

[97] Ernst-Wolfgang Böckenförde, *The Significance of the Distinction between State and Society in the Democratic Welfare State of Today*, in State, Society and Liberty: Studies in Political Theory and Constitutional Law 147–74 (Ernst-Wolfgang Böckenförde ed., J.A. Underwood trans., 1991).

[98] Helmut Willke, Smart Governance: Governing the Global Knowledge Society (2007).

[99] Peer Zumbansen, *Law After the Welfare State: Formalism, Functionalism and the Ironic Turn of Reflexive Law*, 56 Am. J. Comp. L. 769 (2008).

superiority or primacy before another, from the perspective of systems theory, law becomes a broker, a mediator, and translator of competing, intersecting bodies of knowledge.[100] One consequence of this reorientation is law's turn to an *openness* of goals, as its primary function is no longer defined – as from a critical theory perspective[101] – as one to bring about desired (normative) results, but to open up, to facilitate, institutionalize and consolidate *learning opportunities*.[102] Seen through this lens, the primary task for law is to reflexively facilitate the mediation of and between possibly very diverse and complex societal rationalities, without being able, in that process, to rely on previously established, hierarchically structured ordering patterns.[103]

It is difficult to overstate the methodological consequences of this shift of perspective, from which law is seen to assume a fundamentally different role than that which we would ascribe to it on the basis of both a positivist, Kelsenian, or a normative, Fullerian or Dworkinian, model. If law's function could adequately be described as one of mediating, translating, and brokering competing and conflicting societal rationalities and meanings, the question with regard to law's proper *core* would become urgent. This concern with an allegedly fundamental and inherent normative orientation of law[104] becomes the more pressing the more law is placed on the same level as other forms of societal communication, as a systems theory approach would suggest.

---

[100] Gunther Teubner, *Altera pars audiatur: Law in the Collision of Discourses, in* LAW, SOCIETY AND ECONOMY 149–76 (Richard Rawlings ed., 1997).

[101] Erhard Blankenburg, *The Poverty of Evolutionism: A Critique of Teubner's Case for "Reflexive Law,"* 18 L. & SOC'Y REV. 273 (1984); and Teubner's response: Gunther Teubner, *Autopoiesis in Law and Society: A Rejoinder to Blankenburg*, 18 L. & SOC'Y REV. 291 (1984).

[102] Niklas Luhmann, *Die Weltgesellschaft*, 57 ARCHIV FÜR RECHTS- UND SOZIALPHILOSOPHIE 1 (1970), *reprinted in* 2 NIKLAS LUHMANN, SOZIOLOGISCHE AUFKLÄRUNG 51, at 55 (2d ed. 2005). ("Kognitives Erwarten sucht sich selbst, normatives Erwarten sucht sein Objekt zu ändern. Lernen oder Nichtlernen – das ist der Unterschied.").

[103] Karl-Heinz Ladeur, *Die rechtswissenschaftliche Methodendiskussion und die Bewältigung des gesellschaftlichen Wandels* 64 RABELSZ 60 (2000); Karl-Heinz Ladeur, *Constitutionalism and the State of the "Society of Networks": The Design of a New "Control Project" for a Fragmented Legal System*, 2 TRANSNAT'L LEGAL THEORY 463 (2011). *See also* Luhmann, *Weltgesellschaft*, *supra* note 101, at 57 ("Offensichtlich ist mit Hilfe der normativen Mechanismen, vor allem des Rechts, auf der Ebene politisch konstituierter Regionalgesellschaften eine evolutionär unwahrscheinliche Hochleistung stabilisiert und damit erwartbar gemacht worden – nämlich die verlässliche Motivation zu nahezu beliebig spezialisierbarem Handeln. . . . Es könnte sein, daß diese eigentümliche Kombination von Recht und Politik gerade in ihrer besonderen Leistungsfähigkeit eine Fehlspezialisierung der Menschheitsentwicklung war, die sich, vorläufig jedenfalls, nicht auf das System der Weltgesellschaft übertragen lässt.")

[104] *See* Lon L. Fuller, THE MORALITY OF LAW (1964).

TRANSNATIONAL PRIVATE REGULATORY GOVERNANCE
AND THE EMPTY PLACE OF POLITICS

In light of the foregoing, it would appear that there are significant obstacles for a political, critical engagement with the ideological underpinnings of the purportedly market-oriented thinking that characterizes much of today's discourse around transnational economic governance. Not only are many of the avenues of political will formation and contestation that have developed in the state's constitutional system unavailable in the context of transnational regulatory regimes,[105] but also the interest constellations of affected parties and stakeholders in many of the instances alluded to before are of such complexity that traditional political discourse does not seem adequately equipped to provide this diversity with consequential voice.

Against this background, then, it seems that there is some merit in drawing on learning experiences with legal-political critique and legal sociological insights from within the nation state as we ascertain the opportunities for a political critique of the fragmented, transnational regulatory governance landscape. In particular, the insights from postinterventionist, postregulatory law[106] as these theoretical approaches evolved in response to the transformation of the Western welfare state[107] during the last decades of the twentieth century, relate to the far-reaching proliferation of alternative and hybrid forms of regulation. These transformations have left deep imprints in law in general, but particularly in the taught and practiced discipline of administrative law.[108]

---

[105] For a fine analysis of the transnational realm, see Daniela Caruso, *Private Law and State-Making in the Age of Globalization*, 39 N.Y.U. J. INT'L L. & POL. 1 (2006).

[106] Gunther Teubner, *Regulatory Law: Chronicle of a Death Foretold*, 1 SOC. & LEGAL STUD. 451 (1992) (orig.: Gunther Teubner, *Regulatorisches Recht: Chonik eines angekündigten Todes*, 54 ARSP BEIHEFT 140 (1992); *see also* Peer Zumbansen, *Post-regulatorisches Recht: Chronik einer angekündigten Karriere*, *in* SOZIOLOGISCHE JURISPRUDENZ. FESTSCHRIFT FÜR GUNTHER TEUBNER ZUM 65. GEBURTSTAG 629–43 (Gralf-Peter Calliess, Andreas Fischer-Lescano, Dan Wielsch & Peer Zumbansen eds., 2009), English version: Peer Zumbansen, Post-Regulatory Law: Chronicle of a Career Foretold, Faculty Seminar at McGill University Faculty of Law (Feb. 18, 2009), *available at* http://www.mcgill.ca/files/legal-theory-workshop/PZumbansen_Post-Regulatory-Law.pdf (last accessed Feb. 16, 2015).

[107] Gunther Teubner, *Autopoiesis in Law and Society: A Rejoinder to Blankenburg*, 18 L. & SOC'Y REV. 291 (1984).

[108] *See, e.g.*, Matthias Schmidt-Preuss, *Verwaltung und Verwaltungsrecht zwischen gesellschaftlicher Selbstregulierung und staatlicher Steuerung*, 56 VERÖFFENTLICHUNGEN DER VEREINIGUNG DER DEUTSCHEN STAATSRECHTSLEHRER 160 (1996); Alfred C. Aman, Jr., *Administrative Law for a New Century, in* THE PROVINCE OF ADMINISTRATIVE LAW 90–107 (Michael Taggart ed., 1997); Thomas Vesting, *Zwischen Gewährleistungsstaat und Minimalstaat: Zu den veränderten Bedingungen der Bewältigung öffentlicher Aufgaben in der Informations – oder Wissensgesellschaft, in* VERWALTUNGSRECHT IN DER INFORMATIONSGESELLSCHAFT 101–31 (Wolfgang Hoffmann-Riem & Ebehard Schmidt-Assmann eds., 2000).

At the same time, private law scholars have been very prolific in tracing and further theorizing the shifts between public and private governance forms, which have greatly increased over the past decades.[109]

This constellation, arguably, offers considerable opportunities also for a critical-political engagement, which at first sight seemed elusive from the perspective of a sociological account of the world society.[110] In the larger context of lex mercatoria, such opportunities for contestation have become more frequent. In this respect, prominent and lively fields of engagement include bilateral investment treaties,[111] financial regulation[112] and corporate law,[113] in law and development[114] as well as the growing intensification in transnational human rights litigation in the context, for example, of mining operations in Latin America or North Africa.[115] These efforts are of particular importance in our context, as they testify to both inroads and challenges in connecting discourses with a focus on nation-state based changes in regulatory governance with those that at first sight appear to be of a distinctly, if not exclusively global and transnational nature.

---

[109] Rudolf Wiethölter, *Die Wirtschaftspraxis als Rechtsquelle, in* Paul Bockelmann, Werner Maihofer & Fabian von Schlabrendorff, Das Rechtswesen – Lenker oder Spiegel der Gesellschaft? 165–85 (1971); Rudolf Wiethölter, *Recht-Fertigungen eines Gesellschafts-Rechts, in* Rechtsverfassungsrecht. Recht-Fertigung zwischen Privatrechtsdogmatik und Gesellschaftstheorie 11–22 (Christian Joerges & Gunther Teubner eds., 2003).

[110] *See* Marc Amstutz, Ibi Societas, Ibi Ius: The Conundrum of the Concept of World Law. Comments on Calliess and Zumbansen, Rough Consensus and Running Code: A Theory of Transnational Private Law (2010).

[111] Muthucumaraswamy Sornarajah, *Power and Justice: Third World Resistance in International Law*, 10 Singapore Y.B. Int'l L. 19 (2006); Gus Van Harten & Martin Loughlin, *Investment Treaty Arbitration as a Species of Global Administrative Law*, 17 Eur. J. Int'l L. 121 (2006); George K. Foster, *Foreign Investment and Indigenous Peoples: Options for Promoting Equilibrium between Economic Development and Indigenous Rights*, 33 Mich. J. Int'l L. 627 (2012).

[112] See, for example, the description of transnational financial regulation by Julia Black & David Rouch, *The Development of Global Markets as Rule-Makers: Engagement and Legitimacy*, L. & Fin. Markets Rev. 218 (2008).

[113] *See, e.g.,* Larry Catá Backer, *The OECD Guidelines for Multinational Corporations: Using Soft Law to Operationalize a Transnational System of Corporate Governance*, Law at the End of the Day Blog (Mar. 5, 2009), http://lcbackerblog.blogspot.com/2009/03/oecd-guidelines-for-multinational.html (last visited Dec. 1, 2012), and Gregory Shaffer, Discussion Forum, *On Terence C. Halliday and Bruce G. Carruthers, Bankrupt: Global Lawmaking and Systemic Financial Crisis*, 9 Socio-Economic Rev. 371 (2011).

[114] Kerry Rittich, *Functionalism and Formalism: Their Latest Incarnations in Contemporary Development and Governance Debates*, 55 U. Toronto L.J. 853 (2005), and Sundhya Pahuja, Decolonising International Law (2011).

[115] *See, e.g.,* Rodríguez-Garavito, *supra* note 21; *see also* Charis Kamphuis, *Canadian Mining Companies and Domestic Law Reform: A Critical-Legal Account*, 13 German L.J. 1459 (2012), and Sara L. Seck, *Home State Regulation of Environmental Human Rights Harms as Transnational Private Regulatory Governance*, 13 German L.J. 1363 (2012).

To be sure, international economic law is deeply impregnated by the socio-economic imagination of market governance and as such sits only uneasily with regard to a confinement to territorial boundaries or, levels of governance.[116] With a view to the referenced areas in international economic law, we can witness a growing number of efforts to initiate and consolidate processes of political and legal advocacy[117] – all of which seem to be characterized by a focus on process, facilitation of discourse and contestation, but not on a narrowly defined set of principles or values.[118] These examples testify to a significant opening up of opportunities for legal-political critique. To the degree, however that governance challenges are identified as emerging on either a national or a global level, the relevance of approximating national and transnational governance discourses[119] lies in making visible the parallels between struggles in both spheres over an adequate identification and representation of affected interests. Here, and there, the question is how to identify and to verbalize *what is at stake* – and, *for whom.* And yet, in light of the foregoing, to place the question, *What is at stake?*, at the center of such a parallel reading of national and transnational governance discourse is enormously ambitious, if not ill-directed. Because, what should be the reference point for the related assertion of those interests that testify to what *is* at stake? How can we assume to identify the correct starting point in a world of contested identities and meanings?

TRANSNATIONAL PRIVATE REGULATORY GOVERNANCE:
STILL A CASE IN POINT FOR "LEGITIMACY"?

Looking back, what have we learned in terms of identifying starting points for a critical engagement with highly specialized regimes of transnational private regulatory governance? As noted, much of the work done by lawyers in this global governance realm has called for a public interest defense or singled

---

[116] MULTI-LEVEL GOVERNANCE (Ian Bache & Matthew Flinders eds., 2004).

[117] *See* Charis Kamphuis, *Canadian Mining Companies and Domestic Law Reform: A Critical-Legal Account*, 13 GERMAN L.J. 1459 (2012), and Sara L. Seck, *Home State Regulation of Environmental Human Rights Harms as Transnational Private Regulatory Governance*, 13 GERMAN L.J. 1363 (2012).

[118] *See* Rodríguez-Garavito, *supra* note 21; *see also* Boaventura de Sousa Santos, *Beyond Abyssal Thinking*, EUROZINE, *available at* http://www.eurozine.com/articles/2007-06-29-santos-en .html (last visited Dec. 1, 2012); Larry Catá Backer, *The United Nations' "Protect-Respect-Remedy" Project: Operationalizing a Global Human Rights Based Framework for the Regulation of Transnational Corporations*, 9 SANTA CLARA J. INT'L L. 37 (2011).

[119] Saskia Sassen, *Globalization or denationalization?*, 10 REV. INT'L POL. ECON. 1 (2003); Peer Zumbansen, *Neither "Public" nor "Private," "National" nor "International": Transnational Corporate Governance from a Legal Pluralist Perspective*, 38 J.L. & SOC'Y 50 (2011).

out "legitimacy" as a potentially effective lever to scrutinize the legal nature of these transnational regulatory structures. But it is here that the complexity of the global governance context in relation to any encompassing concept of legitimacy has become more visible. In the transnational regulatory context, the pursuit of legitimacy depends on a comprehensive assessment of the different dimensions of this idea that lie beyond otherwise routinely assumed linkages between legality and its grounding in, say, democratic legitimacy.[120] Not only has law become disembedded, but also law's approaches to address its perennial legitimacy concerns[121] have also lost a lot of their footing.[122] Legitimacy concerns for the law today are inextricably caught up in law's existential efforts to redefine and to ascertain its role in societal governance altogether. As such, legitimacy in law and of law has become a laboratory for a multidisciplinary and interdisciplinary engagement with law's relation to and place in society.[123] Following the differentiation of modern world society, legitimacy concerns for law arise and are being addressed within highly sectionalized and specialized areas of regulatory governance; that is to say, they arise in a context that puts enormous pressure on any attempt to submit this constellation to an overarching theory of politics, or justice.[124] But, at the same time, one can discern a distinct and pressing concern with this move away from an embedded system of law to a "global," decentralized regulatory governance framework. This concern is fuelled, partly, by anxieties over a possibly empty place of politics in the evolving global governance landscape.[125] Albeit, neither the concept of politics itself nor the institutional or procedural framework in

---

[120] CARL SCHMITT, THE CRISIS OF PARLIAMENTARY DEMOCRACY (MIT Press, 1988) (Ellen Kennedy trans., 1926).

[121] An illustration of this continues to be the debate between H.L.A. Hart and L. Fuller. *See* Herbert Lionel Adolphus Hart, *Positivism and the Separation of Law and Morals*, 71 HARV. L. REV. 593 (1958), and Lon L. Fuller, *Positivism and Fidelity to Law – A Reply to Professor Hart*, 71 HARV. L. REV. 630 (1958). See the essays concerning this debate in THE HART-FULLER DEBATE IN THE TWENTY-FIRST CENTURY (Peter Cane ed., 2010).

[122] For an elaboration, see Peer Zumbansen, Lochner *Disembedded: The Anxieties of Law in a Global Context*, 20 IND. J. GLOBAL LEGAL STUD. 29 (2013), abstract *available at* http://ssrn.com/abstract=2174017.

[123] One of the best studies outlining this context is by E. DARIAN-SMITH, LAWS AND SOCIETIES IN GLOBAL CONTEXTS. CONTEMPORARY APPROACHES (2013).

[124] Niklas Luhmann, *Globalization or World Society: How to Conceive of Modern Society?*, 7 INT'L REV. SOC. 67 (1997); Gunther Teubner, *The King's Many Bodies: The Self-Deconstruction of Law's Hierarchy*, 31 L. & SOC. REV. 763 (1997).

[125] Kenneth W. Abbott & Duncan Snidal, *Hard and Soft Law in International Governance*, (2000) 54 INT'L ORG. 421 (2000); Peer Zumbansen, *Comparative, Global and Transnational Constitutionalism: The Emergence of a Transnational Constitutional Pluralist Order*, 1 GLOBAL CONST. 16 (2012).

which we would have to resituate politics today are evident.[126] This leaves lawyers, in particular, as they set out to redraw the map of law's legitimacy in a global context from the perspective of a proliferating transnational private regulatory governance framework, in a considerable dilemma. Faced with a multitude of overlapping, fast-evolving private regulatory governance regimes in areas ranging from financial[127] to environmental[128] regulation, investment law[129] or commercial transfers,[130] lawyers must continue to both expand their expertise with regard to specialized, technical transactional areas and appreciate the relevance of nonlegal ordering and regulatory concepts that underlie and inform many of the emerging governance regimes.[131]

Transnational private regulatory governance as a field of research sits squarely in the discursive context of state transformation, both from a national[132] and a transnational[133] perspective, as it addresses a fundamental decentering of both rule creation, dissemination, and adjudication processes and of the conceptual

[126] For an insightful scrutiny, see GUNTHER TEUBNER, CONSTITUTIONAL FRAGMENTS: SOCIETAL CONSTITUTIONALISM AND GLOBALIZATION (2012); see the comprehensive engagement with this work by Karl-Heinz Ladeur, *The Evolution of the Law and the Possibility of a "Global Law" Extending Beyond the Sphere of the State – Simultaneously, a Critique of the "Self-Constitutionalisation" Thesis*, 2012 ANCILLA IURIS 220, *available at* http://www.anci.ch/_media/beitrag/ancilla2012_220_ladeur.pdf (last visited Dec. 1, 2012).

[127] *See* Katharina Pistor, *Towards a Legal Theory of Finance* (Columbia Pub. Law Research Paper No. 12-323, 2012), *available at* http://ssrn.com/abstract=2178000; John Biggins, *"Targeted Touchdown" and "Partial Liftoff": Post-Crisis Dispute Resolution in the OTC Derivatives Markets and the Challenge for ISDA*, 13 GERMAN L.J. 1297 (2012); Colin Scott, *Beyond Taxonomies of Private Authority in Transnational Regulation*, 13 GERMAN L.J. 1329 (2012).

[128] Kirsten Mikadze, *Public Participation in Global Environmental Governance and the Equator Principles: Potentials and Pitfalls*, 13 GERMAN. L.J. 1383 (2012); John M. Conley & Cynthia A. Williams, *Global Banks as Global Sustainability Regulators? The Equator Principles*, 33 L. & POL'Y f 542 (2011); Andrian Lozinski, *The Equator Principles: Evaluating the Exposure of Commercial Lenders to Socio-Environmental Risk*, 13 GERMAN L.J. 1487 (2012); Gail Henderson, *Institutional Investors as Transnational Environmental Regulators? The Limits of Responsible Investing as Environmental Regulation*, 13 GERMAN L.J. 1409 (2012).

[129] Douglas Sarro, *Do Lenders Make Effective Regulators? An Assessment of the Equator Principles on Project Finance*, 13 GERMAN L.J. 1525 (2012).

[130] Agnieszka Janczuk-Gorywoda, *Public-Private Hybrid Governance for Electronic Payments in the European Union*, 13 GERMAN L.J. 1435 (2012).

[131] Tony Porter, *Transnational Private Regulation and the Changing Media of Rules*, 13 GERMAN L J. 1511 (2012); Mathew Chan, *What About Psychological Actors? Behavioral Analysis of Equator Principles Adoption and Its Implications*, 13 GERMAN L.J. 1339 (2012).

[132] TRANSFORMATIONS OF THE STATE? (Stephan Leibfried & Michael Zürn eds., 2005); Peer Zumbansen, *Law After the Welfare State: Formalism, Functionalism and the Ironic Turn of Reflexive Law*, 56 AM. J. COMP. L. 769 (2008), *available at* http://ssrn.com/abstract=1128144, *reprinted in* BEYOND THE STATE: RETHINKING PRIVATE LAW 349–86 (Nils Jansen & Ralf Michaels eds., 2008).

[133] Gregory Shaffer, *Transnational Legal Process and State Change*, 37 L. & SOC. INQUIRY 229 (2011).

frameworks with which we have learned to measure the legality and legitimacy of these processes.[134] This unsettling of the state-law nexus has come under broad scrutiny, a development that finds expression in numerous iterations under titles such as *Law and Globalization*,[135] *Global Legal Pluralism*[136] as well as *Transnational Law*.[137] Notwithstanding their analytical and conceptualizing function, such frameworks are drawn upon in an attempt to address the contested nature, form and scope of law in a global context, that is a context that has greatly amplified law's normative and pluralist challenges. The multifaceted phenomenon of transnational private regulatory governance can here serve as a powerful illustration of how the analytical interest in the maintenance of the state-law nexus must move away from law itself and toward an engagement with the *Actors, Norms* and *Processes* [ANP] in which law appears to be caught up.[138] These three categories, then, assume the role of *translation devices* through which governance discourses as they have unfolded in the nation-state context can be put in relation to governance discourses on the transnational level. Instead of transposing nation-state originating concepts such as the rule of law, judicial review or separation of powers onto the global scale, a the use of ANP might help to highlight the parallels but also the distinct differences and incompatibilities between known regulatory concepts and those which seem to be emerging on the transnational level. From the perspective of an ANP approach to the study of "law and globalization," transnational private regulatory governance offers numerous crucial insights into the newly forming relations between law and society in a global context. Part of the reason for the lively scholarly interest in these processes can be found in the way, that these transnational regulatory regimes appear

---

[134] Julia Black, *Decentering Regulation: The Role of Regulation and Self-Regulation in a 'Post-Regulatory' World*, 54 Current Legal Probs. 103 (2001).

[135] Paul Schiff Berman, *From International Law to Law and Globalization*, 43 Colum J. Transnat'l L. 485 (2005); Ulrich Sieber, *Rechtliche Ordnung in einer Globalen Welt*, 41 Rechtstheorie 151 (2010).

[136] Ralf Michaels, *Global Legal Pluralism*, 5 Ann. Rev. L. & Soc. Sci. 243 (2009); Paul Schiff Berman, *Global Legal Pluralism*, 80 S. Cal. L. Rev. 1155 (2007).

[137] Philip C. Jessup, Transnational Law (1956); Clive M, Schmitthoff, *Nature and Evolution of the Transnational Law of Commercial Transactions, in* The Transnational Law of International Commercial Transactions 19–31 (Norbert Horn & Clive M. Schmitthoff eds., 1982); Christian Tietje & Karsten Nowrot, *Laying Conceptual Ghosts of the Past to Rest: The Rise of Philip C. Jessup's "Transnational Law" in the Regulatory Governance of the International Economic System*, 50 Essays in Transnational Economic Law (2006).

[138] Zumbansen, Lochner *Disembedded*, 17, *supra* note 121; Peer Zumbansen, *What Lies Before, Behind and Beneath a Case? Five Minutes of Transnational Lawyering and the Consequences for Legal Education, in* Stateless Law: Evolving Boundaries of a Discipline (Helge Dedek & Shauna Van Praagh eds., 2015).

to enunciate and embody all these transformations that are associated today with the nation state in a globalized setting. The state's alleged retreat, its loss of regulatory ability, reach and implementation are frequently invoked as mere mirror effects of a widely encompassing privatization and autono-mization of regulatory regimes, associated with a neo-liberal transformation of public governance.[139] It is against that background, that a legal theoretical engagement with transnational regulatory governance becomes crucial. Such a legal theory must adopt a perspective of *methodological transnationalism* in view of the differentiation of regulatory systems across spatial boundaries in an attempt to more effectively engage with the contested aspects of legality, accountability, and legitimacy.

[139] Alfred C. Aman, Jr., *Law, Markets and Democracy: A Role for Law in the Neo-Liberal State*, 51 N.Y.L. Sch. L. Rev. 801 (2007); Levi-Faur, *supra* note 7.

5

International Human Rights Law as a Catalyst for the Recognition and Evolution of Non-State Law

*Helen Quane**

All legal systems are molded by the particular context in which they operate. Non-state law is no different in this regard. The impact of historical, political, economic, and cultural factors on the existence and operation of non-state law is well documented.[1] When analyzing non-state law, it is clear that it cannot be viewed in isolation from state law with which it coexists or from the broader context in which it operates. There is true particularly of religious and customary law, which is the focus of the present inquiry. The tendency to date has been to focus on the range of factors that exist *within* the state that can influence the evolution of these types of non-state law. This approach is unduly limiting, however, and needs to be expanded so as to include an explicitly international law dimension.

The objective of the present chapter is to analyze the impact of international law on the development of non-state law. This may seem a little unorthodox particularly when international law is concerned primarily, albeit not exclusively, with states. This focus becomes more understandable if the state is seen as mediating the relationship between international law and non-state law. Irrespective of the state's willingness to do so, it is a role that it cannot evade completely. It is well established that non-state law can give rise to state responsibility under international law. Where this occurs, the state can be held accountable for any violation of its international obligations and can be required to undertake a range of measures to remedy the violation. These

---

* Associate Professor, Swansea University, United Kingdom (h.quane@swansea.ac.uk).

[1] *See, e.g.*, INTERNATIONAL COUNCIL ON HUMAN RIGHTS POLICY, WHEN LEGAL WORLDS OVERLAP: HUMAN RIGHTS, STATE AND NON-STATE LAW 7–14 (2009); Kwame Akuffo, *The Conception of Land Ownership in African Customary Law and Its Implications for Development* (2009) AFR. J. INT'L & COMP. L. 57, 63–65; Adriaan Bedner & Stijn van Huis, *Plurality of Marriage Law and Marriage Registration for Muslims in Indonesia: A Plea for Pragmatism* 6 UTRECHT L. REV. 175, 177–83 (2006).

measures can have important implications in terms of the recognition, continued existence, and/or reform of non-state law. In effect, state responsibility becomes the gateway for an interesting dynamic to emerge between international and non-state law.

Admittedly, the prospect of any positive engagement between international and non-state law does call into question the common perception that these two bodies of law are mutually incompatible.[2] This is true particularly of international human rights law and non-state law.[3] One can think of numerous instances where the treatment of women under religious or customary law in relation to inheritance rights, marriage, divorce, custody of minors, and the taking of evidence in trial proceedings conflicts with the right to equality and non-discrimination under international human rights law.[4] One can also think of certain punishments that may be administered under religious or customary law, such as amputations, floggings, and stonings, which conflict with the international prohibition on torture, inhuman, and degrading treatment or punishment.[5] These examples reflect traditional views of gender relations and punishments for transgressing community mores but they do more than that. They also reflect more deep-seated beliefs that are not entirely easy to reconcile with the fundamental principles of international human rights law. The emphasis in international human rights law on individual rights grounded in the inherent dignity and worth of every human being does not always sit well with the moral and philosophical underpinnings of religious

[2] See, for example, the discussion in Lisa Hajjar, *Religion, State Power, and Domestic Violence in Muslim Societies: A Framework for Comparative Analysis,* 29 L. & SOC., INQUIRY 1, 16–19 (2004); Amira Mashhour, *Islamic Law and Gender Equality – Could There Be a Common Ground? A Study of Divorce and Polygamy in Sharia Law and Contemporary Legislation in Tunisia and Egypt,* 27 HUM. RTS. Q. 562 (2005).

[3] This is sometimes attributed to a misreading of non-state law. *See, e.g.,* IBRAHIM N. SADA, FATIMA L. ADAMU & ALI AHMAD, CENTRE FOR ISLAMIC STUDIES, PROMOTING WOMEN'S RIGHTS THROUGH SHARIA IN NORTHERN NIGERIA (2006), *available at* http://www.ungei.org/resources/files/dfid_promoting_womens_rights.pdf (last visited May 28, 2014).

[4] *See, e.g.,* Perry S. Smith, *Silent Witness: Discrimination Against Women in the Pakistani Law of Evidence,* 11 TUL. J. INT'L & COMP. L. 21, 30–39, 48–49 (2003); Mark J. Calaguas, Cristina M. Drost & Edward R. Fluet, *Legal Pluralism and Women's Rights: A Study in Postcolonial Tanzania,* 16 COLUM. J. GENDER & L. 471, 472, 518, 520, 522, 527–28, 538 (2007); Sue Farran, *Is Legal Pluralism an Obstacle to Human Rights? Considerations from the South Pacific,* 52 J. LEGAL PLURALISM & UNOFFICIAL L. 77, 87, 97–99 (2006); Robin Perry, *Balancing Rights or Building Rights? Reconciling the Right to Use Customary Systems of Law with Competing Human Rights in Pursuit of Indigenous Sovereignty,* 24 HARV. HUM. RTS. J. 71, 101 (2011).

[5] *See, e.g.,* Calaguas, *supra* note 4, at 472; Janet Afary, *The Human Rights of Middle Eastern and Muslim Women: A Project for the 21st Century,* 26 HUM. RTS. Q. 106, 110 (2004); Curtis Francis Doebbler v. Sudan, African Comm'n on Hum. & Peoples' Rights, Comm'n No. 236/2000 (2003).

law[6] or the communitarian focus of customary law. Taken in the round, these considerations may suggest an irreconcilable conflict between international human rights law and non-state law. While acknowledging the potential for considerable conflict between them, it would be overly simplistic to view the relationship in such one-dimensional terms particularly when it seems to be based on perceptions of non-state law as a homogenous and static body of law[7] and international human rights law as a series of absolute and unyielding human rights norms.

Any fruitful inquiry into the impact of international human rights law on non-state law must start by recognizing the dynamic nature of the latter[8] and the potential inherent in the former to accommodate national and regional variations without compromising its fundamental tenets.[9] Although international human rights law can certainly act as a constraint on particular aspects of non-state law, it can also act as a catalyst for the more widespread use and evolution of non-state law. It is also important to acknowledge that it is not a one-way relationship. Non-state law can inform the interpretation of international human rights law. In doing so, it can heighten the relevance of international human rights law to the everyday lives of a considerable proportion of the world's population and increase its efficacy on the ground. Although this perception of the relationship between international and non-state law may seem overly optimistic, recent developments in international practice lend credence to it.

This chapter tracks these developments and draws out their significance primarily for non-state law. It begins with a brief discussion of the concept of non-state law to establish some parameters to the present inquiry. It also maps the role of the state in mediating the relationship between international and non-state law. The chapter then analyzes two case studies that are fairly representative of recent developments concerning this relationship. The first relates to developments within the U.N. Charter-based system[10] and concerns the rights of indigenous peoples. The second relates to developments within

---

[6] *See also,* Jerome J. Shestack, *The Jurisprudence of Human Rights, in* HUMAN RIGHTS IN INTERNATIONAL LAW: LEGAL AND POLICY ISSUES (Theodor Meron, ed., 1984).

[7] In this regard, it is important to bear in mind that it is possible for different interpretations of non-state law to exist. See, for example, the discussion in Anat Scolnicov, *Religious Law, Religious Courts and Human Rights within Israeli Constitutional Structure* 4 INTERNATIONAL JOURNAL OF CONSTITUTIONAL LAW 732, 733 (2006); Mashhour *supra* note 2.

[8] See also in a similar vein, Calaguas, *supra* note 4, at 534; Perry, *supra* note 4, at 77–79.

[9] *See also* Perry, *supra* note 4, at 72–73.

[10] This is the system that is derived from the U.N. Charter and includes the work of the U.N. Human Rights Council and the system of Special Procedures that includes Special Rapporteurs, Special Representatives and Working Groups. The relevant official documents are

the U.N. Human Rights Treaty Body System,[11] in particular, the U.N. Convention on the Elimination of All Forms of Discrimination against Women. Both case studies demonstrate not only the very real tensions that can exist between international and non-state law but also, more important, the emergence of a coherent conceptual framework for the development of a more constructive relationship between them. This chapter concludes with a series of observations concerning the relationship between international human rights law and non-state law and its significance in terms of the recognition and evolution of non-state law.

DEFINING NON-STATE LAW: THE "NOT A CAT" SYNDROME

A preliminary issue that arises is how to define non-state law. This brings to mind Philip Alston's comments about the definition of non-state actors. Drawing on his experience with his eighteen-month old daughter who described every rabbit, mouse, or kangaroo as "not a cat," he found that an almost identical technique was pervasive in international law discussions of non-state actors.[12] Essentially, this tendency to define something by reference to what it is not, can, as he observed, obfuscate almost any debate.[13] Similar considerations apply to the definition of non-state law. Defining non-state law by what it is not is unlikely to further our understanding of this phenomenon in

available at http://www.ohchr.org/EN/HRBodies/Pages/HumanRightsBodies.aspx (last visited May 29, 2014).

[11] This system is concerned with the implementation of the core international human rights treaties. These are the International Covenant on Civil and Political Rights, 999 U.N.T.S. 171 (adopted Dec. 16, 1966, entered into force Mar. 23, 1976 (ICCPR); the International Covenant on Economic, Social and Cultural Rights, 993 UN.T.S. 3 (adopted Dec. 16, 1966, entered into force Jan. 3, 1976) (ICESCR); the International Convention on the Elimination of All Forms of Racial Discrimination, 660 U.N.T.S. 195 (adopted Mar. 7, 1966, entered into force Jan. 4, 1969); the Convention on the Elimination of All Forms of Discrimination against Women, 1249 U.N.T.S. 13 (adopted Dec. 18, 1979, entered into force Sept. 3, 1981); the Convention Against Torture and Other Cruel, Inhuman or Degrading Treatment or Punishment, 1465 U.N.T.S. 85 (adopted Dec. 10, 1984, entered into force June 16, 1987); the Convention on the Rights of the Child, 1577 U.N.T.S. 3 (adopted Nov. 20, 1989, entered into force Sept. 2, 1990); the International Convention on the Protection of the Rights of All Migrant Workers and Members of Their Families, 2220 U.N.T.S. 3 (adopted Dec. 18, 1990, entered into force July 1, 2003); the Convention on the Rights of Persons with Disabilities, 2515 U.N.T.S. 3 (adopted Dec. 13, 2006, entered into force May 3, 2008); the International Convention for the Protection of All Persons from Enforced Disappearances U.N. Doc. A/61/488 (adopted Dec. 20, 2006, entered into force Dec. 23, 2010).

[12] Philip Alston, *The "Not-a-Cat" Syndrome: Can the International Human Rights Regime Accommodate Non-State Actors?, in* NON-STATE ACTORS AND HUMAN RIGHTS 3 (Philip Alston, ed., 2005).

[13] *Id.*

any significant or meaningful way. Indeed, it is highly unlikely that such an approach is sustainable as it is predicated on the existence of a clear dichotomy between state and non-state law.[14]

For the most part, enquiries into the concept of non-state law focus on the nature or characteristics of the norms under consideration. There are various dimensions to this. At one level, there is the preliminary question of what is *law* and how to establish the *definitional stop* between legal norms and norms of a more diffuse social nature.[15] Having established what constitutes law or law-like norms, the inquiry then tends to shift to whether they are state or non-state legal norms. At this point, attention often focuses on the manner in which these norms are enforced. Where the norms rely on the political authority of the state or its coercive powers for enforcement, there is a tendency to classify them as state rather than non-state legal norms.[16]

This chapter adopts a somewhat different approach. At the outset, it must be said that the present author, like many international lawyers, adopts a fairly pragmatic approach to the definition of a legal norm. According to this approach, if the principal addressees of a norm and the third-party decision makers applying that norm view it as a "legal" norm, then the classification of the norm as a legal norm will be accepted.[17] This then raises the question as to whether the norm should be classified as a state or non-state legal norm. Adopting a functional approach to normative legal orders can provide a useful way of thinking about this issue. In the present context, a functional approach means looking at the range of functions that are integral to the operation of the official legal system in a state. Broadly speaking, these functions can be located along a continuum whereby at one end there is the formation of norms, through to the recognition and interpretation of norms, until finally there is the enforcement of norms. The extent to which non-state law is engaged by the performance of one or more of these functions can reinforce or lessen

---

[14] See also, in a similar vein, Winifred Kamau, *Law, Pluralism and the Family in Kenya: Beyond Bifurcation of Formal Law and Custom*, 23 INT'L J.L. POL'Y & FAM. 133 (2009); INTERNATIONAL COUNCIL ON HUMAN RIGHTS POLICY, *supra* note 1, at 44–49.

[15] See, for example, the discussion in Brian Z. Tamanaha, *Understanding Legal Pluralism: Past to Present, Local to Global*, 30 SYDNEY L. REV. 375, 391–96 (2008); William Twining, *Normative and Legal Pluralism: A Global Perspective*, 20 DUKE J. COMP. & INT'L L. 473 (2010).

[16] *See, e.g.,* Abdullah Ahmed An-Na'im, *Religion, the State, and Constitutionalism in Islamic and Comparative Perspectives* 57 DRAKE L. REV. 829, 830, 840 (2009). *See also* INTERNATIONAL COUNCIL ON HUMAN RIGHTS POLICY, *supra* note 1, at 43.

[17] *See, e.g.,* Ian Brownlie, *The Reality and Efficacy of International Law*, 52 BRIT. Y.B. INT'L L. 1, 1–2 (1981). *See also*, in a similar vein, Tamanaha, *supra* note 15, at 396. The latter refers to law as a "'folk concept,' that is, law is what people within social groups have come to see and label as 'law.'"

the impression that it may or may not be classified as state law. For instance, at any one time and in relation to any one topic, non-state law may be co-opted into performing or assisting in the performance of one of the functions on this continuum. Where this occurs, it may acquire the mantle of state law in relation to that particular function and for so long as it performs that function while continuing to retain its character as non-state law in all other respects.

Although a full exposition of this approach is beyond the remit of the present chapter, this brief overview is intended to highlight the fluidity that can exist in relation to the definition of non-state law in both a temporal and functional sense. Admittedly, it does not avoid completely the not-a-cat syndrome. At the very least, however, it should caution against seeing non-state law in overly rigid and unitary terms and raise the possibility of multiple, concurrent classifications. Ultimately, there is a vast array of opportunities for state and non-state law to interact. When they do, the nature and extent of these interactions may be such as to influence the classification of what would otherwise be regarded as non-state law. This is significant not only in terms of how we define non-state law but also in terms of establishing state responsibility. As the following section will establish, state responsibility is the gateway through which international human rights law can influence non-state law.

MEDIATING THE RELATIONSHIP BETWEEN INTERNATIONAL HUMAN RIGHTS LAW AND NON-STATE LAW: THE ROLE OF THE STATE

To understand the potential of international human rights law to influence non-state law, it is necessary to factor in the role of the state. This is because international human rights law still adheres very much to a state-centered approach.[18] For the most part, it imposes direct legal obligations only on states.[19] To the extent that it can impact on non-state law, it can do so essentially

---

[18] Notwithstanding some recent developments concerning the responsibility of non-state actors for human rights harm; *see, e.g.*, John Ruggie, *Protect, Respect, and Remedy: A Framework for Business and Human Rights: Rep. of the Special Rep. of the Secretary-General on the Issue of Human Rights and Transnational Corporations and Other Business Enterprises*, U.N. Doc. A/HRC/8/5 (Apr. 7, 2008).

[19] A very small number of international human rights treaties now allow regional intergovernmental organizations to become parties. *See, e.g.*, Convention On the Rights of Persons with Disabilities art. 44, Dec. 13, 2006, 2515 U.N.T.S. 3. The European Union ratified the Convention on Dec. 23, 2010. *See* http://treaties.un.org/Pages/ViewDetails.aspx?src=TREATY&mtdsg_no=IV-15&chapter=4&lang=en (last visited May 29, 2014).

only via the state. This means that before international human rights law can require the state to recognize, abolish or instigate reform of non-state law, there must be a preliminary finding that the responsibility of the state is engaged. In the absence of this nexus, it is difficult to discern any basis for a relationship between international human rights law and non-state law. As every state has acceded to at least one international human rights treaty, there is at least a potential gateway for establishing such a relationship.[20]

It is well established in international law that the state can be held responsible for any human rights harm caused by non-state law in a number of instances.[21] The first is where non-state law is co-opted into the state justice system, for example, when religious or customary law is used to regulate certain disputes either within the state as a whole or one of its regions.[22] The second is where decisions of religious or customary courts are enforced in the state courts, for example, as a form of alternative dispute resolution[23] or as a result of a specific agreement between the state and non-state institution in question.[24] The third is where non-state law involves the exercise of elements of governmental authority carried out in the absence of the official authorities. The decisive factor here is that non-state law must involve the exercise of "governmental authority in the absence of official authorities, in operations of which the [government] must have had knowledge and to which it did not specifically object."[25] This third scenario is clearly relevant to the situation where non-state law operates in the absence of any official authorities due,

---

[20] For the status of ratifications, see http://treaties.un.org/Pages/Treaties.aspx?id=4&subid=A&lang=en (last visited May 29, 2014).

[21] *See* International Law Commission, Draft Articles on the Responsibility of States for Internationally Wrongful Acts, with Commentaries arts 4, 5, 9 (2001), *available at* http://legal.un.org/ilc/texts/instruments/english/commentaries/9_6_2001.pdf (last visited May 29, 2014).

[22] See, for example, the concurrent recognition of religious and customary law in parts of the Philippines. June Prill-Brent, *Contested Domains: The Indigenous Peoples Rights Act (IPRA) and Legal Pluralism in the Northern Philippines*, 55 J. LEGAL PLURALISM & UNOFFICIAL L. 11 (2007); see also Republic Act No. 6734, which first created the Autonomous Region of Muslim Mindanao on Aug. 1, 1989.

[23] See, for example, the position in the United Kingdom: Dominic McGoldrick, *Accommodating Muslims in Europe: From Adopting Sharia Law to Religiously Based Opt Outs from Generally Applicable Laws*, 9 HUM. RTS. L. REV. 603, 637–38 (2009).

[24] See, for example, the position in Italy concerning the enforcement in state courts of decisions of the ecclesiastical courts of the Catholic Church discussed in *Pellegrini v. Italy*, 35 Eur. H.R. Rep. 2 (2002).

[25] See extract from the *Yeager* case decided by the Iran-United States Claims Tribunal discussed in International Law Commission, *Draft Articles on Responsibility of States for Internationally Wrongful Acts, with Commentaries* (2001), *available at* http://legal.un.org/ilc/texts/instruments/english/commentaries/9_6_2001.pdf (last visited May 29, 2014).

for example, to the remoteness of the geographical terrain or to the limited resources of the state in establishing a presence in the region.[26] In all three situations, the state can be held responsible for any human rights harm caused by the existence or operation of non-state law. In these circumstances it will be difficult for non-state law to evade the impact of international human rights law as the state will be required to undertake the necessary measures to render it compatible with its international obligations.[27]

The situation is more complex when non-state law operates in parallel to the state justice system without any form of official recognition. Take, for example, the situation where an individual submits voluntarily to the jurisdiction of a religious court even though the court does not comply with the international requirements of a fair trial and notwithstanding the existence of state courts that are fully rights compliant. If the court is simply operating de facto without any official recognition, the state cannot be held directly responsible for its conduct. This raises the question whether international law provides a somewhat perverse incentive to states to avoid engaging with non-state law. This would lead to the curious result that international law could help to insulate non-state law from state intervention notwithstanding the human rights harm that may be caused by non-state law. It is doubtful whether this is correct at least to the extent that it is asserted in unqualified terms. This is because international human rights law imposes obligations on the state not only to respect human rights but also to protect these rights against interferences by private individuals and organisations.[28] In the example given, it is possible that there may be a positive obligation on the state to protect the individual against any interference with her right to a fair trial by the religious court. The difficulty is that the extent of the state's positive obligations to protect human rights is far from clear. According to the international jurisprudence, the scope of these positive obligations are determined in the light of all the circumstances of the case and, in no case, can they result in the imposition of an impossible or disproportionate burden on the state.[29] With

---

[26] See, for example, the type of situation that arose in *Case of Aloeboetoe v. Suriname (Reparation and Costs)*, Inter-Am. Ct. H.R. (Sept. 10, 1993), where the state failed to establish its laws in a particular territory albeit this was not central to the merits of the case.

[27] *See, e.g.*, Concluding Observations of the Human Rights Committee: Canada, U.N. Doc. CCPR/C/79/Add.105 para. 19 (1999).

[28] See, for example, the approach adopted by the U.N. Committee on the Elimination of Discrimination Against Women, General Recommendation No. 28 on the Core Obligations of States Parties under Article 2 of the Convention on the Elimination of All Forms of Discrimination Against Women, U.N. Doc. CEDAW/C/GC/28 (2010).

[29] *See, e.g.*, Osman v. United Kingdom, 29 Eur. H.R. Rep. 245, para. 116 (2000); Case of the Sawhoyamaxa Indigenous Community v. Paraguay, Inter-Am. Ct. H.R. ¶ 155 (Mar. 29, 2006).

this in mind, the most that can be said is that it is possible that the de facto operation of non-state law can engage the responsibility of the state depending on the particular circumstances of the case. Where this occurs, it can open the way for international human rights law to exert some influence on non-state law.

Admittedly, there are several ways that state responsibility can be limited thereby restricting the potential influence of international law on non-state law. The first is that the state can enter a reservation to a human rights treaty, for example, to the effect that a particular provision will be applied only to the extent that it does not affect the prescriptions of religious law. This is not uncommon in international practice. It is interesting in the present context for several reasons. At one level, it demonstrates how a particular form of non-state law can be invoked by the state to justify its selective acceptance of treaty obligations and to block the full implementation of a treaty regime. At another level, it can be seen as a way for the state to insulate non-state law from the full impact of international human rights law. Whether this strategy is a viable one depends on a range of factors, not least whether the reservation is valid in terms of being compatible with the object and purpose of the treaty.[30]

The second way is to argue that even though the state is bound by the obligation under international human rights law, it has not violated that obligation. There are various strands to this argument. The state may claim that there is no interference with human rights on the basis that the individual could have avoided any negative impact on the exercise of her human rights but chose not to do so. For example, it may deny any interference with the right to a fair trial because the individual submitted voluntarily to the jurisdiction of a religious court even though she knew that the court did not comply with this right and notwithstanding the fact that she could have accessed state courts that were rights compliant. In the past, this line of argument has been successful but it is questionable whether it will continue to be.[31] Recent case law suggests that even though the individual could have acted to minimize any negative impact on the exercise of her rights, there may still be an interference with her human rights for which the state will be answerable at the international level.[32]

---

[30] *See* Vienna Convention on the Law of Treaties art. 19(c), 1155 U.N.T.S. 331 (adopted May 22, 1969, entered into force Jan. 27, 1980).

[31] See, for example, the review of the jurisprudence in *Eweida and Others v. United Kingdom*, App. Nos. 48420/10, 59842/10, 51671/10 and 36516/10, para. 83 (Jan. 15, 2013).

[32] *Id.* paras. 83, 109. In assessing whether the interference is justified, the court will take into account the individual's ability to circumvent the negative impact on the exercise of his rights. Nevertheless, the key point is that the state is held to account even in these circumstances.

Another strand to this argument is the claim that the individual has waived the exercise of her human rights by submitting to the jurisdiction of the religious court rather than to the state courts. According to the international jurisprudence, it is possible to waive the exercise of a human right but it is subject to several conditions. To the extent that the waiver is "permissible" it "must not run counter to any important public interest, must be established in an unequivocal manner and requires minimum guarantees commensurate to the waiver's importance."[33] This suggests several factors that must be taken into account when considering the validity and efficacy of a waiver. The waiver must (a) be permissible although there is little guidance in the jurisprudence on when a waiver will be prohibited in principle,[34] (b) not be contrary to any important public interest,[35] (c) be established in an "unequivocal manner" with the onus on the state to establish its existence,[36] and (d) be consented to by the individual in a very real and genuine sense.[37] It follows that the state cannot be complacent even where the individual submits voluntarily to the jurisdiction of a religious or customary court and seemingly waives the exercise of her human rights. Depending on the particular circumstances of a case, there is a very real possibility that the state may be held responsible for any human rights harm. It shows that even where non-state law is completely independent of the state, international human rights law may still exert some influence on its existence and operation.

The possibility of justifying an interference with a human right provides another way for the state to deny any violation of its international obligations and to limit the impact of international human rights law on non-state law. Aside from a small number of absolute rights, most human rights can be subject to restrictions provided certain conditions are met. In order to justify a restriction, the state must demonstrate that it (a) is prescribed by law, (b) pursues a legitimate objective, (c) is necessary to achieve that objective, and (d) is not discriminatory. In respect of the latter, it is well established in international human rights law that not every difference in treatment will be discriminatory. Instead, discrimination occurs when the state treats persons in analogous positions differently without objective and reasonable justification or when it

---

33 *See, e.g.*, Thompson v. United Kingdom, 40 Eur. H.R. Rep. 11, para. 43 (2005).
34 One possible example is suggested in the case of *Refah Partisi (The Welfare Party) v. Turkey*, 37 Eur. H.R. Rep. 1, para. 128 (2003) (decision of the Grand Chamber), where the waiver encroaches on "the state's role as the neutral and impartial organiser of the exercise of religions."
35 *See, e.g.*, Ozerov v. Russia, App. No. 64962/01, para. 57 (Eur. Ct. H.R., May 18, 2010).
36 *See, e.g.*, Colozza v. Italy, 7 Eur. H.R. Rep. 516, para. 28 (1985).
37 *See, e.g.*, Deweer v. Belgium, 2 Eur. H.R. Rep. 439, paras. 49–51, 54 (1980); Pfeifer and Plankl v. Austria, 14 Eur. H.R. Rep. 692, para. 39 (1992); *Thompson, supra* note 33, para. 44.

fails "to treat differently persons whose positions are significantly different" without objective and reasonable justification.[38] It follows that although there are some absolutes in international human rights law, there is also considerable potential for it to accommodate a range of competing rights and interests. This has to be factored in to any consideration of its possible impact on non-state law.

What emerges from this brief overview is that there are various ways in which international human rights law can exert some influence on non-state law. Admittedly, the relationship between the two is one that is conducted effectively at arms' length and with the state acting as intermediary. Drawing largely on principles of state responsibility, the state can be cast in the role of mediating the relationship between the two bodies of law. Depending on the range of obligations undertaken by the state, international human rights law may require the state to recognize, restrict, or instigate reform of non-state law. The extent to which it actually does so will depend on several factors.

One is the nature and range of international human rights obligations undertaken by the state. The greater the number of human rights obligations undertaken by the state, the greater the prospects for the relationship between international and non-state law taking hold. In recent years, there has been a considerable expansion in the number of ratifications of human rights treaties by states.[39] This suggests that the potential for international human rights law to influence non-state law will increase rather than diminish in the coming years.

A second factor is the extent to which the state is prepared to comply with its international obligations in good faith. The state may simply refuse to engage with the international human rights bodies or ignore their recommendations. If it does, the impact of international human rights law on non-state law will be minimal, at best. This raises issues concerning the general efficacy of international human rights law. Although it is important to appreciate the shortcomings of the law in this respect, it is also important not to be too bleak in one's assessment of its potential efficacy. When considering this issue, it is

[38] *See, e.g.*, U.N. Human Rights Committee, General Comment No. 18 in Note by the Secretariat, Compilation of General Comments and General Recommendations adopted by Human Rights Treaty Bodies, U.N. Doc. HRI/GEN/1/Rev.7 (2004).

[39] *See, e.g.*, Navanethem Pillay, Report by the U.N. High Commissioner for Human Rights, *Strengthening the United Nations Human Rights Treaty Body System* (2012), http://www2 .ohchr.org/english/bodies/HRTD/docs/HCReportTBStrengthening.pdf (last visited May 29, 2014). According to this report, the six core international human rights treaties in force in 2000 had attracted 927 ratifications. By 2012, this total had increased by more than 50 percent to 1,586 ratifications.

best to see the situation as a moving image. Even if international human rights law does not deliver immediate results it can still exert an influence over the medium to long term.[40] In exploring the relationship between international human rights law and non-state law, it is necessary to factor in this time component and to stress that what we are witnessing are the very early stages in an evolving relationship.

THE RIGHTS OF INDIGENOUS PEOPLES UNDER INTERNATIONAL HUMAN RIGHTS LAW: A CATALYST FOR THE GREATER RECOGNITION AND USE OF NON-STATE LAW

Normative developments concerning the rights of indigenous peoples have the potential to exert considerable influence on the recognition and development of their customary laws and juridical systems. This is evident from the U.N. Declaration on the Rights of Indigenous Peoples, which was adopted by the U.N. General Assembly in 2007.[41] According to this Declaration, indigenous peoples have the "right to maintain and strengthen their distinct . . . legal . . . institutions."[42] Where juridical systems or customs exist, indigenous peoples have the "right to promote, develop and maintain" them.[43] This should afford some protection against any attempts by the state to suppress or eliminate this form of non-state law. The Declaration also requires the state to adopt positive measures to give greater effect to customary law. In particular, it requires the state "to give due recognition to" customary law in adjudicating the rights of indigenous peoples relating to their lands, territories, and resources.[44] In addition to this, any decision concerning the resolution of a dispute between an indigenous people and the state or other third party must give "due consideration to the . . . rules and legal systems of the indigenous peoples concerned."[45] In this respect, the Declaration should act as an important catalyst for the greater recognition and use of this form of customary law.

The precise implications of these provisions become more apparent from the drafting history of the Declaration. The drafting history shows that the

---

[40] *See, e.g.*, Philip Alston, *Beyond "Them" and "Us": Putting Treaty Body Reform into Perspective, in* THE FUTURE OF U.N. HUMAN RIGHTS TREATY MONITORING (Philip Alston & James Crawford eds., 2000).

[41] The United Nations Declaration on the Rights of Indigenous Peoples, G.A. Res. 61/295 (Sept. 13, 2007) (adopted by 143 votes, with 4 votes against and 11 abstentions).

[42] Art. 5.

[43] Art. 34.

[44] Art. 27. The relevance of indigenous peoples' laws to land rights is also recognized in art. 11(2).

[45] Art. 40.

provisions were not intended to create new legal systems.[46] Nor, it seems, were they intended to establish parallel legal systems or to allow indigenous peoples to opt out of the state system.[47] Admittedly, concerns were expressed about the creation of "parallel and . . . contradictory legal systems within the state"[48] but these concerns seem to have been dispelled.[49] This may be attributed, in part, to some of the amendments made during the drafting process.[50] For example, the original draft referred to the right of indigenous peoples to maintain and strengthen their "legal systems," but this was subsequently changed to "legal institutions," apparently to diminish the risk of creating separate and competing legal systems within the state. There are some references to indigenous peoples' "legal" or "juridical systems" in the final draft but only in the context of states giving "due recognition" or having "due regard" to them.[51] The duty on the state to take account of these non-state systems was also intended to ensure that state and non-state law "operated in a compatible way."[52] What emerges from the drafting history is that although the Declaration can act as an important catalyst for the greater recognition of non-state law, it does not go so far as to require the recognition of new legal systems or the right to establish parallel and competing legal systems within the state.

The drafting history also provides useful insights into the relationship between this particular form of non-state law and international human rights law. The need for customary law to be consistent with international human rights law was emphasized by several states during the drafting of the Declaration.[53] This was not contested by the representatives of indigenous peoples themselves. Indeed, they pointed out that compatibility was assured

---

[46] Report of the Working Group established in accordance with Commission on Human Rights Res. 1995/32 of Mar. 3, 1995, U.N. Doc. E/CN.4/2004/81 para. 91 (Jan. 7, 2004) [hereinafter 2004 Report].

[47] Report of the Working Group established in accordance with Commission on Human Rights Res. 1995/32 of Mar. 3, 1995, U.N. Doc. E/CN.4/1996/84 paras. 92, 97 (Jan. 4, 1996) [hereinafter Jan. 1996 Report]. *See also* Report of the Working Group established in accordance with Commission on Human Rights Res. 1995/32 of Mar. 3, 1995, U.N. Doc. E/CN.4/1997/102 para. 230 (Dec. 10, 1996) (Malaysia) [hereinafter Dec. 1996 Report].

[48] 2004 Report, para. 85. *See also* Dec. 1996 Report, paras. 244, 233 (Ukraine, Brazil).

[49] Australia continued to express concerns and voted against the Declaration on this and other grounds. *See* U.N. GAOR, 61st sess., 108th plen. mtg., U.N. Doc. A/61/PV.107, at 12 (Sept. 13, 2007). Australia subsequently accepted the Declaration.

[50] 2004 Report, para. 86. *See also* Draft Declaration on the Rights of Indigenous Peoples, Amended Text, prepared by Denmark, Finland, Iceland, New Zealand, Norway, Sweden, and Switzerland, U.N. Doc. E/CN.4/WG.15/CRP.1 art. 4 (Sept. 6, 2004); Report of the Working Group established in accordance with Commission on Human Rights Res. 1995/32 of Mar. 3, 1995, U.N. Doc. E/CN.4/2006/79 art. 4 (Mar. 22, 2006) [hereinafter 2006 Report].

[51] Arts. 34, 40.

[52] 2004 Report, para. 89.

[53] *See, e.g.*, Dec. 1996 Report, para. 232 (Colombia). *See also* Jan. 1996 Report, para. 92.

not only by virtue of the wording of the Declaration[54] but also by the dynamic character of their customary law and the fact that they considered themselves bound by international human rights law.[55] Aside from this, the drafting history demonstrates how concern for human rights played such an important role in the drafting of the Declaration. There was a general consensus that existing formulations of human rights had proved inadequate in addressing the serious deprivations suffered by indigenous peoples who remain among the poorest and most marginalized in the world. Against this backdrop, the provisions on indigenous peoples' law can be seen as a way of ensuring greater respect for the rights of indigenous peoples, most notably, their right to respect for their identity[56] and their right to self-determination.[57] It demonstrates a strong justificatory basis for these provisions, one that is firmly rooted in international human rights norms and linked very much to the specific characteristics of indigenous peoples. When combined with the requirement that indigenous peoples' laws must be compatible with international human rights laws, it shows how non-state law has the potential to reinforce rather than weaken the global system for the protection of human rights.

Of course, it may be argued that as the Declaration is not legally binding, its significance is limited. This is questionable for several reasons. The Declaration is the product of over twenty years of negotiation and represents an important standard-setting exercise. As such, it is capable of influencing state behavior and contributing to the formation of customary international law. It is also important to note that its provisions on indigenous customary law are very much in line with developments concerning the rights of indigenous peoples in numerous global and regional human rights treaties.[58] The International Labour Organisation's Indigenous and Tribal Peoples Convention No. 169 of 1989, for example, requires states to have "due regard" to customary law when applying national laws to indigenous and tribal peoples.[59] To the extent that they are compatible with human rights, indigenous and tribal peoples have the right to retain their own customs and institutions[60] and specifically to

---

[54] *See, e.g.*, arts. 46(2)(3), 40, 1.

[55] *See, e.g.*, Dec. 1996 Report, paras. 92, 224.

[56] *Id.* para. 237 (Aboriginal and Torres Strait Islander Social Justice Commissioner).

[57] *See, e.g.*, Indigenous Issues: Working Group established in accordance with Commission on Human Rights Res. 1995/32 of Mar. 3, 1995, Chairperson's Summary of Proposals, 62nd sess., U.N. Doc. E/CN.4/2005/WG.15/CRP.7 art. 33 (Dec. 20, 2005).

[58] On the significance of the Declaration, see also U.N. Human Rights Council, Report of the Special Rapporteur on the Rights of Indigenous Peoples, U.N. Doc. A/HRC/21/47/Add.1 paras. 79–82 (2012).

[59] Art. 8(1).

[60] Art. 8(2).

have their customs regarding penal matters respected and taken into consideration by state authorities when dealing with criminal cases.[61] Although the Convention has been ratified by a relatively small number of states, its influence has extended beyond these states and can be linked to developments at the regional and global levels.[62]

It is possible to identify similar trends at the regional level, specifically, within the Inter-American human rights system.[63] In several landmark cases, the Inter-American Court of Human Rights has held that the recognition of customary law in the demarcation and titling of ancestral land is legally required under the American Convention on Human Rights.[64] At first sight, this may seem discriminatory as it seems to introduce different systems of regulation of land ownership depending on whether or not one is a member of an indigenous people. The better view is that this is an example of where differently situated people must be treated differently.[65] In addition to this, the adoption of an exclusively civil law concept of "property" would operate to exclude a significant proportion of humanity from the protection of the right to respect for one's property and this, in itself, would be discriminatory.[66] It is also important to bear in mind that a failure to recognize customary law could undermine or even destroy the ability of indigenous peoples to maintain their traditional relationship with their ancestral lands. This, in turn, could have far reaching implications for their other human rights, notably, their right to life, to food, and to respect for their indigenous identity.[67] Recognizing customary law in these circumstances can be vital to maintaining the physical

---

[61] Art. 9.

[62] *See, e.g.*, INT'L LABOUR ORG., HANDBOOK FOR ILO TRIPARTITE CONSTITUENTS, UNDERSTANDING THE INDIGENOUS AND TRIBAL PEOPLES CONVENTION, 1989 (No. 169),(2013), at xi, 5, *available at* http://www.ilo.org/wcmsp5/groups/public/---ed_norm/---normes/documents/publication/wcms_205225.pdf (last visited Jan. 15, 2015).

[63] On this point, see further Luis Rodriquez-Pinero, *The Inter-American System and the U.N. Declaration on the Rights of Indigenous Peoples: Mutual Reinforcement, in* REFLECTIONS ON THE U.N. DECLARATION ON THE RIGHTS OF INDIGENOUS PEOPLES (Stephen Allen & Alexandra Xanthaki eds., 2011).

[64] *See, e.g.*, Case of the Mayagna (Sumo) Awas Tingni Community v. Nicaragua, Inter-Am. Ct. H.R.¶¶ 138, 151 (Aug. 31, 2001). *See also id.*, Separate Opinion of Judge Sergio Garcia Ramirez, ¶ 6.

[65] *See, e.g.*, Case of the Saramaka People v. Suriname, Inter-Am. Ct. H.R. ¶¶ 85, 103 (Nov. 28, 2007); Case of the Yakye Axa Indigenous Community v. Paraguay, Inter-Am. Ct. H.R. ¶ 63 (June 17, 2005).

[66] *Awas Tingni, supra* note 64 ¶¶ 148–49, 151, 153; *see* especially the Separate Opinion of Judge Sergio Garcia Ramirez, ¶¶ 11–14.

[67] See the particular facts in *Sawhoyamaxa, supra* note 30. Indeed, the Inter-American Court has found that it could threaten the very physical and cultural survival of an indigenous people: *See, e.g., Saramaka, supra* note 65, ¶¶ 121–22, 128.

and cultural wellbeing of indigenous peoples that might not be achievable by other means. Although this is a powerful argument for the recognition of the customary law of indigenous peoples, it is doubtful whether this argument can be deployed in support of the more widespread recognition of other forms of non-state law. It will be difficult to establish such a direct link between the failure to recognize non-state law and such grave human rights violations occurring outside an indigenous context. Furthermore, international practice to date reveals that current interpretations of the right to respect for identity and the right to freedom of religion do not compel the state to recognize other forms of customary or religious law.[68]

THE CONVENTION ON THE ELIMINATION OF ALL FORMS OF DISCRIMINATION AGAINST WOMEN: A CATALYST FOR THE REFORM AND EVOLUTION OF NON-STATE LAW

The negative impact of non-state law on the rights of women is well documented.[69] Indeed, it often seems that the principle of gender equality is an insurmountable obstacle to any attempt to reconcile non-state law and international human rights law. This issue is explored in the present section with particular reference to developments relating to the Convention on the Elimination of All Forms of Discrimination against Women. As there are currently 188 state parties to this Convention,[70] it is a useful global benchmark against which to assess the potential impact of international human rights law on non-state law in the particular area of gender equality.

At the outset, it is important to note that a sizeable number of states have made reservations to the Convention based on religious or customary law.[71] For the most part, the reservations are based on religious law, especially Sharia law.[72] They stipulate either that the state is not bound by certain articles of the Convention or that it is bound insofar only as the Convention does not

---

[68] For a review of the practice of regional and global human rights bodies in this area, see, Helen Quane, *International Human Rights Law and Legal Pluralism: Inherently incompatible, Mutually Reinforcing or Something In Between?*, 33 OXFORD J. STUD. 675 (2013).

[69] See sources cited *supra* note 4.

[70] For a complete list of ratifications, reservations, and objections to reservations, see U.N. Treaty Collection, ch. IV. ("Human Rights"), sec. 8, "Convention on the Elimination of All Forms of Discrimination against Women," *available at* http://treaties.un.org/Pages/ViewDetails.aspx?src=TREATY&mtdsg_no=IV-8&chapter=4&lang=en (last visited May 28, 2014).

[71] Namely, Bahrain, Bangladesh, Brunei, Egypt, India, Iraq, Israel, Kuwait, Libya, Malaysia, the Maldives, Mauritania, Morocco, New Zealand, Niger, Pakistan, Oman, Qatar, Saudi Arabia, Singapore, Syria, and the United Arab Emirates.

[72] Reservations based on other forms of religious or customary law have been entered by India, Israel, New Zealand, and Niger.

conflict with religious or customary law. They are a concrete illustration of how non-state law can be invoked to limit a state's international obligations. For this reason, these reservations may be seen to cast doubt on the ability of international human rights law to influence religious and customary law. This is doubtful for several reasons.

The first is due to what these reservations tell us about non-state law and its capacity to evolve and adapt to the requirements of international human rights law. Take the reservations based on Sharia law as an example. The number and identity of Convention provisions that are subject to reservations on the basis that they may conflict with Sharia law tend to vary.[73] Although some states enter a general reservation, others refer only to specific articles and, then, not always to the same ones.[74] At the very least, this suggests that there are different interpretations of Sharia law, some of which are more compatible than others with the requirements of the Convention.[75]

The second is due to the international response to these reservations. A substantial number of states have entered formal objections to them.[76] The Committee on the Elimination of Discrimination against Women, which monitors and promotes compliance with the Convention, has also objected to these reservations.[77] For the most part, these objections are based on the perception that the reservations are incompatible with the object and purpose of the Convention.[78] As such, they call into question the validity of the reservations and the viability of attempts to use non-state law to limit a state's

---

[73] Compare the reservations entered by Bahrain (arts. 2, 16); Bangladesh (arts. 2 and 16(1)(c)); Brunei (general reservation); Egypt (arts. 2, 16); Iraq (art. 16); Kuwait (art. 16(f)); Libya (arts. 2, 16(c)(d)); Malaysia (general reservation); Maldives (art. 16); Mauritania (general reservation); Morocco (art. 2); Pakistan (general reservation); Qatar (arts. 15(1), 16(1)(a)(c)(f)); Saudi Arabia (general reservation); Singapore (arts. 2, 9(2), 15(4), 16(1)(c)(d)(f)(g)(2)); and the United Arab Emirates (arts. 2(f), 15(2), 16).

[74] *Id.*

[75] On the potential to reconcile Sharia law with women's human rights more generally, see, for example, SADA, ADAMU & AHMAD, *supra* note 3.

[76] See the objections entered by Austria, Belgium, Canada, Czech Republic, Denmark, Estonia, Finland, France, Germany, Greece, Hungary, Ireland, Italy, Latvia, Mexico, the Netherlands, Norway, Poland, Portugal, Romania, Slovakia, Spain, Sweden, and the United Kingdom.

[77] *See, e.g.*, Committee's Recommendations to Bangladesh, Iraq, Kuwait, Maldives, Saudi Arabia, Singapore, Syria, and the United Arab Emirates: U.N. Docs. A/52/38/Rev.1 (Supp.) para. 433 (1997); A/55/38 para. 186 (Supp.) (2000); CEDAW/C/KWT/CO/3–4 (2011); A/56/38 (Supp.) paras. 130–131 (2001); CEDAW/C/SAU/CO/2 (2008); A/56/38 (Supp.) paras. 73–74 (2001); CEDAW/C/SYR/CO/1 (2007); CEDAW/C/ARE/CO/1 (2010).

[78] Other reasons given for the objections include (a) that the reservation was of limited scope and undefined character thereby giving rise to questions about the state's commitment to the treaty and the extent of the obligations it was undertaking, (b) that it would cause sex discrimination, and (c) that the state cannot rely on the provisions of internal law to restrict its international obligations.

international human rights obligations. This sustained pressure has led to the withdrawal of some of these reservations either in whole or in part.[79] The withdrawal of these reservations is significant as it suggests that religious and customary law is not set in stone but is capable of being interpreted in an evolving manner and in a way that is compatible with international human rights law.

Notwithstanding the existence of the reservations, the Committee reviews each state's compliance with all the provisions of the Convention and makes a number of concluding recommendations. Although these recommendations are not legally binding they provide an authoritative interpretation of the Convention and can influence state behavior. Several trends emerge from these recommendations. The first is that there are some religious and customary laws that are deemed to be completely incompatible with the Convention. This is true, for example, of laws permitting polygamy and child marriages. In these instances, the state concerned is called upon to eliminate these laws.[80] Several states have already taken measures to do so.[81] It is just one example of how international human rights law can impact on non-state law. However, it is important not to lose sight of the bigger picture. There is no evidence to suggest that the Convention requires the wholesale abolition of religious or customary law. For the most part, attention is directed to rendering this law compatible with the Convention.

A second trend is that religious and customary law is regarded as having the capacity to evolve in line with international standards.[82] Attempts to portray

[79] *See, e.g.,* Bangladesh, Syria, Singapore, and Kuwait: U.N. Docs. A/52/38/Rev.1 (Supp.) para. 411 (1997); CEDAW/C/SYR/CO/1 para. 11 (2007); CEDAW/C/SGP/CO/4 (2011); CEDAW/C/KWT/CO/3–4 (2011). Others made commitments during the first Universal Periodic Review to withdraw or review their reservations to the Convention. *See, e.g.,* Oman: U.N. Doc. CEDAW/C/OMN/CO/1 (2011). Several states have signaled their intention to withdraw at least some of their reservations. *See, e.g.,* Mauritania, Morocco, and Malaysia: U.N. Docs. CEDAW/C/MRT/CO/1 (2007); CEDAW/C/MAR/CO/4 (2008); CEDAW/C/MYS/CO/2 (2006).

[80] *See, e.g.,* Committee's Recommendations to Iraq, Israel, Kuwait, Mauritania, Morocco, Oman, Saudi Arabia, Syria, Uganda, Kenya, Myanmar, Madagascar, and Singapore: U.N. Docs. A/55/38 (Supp.) para. 192 (2000); A/52/38/Rev.1 Pt. II para. 178 (1997); CEDAW/C/KWT/CO/3–4 (2011); CEDAW/C/MRT/CO/1 (2007); CEDAW/C/MAR/CO/4 (2008); CEDAW/C/OMN/CO/1 (2011); CEDAW/C/SAU/CO/2 (2008); CEDAW/C/SYR/CO/1 (2007); CEDAW/C/UGA/CO/7 (2010); CEDAW/C/KEN/CO/6 (2007); CEDAW/C/MMR/CO/3 (2008); CEDAW/C/MDG/CO/5 (2008); CEDAW/C/SGP/CO/4 (2011).

[81] *See, e.g.,* introduction of a minimum age of marriage in Morocco and Singapore: U.N. Docs. CEDAW/C/MAR/CO/4 (2008); CEDAW/C/SGP/CO/4 (2011).

[82] *See, e.g.,* Committee's Recommendations to Morocco, Singapore, and Kuwait: UN Docs. A/52/38/Rev.1 (Supp.) para. 71 (1997); CEDAW/C/SGP/CO/4 (2011); CEDAW/C/KWT/CO/3–4 (2011).

religious or customary law as incapable of reform are consistently challenged and rejected by the Committee.[83] Instead, the Committee focuses on encouraging a more flexible interpretation of these laws and a sharing of best practice. For example, it has commented positively on one state's "gradual, greater flexibility in the interpretation of Sharia"[84] and on another state "leading the way" for other states with similar reservations to lift their reservations.[85] On a number of occasions, the Committee refers to the existence of a "comparative jurisprudence seeking to interpret Islamic law in harmony with international human rights standards"[86] and frequently calls on states to "study reforms in other countries with similar legal traditions with a view to reviewing and reforming personal laws" so that they conform to the Convention.[87] These recommendations highlight the Committee's firm belief in the capacity of non-state law to develop in line with international standards but they do more than that. They also demonstrate the potential normative significance of developments taking place at the *national* level. These developments merit further study given their potential to contribute to an *international* consensus on how best to develop religious and customary law in line with international human rights law.

A third trend is that states are required to harmonize statutory, religious, and customary law with the Convention.[88] States have been called upon to raise awareness of the precedence of international human rights law over religious and customary laws that discriminate against women.[89] They have also been called upon to adopt awareness-raising measures to ensure that customary or religious courts are familiar with the concept of equality under

[83] *See, e.g.*, Committee's Recommendations to Israel and Niger: U.N. Docs. CEDAW/C/ISR/CO/3 (2005); CEDAW/C/NER/CO/2 (2007).

[84] *See, e.g.*, Committee's Recommendations to United Arab Emirates and Singapore: U.N. Docs. CEDAW/C/ARE/CO/1 (2010); A/56/38 (Supp.) para. 74 (2001); CEDAW/C/SGP/CO/4 (2011).

[85] *See* Committee's Recommendations to Bangladesh: U.N. Doc. A/52/38/Rev.1 (Supp.) para. 424 (1997).

[86] *See* Committee's Recommendations to Maldives: U.N. Doc. A/56/38 (Supp.) para. 141 (2001).

[87] *See* Committee's Recommendations to Singapore: U.N. Doc. A/56/38(Supp.) para. 74 (2001). *See also* its Recommendations to Kuwait, Oman, Malaysia, Sri Lanka, Jordan, and Djibouti: U.N. Docs. CEDAW/C/KWT/CO/3–4 (2011); CEDAW/C/OMN/CO/1 (2011); CEDAW/C/MYS/CO/2 (2006); A/57/38 (Supp.) (2002); CEDAW/C/JOR/CO/5 (2012); CEDAW/C/DJI/CO/1–3 (2011).

[88] *See, e.g.*, Committee's Recommendations to Niger, Kenya, Myanmar, Ghana, Madagascar, Zambia, Tanzania, Uganda, and Malaysia: U.N. Docs CEDAW/C/NER/CO/2 (2007); CEDAW/C/KEN/CO/6 (2007); CEDAW/C/MMR/CO/3 (2008); CEDAW/C/GHA/CO/5 (2006); CEDAW/C/MDG/CO/5 (2008); CEDAW/C/ZMB/CO/5–6 (2011); CEDAW/C/TZA/CO/6 (2009); CEDAW/C/UGA/CO/7 (2010); CEDAW/C/MYS/CO/2 (2006).

[89] *See, e.g.*, Committee's recommendations to Botswana, Congo, and Tanzania: U.N. Docs. CEDAW/C/BOT/CO/3 (2010); CEDAW/C/COG/CO/6 (2012); CEDAW/C/TZA/CO/6 (2009).

the Convention and adopt decisions consistent with it.[90] On occasion, the Committee has called on the state to ensure that the procedure of customary courts is "brought into line with statutory courts," to ensure that individuals are aware that they can request the transfer of a case to a state court[91] or to introduce a choice of court where none exists.[92] All these recommendations, if implemented, could have significant implications not only on customary and religious law but also on the non-state institutions that interpret and apply it.

More generally, the Committee has called on states to undertake a "comprehensive review process" with a view to ensuring the removal of all discriminatory provisions against women "within customary, religious and modern laws."[93] Attempts by states to evade this role have been unsuccessful. For example, a state's policy of non-intervention in the personal laws of any community without the community's initiative and consent did not insulate it from criticism by the Committee. Noting that "steps have not been taken to reform the personal laws of different religious and ethnic groups" to ensure that they conform to the Convention, the Committee expressed concern that the state's policy of non-intervention "perpetuates . . . discrimination against women" and recommended that it should work with the communities concerned to review and reform these personal laws.[94] It demonstrates how international human rights law can require the state to intervene in the development of non-state law notwithstanding that it may have refrained from doing so in the past. Once again, it highlights the potential significance of international law as one of several factors that can influence the evolution of religious and customary law.

It is clear from the recommendations that the Committee does not expect any transformation of religious or customary law overnight. The Committee acknowledges the need for the population to support any reform of existing laws concerning women's human rights.[95] This does not mean, however, that the

<hr>

[90] *See, e.g.*, Committee's Recommendations to Vanuatu: U.N. Doc. CEDAW/C/VUT/CO/3 (2007). *See also* its Recommendations to Zambia: U.N. Doc. CEDAW/C/ZMB/CO/5–6 (2011).

[91] *See, e.g.*, Committee's Recommendations to Botswana: U.N. Doc. CEDAW/C/BOT/CO/3 (2010). *See also* its Recommendations to Vanuatu: U.N. Doc. CEDAW/C/VUT/CO/3 (2007).

[92] *See* Committee's Recommendations to Singapore: U.N. Doc. CEDAW/C/SGP/CO/4 (2011).

[93] *See* Committee's Recommendations to Chad: U.N. Doc. CEDAW/C/TCD/CO/1–4 (2011). *See also* its Recommendations to Niger, Botswana, and Zimbabwe: U.N. Docs. CEDAW/C/NER/CO/2 (2007); CEDAW/C/BOT/CO/3 (2010); CEDAW/C/ZWE/CO/2–5 (2012).

[94] *See* Committee's Recommendations to India: U.N. Docs. A/55/38 (Supp.) paras. 60–61 (2000); CEDAW/C/IND/CO/3 (2007).

[95] *See, e.g.*, Committee's Recommendations to Morocco: U.N. Doc. A/52/38/Rev.1 (Supp.) para. 71 (1997).

state can stand by and wait until such time as this support materializes. Instead, the state is given the role of generating support for law reform, for example, through "partnerships and collaboration with religious and community leaders, lawyers and judges, civil society organizations and women's ngos."[96] States are expected to "proactively initiate and encourage debate within the relevant communities on . . . the human rights of women"[97] and conduct awareness raising campaigns "among all sections of society, particularly traditional leaders [and] religious clerics" on the importance of gender equality.[98] The law reform process itself must be fully inclusive,[99] with the effective participation of traditional and religious leaders, civil society representatives, and women's organizations.[100] Beyond this, the modalities are left to the state and communities concerned to develop religious and customary law in a manner that is consistent with the Convention. This is a pragmatic and conceptually coherent approach. It allows local variations to be factored into the process of reform without compromising the fundamental tenets of the Convention.[101] Further by co-opting traditional and religious leaders into this process, it can heighten the prospects for a greater understanding and more effective implementation of international human rights law on the ground.

CONCLUSION

The starting point for this chapter was the recognition that non-state law is molded by the specific context in which it operates. This is commonly recognized but what is not always recognized is that this context now has an international law dimension, specifically, one based on international human

---

[96] *See* Committee's Recommendations to Syria: U.N. Doc. CEDAW/C/SYR/CO/1 (2007). *See also* its Recommendations to Malaysia, Morocco, Jordan, Myanmar, Tunisia, and Egypt: U.N. Docs. CEDAW/C/MYS/CO/2 (2006); A/52/38/Rev.1 (Supp.) para. 71 (1997); CEDAW/C/JOR/CO/4 (2007); CEDAW/C/MMR/CO/3 (2008); CEDAW/C/TUN/CO/6 (2010); CEDAW/C/EGY/CO/7 (2010).

[97] *See* Committee's Recommendations to India: U.N. Doc. CEDAW/C/IND/CO/3 para. 11 (2007).

[98] *See, e.g.,* Committee's Recommendations to Bahrain, Chad, Lesotho, and Kuwait: U.N. Docs. CEDAW/C/BHR/CO/2 (2008); CEDAW/C/TCD/CO/1 4 (2011), CEDAW/C/LSO/CO/1-4 (2011); CEDAW/C/KWT/CO/3-4 (2011).

[99] On the potential challenges to participatory law reform processes as well as possible ways forward, see, for example, SADA, *supra* note 3. On the viability of such an approach, see Perry, *supra* note 4, at 107–13.

[100] *See, e.g.,* Committee's Recommendations to Singapore, Papua New Guinea, and Sri Lanka: U.N. Docs. CEDAW/C/SGP/CO/4 (2011); CEDAW/C/PNG/CO/3 (2010); CEDAW/C/LKA/CO/7 (2011).

[101] *See also* Committee's General Recommendation No. 28, *supra* note 28, para. 23. The importance of framing reform "within local traditions" is also recognized in the literature. *See, e.g.,* Calaguas, *supra* note 4, at 539.

rights law. This oversight is understandable given the state-centered approach that still dominates international human rights law and the very nature of non-state law. Through the concept of state responsibility, however, there is a gateway for the emergence of a relationship between the two bodies of law. Admittedly, what we are witnessing are the very early stages in this relationship. Nevertheless, recent developments suggest that the level of engagement between the two is set to increase rather than diminish in the coming years and that international human rights law may exert a growing influence on non-state law.

This raises the question as to how to characterize the relationship between international human rights law and non-state law. It is all too easy to portray it as an inherently hostile one. Examples abound of particular forms of human rights harm caused by non-state law. They seem to offer little grounds for optimism for any constructive engagement between international human rights law and non-state law. This chapter calls into question such a one-dimensional view of this relationship. Certainly, there are aspects of non-state law that cannot be reconciled with international human rights law. To the extent that the state complies with its international obligations in good faith, it will mean that non-state law will come under considerable pressure to change these particular laws. At the same time, focusing exclusively on these particular aspects of non-state law ignores the potential for positive engagement with international human rights law and presents a somewhat distorted view of the relationship between them.

International human rights law can require the elimination of some non-state laws but it can also act as a catalyst for the recognition and evolution of other aspects of this body of law. As the case study of indigenous peoples' rights demonstrates, it can lead to the greater recognition and use of their customary laws and juridical systems. In this way, international human rights law can contribute to the growth of the customary law of indigenous peoples. It is doubtful whether it will have a similar impact on other forms of non-state law. In the case of indigenous peoples, there is a strong justificatory basis for recognizing their customary laws and systems. It helps to ensure the more effective exercise of human rights by one of the most marginalized groups of peoples in the world. In these circumstances, the rationale for the recognition of non-state law is one that is rooted firmly in the basic principles of international human rights law. When viewed in combination with the requirement to respect human rights, it demonstrates how non-state law has the potential to strengthen rather than undermine international human rights law.

Although the case study on indigenous peoples focused on how international human rights law can act as a catalyst for the recognition of non-state law, the case study on gender equality focused on how it could lead to its reform. Even though international human rights law can act as the catalyst for reform, it does not attempt to micromanage the process. Instead, it stipulates the need for a participatory and inclusive reform process and establishes the broad objectives to be achieved by this process. Beyond this, it is left to the relevant stakeholders at the national level to develop non-state law in a way that respects human rights. This enables the law to be developed in a way that is sensitive to local values while remaining consistent with international human rights standards. This demonstrates the potential significance of developments at the national level not only for the population concerned but also for the international community as a whole. These developments at the national level can generate an international consensus on how religious and customary law should be interpreted so that it respects human rights. In doing so, they can also inform the interpretation of international human rights law. In this way, they can help international human rights law to move beyond debates about cultural relativism and toward more constructive discussions about how it should be interpreted and implemented.

Clearly, it would be misleading to portray the relationship between international human rights law and non-state law as an entirely harmonious one. There remains considerable scope for tension and conflict between the two. However, recent developments suggest that there is a coherent, conceptual framework for the emergence of a more constructive relationship between them. By harnessing the pull of non-state law and institutions, international human rights law can ensure its own, more widespread acceptance and effective implementation on the ground. By encouraging an inclusive and participatory process of developing religious and customary laws, international human rights law can help ensure that these laws retain their ongoing relevance and genuine support among all sections of the communities to which they apply. More fundamentally, these developments call into question common perceptions of the impact of international human rights law on non-state law. International human rights law will not lead inevitably to the wholesale decline or demise of non-state law. Instead, in many instances, it can act as a catalyst for the greater recognition of some types of non-state law and, more generally, for the evolution of non-state law in a manner that is sensitive to local traditions and values while remaining consistent with the fundamental tenets of international human rights law.

6

The Administrative State Goes Global

Daphne Barak-Erez and Oren Perez**,*[1]

Classical works in the field of administrative law emphasized the problems that arise from endowing the executive branch with broad administrative discretion.[2] Generally speaking, the conventional narrative of administrative law has conceptualized agencies as omnipotent decision makers with vast bureaucratic power. In his *Ideology of Bureaucracy in American Law*, Gerald Frug stated, "bureaucracy is the primary form of organized power in America today."[3] This organized bureaucratic power has been perceived as a threat to human freedom and to constitutional principles.[4] Thus, controlling the discretion of unelected bureaucrats has been seen as the guiding principle of traditional administrative law.[5] According to this approach, administrative law should be understood as an attempt to legitimize modern bureaucratic power by providing "a series of assurances that the legal system can overcome the perennial concerns about bureaucratic organizations"; by ensuring that "bureaucratic organizations are under control."[6] This chapter challenges the traditional narrative of administrative law in two ways. First, it argues that

* Justice, Supreme Court of Israel, Formerly Professor of Law, Tel Aviv University, Israel.

** Professor of Law, Bar-Ilan University, Israel.

[1] This chapter draws on Daphne D. Barak-Erez and Oren O. Perez, *Whose Administrative Law Is It Anyway? How Global Norms Reshape the Administrative State*, 46 CORNELL INT'L L.J. 455 (2013). We would like to thank Einav Tamir for excellent research assistance.

[2] Gerald E. Frug, *The Ideology of Bureaucracy in American Law*, 97 HARV. L. REV. 1276 (1984); Gary Lawson, *The Rise and Rise of the Administrative State*, 107 HARV. L. REV. 1231 (1994).

[3] Frug, *supra* note 2, at 1295. Recognizing the broad discretion exercised by administrative agencies also meant that – for better or worse – policy has been continuously shaped by these agencies; Colin S. Diver, *Policymaking Paradigms in Administrative Law*, 95 HARV. L. REV. 393 (1981).

[4] Frug, *supra* note 2, at 1295; Lawson, *supra* note 2, at 1232–33.

[5] CHRISTOPHER F. EDLEY, JR., ADMINISTRATIVE LAW: RETHINKING JUDICIAL CONTROL OF BUREAUCRACY 11 (1990).

[6] Frug, *supra* note 2, at 1284.

the strong state-centric character of traditional administrative law,[7] which associates bureaucratic power with the state apparatus and problematizes this power in the context of domestic constitutional law, disregards the increasingly globalized legal environment in which administrative action is embedded. Many local administrative decisions affect not only citizens but also foreign entities, such as investors, immigrants, and foreign laborers. Moreover, as a result of globalization processes, the state has lost its exclusive power to regulate matters that lie within the traditional realm of administrative law. In many areas, covering diverse topics such as trade, financial regulation, public health, and the environment, various international agencies have acquired increasing influence over domestic regulatory processes. The integration with the global arena, together with the economic promises it contains, requires the state, as will be elaborated below, to forgo some of its regulatory powers.[8]

Second, this decoupling between bureaucratic power and the state apparatus also challenges the mechanisms of control developed by administrative law to counter potential abuse of administrative power. The main mechanisms of control – the nondelegation doctrine and judicial review of administrative action – by their very nature are not equipped to regulate the actions of transnational regulatory bodies. The nondelegation doctrine assumes that the legitimacy of government bureaucracies is derived from legislation. According to this doctrine, "the legislature must retain primary decision making authority for governmental activity because it represents the subjective desires of the democratic electorate. Bureaucrats must carry out the wishes of the people (as expressed by their chosen representatives), not their own personal conceptions of the good."[9] But this doctrine becomes irrelevant once its basic premise no longer holds in the era of globalization. Judicial review by domestic courts also lacks the power to control transnational regulatory processes, due to jurisdictional limitations.

The normative reality generated by globalization calls for the reexamination of the basic theoretical and doctrinal conceptualizations of administrative law. This chapter critically examines these conceptualizations and adapts them to the challenges administrative law faces in today's globalized society. Our argument builds on the paradigm of global administrative law,[10] but seeks to

---

[7] *See, e.g.,* Frug, *supra* note 2, at 1284; Lawson, *supra* note 2.

[8] *See* Thomas L. Friedman, The Lexus and the Olive Tree 105–06 (1999); H.W. Arthurs, *The Administrative State Goes to Market (and Cries 'Wee, Wee, Wee' All the Way Home)*, 55 U. Toronto L.J. 797, 818 (2005).

[9] Frug, *supra* note 2, at 1300–01.

[10] Benedict Kingsbury, Nico Kirsch & Richard B. Stewart, *The Emergence of Global Administrative Law*, 68 Law & Contemp. Probs. 15, 17 (2005). For a preliminary discussion of these

transcend it. Whereas the global administrative law literature typically focuses on the meta-norms that regulate the activities of global administrative bodies in their capacity as global norm-makers and regulators,[11] we focus on the way in which international norms *intervene* and *reshape* decision-making processes within domestic bureaucracies. Our argument thus exposes a certain blind spot of the global administrative law scholarship, which has not given sufficient attention to the dynamic of global–national interactions. To the extent that current research examines the influence of global administrative law on national processes it mainly focuses on the work of domestic courts, drawing on classical doctrinal notions such as "incorporation" or "legal transplants," or on the formal questions of the status of public international norms in the domestic sphere.[12] In contrast, this chapter seeks to uncover the impact of international norms on domestic bureaucracies, taken as semiautonomous systems, and on the potential reciprocal dynamic this impact could unleash between the national and international bureaucratic orders.

This chapter develops an analytical schema that provides a framework for analyzing the influence of global administration law on domestic regulatory processes. This schema distinguishes among three forms of influence (which have not been clearly articulated before): *the substitution of domestic administrative discretion by global standards, the emergence of universal standards of administrative due process,* and *the globally inspired transference of enforcement*

challenges from the perspective of internal law, focusing on the U.S. context, see Richard B. Stewart, *The Global Regulatory Challenge to U.S. Administrative Law,* 37 N.Y.U. J. INT'L L. & POL. 695 (2005).

[11] *See, e.g.,* Kingsbury et al., *supra* note 10, at 17 (defining global administrative law as "comprising the mechanisms, principles, practices, and supporting social understandings that promote or otherwise affect the accountability of global administrative bodies, in particular by ensuring they meet adequate standards of transparency, participation, reasoned decision, and legality, and by providing effective review of the rules and decisions they make"); Benedict Kingsbury & Lorenzo Casini, *Global Administrative Law Dimensions of International Organizations Law,* 6 INT'L ORG. L. REV. 319, 326–34 (2009). This is also how external observers perceive the field of global administrative law. *See. e.g.,* GUNTHER TEUBNER, CONSTITUTIONAL FRAGMENTS: SOCIETAL CONSTITUTIONALISM AND GLOBALIZATION 50–51 (2012). For a preliminary discussion of the influence of GAL on internal law, focusing on the U.S. context, see Richard B. Stewart, *The Global Regulatory Challenge to U.S. Administrative Law,* 37 N.Y.U. J. INT'L L. & POL. 695 (2005) and David Y. Livshiz, *Updating American Administrative Law: WTO, International Standards, Domestic Implementation and Public Participation,* 24 WISC. INT'L L.J. 961 (2007).

[12] *See, e.g.,* Benedict Kingsbury, *Weighing Global Regulatory Rules and Decisions in National Courts,* ACTA JURIDICA 90, 99 (2009); Andrew P. Cortell & James W. Davis, *When Norms Clash: International Norms, Domestic Practices, and Japan's Internalisation of the GATT/WTO,* 31 REV. INT'L STUD. 3, 6 (2005); Andrew P. Cortell & James W. Davis, Jr., *Understanding the Domestic Impact of International Norms: A Research Agenda,* 2 INT'L STUD. REV. 65, 68–84 (2000).

responsibilities. We focus in particular on the emergence of *universal standards of the administrative process.* Here, we address the fact that beyond the particular norms generated by global bodies, transnational norm-production processes also establish basic standards of procedural and institutional integrity, which together form an emerging body of *universal administrative law.* By standards of procedural and institutional integrity we refer to those rules that regulate the procedure and structure through which decisions are being made. These include both *due-process rules,* which focus on the fairness of the administrative process, and *perfecting rules,* which seek to improve the decision outcome in terms of some overarching principle.[13]

The first part of this chapter maps the various mechanisms through which transnational regulatory processes intervene in the local realm, reshaping the contours of domestic administrative law. In doing so, it responds to a lacuna in the literature on globalization that has tended to disregard the exact analytical and empirical features of this process.[14] Our analysis draws on the literature on global legal pluralism by noting the diverse sources and paths through which global law influences the domestic realm. Thus we focus not only on the influence of the World Trade Organization (WTO) framework, as reflected in the three recent rulings against the United States in the *Tuna Labeling, Clove Cigarettes,* and *Country of Origin Labeling (COOL) Requirements* cases, but also on the influence of private transnational institutions such as the International Organization for Standardization and the International Commission on Non-Ionizing Radiation Protection (ICNIRP) and global certification bodies such as Social Accountability International (SAI) and the Global Food Safety Initiative. As we will demonstrate, some of these global bodies provide also meta-regulatory rules that govern the actions of other transnational bodies (which in turn influence the domestic realm).

---

[13] We use the concept of "universality" here in a somewhat tentative fashion to designate the emergence of global administrative law norms that apply at the domestic level. Our use of the term is tentative because we are describing an evolving process: there is still substantial diversity and discord in this emerging body of law. Further, some of the processes we describe are soft law phenomena, and thus cannot be analyzed using the conventional doctrine of validity in international law. Therefore, the validity of some of the norms we describe cannot be articulated using the conventional theory of the secondary rules of recognition of international law. *See* Jonathan I. Charney, *Universal International Law,* 87 Am. J. Int'l L. 529, 531 (1993); Oren Perez, *Purity Lost: The Paradoxical Face of the New Transnational Legal Body,* 33 Brooklyn Int'l L.J. 1 (2007); Paul Schiff Berman, Global Legal Pluralism: A Jurisprudence of Law Beyond Borders (2012).

[14] See, for example, the discussion in Michael Goodhart & Stacy Bondanella Taninchev, *The New Sovereigntist Challenge for Global Governance: Democracy without Sovereignty,* 55 Int'l Stud. Q. 1047, 1055 (2011); David Held, *Restructuring Global Governance: Cosmopolitanism, Democracy and the Global Order,* 37 Millennium – J. Int'l Stud. 535, 537 (2009); Teubner, *supra* note 11, at 5; Arthurs, *supra* note 8.

The second part of this chapter proceeds to examine the normative challenges posed by these processes of transnational rule making. We argue that this new reality requires administrative law to develop new legitimization devices that would supplement and even replace traditional devices. Our argument thus sheds new light on the classic critique of administrative law.[15] We start by criticizing the hidden ideological agenda of this transnational legal body, highlighting especially its propensity for neo-liberal, capitalist ideas. This bias undermines any attempt to ground the legitimacy of global administrative law on some universal rationality. We explore how this ideological bias can be countered at the global level. We then move to discuss the problematic posed by the fragmented accountability regimes that characterize today's global legal system. This fragmentation calls into question the legitimacy of global administrative law by exposing the lack of efficient control mechanisms on both the domestic level and the global level. Finally, we examine the challenge posed by the expanding influence of universal administrative law norms on our democratic conceptions of legitimization. Although modern administrative law has developed sophisticated methods of public participation, these mechanisms have remained confined to the domestic level, disregarding the extent to which domestic administrative law is influenced by external norms. We assess the challenge of developing new decision-making processes and forms of participation that will be better attuned to the new global reality and at the same time meet democratic standards. In this context, our approach steers a middle course between the extremes of sovereign exceptionalism and global constitutionalism by focusing on the potential of administrative law for democratic innovativeness at the micro level of administrative praxis.[16]

The analysis leads us to the conclusion that global processes have drastically changed the realm of administrative law. Administrative law can no longer be studied by using only traditional assumptions of absolute sovereignty and autonomous administrative discretion. The study of transnational regulatory processes should become an integral part of administrative law research.

THE MULTIFACETED INFLUENCE OF INTERNATIONAL NORMS ON NATIONAL ADMINISTRATIVE LAW

The influence of international norms on national administrative law is multifaceted both in terms of its sources or institutional background and in terms of

---

[15] *See* Frug, *supra* note 2.

[16] *See* Peter J. Spiro, *The New Sovereigntists: American Exceptionalism and Its False Prophets*, 79 FOREIGN AFF. 9 (2000); Anne Peters, *The Merits of Global Constitutionalism*, 16 IND. J. GLOBAL LEGAL STUD. 397 (2009).

its routes of implementation. In this part we want to offer an in-depth description of this multidimensional causality, drawing on the analytical framework that was previously introduced. This framework will assist us in developing a better understanding of the interlinkages between the evolving body of globalized administrative law and domestic administrative law, and it should pave the way for more detailed comparative studies.[17]

Global Standards Replacing Local Administrative Discretion

The substitution of local administrative discretion by particular global standards happens when particular international standards are adopted by national systems. This process reflects, by its very nature, a contraction of the discretion of domestic regulators, which had traditionally included the freedom to design a regulatory policy, to set the necessary standards, and to enforce their implementation. The influence of international norms on national administrative law has undergone remarkable changes in recent years, in terms of both the extent and scope of that influence. International norms influence domestic administrative law not just through the realm of public international law but also through private and hybrid sources of transnational law.[18]

The first pathway by which international law affects local administrative law is the classic channel of treaties.[19] Countries are subscribed to an increasing number of international treaties in many areas (e.g., trade, environment, intellectual property), which limit the discretion of their bureaucratic agencies in multiple areas. Of these, especially important are treaties in the international economic and trade spheres, particularly the WTO Agreement.[20] Membership in the WTO binds member states to a complex system of agreements,[21] which constrains the discretion of their administrative agencies across multiple dimensions. Other economic agreements that constrain the discretion of national administrative authorities are regional and bilateral trade treaties, as well as bilateral investment treaties. The Organization for Economic Cooperation and Development (OECD) is another example of a multilateral treaty that has broad-ranging influence over domestic administrative law

---

[17] *See* Peer Zumbansen, *Transnational Comparisons: Theory and Practice of Comparative Law as a Critique of Global Governance* 16 (Osgoode CLPE Research Paper No. 1/2012, Feb. 7, 2012), *available at* http://ssrn.com/abstract=2000803.

[18] Perez, *supra* note 13.

[19] We do not focus on customary international law because customary norms affect only limited areas, primarily in the law of war and human rights.

[20] Agreement Establishing the World Trade Organization, Apr. 15, 1994, 1867 U.N.T.S. 154.

[21] *See generally id.*

in diverse areas, from the struggle against corruption to environment protection. Another important development in this context is the emergence of judicial tribunals with normative authority exceeding the conventional conceptions of the authority of public international law.[22] Prominent examples are the tribunals of the WTO and the International Criminal Court (ICC).[23]

Administrative law is affected not only by standards associated with international treaties but also by norms produced by private international governance organizations (PIGOs) – international organizations that are not the product of international treaties.[24] This route is the result of the increasing complexity of the global legal map, and the emergence of "regime complexes" – a new form of transnational governance in which treaty-based bodies and private or hybrid bodies combine to co-produce a governance regime in a particular field.[25] Prominent examples of such actors include standard-setting organizations such as the ISO, which constitutes an important source for technical and organizational standards;[26] the Global Reporting Initiative (GRI), which is the global leader in the area of environmental reporting;[27] and hybrid regulatory-scientific bodies such as ICNIRP, which promulgate exposure guidelines for nonionizing radiation.[28] Other important certifying schemes are the SA8000

---

[22] The authority of these tribunals extends beyond the classical sources of international law as envisioned in Article 38 of the Statute of the International Court of Justice. See the discussion in Perez, *supra* note 13.

[23] The Rome Statute that founded the ICC represents an exceptional case in which an international organization was created that has judicial authority even over citizens of countries that did not ratify the treaty.

[24] The institutional structure of these organizations varies. Some are controlled by private entities; others are controlled jointly by governments and private entities. We will use the term IGOs (Intergovernmental Organizations) to designate the institutions established by multilateral treaties (e.g., WTO, ICC, UN).

[25] *See also* Robert O. Keohane & David G. Victor, *The Regime Complex for Climate Change*, 9 PERSP. POL. 7, 7 (2011); Kenneth W. Abbott, *The Transnational Regime Complex for Climate Change*, 30 ENV'T & PLAN. C: GOV'T & POL'Y 571 (2012).

[26] Oren Perez, Yair Amichai-Hamburger & Tammy Shterental, *The Dynamic of Corporate Self-Regulation: ISO 14001, Environmental Commitment, and Organizational Citizenship Behavior*, 43 L. & SOC'Y REV. 593, 593–630 (2009).

[27] *Sustainability Reporting Guidelines*, G3.1 GLOBAL REPORTING INITIATIVE (2011), *available at* https://www.globalreporting.org/resourcelibrary/G3.1-Sustainability-Reporting-Guidelines .pdf (last visited June 15, 2013).

[28] ICNIRP generates exposure guidelines routinely adopted by the United Nations' World Health Organization (WHO) and subsequently used as a basis for local regulation by many nation-states. *See* Adi Ayal, Ronen Hareuveni & Oren Perez, *Science, Politics and Transnational Regulation: Regulatory Scientific Institutions and the Dilemmas of Hybrid Authority*, 2 TRANSNAT'L ENVTL. L. 45 (2013); Oren Perez, *Private Environmental Governance as Ensemble Regulation: A*

social certification standards for a decent workplace[29] and the Global Food Safety Initiative (GFSI), which provides benchmarking for global food-safety standards.[30]

Norms of this type penetrate the local legal sphere through two main conduits. First, in some cases administrative authorities adopt standards that were developed by international organizations. Such adoption usually takes place through either secondary legislation or by administrative directives.[31] A second conduit is a voluntary incorporation by firms. This route has become a significant source of legal incorporation as more and more firms subscribe to transnational codes.[32] Such voluntary incorporation tends to have a network effect, especially as market leaders — such as Wal-Mart (in the food market) or Karstadt-Quelle, Argos, and Woolworth (in the toys market) – adopt certain standards.[33]

A fascinating recent development in the field of private transnational regulation is the evolution of metaregulatory processes: legal schemes that seek to regulate the global standard-setting process itself. Thus, for example, ISEAL Alliance, which is a global association of standard-setting organizations and accreditation bodies focusing on sustainability standards, has developed a Standard-Setting Code (ISEAL Code of Good Practice for Setting Social and Environmental Standards) that defines good-practice standard-setting processes with the objective of increasing the credibility of the resulting standard.[34] The GFSI developed general benchmarking criteria for food safety schemes, which define the process by which food safety schemes may gain

---

Critical Exploration of Sustainability Indexes and the New Ensemble Politics, 12 THEORETICAL INQUIRIES L. 543, 566 (2011).

[29] *See* SOCIAL ACCOUNTABILITY 8000, http://www.sa-intl.org/.

[30] *See What Is GFSI*, GLOBAL FOOD SAFETY INITIATIVE, http://www.mygfsi.com/about-gfsi.html (last visited June 1, 2014).

[31] Such incorporation is particularly prominent in the areas of occupational safety, environment and health, securities regulation (IFRS rules) and banking (Basel rules).

[32] *See* Tim Bartley, *Institutional Emergence in an Era of Globalization: The Rise of Transnational Private Regulation of Labor and Environmental Conditions*, 113 AM. J. SOC. 297 (2007); Perez, *supra* note 28.

[33] Walmart had adopted the GFSI scheme. *See* WALMART 2012 GLOBAL RESPONSIBILITY REPORT 24, WALMART (2012), *available at* http://c46b2bccodb5865f5a76-91c2ff8eba65983a1-c33d367b8503d02.-r78.cf2.rackcdn.com/d3/35/66be9cc44c2b8d096565166e79f4/2012-global-responsibility-report_129823695403288526.pdf; *Code of Business Practices*, INT'L COUNCIL OF TOY INDUS., *available at* www.toy-icti.org/info/codeofbusinesspractices.html (last visited June 15, 2013). *See also* Reinhard Biedermann, *From a Weak Letter of Intent to Prevalence: The Toy Industries' Code of Conduct*, 6 J. PUB. AFF. 197, 206–07 (2006).

[34] See *Standard-Setting Code*, ISEAL ALLIANCE, *available at* http://www.isealalliance.org/our-work/defining-credibility/codes-of-good-practice/standard-setting-code (last visited January 21, 2015). The standard draws, partially, from the ISO/IEC Guide 59 Code of Good

recognition by GFSI.[35] These metaregulatory schemes have gained recognition by significant global actors.[36]

The incorporation of private transnational norms into domestic law is driven by two concepts of authority: epistemological authority, that is, recognition of the superior knowledge and expertise of the rule-making body, and normative authority, which reflects recognition of the authority of these transnational bodies to produce binding norms.[37] In some cases, especially in the field of technical standards, the normative authority is created through endorsement by public treaties. The establishment of the WTO was particularly important in this context: the Agreement on Technical Barriers of Trade (TBT) and the Agreement on the Application of Sanitary and Phytosanitary Measures (SPS) encourage WTO Members to adopt international standards set by organizations such as the ISO and the Codex Commission.[38] The adoption of private transnational norms is also motivated by economic interests, especially in nonhegemonic states, in which local decision makers (regulators or company managers) may have little choice but to adopt the international standards.

Global Standards Affecting the Administrative Process: Due Process and Beyond

The concept of *universal standards of the administrative process* sheds light on a distinct type of influence on national administrative law. It calls attention to the fact that beyond the particular norms generated by global administrative bodies – both public and private – transnational norm-production processes also establish general standards of procedural and institutional integrity, which together form an evolving body of *global general administrative law*. By standards of procedural and institutional integrity we refer to those rules that

---

Practice for Standardization and the WTO Technical Barriers to Trade (TBT) Agreement, Annex 3.

[35] *See* The Global Food Safety Initiative, GFSI Guidance Document, *available at* http://www.mygfsi.com/schemes-certification/benchmarking/gfsi-guidance-document.html. The core criteria of the GFSI framework are included in Part III of the Guidance Document, which specifies the requirements for the recognition of food safety schemes (*Requirements for the Management of Schemes Contents*). *Id.* at 101–47.

[36] *See* Fabrizio Cafaggi & Andrea Renda, *Public and Private Regulation: Mapping the Labyrinth* 20 (Ctr. for Eur. Pol'y Stud., Working Paper No. 370, 2012); Global Responsibility Report, *supra* note 33.

[37] *See* Ayal, Hareuveny & Perez, *supra* note 28, and Kevin E. Davis, Benedict Kingsbury & Sally Engle Merry, *Indicators as a Technology of Global Governance*, 46 L. & Soc'y Rev. 71 (2012).

[38] David A. Wirth, *The International Organization for Standardization: Private Voluntary Standards as Swords and Shields*, 36 B.C. Envtl. Aff. L. Rev. 79, 95 (2009).

regulate the procedure and structure through which decisions are made. What we have in mind are both *due process rules* that focus on the fairness of the administrative process (e.g., notice-and-comment rules, transparency rules),[39] and *perfecting rules*[40] that seek to improve the decision outcome in terms of some overarching principle such as collective welfare (e.g., proportionality, cost-benefit analysis, risk-assessment).[41]

Among the diverse sources driving this process, the WTO takes a prominent role. The WTO adds to the development of both due process rules and perfecting rules. But the WTO is not alone in this process. It is part of a broader transnational network of law-making bodies, consisting of both public and private institutions that take part in the promulgation of this new universal administrative law rulebook. What distinguishes this network from global administrative law is that it claims to directly shape the discretion of national administrative bodies. Below we provide an overview of this new body of law and elaborate on the way its impact takes place.

The Development of Universal Due Process Norms

The WTO legal system plays a key role in the development of this network of universal due process rules. Article X of the GATT establishes a general framework for regulatory due process in trade regulation, which consists of rules on transparency of trade-related regulatory measures and the uniform, impartial, and reasonable administration of these rules. Similar requirements about transparency can be found in the SPS and TBT Agreements. The WTO rulebook also includes provisions that seek to protect the fairness of the legal processes that take place within the regulatory systems of WTO Members in areas governed by WTO law. Thus, for example, the Anti-Dumping Agreement contains provisions for issuing notices to interested parties and to the public

---

[39] *See* Robin Creyke, *Administrative Justice – Towards Integrity in Government*, 31 MELBOURNE U. L. REV. 705, 710 (2007).

[40] Alice Woolley, *Legitimating Public Policy*, 58 UNIV. TORONTO L.J. 153, 176 (2008).

[41] The distinction between fairness procedures and perfecting procedures is not exact. Some perfecting procedures can also serve fairness goals (e.g., cost-benefit analysis contributes to the ideal of fairness by facilitating comparison thus making discrimination more difficult). "Due process" rules could be considered perfecting since they contribute to the total fairness of the administrative system as a whole as well – at least by some observers – to its epistemic perfectness by bringing to the process the views of people outside the regulatory circle. Perfecting procedures are commonly driven by a particular worldview, and thus can also be a source of ideological conflict. *See* Amy Sinden, Douglas A. Kysar, & David M. Driesen, *Cost–Benefit Analysis: New Foundations on Shifting Sand*, 3 REG. & GOVERNANCE 48 (2009).

about the launching of dumping investigations (Article 12), as well as regarding the review of administrative decisions concerning anti-dumping duties (Article 13).[42] Interestingly the new Agreement on Trade Facilitation, which was agreed to on Bali on December 11, 2013, includes provisions regarding not only the transparency of domestic regulations pertaining to international trade but also provisions requiring states to establish participatory procedures that would allow interested parties to comment on proposed regulations.[43] Transparency rules have also been introduced by other international treaties such as the Aarhus Convention.[44]

The rulings of WTO tribunals have served as another source of due process rules.[45] A good example of the potential influence of the WTO on the procedural standards of domestic administrative law is the decision in the *Shrimps* case.[46] In that case, the Appellate Body accepted the American position whereby the regulatory regime that it established, which prevented the import of shrimps without certification concerning the use of methods that protect sea turtles, was entitled to the exemption specified in Article 20 of the GATT (starting, among others, with limitations required for the protection of the lives and health of people, animals, and plants).[47] Nevertheless, the ruling of the Appellate Body contained substantial criticism of the decision-making processes, and it is likely to affect the shaping of universal standards of due process. The original decision of the Panel noted that, in this matter, the American regulatory arrangement suffered from administrative flaws. Thus, as part of the process of obtaining an import license, the applicants (India, Pakistan, Malaysia, and Thailand) were not given the opportunity to be heard (which could have been the cause of the denial of the import license), they did not receive a reasoned decision, and they had no proper way of

---

[42] *See* GATT 1994 (the Anti-Dumping Code), Annex 1, at arts. 12–13.

[43] WT/MIN(13)/36, WT/L/911, arts. 1 and 2 respectively.

[44] Aarhus Convention on Access to Environmental Information, arts. 3.1–5.2, 7, June 25, 1997, *available at* http://www.unece.org/fileadmin/DAM/env/pp/documents/cep43e.pdf; Aarti Gupta, *Transparency under Scrutiny: Information Disclosure in Global Environment Governance*, 8 GLOBAL ENVTL. POL. 1, 2 (2008).

[45] According to WTO law, the rulings of the WTO tribunals are binding upon WTO Members. The influence on local law is usually indirect since in most jurisdictions, these WTO rulings do not have direct effect in the local realm. In many jurisdictions, however, local courts will take such ruling as guidance for interrelating local law, in order to prevent prospective breaches of the state's international obligations.

[46] Appellate Body Report, *United States – Import Prohibition of Certain Shrimp and Shrimp Products*, WT/DS58/AB/R (Oct. 12, 1998) [hereinafter The Shrimps case].

[47] GATT 1994, at art. 20.

appealing the administrative decision.[48] Subsequently, the Appellate Body also discussed the fairness of the process, but in doing so it did not base its decision on the American administrative law but on the interpretation of the expression "arbitrary discrimination between countries where the same conditions prevail," found in Article 20 of the GATT.[49] The recent decision of the WTO Panel in the dispute over the COOL requirements for imported livestock in the Unites States provides another illustration of this form of intervention, as the Panel noted the failure of the Unites States to meet the WTO transparency requirements.[50] In *United States – Clove Cigarettes*, the United States was found in breach of both the notification and the "reasonable interval" requirements of the TBT Agreement.[51]

But due process norms can also be found in other fields of international law, such as international investment law and private transnational regulation.[52] Thus, standards such as GRI, ISO 14001, ISO 26000, Equator Principles, OECD Multinational Guidelines and Accountability standards all include provisions on disclosure and stakeholder participation.[53] Although the details vary, they all seem to share a similar principled commitment to procedural fairness. Unlike the WTO rules, which have universal application due to the WTO's broad membership, these private rules apply only to the firms that choose to adopt them.[54] However, taken together, these private rules contribute to the consolidation of norms regarding transparency and public

---

[48] *See also* Benedict Kingsbury, *The Concept of "Law" in Global Administrative Law*, 20 Eur. J. Int'l L. 23, 37 (2009).

[49] GATT 1994, at art. 20.

[50] The Panel found that a letter sent by U.S. Secretary of Agriculture, Thomas Vilsack, to the agriculture industry addressing how companies could implement the COOL measure, has breached Article X:3(a) of the General Agreement on Tariffs and Trade 1994 by failing to meet the requisite standards of transparency and procedural fairness; Panel Report, *United States – Certain Country of Origin Labeling (COOL) Requirements*, para. 7.864 WT/DS384/AB/R, WT/DS386/AB/R.

[51] Panel Report, United States – Clove Cigarettes, paras. 7.550, 7.595. According to Article 2.12 of the TBT Agreement, members must also allow a "reasonable interval" between publication and entry into force of a measure "in order to allow time for producers... particularly in developing country Members, to adapt their products or methods of production...."

[52] For the case of international investment law, see *Metalclad v. United Mexican States*, ICSID Case No. ARB/AF/97/1, Award, 30 August 2000. *See also* Vicki Been & Joel C. Beauvais, *The Global Fifth Amendment? NAFTA's Investment Protection and the Misguided Quest for an International Regulatory Takings Doctrine*, 30 N.Y.U. L. Rev. 83 (2003).

[53] Basel Banking rules also include rules on transparency.

[54] *See, e.g.*, The Equator Principles (June 2006), *available at* http://www.equator-principles.com/resources/equator_principles.pdf.

participation and thus to the creating of a new global body of due process norms.[55]

Reaching beyond Classical Due Process: The Evolution of Perfecting Procedures Allowing Deep Intervention into Regulatory Discretion

The contribution of the WTO to the development of global general standards of administrative law also extends to issues that lie beyond the procedural concept of due process, to what we suggest calling *perfecting rules*. This development is manifested in three main areas, most prominently realized in the context of the TBT and SPS Agreements and in the jurisprudence of Article XX of the GATT 1947: (a) general perfecting principles such as necessity, proportionality, and even-handedness used to review regulatory decisions with antitrade effects;[56] (b) principles of risk assessment and scientific justification in the context of the SPS Agreement; and (c) detailed perfection procedures (risk assessment) developed by global standardization bodies.[57]

To illustrate our argument we focus on the TBT and SPS Agreements. These agreements give the WTO extraordinary powers to intervene in regulatory discretion in areas that fall outside the domain of trade, such as public health and environmental quality. Generally, the SPS and TBT agreements endow three distinct types of transnational bodies with the authority to intervene in the discretion of national authorities, covering different phases of the regulatory process: *international standards setting bodies* (standards content), *the WTO judicial tribunals* (through the doctrines of even-handedness, necessity, risk-assessment and scientific justification), and *foreign laboratories and accreditation bodies* (compliance assurance).[58]

---

[55] On the interlinkages between private CSR rules, see Perez, *supra* note 28.

[56] *See* Mads Andernas & Stefann Zleptnig, *Proportionality: WTO Law: In Comparative Perspective*, 42 Tex. Int'l L.J. 371, 372 (2007).

[57] We do not claim that these rules have, at this point of time, a clear meaning; they are still at the process of consolidation. They represent, however, a new and unprecedented development in international law. For a discussion of the interpretative dilemmas underlying, for example, the Appellate Body Article XX(b) jurisprudence, see Chad P. Bown & Joel P. Trachtman, *Brazil – Measures Affecting Imports of Retreaded Tyres: A Balancing Act*, 8 World Trade Rev. 85, 89 (2009).

[58] On the latter point, see *infra* subsection C titled, "Transnational Transfer of Enforcement Responsibilities." *See also* Tim Buthe, *The Globalization of Health and Safety Standards: Delegation of Regulatory Authority in the SPS Agreement of the 1994 Agreement Establishing the World Trade Organization*, 71 L. & Contemp. Probs. 219 (2008); Gstöhl Sieglinde, *Blurring Regime Boundaries: Uneven Legalization of Non-Trade Concerns in the WTO* 9 J. Int'l Trade L. & Pol'y 275 (2010).

Overall, the SPS and TBT Agreements have considerably expanded the grounds on which the WTO can intervene in local regulatory processes, by creating a regulatory system that reaches beyond the traditional concerns of the international trade system, and provides grounds for intervention in the regulation of nontrade issues such as environmental and health risks.[59] The SPS Agreement deals primarily with regulation focusing on food safety and agricultural products;[60] the TBT Agreement deals with technical standards in general.[61]

The SPS and TBT agreements deviate from the traditional focus of the GATT agreement on nondiscrimination[62] by focusing not only on matters of transparency[63] and consistency,[64] but also, and most important, on the manner in which national administrative authorities exercise discretion in setting and implementing their public health and environmental regulatory regimes – topics that until the establishment of the WTO had been considered to lie exclusively within the jurisdiction of the sovereign state. The SPS and TBT agreements establish two sets of principles that help determine the legitimacy (trade-wise) of a given regulatory measure. The first set is based on the classical GATT principle of nondiscrimination encapsulated in the doctrines of "most favored nation" and "national treatment."[65] The second set examines the substantive justification of the regulatory measure, from the points of view of both scientific justification and proportionality (in the sense of being least trade restrictive).[66]

A recent illustration of WTO's capacity to intervene in domestic regulatory processes can be found in a series of cases dealing with the TBT Agreement.

---

[59] For additional details, see OREN PEREZ, ECOLOGICAL SENSITIVITY AND GLOBAL LEGAL PLURALISM: RETHINKING THE TRADE AND ENVIRONMENT CONFLICT ch. 4 (2004).

[60] Agreement on the Application of Sanitary and Phytosanitary Measures, Apr. 15, 1994, Annex A, 1867 U.N.T.S. 493 [hereinafter SPS Agreement].

[61] Agreement on Technical Barriers to Trade, Apr. 15, 1994, app. 1, 1868 U.N.T.S. 120 [hereinafter TBT Agreement].

[62] Tuerk and Howse refer to this as the anti-protection norm that is at the basis of Article III (4) of the GATT. *See* Robert Howse & Elisabeth Tuerk, *The WTO Impact on Internal Regulations: A Case Study of the Canada-EC Asbestos Dispute, in* THE EU AND THE WTO: LEGAL AND CONSTITUTIONAL ISSUES 283, 309 (Gráinne de Búrca & Joanne Scott eds., 2001).

[63] For example, the TBT Agreement created a strict regime of reporting that obligates countries to disclose any technical standard that can affect trade. The various notifications are stored in a searchable database. *See TBT Information Management System*, WTO, *available at* http://tbtims.wto.org/.

[64] The demand for consistency was applied, for example, with respect to regulatory requirements applicable to materials of similar qualities. This issue arose in the Hormones Case, *infra* note 91, when it became clear that the EC enacted an incoherent regime with regard to the use of synthetic hormones in cattle vis-à-vis pigs. *See* PEREZ, *supra* note 59, at 132–37.

[65] *See id.* at 148–51.

[66] Howse & Tuerk, *supra* note 62, at 309–10.

In these cases, involving U.S. internal regulation of the labeling of tuna products, the labeling requirements for imported livestock and the ban on the sale of "flavored" cigarettes (cigarettes containing a flavor or herb or spice, excluding menthol cigarettes), the WTO tribunals have demonstrated their willingness to delve deeply into the rationale and architecture of U.S. domestic regulation.[67]

The *Tuna Labeling* case provides a good illustration of our argument.[68] In that case, Mexico challenged the U.S. labeling scheme regarding tuna products (U.S. Dolphin Protection Consumer Information Act, (DPCIA)). It argued that the DPCIA, despite its nonprescriptive nature, is a "technical regulation" and subject to the provisions of the TBT Agreement.[69] Further, Mexico argued that the DPCIA is discriminatory (TBT Article 2.1), more trade-restrictive than necessary (TBT Article 2.2), and unjustifiably fails to use an international standard – the 1999 Agreement on the International Dolphin Conservation Program (AIDCP) as the basis for labeling (TBT Article 2.4).[70]

The decision of the Appellate Body on these issues serves as an example of the potential influence of the WTO on domestic regulatory dilemmas. First, the Appellate Body adopted an expansive reading of the definition of "technical regulation."[71] This expansive reading has far-reaching consequences because it extends the regulatory ambit of the TBT Agreement. The Appellate Body rejected the U.S. argument that "compliance with a labeling requirement is not mandatory in situations where producers retain the option of not using the label but nevertheless are able to sell the product on the market."[72] The Appellate Body noted that the restrictive U.S. interpretation is not supported by the text of TBT Annex 1.1. It attached significance to the fact that "while it is possible to sell tuna products without a 'dolphin-safe' label in the United States, any 'producer, importer, exporter, distributor or seller' of tuna products must comply with the measure at issue in order to make any 'dolphin-safe' claim."[73]

---

[67] *See* Appellate Body Report *United States – Measures Concerning the Importation, Marketing and Sale of Tuna and Tuna Products* (WT/DS381/AB/R) [hereinafter the *Tuna Labeling* case]; Appellate Body Report, *United States – Clove Cigarettes* Measures Affecting the Production and Sale of *Clove Cigarettes*, WT/DS406/AB/R (Apr. 4, 2012) [hereinafter *Clove Cigarettes* case]; and Appellate Body Report, *United States – Certain Country of Origin Labeling (COOL) Requirements*, WT/DS384/AB/R, WT/DS386/AB/R (June 29, 2012) [hereinafter *COOL* case].

[68] A detailed discussion of the three cases is beyond the scope of this article, although we will briefly comment also on the other two cases.

[69] *Tuna Labeling* case, *supra* note 67.

[70] *Id.*

[71] *Id.*

[72] *Id.* para. 196.

[73] *Id.*

Second, the Appellate Body accepted the Mexican claim that the U.S. "dolphin-safe" labeling provisions modify the conditions of competition in the U.S. market to the detriment of Mexican tuna products and thus are inconsistent with TBT Article 2.1.[74] The Appellate Body examined whether that detrimental impact of the regulations stems from a legitimate regulatory distinction. It focused on the U.S. claim that the different criteria that were used to substantiate "dolphin-safe" claims have been "calibrated" to the risk that dolphins may be killed or seriously injured when tuna are caught.[75] In this regard, the United States emphasized the uniqueness of the Eastern Tropical Pacific (ETP), which, due to the phenomenon of tuna–dolphin association, exhibits more cases of dolphin mortalities than areas outside the ETP.[76] This uniqueness, the United States argued, justifies the unqualified ban on tuna products originating from the ETP from applying for a "dolphin-safe" label. The panel concluded that although the United States had demonstrated that the fishing technique of setting on dolphins is indeed particularly harmful to dolphins, it had failed to demonstrate that the risks to dolphins from *other* fishing techniques are insignificant[77] and do not, under some circumstances, rise to the *same level* as the risks from setting on dolphins.[78]

The Appellate Body ruled that United States had therefore failed to demonstrate that "the detrimental impact of the US measure on Mexican tuna products stems exclusively from a legitimate regulatory distinction."[79] The Appellate Body noted, in particular, that whereas "the US measure *fully* addresses the adverse effects on dolphins resulting from setting on dolphins in the ETP," *it does not* "address mortality (observed or unobserved) arising from fishing methods other than setting on dolphins outside the ETP."[80] In these circumstances, even if the fishing technique used by Mexican fishermen is particularly harmful to dolphins, the Appellate Body noted that it is not "persuaded that the United States has demonstrated that the measure is even-handed in the relevant respects."[81] The Appellate Body reached similar conclusions in the *Clove Cigarettes* and *COOL* cases.

The Appellate Body's rejection of the argument that the U.S. measure in the *Tuna Labeling* case (as well as in the *Clove Cigarettes* and *COOL* cases) was

---

[74] *Id.* para. 298.
[75] *Id.* para. 282.
[76] *Id.*
[77] *Id.* para. 289 and Tuna Panel Report, paras. 7.529, 7.531, and 7.562.
[78] *Id.* para. 289 and Tuna Panel Report, para. 7.562.
[79] *Id.* para 297.
[80] *Id.* (emphasis added).
[81] *Id.*

not more trade-restrictive than necessary to fulfill its legitimate objectives, and thus not inconsistent with Article 2.2 of the TBT Agreement, could be seen as reflecting a policy of deference to the discretion of domestic regulators – counter to our thesis.[82] It would be wrong, however, to overstate the deference component of this decision. The Appellate Body's conservative reading of Article 2.2 is in fact overshadowed by its ruling that the U.S. regulatory measures in all the three cases were incompatible with Article 2.1 of the TBT Agreement due to their discriminatory nature. This ruling reflects a de facto interventionist approach, inconsistent with the Appellate Body's ostensibly deferential reading of Article 2.2. First, the application of Article 2.1 by the Appellate Body involved an in-depth scrutiny of the regulatory measure, as demonstrated by the critique of the "calibration" argument presented by the United States in the *Tuna Labeling* case (the "even-handedness" requirement). Second, correcting the discriminatory aspect of local regulation may be difficult to achieve, due to internal regulatory complexities. Such difficulties could ultimately undermine the capacity of the state to achieve its legitimate regulatory objectives.

Thus, for example, in the *United States – Clove Cigarettes* case, the capacity of the U.S. authorities to achieve the objective of reducing smoking rates is mired by the implications of the Supreme Court ruling in *Food and Drug Administration v. Brown & Williamson Tobacco Corp.*,[83] which stated that the FDA did not have the power to regulate tobacco, and the political entanglements in Congress following it.[84] The United States could theoretically implement the WTO ruling by banning menthol cigarettes,[85] but this proposal is unlikely to pass Congress and would not assist Indonesian exports of clove cigarettes.[86] The United States could repeal the current ban on cigarettes with flavoring other than menthol or tobacco, but this move is again likely

---

[82] *Id. paras* 323–331; *COOL* case, *supra* note 67, paras. 462–469; *Clove Cigarettes* case, *supra* note 67, paras. 7.353–7.432.

[83] Food & Drug Admin. v. Brown & Williamson Tobacco Corp., 529 U.S. 120, 120 (2000); *see* J. Christopher Baird, *Trapped in the Greenhouse? Regulating Carbon Dioxide after* FDA v. Brown & Williamson Tobacco Corp., 54 DUKE L.J. 147 (2004).

[84] *See* Memorandum from Todd Tucker, PUBLIC CITIZEN, to Consumer and Health Groups (Apr. 27, 2012), Summarizing WTO Appellate Body Decision on U.S. Flavored Tobacco Ban 16 (Apr. 27, 2012), *available at* www.citizen.org/documents/memo-appellate-body-clove-ruling-04-12.pdf.

[85] The 2009 Family Smoking Prevention and Control Act (Tobacco Control Act), which expressly grants the FDA the power to regulate the tobacco industry, does not apply to menthol cigarettes. Tobacco Control Act, § 907(1)(A), 123 Stat. 1776 (2009); *see also* Elisa Solomon, *WTO Creates Roadblock to Administration's Anti-Smoking Initiative*, REGBLOG (Apr. 11, 2012), http://www.regblog.org/2012/04/11/wto-creates-roadblock-to-adminis-trations-anti-smoking-initiative/; Tania Voon, *The WTO Appellate Body Outlaws Discrimination in U.S. Flavored Cigarette Ban*, 16 AM. SOC'Y INT'L L. INSIGHTS 1, 1–7 (2012).

[86] Tucker, *supra* note 84.

to meet political resistance in Congress.[87] Although the discrimination-based argument of the Appellate Body may seem less interventionist than the "least-trade restrictive" argument of Article 2.2, the way in which it was applied by the Appellate Body in these three cases was ultimately similarly interventionist, both because it involved an in-depth critique of domestic regulatory decisions and because of its potential detrimental impact on the capacity of domestic regulators to accomplish their legitimate goals.[88]

A further illustration of the way in which the SPS and TBT agreements extend the intervention horizon of WTO law beyond its traditional focus on nondiscrimination can be found in the risk jurisprudence of the SPS Agreement. According to the SPS Agreement, WTO members cannot impose limitations on the importation, marketing, and sale of any materials or products, even if the limitations are imposed equitably, if the national regulation is not based on sound scientific justification[89] and a detailed process of risk assessment.[90] The influence of the SPS Agreement on the substantive discretion of state authorities was addressed in several cases by the WTO judicial bodies. The best-known case is the *beef hormones* dispute,[91] which began in the 1980s, when the EC prohibited the importation of beef injected with synthetic growth hormones. The prohibition was enshrined in a Directive stating that no beef that has been treated with synthetic or natural hormones is to be sold in EC countries, whether produced locally or imported.[92] The United States claimed that this position was inconsistent with the SPS Agreement.

[87] *See* Press Release, Energy & Commerce Comm., Rep. Waxman Statement on the WTO Ruling on Clove Cigarettes (Apr. 4, 2012), *available at* http://democrats.energycommerce .house.gov/index.php?q=news/rep-waxman-statement-on-the-wto-ruling-on-clove-cigarettes.

[88] For a discussion of the U.S. regulatory response to these three cases, see Jamie Strawbridge, *U.S. Implementation of Adverse WTO Rulings: A Closer Look at the Tuna-Dolphin, COOL, and Clove Cigarettes Cases*, 17 AM. SOC'Y INT'L L. (2013), *available at* http://www.asil.org/ insights/volume/17/issue/23/us-implementation-adverse-wto-rulings-closer-look-tuna-dolphin-cool-and.

[89] SPS Agreement, *supra* note 60, at art. 2.

[90] *Id.* at art 5. Article 2.2 of the SPS Agreement states: "Members shall ensure that any sanitary or phytosanitary measure is applied only to the extent necessary to protect human, animal or plant life or health, is based on scientific principles and is not maintained without sufficient scientific evidence, except as provided for in paragraph 7 of Article 5." *Id.* at art. 2.2. Article 5.1 states: "Members shall ensure that their sanitary or phytosanitary measures are based on an assessment, as appropriate to the circumstances, of the risks to human, animal or plant life or health, taking into account risk assessment techniques developed by the relevant international organizations." *Id.* at art. 51. *See also id.* at app. A, at art. 4 (defining risk assessment). Article 2.2 of the TBT Agreement is based on a similar logic. For commentary on this article, see Howse & Tuerk, *supra* note 62, at 313–20.

[91] Appellate Body Report, *European Communities – Measures Concerning Meat and Meat Products (Hormones)*, WT/DS26/AB/R, WT/DS48/AB/R (Jan. 16, 1998) (adopted Feb. 13, 1998) [hereinafter Hormones case].

[92] *Id.*

The Appellate Body accepted the United States and Canadian claims that the Directive was inconsistent with the principles of the SPS Agreement, which require that regulation in the area of food safety[93] be based on scientific justification and a proper process of scientific assessment.[94] Another example is the U.S.–E.U. conflict concerning genetically engineered food (GMOs).[95]

As noted, a further important source of perfecting rules are the general guidelines on risk assessment promulgated by global standard setting bodies. Article 5.1 of the SPS Agreement states that member countries, as part of their internal regulatory process, must take into account risk-assessment techniques developed by the relevant international organizations.[96] In other words, when they promulgate domestic regulations, member countries must take into consideration not only the international standards relevant to the specific regulatory problem being addressed, but also the methodology of risk assessment developed by such organizations.[97] The organizations listed in Article 5 include the International Office of Epizootics (OIE), Codex Alimentarius Commission (Codex), and the International Plant Protection Convention (IPPC).[98]

Another body of law that influences the scope of regulatory discretion is international investment law. This influence derives from the concept of

---

[93] The legal principle is formulated in the decision of the Appellate Body as follows: "We believe that Article 5.1 ... with ... Article 2.2 of the SPS Agreement requires that the results of the risk assessment must sufficiently warrant – that is to say, reasonably support – the SPS measure at stake. The requirement that an SPS measure be 'based on' a risk assessment is a substantive requirement that there be a rational relationship between the measure and the risk assessment." *Id.*, Article 193. For a discussion of the directives of this agreement, see PEREZ, *supra* note 59, ch. 4.

[94] The case was debated again by the Appellate Body: Appellate Body Report, *United States – Continued Suspension of Obligations in the EC-Hormones Dispute*, WT/DS320/AB/R (Oct. 16, 2008) (adopted Nov. 14, 2008); Appellate Body Report, *Canada – Continued Suspension of Obligations in the EC-Hormones Dispute*, WT/DS321/AB/R (Oct. 16, 2008) (adopted Nov. 14, 2008). For further discussion of these decisions, see Bernard Hoekman & Joel Trachtman, *Continued Suspense: EC–Hormones and WTO Disciplines on Discrimination and Domestic Regulation Appellate Body Reports: Canada/United States–Continued Suspension of Obligations in the EC–Hormones Dispute, WT/DS320/AB/R, WT/DS321/AB/R, adopted 14 November 2008*, 9 WORLD TRADE REV. 151 (2010) (noting the weakening of the scientific justification standard).

[95] *See* Oren Perez, *Anomalies at the Precautionary Kingdom: Reflections on the GMO Panel's Decision*, 6 WORLD TRADE REV. 265 (2007).

[96] SPS Agreement, *supra* note 60, at art. 5.1.

[97] PEREZ, *supra* note 59, at 115–50; Jacqueline Peel, *A GMO by Any Other Name ... Might Be an SPS Risk!: Implications of Expanding the Scope of the WTO Sanitary and Phytosanitary Measures Agreement* 17 EUR. J. INT'L L. 1009 (2006).

[98] *See, e.g., Terrestrial Animal Health Code*, OIE ch. 2.1 (2011), *available at* http://www.oie.int/doc/ged/D10905.PDF (regarding import risk analysis); *see also Procedural Manual*, CODEX ALIMENTARIUS 85–91, 180 (19th ed. 2010), *available at* http://www.fao.org/docrep/012/i1400e/i1400e01.pdf [hereinafter the Codex Manual]; *see also International Standards for Phytosanitary Measures: Framework for Pest Risk Analysis*, IPPC (2011), *available at* www.ippc.int/

regulatory expropriation, based on the expropriation provision present in one form or another in all bilateral investment treaties.[99] In making decisions regarding disputes involving regulatory expropriation, several arbitral panels have made reference to proportionality in the evaluation of the relationship between the purpose of the impugned measure and the effect of the measure on the investor.[100] Some authors have argued that the capacity of international investment law to intervene in national regulatory discretion is inconsistent with the public interest and could lead to (socially unjustified) regulatory chill.[101] At the same time, others have argued that this intervention can improve domestic regulatory failures.[102] At any rate, what we want to emphasize is that international investment law, just like the WTO, intervenes not just in classic questions of due process but also in issues relating to the rationale of regulatory decisions.

Transnational Transfer of Enforcement Responsibilities

The transference of enforcement responsibilities occurs in several arenas involving both public and private forms of international law. Taken together, these different processes reflect a further significant impact of global administrative law on the domestic arena. One area in which this transference takes place is conformity assessment of technical standards. As described, one of the ways through which the TBT and SPS agreements seek to advance the goal of international harmonization is to encourage WTO members to sign agreements on mutual recognition of conformity assessment carried out in the

---

publications/framework-pest-risk-analysis; *ISO/TR 13121:2011: Nanotechnologies – Nanomaterial Risk Evaluation*, ISO (2011), *available at* http://www.iso.org/iso/catalogue_detail.htm?csnumber=52976.

[99] *See* Caroline Henckels, *Indirect Expropriation and the Right to Regulate: Revisiting Proportionality Analysis and the Standard of Review in Investor-State Arbitration*, 15 J. INT'L ECON. L. 223 (2012); Justin R. Marlles, *Public Purpose, Private Losses: Regulatory Expropriation and Environmental Regulation in International Investment Law*, 16 J. TRANSNAT'L L. & POL'Y 275, 278 (2007). A recent example of this problem is the struggle of tobacco companies against a new wave of anti-smoking law, *See* Sabrina Tavernise, Big Tobacco Steps Up Its Barrage of Litigation, INT'L N.Y TIMES, Dec. 13, 2013, at 1; Crawford Moodie, Allison Ford, Anne Marie Mackintosh & Gerald Hastings, *Young People's Perceptions of Cigarette Packaging and Plain Packaging: An Online Survey*, 14 NICOTINE & TOBACCO RES. 98 (2012); Harry Clarke & David Prentice, *Will Plain Packaging Reduce Cigarette Consumption?*, 31 ECON. PAPERS: J. APPLIED ECON. & POL'Y 303 (2012).

[100] *See* Henckels, *supra* note 99, at 225–26.

[101] *See* David Schneiderman, *Investing in Democracy: Political Process and International Investment Law*, 60 U. TORONTO L.J. 909 (2010).

[102] Thanh Tra Pham, *The Impact of Treaty-Based Investment Protection upon Host States' Regulatory Autonomy*, KU LEUVEN (May 11, 2011), *available at* https://lirias.kuleuven.be/handle/123456789/307494.

laboratories of the other country.[103] These agreements complement another type of harmonization mechanism advocated by the TBT and SPS Agreements: mutual recognition of standards.[104] Conformity assessment agreements seek to reduce the cost of international trade by allowing exporters to test the conformity of their products with local (or international) standards in laboratories located outside the target country (e.g., in the country of origin). These agreements erode the power of domestic administrative agencies, even when the standard remains local, because they transfer the power to supervise and implement the domestic norm from the national administrative agency to an external body.

The scale of this phenomenon at the global level can be ascertained from the work of the CASCO Committee (Committee on Conformity Assessment) established by the ISO in order to encourage international harmonization of conformity assessment procedures. The committee both works on the principles and the practice of conformity assessment[105] and develops documents that are published as ISO/IEC international standards or guides.[106] CASCO's main objectives are (1) to prepare international guides and international standards relating to the practice of testing, inspection, and certification of products, processes, and services, and (2) to promote mutual recognition and acceptance of national and regional conformity assessment systems, and the appropriate use of International Standards for testing, inspection, certification, assessment and related purposes.[107] So far, CASCO has been involved in the publication of twenty-seven standards.[108] It has seventy-one participating countries and forty-eight observing countries.[109]

---

[103] *See* TBT Agreement, *supra* note 61, at art. 6 (mutual recognition of conformity assessment). Conformity assessment is "the demonstration that specified requirements relating to a product process, system, person or body are fulfilled." *ISO/IEC 17000:2004(E): Conformity Assessment – Vocabulary and General Principles*, ISO, cl. 2.1 (2004), *available at* http://www.iso.org/ iso/catalogue_detail.htm?csnumber=29316. *See also What is Conformity Assessment?*, ISO, *available at* www.iso.org/iso/resources/conformity_assessment.htm (last visited July 26, 2013). Further work in this field is conducted by International Laboratory Accreditation Cooperation (ILAC) and the International Accreditation Federation (IAF).

[104] The idea behind these agreements is that in the presence of equivalence between two standards, there is no need to impose additional technical demands that would increase the cost of the transaction without serving the substantive purpose of the regulation. *See* SPS Agreement, *supra* note 60, at art. 4.1; *see also* TBT agreement, *supra* note 61, at art. 2.7.

[105] *ISO and Conformity Assessment*, ISO (2005), *available at* www.iso.org/iso/casco_2005-en.pdf.

[106] *Standards Catalogue*, ISO, *available at* www.iso.org/iso/home/store/catalogue_tc/catalogue_ tc_browse.htm?commid=54998.

[107] *ISO/CASCO Committee on Conformity Assessment*, ISO, www.iso.org/iso/iso_technical_ committee.html?commid=54998.

[108] *Id.*

[109] *Id.*

Similar processes occur also in the domain of corporate social responsibility (CSR). Many of the global CSR codes have developed an intricate system of private verifications and accreditation, which is operated and managed outside the boundaries of state control. Prominent examples of this process are the environmental management system – ISO 14001,[110] the Sustainability Disclosure Guidelines of GRI,[111] and the social accountability standard for ethical working conditions, SA8000.[112] The certification procedures of the SA8000 standard came under scrutiny following the 2012 tragic accident in Ali Enterprises textile factory in Karachi, already mentioned in the introduction. We will further examine the implications of this incident below.[113]

The transference of regulatory powers also occurs at the metaregulatory level: the transnational system also provides the framework that supervises and monitors the multiple bodies – laboratories, accreditation bodies, external verifiers – that provide those various enforcement services. For example, one of CASCO's main goals is to develop international guides and international standards relating to the operation and acceptance of testing laboratories, inspection bodies, certification bodies, and accreditation bodies.[114] In a similar manner, the ISEAL Code of Good Practice for Assuring Compliance with Social and Environmental Standards provides general guidance for assurance compliance processes.[115] The global organization AccountAbility

---

[110] *See* Matthew Potoski & Aseem Prakash, *Covenants with Weak Swords: ISO 14001 and Facilities' Environmental Performance*, 24 J. POL'Y ANALYSIS & MGMT. 745 (2005).

[111] *GRI Sustainability Reporting Guidelines, Version 3.1*, GLOBAL REPORTING INITIATIVE (2000–2011), *available at* https://www.globalreporting.org/resourcelibrary/g3.1-guidelines-incl-technical-protocol.pdf. The GRI Guidelines offer two complementary compliance mechanisms. GRI can check the reporter's self-declaration of its reporting application level. Another alternative is to have the report reviewed by a third party. *Id.* at 6, 41.

[112] The accreditation and monitoring of organizations certifying for SA8000 is carried out by the international accreditation agency Social Accountability Accreditation Services (SAAS), which was founded in 2007 to accredit and monitor organizations as certifiers of compliance with social standards, including the Social Accountability 8000. *See* SOC. ACCOUNTABILITY ACCREDITATION SERVS., *available at* http://www.saasaccreditation.org/. *See also* Ingrid Gustafsson & Kristina Tamm Hallström, *Unpacking the Certification Revolution – The Construction of Legitimacy* (2012), *available at* http://carbsdrupal.hosting.cf.ac.uk/sites/default/files/ipa2012/Final_Version_IPA_Paper_Reference_163.pdf; Rainer Braun, *Social Accountability International*, in THE HANDBOOK OF TRANSNATIONAL GOVERNANCE: INSTITUTIONS AND INNOVATIONS 338 (Thomas Hale & David Held eds., 2011).

[113] *See infra* notes 169–172 and accompanying text.

[114] The primary references in this context are *ISO/IEC 17021:2006: Conformity assessment – Requirements for Bodies Providing Audit and Certification of Management Systems*, ISO (2006); *ISO/IEC Guide 62:1996 General Requirements for Bodies Operating Assessment and Certification/Registration of Quality Systems*, ISO (1996).

[115] *See* ISEAL ALLIANCE, http://www.isealalliance.org/our-work/defining-credibility/codes-of-good-practice/assurance-code.

developed a general framework for assurance compliance for organizations.[116] Such metaregulatory frameworks can also be found in more specific contexts. For example, SAAS has developed metarules regarding the accreditation of certification bodies in the context of social standards such as SA8000.[117]

CHALLENGES FOR ADMINISTRATIVE LAW IN THE ERA OF GLOBALIZATION

The increasing influence of global law on national administrative law raises important normative and policy dilemmas. In particular, we argue that it challenges the traditional mechanisms of control developed by administrative law in order to counter potential abuse of administrative power. The new reality of increasing transnational intervention in the domestic sphere requires administrative law to develop new legitimization devices.

We start by examining the possibility to ground the legitimacy of this new body of transnational administrative law in (some) universal rationality, exploring, in particular, and in this context criticizing, its ideological undercurrents. We then move to discuss the problematic of fragmented accountability regimes. This fragmentation questions the legitimacy of global administrative law by pointing to the lack of efficient control mechanisms. Finally, we examine the challenge posed by the expanding influence of universal administrative law norms on our democratic conceptions of legitimization.

The Ideological Undercurrents of Global General Administrative Law

The norms of this evolving system of global general administrative law are not ideologically neutral. They are driven by certain perceptions regarding the nature of a good and just society, more specifically by a neoliberal, capitalist vision, which privileges efficiency, competition, and market, as both goals and mechanisms of control, over alternative conceptions of value and governance (e.g., robust conceptions of sustainability and democracy). This vision is particularly problematic when it is promoted by corporate players who use it to advance their own interests, turning capitalism into what José Gabriel Palma has termed "rentiers' delight": a world in which the constraints of "competitive market" are imposed selectively to the benefit of big corporations and to the

---

[116] *See* ACCOUNTABILITY, www.accountability.org/standards/aa1000as/index.html.
[117] *See Accreditation of Certification Bodies of Social Accountability Systems*, SAAS (Jan. 18, 2008), *available at* http://www.saasaccreditation.org/?q=node/43.

detriment of politically weak agents (e.g. workers, small firms).[118] This ideological dimension is problematic mainly because it remains concealed behind a discourse of rationality and objectivity. Exposing the way in which the ideological presuppositions underlying this new body of law are manifested in its intricate doctrinal structure is thus an important contribution to the project of "placing political controls on a globally unleashed capitalism."[119] This ideological bias undermines any attempt to ground the legitimacy of global administrative law on some universal rationality.[120]

The neoliberal, capitalist vision is particularly dominant in the regimes of WTO law and international investment law. Because of the institutional ties between the WTO and some of the global standardization regimes (through the TBT and SPS Agreements), this ethos also influences the norm-production process in their respective spheres. The way in which the capitalist ethos influences the structure of the new universal regime of administrative law is not always obvious or transparent. It is beyond the scope of this article to provide a complete exposition of this influence, and we will focus on two recent examples – the decisions of the Appellate Body in the *Tuna Labeling* case and the *Clove Cigarettes* case – which illustrate this point.[121] In the *Tuna Labeling* case the Appellate Body ruling was driven by the understanding that "the lack of access to the 'dolphin-safe' label of tuna products containing tuna caught by setting on dolphins has a detrimental impact on *the competitive opportunities* of Mexican tuna products in the U.S. market."[122] The Appellate Body did not consider an alternative approach that would focus on the possibility of achieving a better environmental response to this dilemma. Thus, it did not ask itself how to combine the U.S. regulatory regime (the DPCIA) with the AIDCP in order to produce a better regime for protecting dolphins in the ETP and elsewhere.

Exposing the capitalist undercurrents of the universal administrative law norms highlights the need to develop new institutional venues in which the ideological presuppositions of this new body of law could be subject to public

---

[118] *See* José G. Palma, *The Revenge of the Market on the Rentiers: Why Neo-Liberal Reports of the End of History Turned Out to Be Premature*, 33 Cambridge J. Econ. 829 (2009); Wendy Brown, *American Nightmare Neoliberalism, Neoconservatism, and De-Democratization*, 34 Pol. Theory 690 (2006).

[119] *See* Jurgen Habermas, *Toward a Cosmopolitan Europe*, 14 J. Democracy 86, 87 (2003); Teubner, *supra* note 11, at 85, 93.

[120] The depiction of this ethos by Max Weber is still relevant. *See* Max Weber, The Protestant ethic and the "spirit" of capitalism 18–19 (Talcott Parsons trans., Routledge 2005) (1904).

[121] For more detailed discussion see Perez, *supra* note 59; Schneiderman, *supra* note 101; Habermas, *supra* note 119, at 91.

[122] Tuna Labeling case, *supra* note 67, para 235 (emphasis added).

contestation.[123] What is needed, in other words, are institutionalized mechanisms that could support reflexive deliberation regarding these rule-making processes, in a way that will enable the public to unveil and criticize their underlying presuppositions. One way to promote this goal is to create a *new global alliance* (or alliances) of transnational institutions that pursue noneconomic objectives. Such alliances should include both treaty-based international organizations such as UNEP and WHO and private transnational organizations such as GRI and Social Accountability International.[124] Creating such *sustainability-based alliances* could counter the economic-driven logic of the WTO with a more holistic thinking that gives due regard to social and environmental/health concerns. Such an alliance also has the potential to promote sustainability thinking in the emerging global general standards of administrative law. Two examples are the subjection of the SPS principle of scientific justification to the precautionary principle and the extension of the transparency principle to environmental and labor issues as promulgated by the GRI G3.1 Sustainability Reporting Guidelines.[125]

Sustainability-based alliances have already emerged in various contexts. Various global initiatives follow this vision: the United Nations Environment Programme Finance Initiative (UNEP FI), which is a global partnership between the UNEP and the global financial sector; the GRI global strategic partnerships with the OECD, the UNEP and the United Nations Global Compact; ISO 26000 Guidance on social responsibility was developed through a wide range consultation, drawing on a network of sustainability organizations.[126]

---

[123] *See* Habermas, *supra* note 119, at 94; Peter Wagner, *The Democratic Crisis of Capitalism: Reflections on Political and Economic Modernity in Europe* 23–24 (LEQS Paper No. 44, 2011), *available at* http://ssrn.com/abstract=1969031.

[124] Two prominent examples of such public–private alliances include the GRI – which has global strategic partnerships with the OECD, UNEP, and the United Nations Global Compact – as well as the UNEP Finance Initiative, which is a global partnership between UNEP and the financial sector. GRI's *Alliances and Synergies*, GLOBAL REPORTING INITIATIVE, www .globalreporting.org/information/about-gri/alliances-and-synergies/Pages/default.aspx; *What We Do*, UNEP FINANCE INITIATIVE, www.unepfi.org/.

[125] One possible interpretation of the precautionary principle (PP) is the imposition of greater sensitivity to false negative. In some environmental-health contexts involving severe hazards, the possibility of false negative (Type II error) – that is, failing to detect a true hazard – could be considered much worse than the possibility of false positive (Type I error) – that is, falsely describing something as a hazard. Type I errors drive the conventional scientific work, and, by imposing greater sensitivity to Type II errors, the PP could reform the nature of scientific justification in the specific context of health and environmental hazards. *See* Steve E. Hrudey & William Leiss, *Risk Management and Precaution: Insights on the Cautious use of Evidence*, 113 ENVTL. HEALTH PERSP. 1577, 1580 (2003).

[126] *See About*, UNEP FINANCE INITIATIVE, http://www.unepfi.org/; GRI's *Alliances and Synergies*, *supra* note 124; *ISO 2600 Social Responsibility*, INT'L ORG. FOR STANDARDIZATION (Sept. 2010), http://www.iso.org/iso/iso_26000_project_overview.pdf.

The main problem facing this idea is the current asymmetry between the institutions of global capitalism and the institutions that have the potential to be part of such a sustainability alliance. A good example of this asymmetry is the failure of the June 2012 Rio+20 Conference to strengthen UNEP, leaving it almost as weak as it was before the conference.[127] The Rio+20 Conference has also failed in its effort to promulgate a clear concept of "green economic growth," which could serve as a counter concept to the vision of growth underlying the WTO.[128] In that respect, the literature celebrating the emergence of new resisting institutions, following the 2008 financial crisis, seems to overstate the impact of these forces of contest.[129]

The Accountability Challenge: Disharmony between the Universalization of Administrative Law Norms and the Fragmentation of Accountability Regimes

The accountability challenge focuses on the tension between the processes of regulatory harmonization and transference of enforcement responsibilities, described above, and the primarily domestic regimes of accountability (tort law, criminal law, and administrative forms of accountability), which are still highly fragmented. In other words, while globalization has triggered a process that requires domestic regulators to exercise their discretion according to globally determined decision-frameworks and to rely on the discretion of external bodies (laboratories and accreditation bodies) in the implementation of local (or global) standards, decisions on liability for the same actions are still governed by domestic systems of accountability.[130]

This accountability gap could distort both global and local decisions regarding risks in a way that may lead to suboptimal policies. First, the fragmentation of accountability regimes could prevent attempts to hold international actors accountable for their negligent actions. This problem arises because

[127] Despite the commitment to "[e]nhance the voice of the United Nations Environment Programme and its ability to fulfil its coordination mandate," the reform suggested in Rio+20 failed to upgrade UNEP to the same level as more powerful U.N. bodies, such as the WTO. *See The Future We Want*, RIO+20, U.N. CONFERENCE ON SUSTAINABLE DEV., (Sept. 11, 2012), *available at* https://sustainabledevelopment.un.org/futurewewant.html; Jonathan Watts, *Rio+20 Earth Summit Moves to Boost UN Environment Programme*, THE GUARDIAN, June 18, 2012, *available at* www.guardian.co.uk/environment/2012/jun/18/rio-20-earth-summit-environment.

[128] *The Future We Want, supra* note 127, at 10 (the section called "Green economy in the context of sustainable development and poverty eradication").

[129] *See, e.g.*, TEUBNER, *supra* note 11, at 94–96; Peter Muchlinski, *The Changing Face of Transnational Business Governance: Private Corporate Law Liability and Accountability of Transnational Groups in a Post-Financial Crisis World*, 18 IND. J. GLOBAL LEGAL STUD. 665 (2011).

[130] *See, e.g.*, Cassandra Burke Robertson, *Transnational Litigation and Institutional Choice*, 51 B.C. L. REV. 1081 (2010); Hannah L. Buxbaum, *Transnational Regulatory Litigation*, 46 VA. J. INT'L L. 251 (2005).

of the inherent mismatch between states' exposure to foreign actors and their capacity to subject them to ex ante regulatory scrutiny or ex post tortious or criminal liability. Transnational regulatory bodies could generate risks that could influence the domestic market in various ways: (1) through the negligent promulgation of a standard (which was followed by local players – whether firms or public officials); (2) by negligently conducting conformity assessments of products designated for export (which were relied upon by local players – whether firms or public officials); (3) by negligently certifying a local firm to some global standard (e.g., the incident in the Ali Enterprises textile factory in Karachi involving SA8000 certification).[131]

The risks associated with the work of transnational regulatory bodies should be analyzed in the context of the primary risks created by foreign firms, through the manufacturing of hazardous products or in engaging in risky production processes. Subjecting these foreign bodies to regulatory scrutiny (both ex ante and ex post) is problematic due to jurisdictional issues (the problem of long arm jurisdiction), as well as to differing standards of liability.[132]

Second, the accountability gap is problematic in that it subjects domestic regulators to contradictory expectations – reflecting the conflict between the forces of trade liberalization and domestic regulatory oversight – which cannot be resolved at the level of a particular regulatory agency. A particularly illuminating manifestation of this conundrum is the case in which a hazardous product has entered the domestic market, drawing on a negligent assessment and certification by a foreign laboratory (drawing on a bilateral conformity assessment procedure). In such circumstances, should the domestic regulatory agency and the domestic importer, which have both relied on the evaluation by the external body, receive immunity from local tortious or criminal liability? Forcing domestic regulators and firms to duplicate tests done abroad could lead to a waste of scarce administrative resources and is also inconsistent with the harmonization effort of the TBT and SPS Agreements.

---

[131] *See* Robert H. Heidt, *Damned for Their Judgment: The Tort Liability of Standard Development Organizations*, 45 WAKE FOREST L. REV. 1227 (2010). A similar problem arises in the context of accreditation bodies. *See* Peter H. Schuck, *Tort Liability to Those Injured By Negligent Accreditation Decisions*, 57 L. & CONTEMP. PROBS. 185, 185–86 (1994). This problem is mitigated due to jurisdictional issues. *See, e.g.,* Hannah L. Buxbaum & Ralf Michaels, *Jurisdiction and Choice of Law in International Antitrust Law – A U.S. Perspective, in* INTERNATIONAL ANTITRUST LITIGATION: CONFLICT OF LAWS AND COORDINATION (Jürgen Basedow, Stéphanie Basedow & Laurence Idot eds., 2012); Sarah C. Kaczmarek & Abraham L. Newman, *The Long Arm of the Law: Extraterritoriality and the National Implementation of Foreign Bribery Legislation*, 65 INT'L ORG. 745 (2011).

[132] For a more detailed analysis of this problematic see, for example, Buxbaum & Michaels, *supra* note 131; Kaczmarek & Newman, *supra* note 131.

However, the accountability gap raises valid concerns regarding the deference to transnational regulatory bodies, especially in the context of certain risk-prone products such as pharmaceutical and food products.

A good example for this problem, taken from the Israeli context, is the *Remedia* affair.[133] The *Remedia* affair[134] dealt with the marketing of baby food products imported from Germany, which did not contain a vitamin necessary for the development of infants (B1) and thus caused severe health issues, some of them irreversible, and even death, to infants whose only source of nutrition was the Remedia baby formula.[135] After the case was made public at the end of 2003, public shock focused the attention on the issue of regulation of imported food products.[136] Ultimately, an Israeli court placed most of the responsibility for the absence B1 in the food on the German manufacturer (Humana) and on the German laboratory that checked the product.[137]

The *Remedia* affair resulted not only in tort actions against the Israeli importer, but also in criminal indictments that were issued against three high-level Remedia officials, as well as against five Israeli Health Ministry officials. The final court ruling was somewhat complex acquitting some of the defendants from several indictments and convicting them of others. Although the court stated that the defendants should have done more to inspect and supervise the importation of the product, it also noted the difficult dilemma underlying this case, as will be elaborated below.[138]

Focusing once again on the accountability challenge, the question raised by the case is whether in a world that is increasingly dominated by free trade, should a domestic regulator formulate a policy that requires the conduct of independent tests of the quality and safety of imported goods, or can it rely on the testing and standards of other countries with which it maintains

---

[133] A parallel U.S. case concerns the growing discontent with the inability of the FDA to supervise the quality and safety of imported products, mainly food, drugs, and cosmetics. The 2008 Chinese Heparin contamination incident is a case in point. *See* Editorial, *The Frightening Heparin Case*, N.Y. TIMES, Apr. 28, 2008, *available at* http://www.nytimes.com/2008/04/28/opinion/28mon2.html. *See also* Marisa A. Pagnattaro & Ellen R. Peirce, *From China to Your Plate: An Analysis of New Regulatory Efforts and Stakeholder Responsibility to Ensure Food Safety*, 42 GEO. WASH. INT'L L. REV. 1, 7 (2010).

[134] *See* Judy Siegel-Itzkovich, *Remedia Owner, CEO Face Indictment*, JERUSALEM POST, Oct. 9, 2006, *available at* www.jpost.com/Israel/Article.aspx?id=34394.

[135] Yonah Jeremy Bob, *Former Technologist Convicted in Baby Formula Case*, JERUSALEM POST, Feb. 13, 2013, *available at* http://www.jpost.com/National-News/Former-technologist-convicted-in-baby-formula-case.

[136] *Id.*

[137] *Id. See also* (Petach Tikva Magistrate) 2613/08 State of Israel v. N. Black & Others (verdict given on Feb. 13, 2013) (in Hebrew).

[138] Bob, *supra* note 135; Case 2613/08, *supra* note 137.

trade relations? This question has two aspects: standards (is it enough to meet a foreign standard?) and testing (is it possible to rely on testing carried out abroad by the manufacturer and/or certified laboratories?). The indictment attributed negligence to the Remedia defendants, among others, because "they adopted a policy of complete and blind reliance on Humana in all matters of product safety, and not only were Humana products not tested by Remedia Marketing, but Humana was not even required to send to Remedia Marketing the results of its analysis of the products that Remedia Marketing had ordered."[139] The indictment of the management of the Health Ministry officials, in particular, addressed the fact that the officials "caused a reduction in the scope of testing carried out by supervisors at the quarantine stations for imported foods," and "caused the formation of an attitude at the quarantine station that resulted in minimal, if any, testing of imported foods."[140] The indictment implies that administrators cannot rely on standards and testing performed in other countries and should act independently. This approach is at odds with the attempt of the TBT and SPS Agreements to remove artificial trade barriers and to encourage processes of reciprocal recognition in standards and conformity assessment.

The indictments issued in *Remedia*, especially those directed at the public officials involved, seem to reflect unwarranted disregard for the tension between the powers and capabilities of domestic administrative agencies and the international trade framework in which they fulfill their regulatory responsibilities. This disregard became apparent not only because of the criminal trial, but also because the Israeli Ministry of Trade has continued to promote a policy of mutual recognition of standards and conformity assessments within the WTO and in other contexts. In fact, the Agreement on Conformity Assessment and Acceptance of Industrial Products, between E.U. and Israel (signed on May 6, 2010 and ratified by the E.U. on October 23, 2012) includes an important annex in the area of pharmaceutical products.[141] Eventually, facing this seeming paradox was left for another day because the indictments against the defendants from the Ministry of Health resulted in plea bargains.[142] Nonetheless, the Court's final ruling regarding the managers of Remedia, given on February 13, 2013, seems to reflect the regulatory complexities underlying this case. The Court acquitted Remedia's CEO from most of the indictments

---

[139] Bob, *supra* note 135; Case 2613/08, *supra* note 137.

[140] Bob, *supra* note 135; Case 2613/08, *supra* note 137.

[141] *See* David Kriss, *European Parliament Approves EU-Israel Agreement to Simplify Trade*, Delegation of the E.U. to Israel (Oct. 25, 2012), *available at* http://eeas.europa.eu/delegations/israel/press_corner/all_news/news/2012/20121025_en.htm.

[142] *See* Bob, *supra* note 135.

against him, noting that his reliance on the German manufacturer and the German laboratory was reasonable under the circumstances and that Remedia was not required to recheck the products' quality in Israel.[143] The Court noted in that context that the German manufacturer adopted strict international standards such as ISO 9000 and HACCP.[144] Finally the Court noted the lack of specific Israeli standards on baby food and quoted the Director General of the Ministry of Health, who noted that when a product certified by a reputable standard is imported to Israel the practice is that Israeli authorities will not check it again.[145]

The solutions available to this regulatory challenge at the domestic level tend to provide only a partial response. Broadening the scope of inspection of foreign producers and imported products is not only economically costly but also seems to be inconsistent with the WTO-inspired effort to reduce the transaction costs associated with divergent standards and compliance assurance processes. This is the route taken by the FDA Food Safety Modernization Act (FSMA), which gives the FDA more authority to ensure that foods consumed in the United States are safe. With this new law, the FDA is required to double the number of foreign food facility inspections each year from 2011 to 2016.[146] A completely opposite approach is to refrain from any inspections and impose the responsibility to inspect foreign producers on importers. This approach, which amounts to the de facto privatization of the regulatory process, is problematic in that it assumes that importers can be completely relied upon to fulfill this regulatory task.[147] A middle-way approach is to develop a

---

[143] *Id.*

[144] *Id.*

[145] *See* Case 2613/08, *supra* note 137, at 855, 905, 982. For details on the plea bargains, see Ron Friedman, *5 Health Ministry Workers Plead Guilty for Remedia Deaths*, JERUSALEM POST, Feb. 28, 2011, *available at* http://www.jpost.com/Health/Article.aspx?id=210139. One of the intriguing facts about this affair is that, whereas the Israeli authorities have initiated criminal proceedings against the managers of Remedia and the Ministry of Health officials, the German authorities satisfied themselves with a very low-key response. On Dec. 10, 2008, the District Court in *Bielefeld* authorized a bargain between the German police and the four Humana employees involved, ordering them to pay very modest fines (in the range of 6,000 to 20,000 euros). *See* Case 2613/08, *supra* note 137, at 25–26.

[146] The FDA Food Safety Modernization Act was enacted by the U.S. Congress and signed into law by President Obama on January 4, 2011. Food Safety Modernization Act (FSMA), Pub. L. No. 111-353, 124 Stat. 3885; *see also* Maria Utecht, *FDA Food Safety Modernization Act: Top 10 New Requirements Food Industry Professionals Need to Know*, REGISTRAR CORP, Mar. 8, 2012, http://fda-news.registrarcorp.com/2012/03/fda-food-safety-modernization-act-top-10-new-requirements-food-industry-professionals-need-to-know/.

[147] Kenneth A. Bamberger & Andrew T. Guzman, *Importers as Regulators: Product Safety in a Globalized World, in* IMPORT SAFETY: REGULATORY GOVERNANCE IN THE GLOBAL ECONOMY (Cary Coglianese, Adam M. Finkel & David Zaring eds., 2010).

risk-based inspection system, which focuses inspection efforts on importers and manufacturers that are more likely to pose a threat (based on recent incidents, reputation, geographical location of the manufacturing sites, characteristics of the product, etc.).[148]

Because the regulatory problems associated with the accountability gap cannot be solved completely by unilateral steps, both regulators and firms have developed solutions that involve transnational efforts. One such approach is to create deeper relations between the regulators of different trading partners. A good example of this approach is the agreement signed between the U.S. Department of Health and Human Services and the Chinese government on cooperation and exchange with regard to the safety of food and feed.[149] The agreement established various mechanisms expected to assist the parties in fulfilling their regulatory objectives, primarily through more open and efficient exchange of information.[150] One of the interesting consequences of the agreement has been the opening of three FDA offices in China in 2008 (the first FDA offices to open outside the United States).[151] Agreements of this type can improve regulatory cooperation but cannot completely resolve the accountability gap that results from the fragmented jurisdictional structure of the international arena.

A different type of response focuses on the transnational arena, seeking to strengthen the regulatory capacities of the relevant international schemes. Two mechanisms are worth noting in this context. The first is the use of metaregulatory schemes, such as the GFSI benchmarking criteria for food safety schemes, discussed previously.[152] The second involves stricter interfirm contractual monitoring. For example, Walmart's manual on Standards for Suppliers states that suppliers may be subject to audits by Walmart and its third-party service providers and must cooperate with such audits.[153] Further, according to Walmart's 2012 CSR Report, since 2007 Walmart requires all private-brand suppliers and select categories of national-brand suppliers to

---

[148] *See* Caitlin E. Fleming, *Overdosed and Contaminated: A Critical Examination of The FDA and Drug Industry's Role in Drug Safety in the Context of the Heparin Catastrophe*, 13 QUINNIPIAC HEALTH L.J. 117, 168 (2002) (stating that during Congress' hearings regarding the Heparin case, congressional staff suggested that Baxter's request to change the manufacturing site of its Heparin from Wisconsin to China should have been considered a high-risk action).

[149] *See generally* Agreement on the Safety of Food and Feed, U.S.-China, Dec. 11, 2007, T.I.A.S. No. 07-1211.1, *available at* http://www.state.gov/documents/organization/108850.pdf.

[150] *See* Pagnattaro & Peirce, *supra* note 133, at 24–26.

[151] *See id.* at 26.

[152] *See* GFSI GUIDANCE DOCUMENT, *supra* note 35 and accompanying text.

[153] WAL-MART STORES, INC., STANDARDS FOR SUPPLIERS MANUAL 2, at 35 (adopted Apr. 2014), *available at* http://cdn.corporate.walmart.com/d1/7e/ee6f5c8942f69ad4183bc0683771/standards-for-suppliers-manual.pdf.

obtain certification from one of the Global Food Safety Initiative's (GSFI) internationally recognized food safety standards.[154] In addition, every international market in which Walmart has retail facilities has required all facilities producing private-brand products to become certified against one of the GFSI standards.[155]

The Democratic Challenge: Toward Diversity of Participation and Consultation Models

The expanding influence of universal administrative law norms poses a challenge to the democratic conceptions of domestic administrative law. Although modern administrative law has developed sophisticated methods of public participation, these mechanisms have remained embedded in a domestic framework, disregarding the extent to which domestic administrative law is influenced by external norms. The ideological undercurrents of the general norms of global administrative law and the accountability gap discussed emphasize the need to cope with this democratic deficit, which questions the legitimacy of the transnational normative network.

In thinking about this democratic dilemma, we suggest to adopt a middle course between the extremes of sovereign exceptionalism and global constitutionalism.[156] The attempt by the advocates of sovereign exceptionalism[157] to reestablish popular democracy by resisting the intrusion of external norms into the constitutional space of the nation-state seems to us to be out of touch with the empirical and normative repercussions of globalization. First, the penetration of global norms into the local realm is so pervasive that it is simply unrealistic, even for powerful countries, to resist this process. Second, the isolationists' approach disregards some positive aspects of the development of global administrative law. For example, the WTO normative framework can correct, in some cases, failures in the internal democratic system that impair the government's ability to act in the public's best interest, due to pressures of interested parties.[158] In the case of developing countries, where poverty runs

---

[154] Maria Utecht, *FDA Food Safety Modernization Act: Top 10 New Requirements Food Industry Professionals Need to Know*, REGISTRAR CORP, Mar. 8, 2012, http://fda-news.-registrarcorp.com/2012/03/fda-food-safety-modernization-act-top-10-new-requirements-food-industry-professionals-need-to-know/?lang=pt.

[155] WALMART 2012 GLOBAL RESPONSIBILITY REPORT, *supra* note 33, at 24.

[156] For further critique of these two positions see Goodhart & Taninchev, *supra* note 14.

[157] These are primarily American scholars. *See* Spiro, *supra* note 16.

[158] Robert O. Keohane, Stephen Macedo & Andrew Moravcsik, *Democracy-Enhancing Multilateralism*, 63 INT'L ORG. 1, 11 (2009). Thus, for example, the limitations resulting from international trade laws (for example, regarding the granting of subsidies) reduce the ability of the government to use its power for the benefit of narrow interests. *See also* Miguel Maduro, *Where*

deep and the regulatory framework is weak, private standards such as SA8000 may be one of the few mechanisms for improving social and environmental practices.[159] Finally, the new sovereigntists also disregard the fact that in our increasingly interconnected world, coping with global problems such as climate change, poverty, and peace keeping requires collaborative action. There is a strong moral argument for transnational collaboration, which must also be reflected in the structuring of domestic regulation.[160]

But the case for global constitutionalism or cosmopolitan democratization seems to us equally problematic. The attempt to solve the democratic deficit of the new body of globalized administrative law by embedding it in an overarching global constitutional framework (with the associated political institutions) is problematic because it disregards the gap between the proposed global constitutional structure and the social–political reality.[161] A constitutional system can survive only if it is supported by a sense of civic solidarity shared by all citizens. Such solidarity does not exist at the global level. Indeed, as Jürgen Habermas argues, "peoples emerge only with the constitutions of their states. Democracy itself is a legally mediated form of political integration."[162] Such a process of integration, however, is full of hurdles and its prospects to succeed at the global level seem to be very low.

We argue that a preliminary response to the democratic challenge might be based on the potential for democratic innovativeness ingrained in administrative law. This thesis is based on three premises:

(1) Modern administrative law has developed sophisticated participatory mechanisms that increasingly draw on web-based platforms.[163] Such platforms can be used to support consultation efforts at the transnational level.

---

to Look for Legitimacy?, in INSTITUTIONAL CHALLENGES IN POST-CONSTITUTIONAL EUROPE: GOVERNING CHANGE 45, 45 (Catherine Moury & Luís de Sousa eds., 2009).

[159] *See* Karin Kreider, *ISEAL Alliance Effective Assurance in Light of Pakistan Fire*, ISEAL ALLIANCE (Dec. 14, 2012), *available at* http://www.sa-intl.org/index.cfm?fuseaction=Page.ViewPage&PageID=1392#.UPoA2G8Uma8.

[160] *See* Held, *supra* note 14, at 542–43.

[161] *Id.*

[162] *See* Habermas, *supra* note 119, at 97 (noting the problems facing the project of political integration within the European Union).

[163] Probably the most prominent example of such mechanisms is President Obama's "Open Government Directive" (OG Directive). A key element of this initiative is Regulations.Gov. Similar initiatives have been developed by other countries. *See, e.g., Open Government,* GOVERNMENT OF CANADA, www.open.gc.ca/index-eng.asp; *Petition the Government,* GOV.UK, www.direct.gov.uk/en/Dioh/DoItOnline/DG_066327; *see also* Oren Perez, *Open Government, Technological Innovation and the Politics of Democratic Disillusionment: (E-)Democracy from Socrates to Obama,* 9 I/S: J.L. & POL'Y FOR INFO. SOC'Y 61 (2013).

(2) Domestic regulators are already deeply involved in transnational processes of norm-production, through both interactions with their peers at other countries and direct interaction with relevant transnational institutions.[164] This expanding transnational regulatory network can serve as a preliminary platform for incorporating civic voices in global regulatory processes.

(3) Global institutions, especially private and hybrid bodies that are involved in the transnational regulatory process have already developed innovative mechanisms of deliberation and consultation.[165] These experiences can serve as a model for a more expansive democratic framework.

Taken together, these three premises constitute a platform for democratic innovation on the global level and, therefore, provide at least a partial response to the problems of ideological bias and accountability gap discussed above. These new forms of democratic governance create a reflexive potential that could counter the adverse effects of uncontrolled capitalism by developing a global regulatory architecture in which the voice of civic players could become more influential. Although this vision represents a latent possibility rather than actual reality, there are nonetheless already varied examples that demonstrate its transformative potential. Global CSR organizations, such as GRI, SAI, or AccountAbility, have developed an intricate platform of governance, which allows a broad spectrum of stakeholders to take part in their daily operations and in the promulgation of new standards.[166] More established bodies, such as the WTO and the World Bank, have also started to give more attention to the link with civic society, creating special venues through which NGOs can voice their concerns.[167] The Open Government Global Partnership, initiated by

---

[164] *See* Pierre-Hugues Verdier, *Transnational Regulatory Networks and Their Limits*, 34 YALE J. INT'L L. 113 (2009); Eleanor M. Fox, *Linked-In: Antitrust and the Virtues of a Virtual Network*, 43 INT'L LAW. 151 (2009).

[165] *See* Oren Perez, *E-Democracy, Transnational Organizations, and the Challenge of New Techno-Intermediation*, in CONNECTING DEMOCRACY: ONLINE CONSULTATION AND THE FLOW OF POLITICAL COMMUNICATION (Stephen Coleman & Peter M. Shane eds., 2011).

[166] *See* GRI's *Governance Bodies*, GLOBAL REPORTING INITIATIVE, https://www.globalreporting .org/network/network-structure/Pages/default.aspx (last visited Jan. 21, 2015); *About SAI*, SOC. ACCOUNTABILITY INT'L, http://www.sa-intl.org/index.cfm?fuseaction=Page.ViewPage& pageId=490 (last visited Apr. 21, 2013); *AA1000 Standards Governance*, ACCOUNTABILITY, http:// www.accountability.org/standards/aa1000-governance/index.html (last visited Jan. 21, 2015).

[167] *See* NGOs and the WTO, WORLD TRADE ORGANIZATION, http://www.wto.org/english/forums_ e/ngo_e/ngo_e.htm (last visited Apr. 21, 2013); *The World Bank and Civil Society*, WORLD BANK, http://web.worldbank.org/WBSITE/EXTERNAL/TOPICS/CSO/0,,pagePK:220469~the SitePK:228717,00.html (last visited June 15, 2013).

168   *Daphne Barak-Erez and Oren Perez*

President Obama in 2011, reflects a vision that links local and global processes of transparency and participation.[168]

The recent tragic accidents in textile factories in Pakistan and Bangladesh illustrate the potential of the foregoing democratic vision. These cases have raised concerns regarding the function and accountability of Social Accountability International (SAI), the global organization that was responsible for the certification of the Pakistani factory (through SAAS and RINA).[169] SAI was not subject to regulatory oversight by either the Pakistani government or any international organization. On September 12, 2012, a fire swept through Ali Enterprises textile factory in Karachi, trapping hundreds of workers in a building with barred windows and just one open exit, causing the deaths of nearly 300 workers.[170] On August 20, 2012, merely a month before the accident, this plant was granted the prestigious Social Accountability 8000 (SA8000) certification, issued by SAI – a prominent international nongovernmental organization.[171]

---

[168] *See About*, Open Gov't P'ship, http://www.opengovpartnership.org/about (last visited June 15, 2013).

[169] Social Accountability Accreditation Services (SAAS) is an independent nonprofit accreditation agency that SAI has empowered to oversee the certification of SA8000. One of the SAAS'21 accredited certification bodies is RINA, the global certification body based in Genova, Italy, that issued the Karachi factory's certificate. As part of the certification process, RINA used a subcontractor, RI&CA, to coordinate and deliver its auditing services. *Q&A: Ali Enterprises Fire in Karachi, Pakistan*, Soc. Accountability Int'l, http://www.sa-intl.org/index.cfm?fuseaction=Page.ViewPage&PageID=1342#.VKh6onuqE5g (updated Dec. 7, 2012).

[170] Just nine months after this event, another disaster hit the garment industry in the east, this time in Bangladesh. A building hosting a garment factory collapsed leaving more than 500 dead. This disaster was again linked to poor safety standards and raised general concerns about the working conditions of more than 3.6 million Bangladeshis working in the garment industry and the role that Western retailers should play in improving those conditions. *See* Amy Kazmin, *Disaster Raises Pressures for Labor Reform*, Wash. Post, May 4, 2013, at A7. These recurring disasters have led to the development of several new transnational regulatory schemes. On July 8, 2013, the EU launched a joint initiative for improving conditions for workers in Bangladeshi garment factories entitled. Press Release, European Commission, EU Trade Commissioner De Gucht Launches Global Sustainability Compact in Response to Bangladesh Tragedy (July 8, 2013), *available at* http://trade.ec.europa.eu/doclib/press/index.cfm?id=935. The textile industry has also initiated schemes seeking to improve conditions at Bangladeshi factories. Across the Atlantic, a group of seventeen North American retailers and clothing makers agreed to a five-year safety pact that calls for inspecting all factories that supply their garments within a year. Anne D'innocenzio, *U.S. Companies Detail Bangladesh Safety Pact*, Seattle Times, July 10, 2013, http://seattletimes.com/html/businesstechnology/2021364945-apbcusbangladeshsafetyaccordusretailers.html; *Canadian, U.S. Retailers Sign Bangladesh Factory-Safety Pact*, CBC News, July 10, 2013, http://www.cbc.ca/news/world/story/2013/07/10/bangalesh-factories.html. European retailers, including Swedish retailer H&M and Italian clothing company Benetton, signed a similar safety pact earlier that month. *See 70 Retailers Agree to New Bangladesh Factory Safety Pact*, CBC News, July 8, 2013, http://www.cbc.ca/news/business/story/2013/07/08/business-bangladesh-factory.html.

[171] Declan Walsh & Steven Greenhouse, *Inspectors Certified Pakistani Factory as Safe Before Disaster*, N.Y. Times, Sept. 19, 2012, http://www.nytimes.com/2012/09/20/world/asia/

The SAI, as a reaction to this tragic event (and several others) released an announcement calling "for broad international cooperation and rapid reforms in Pakistani and Bangladeshi enforcement of their labor laws."[172]

One of the questions raised by this accident – probably one of the worst industrial disasters in history – is whether the Pakistani administration relied on SAI to regulate the health and safety aspects of the Ali Enterprises operations, and thus transferred to SAI (de facto) its administrative duties. Such reliance, to the extent that it has in fact occurred, represents a departure from the classic paradigm of administrative law that places these regulatory responsibilities solely within the administrative agencies of the state.

The SAI has initiated a process of self-reflection, involving all the organizations involved in the certification process. This process of internal review resulted in several concrete actions, including the offering of more advanced fire safety courses for auditors and workplaces and an increase in the number of spot checks and unannounced certification audits by SAAS.[173] In Pakistan, these measures included the suspension of new SA8000 certificates until SAAS can conclude its analysis and make the necessary changes to its accreditation and certification procedures, a decision not to allow RINA to issue SA8000 certificates in Pakistan, and a decision to require all certification bodies undertaking SA8000 certifications in Pakistan to conduct unannounced fire safety inspections and report back to SAAS.[174] This process of self-reflection, which took place despite the absence of formal regulatory requirements, stemmed from SAI's character as a multistakeholder organization whose legitimacy depends on the continuous support of its varied stakeholders.[175] The findings of this investigation have also played a key role in the revision process of SA8000, as part of a completely revised "Health & Safety" section, which will

---

pakistan-factory-passed-inspection-before-fire.html?pagewanted=all&_r=0; *Q&A: Ali Enterprises Fire in Karachi, Pakistan by SAI*, Soc. Accountability Int'l, http://www.sa-intl.org/_data/n_0001/resources/live/Q&A_AliEnterprises_8Dec2012.pdf (updated Dec. 7, 2012).

[172] *Bangladesh & Pakistan: Tragic Fires Underscore Urgent Safety Needs*, Soc. Accountability Int'l, Dec. 2012, http://www.sa-intl.org/index.cfm?fuseaction=Page.ViewPage&PageID=1391#.UshW57Qiqsh.

[173] SAI's multistakeholder Advisory Board (which includes trade unions, business, and NGOs) convened for three days from October 9–11, 2012, to focus on the Ali Enterprises fire and its implications for the SA8000 system. *Fire Safety a Key Focus in SA8000 Revision*, Soc. Accountability Int'l, Mar. 11, 2013, http://www.sa-intl.org/index.cfm?fuseaction=Page.ViewPage&PageID=1435&utm_source=March+2013+Newsletter+-+short+version+&utm_campaign=March+2013+newsletter&utm_medium=archive#.UXSZHKVhyZM.

[174] *Q&A: Ali Enterprises Fire in Karachi, Pakistan*, Soc. Accountability Int'l, http://www.sa-intl.org/index.cfm?fuseaction=Page.ViewPage&PageID=1342#.UxwuJoXJDng (updated Dec. 7, 2012); RINA Services, http://www.rina.org/_files/pdf/Rina_Details/QandA_en.pdf.

[175] *See* Soc. Accountability Int'l, http://www.sa-intl.org/index.cfm?fuseaction=Page.ViewPage&pageId=490.

include new provisions on fire safety.[176] The revised standard was released on spring 2014.[177]

At the same time, it is important to highlight the hurdles expected to face any attempt to develop transnational democratic processes. First, existing transnational regulatory networks tend to be insulated from civic society.[178] These networks currently constitute a closed technobureaucratic system, consisting of experts and bureaucrats who may resist attempts to incorporate civic voices into their working routines. Second, it is important to note the mixed record of global institutions with participatory mechanisms. Some organizations, especially in the technical domain, limit their decision-making processes to experts with little opportunities for civic input. Once again, this technocratic tendency for closure will have to be resisted.[179]

Finally, it is important to clarify the limitations of this vision of administrative-based transnational democratization, which is not expected to meet the ideal of an all-inclusive global democratic framework of the type advocated by David Held.[180] Our vision is more limited in its ambitions and scope. It is based on an experimental vision of direct deliberation, which recognizes the highly fragmented structure of the globalized administrative law. It is likely to produce fragmented regulatory "publics," centered on particular regulatory subject matters. Nonetheless, we think that this vision offers a more realistic response to the need to subject global processes of rulemaking to civic scrutiny than the model of global constitutionalism. Our thesis is based on a vision of fragmented democratization that seeks to expand the reflexivity of this new body of law by subjecting it to diverse processes of critique, taking place simultaneously at multiple venues. This multiplicity, through its defiance of domination and exclusion, is likely to generate creative forms of critique. The appeal of the nexus "creative administrative law" does not depend, therefore, on particular ideological premises, or on the promise of intersubjective rationality, but on the capacity of creative institutions to challenge habitual social structures. In

---

[176] *Fire Safety a Key Focus in SA8000 Revision, available at* http://www.sa-intl.org/index.cfm?fuseaction=Page.ViewPage&PageID=1435#.UshqCLQiqsg.

[177] *See* SA8000: 2014, http://www.sa-intl.org/_data/n_0001/resources/live/SA8000%202014%20Drafters%20Notes2.pdf. Beginning January 1, 2016, certification will only be available to SA8000: 2014. The SAI conducted an extensive public consultation process on the revised standard. *See* Expert Consultation Report: SA8000:2014 Revision (June 2013), http://www.sa-intl.org/_data/n_0001/resources/pending/Discussion%20and%20Analysis%20Paper_August%2017%202013.pdf.

[178] Verdier, *supra* note 164, at 118.

[179] *See* Perez, *supra* note 163.

[180] *See* Held, *supra* note 14, at 542–43.

a world that cherishes diversity of thought and forms of life, this competency could play an important role.[181]

CONCLUSION

Global norms are increasingly reshaping the contours and dynamic of domestic administrative law. We have shown that external influence originating in the global sphere manifests itself in the specific contents of the regulation, in the formulation of global general standards of due process, and in the transference of enforcement powers to global bodies. In this context, we have distinguished between due process rules that focus on the fairness of the administrative process, and perfecting procedures such as rules pertaining to risk assessment. The influence of this emerging body of law is not limited to the economic domain. It also extends to the regulation in other areas such as the regulation of environmental and health risks. The norms of universal administrative law are the product of a highly pluralist transnational regime. This pluralistic framework influences the paths through which these administrative norms penetrate the domestic realm – either by administrative decisions or through voluntary decisions of private corporations.

In light of this complex reality, our analysis has drawn attention to the challenges that administrative law faces at the present juncture: the meta-theoretical challenge associated with hidden ideological presuppositions of the new universal administrative law; the challenge of the fragmentation of accountability regimes; and the democratic challenge. We cannot offer easy solutions to these challenges. However, identifying and mapping them is crucial for any long-term thinking about the administrative state in the twenty-first century.

---

[181] *See* Oren Perez, *Normative Creativity and Global Legal Pluralism: Reflections on the Democratic Critique of Transnational Law*, 10 IND. J. GLOBAL LEGAL STUD. 25 (2003).

7

International Precedent and the Practice of
International Law

*Harlan Grant Cohen**

Precedent presents something of a puzzle for international law. By many accounts, precedent is everywhere. Reports from fields as diverse as international investment arbitration,[1] international criminal law,[2] international human rights,[3] and international trade[4] testify to precedent's apparent authority.

* Associate Professor of Law, University of Georgia School of Law. Thank you to Dené Terry for her invaluable research assistance. A shorter version of some of these ideas was published in Harlan Grant Cohen, *Lawyers and Precedent*, 46 VAND. J. TRANSNAT'L L. 1025 (2013).

[1] *See, e.g.*, Int'l Thunderbird Gaming Corp. v. United Mexican States, Final Award, ¶ 129 (Jan. 26, 2006), *reprinted in* 6 ASPER REV. INT'L BUS. & TRADE L. 419, 571 (2006) ("In international and international economic law – to which investment arbitration properly belongs – there may not be a formal 'stare decisis' rule as in common law countries, but precedent plays an important role. Tribunals and courts may disagree and are at full liberty to deviate from specific awards, but it is hard to maintain that they can and should not respect well-established jurisprudence."); Susan D. Franck, *The Legitimacy Crisis in Investment Treaty Arbitration: Privatizing Public International Law Through Inconsistent Decisions*, 73 FORDHAM L. REV. 1521, 1611–12 (2005) ("The fact is that investment awards are not technically precedential. . . . As a practical matter, however, private investors, governments, and arbitral tribunals rely on previous awards to interpret similar provisions in investment treaties.").

[2] *See, e.g.*, Alexander K.A. Greenawalt, *The Pluralism of International Criminal Law*, 86 IND. L.J. 1063, 1073–78 (2011); William W. Burke-White, *Regionalization of International Criminal Law Enforcement: A Preliminary Exploration*, 38 TEX. INT'L L.J. 729, 757–58 (2003).

[3] *See, e.g.*, Christina Binder, *The Prohibition of Amnesties by the Inter-American Court of Human Rights*, 12 GERMAN L.J. 1203, 1204 (2011) (evaluating the Inter-American Court's dynamic interpretation of rights that "at times, hardly finds a legal basis in the Convention")

[4] *See, e.g.*, Zhu Lanye, *The Effects of the WTO Dispute Settlement Panel and Appellate Body Reports: Is the Dispute Settlement Body Resolving Disputes Only or Making Precedent at the Same Time?* 17 TEMP. INT'L & COMP. L.J. 221, 230 (2003) ("If we regard precedents as decisions furnishing a basis for determining later cases involving similar facts or issues we can say without hesitation that large amounts of such precedents exist in the WTO dispute settlement system."); Raj Bhala, *The Myth about Stare Decisis and International Trade Law (Part One of a Trilogy)*, 14 AM. U. INT'L L. REV. 845, 850 (1999) ("In brief, there is a body of international common law of trade emerging as a result of adjudication by the WTO's Appellate Body. We have yet to recognize, much less account for, this reality in our doctrinal thinking and discussions.").

Across international law, practitioners invoke it and tribunals apply it. Nor is the use of precedent a matter confined simply to specific regimes or arguments before specific bodies. The precedents from one regional body are argued to others;[5] precedents from human-rights courts are argued to investment tribunals;[6] precedents from ad hoc criminal tribunals are applied to domestic civil judgments.[7]

These reports, however, widespread as they may be, butt up against an uncomfortable doctrinal reality: International law today, just like international law a century ago, denies international precedents any doctrinal force. Since at least the establishment of the Permanent Court of International Justice in 1922, judicial decisions have been relegated to the status of "subsidiary means for the determination of rules of law."[8] This understanding, carried into Article 38 of the Statute of the International Court of Justice[9] and reified by casebooks and treatises as part of international law's "doctrine of sources,"[10] has meant that as a matter of international law doctrine, judicial decisions construing international law are generally not in and of themselves law – decisions are not binding on future parties in future cases, even before the same tribunal.[11] Precedent, as a matter of doctrine, exerts no special force.

---

[5] *See, e.g.*, Laurence R. Helfer, *Overlegalizing Human Rights: International Relations Theory and the Commonwealth Caribbean Backlash Against Human Rights Regimes*, 102 COLUM. L. REV. 1832 (2002) (describing the migration of the ECHR *Soering* precedent to other bodies).

[6] *See generally* Andrea K. Bjorklund & Sophie Nappert, *Beyond Fragmentation, in* NEW DIRECTIONS IN INTERNATIONAL ECONOMIC LAW – IN MEMORIAM THOMAS WÄLDE 439 (2011) (discussing cases).

[7] U.S. courts have, for example, turned to the jurisprudence of the ICTY and ICTR to ascertain the standard for aiding and abetting liability under the Alien Tort Statute, 28 U.S.C. § 1350. *Compare* Sarei v. Rio Tinto, PLC, 671 F.3d 736 (9th Cir. 2011) *with* Presbyterian Church of Sudan v. Talisman Energy, Inc., 582 F.3d 244 (2d Cir. 2009).

[8] Statute of the Permanent Court of International Justice art. 38(4), Dec. 16, 1920, 6 L.N.T.S. 380.

[9] Statute of the International Court of Justice art. 38(1)(d), June 26, 1945, 59 Stat. 1055, 1060 [hereinafter ICJ Statute].

[10] *See, e.g.*, LORI F. DAMROSCH ET AL., INTERNATIONAL LAW: CASES AND MATERIALS 56–57 (4th ed. 2001); MARK W. JANIS & JOHN E. NOYES, INTERNATIONAL LAW: CASES AND COMMENTARY 20–21 (2d ed. 2001) ("An ordinary starting point for international lawyers from most any part of the globe when thinking about the formal sources of international law is Article 38 of the International Court of Justice."); HENRY J. STEINER, DETLEV VAGTS & HAROLD KOH, TRANSNATIONAL LEGAL PROBLEMS: MATERIALS AND TEXT 232 (4th ed. 1994) (quoting the statute and commenting that "[t]his list has significance not only for tribunals but also for officials or scholars pursuing the inquiries described above").

[11] ICJ Statute, *supra* note 9, arts. 38(1)(d), 59 ("The decision of the Court has no binding force except between the parties and in respect of that particular case.").

In a sense, precedent is like the embarrassing family member who no one talks about but whose presence is impossible to ignore. How can we explain this "embarrassing" reality?

This chapter outlines the beginnings of an account of international precedent. The first part of the chapter surveys the existing literature on international precedent and argues that traditional accounts of precedent's force have focused too much on the role of states. Most existing accounts take either a positivist or rationalist approach to the emergence of precedent. They focus on either (1) the design of international agreements and institutions and the ex ante choices states make regarding the authority of decision-making bodies or (2) compliance decisions, when state actors choose ex post whether to follow a particular decision-making body's decision. Each of these accounts tells part of the story of precedent's authority, but even together, these accounts seem incapable of explaining the full pattern of precedent's use and the widespread invocation of precedent by international bodies and by advocates on all sides.

What's missing, this chapter argues, is an account of precedent's role in legal argumentation. In focusing on the moments when the law is either "made" or applied, these positivist and rationalist accounts fail to capture the ways in which law is practiced. Law doesn't simply provide rules to be followed. Perhaps distinctively, law also sets the norms or rules for discerning, interpreting, advocating, and debating, the contents of those rules. It provides a set of spoken and unspoken ground-rules that structure an ongoing claim and response over the applicable law. One party argues for one interpretation of the rules; another argues for a different one. The law frames which arguments are better or worse, which arguments will be convincing and which will fail.[12]

In this sense, law is a practice,[13] and understanding the role or authority of precedents requires understanding precedent's role within it. Doing so requires recentering our focus away from the states that make, follow, and break international law, toward the communities of legal practitioners who bandy over the rules on a regular basis and the norms of argumentation and legitimization around which they coalesce. Elsewhere, I have argued that thinking about international law as the product of specific communities of practice can help explain the philosophical, theoretical, and doctrinal differences developing

---

[12] *See* Robert M. Cover, *The Supreme Court, 1982 Term – Foreword: Nomos and Narrative*, 97 HARV. L. REV. 4, 7 (1983) ("The normative universe is held together by the force of interpretative commitments – some small and private, others immense and public. These commitments – of officials and others – do determine what law means and what law shall be.").

[13] *Cf.* JUTTA BRUNNEÉ & STEPHEN J. TOOPE, LEGITIMACY AND LEGALITY IN INTERNATIONAL LAW: AN INTERACTIONAL ACCOUNT 25–26 (2010).

between different areas of international law,[14] like international human rights law,[15] international criminal law,[16] and international investment arbitration.[17] It also helps break free from the state-centered model of international lawmaking. In each of these areas, rules and norms of interpretation have developed that are hard to square with the state-centered model of international law, rules that override state consent or privilege sources other than state practice. In other areas, like global administrative law, transnational law has emerged to govern private regimes like the International Organization for Standardization (ISO), with little or no state involvement.[18]

All these phenomena are better explained, I argue, as a function of specific communities of practice rather than of formal state decisions. As I explain in the second part of this chapter, the communities that practice around a particular area of law will differ from one another. Some areas of law, like international arbitration, may involve relatively small groups of repeat players who know each other well and share common backgrounds and training.[19] Others, like human rights law, will be much looser, involving a range of different actors – states, international advocates, grassroots organizers, expert academics – from a range of cultures who may have little in common other than their intermittent interaction over human rights claims. In some communities, like international humanitarian law or trade, states may be prominent, even dominant, players. In others, states may be just one group of actors or take a marginal role, for example, international accounting standards[20] or anti-doping law.[21] The different shapes of these communities, the different actors who practice within them, and the different training and assumptions they bring to bear on that practice, can help explain the different legal results that emerge.

Key here, focusing on communities of practice can also help unlock the mystery of international precedent. Precedent is hard to understand as an objective fact disconnected from any particular group of actors. A prior decision by a particular legal body is a fact, but how much weight it should be given

---

[14] *See generally* Harlan Grant Cohen, *Finding International Law, Part II: Our Fragmenting Legal Community*, 44 N.Y.U. J. INT'L L. & POL. 1049 (2012).

[15] *Id.* at 1070–78.

[16] *Id.* at 1078–84.

[17] *Id.*

[18] *Id.* at 1084–89.

[19] *See, e.g., generally* YVES DEZALAY & BRYANT G. GARTH, DEALING IN VIRTUE: INTERNATIONAL COMMERCIAL ARBITRATION AND THE CONSTRUCTION OF A TRANSNATIONAL LEGAL ORDER (1998) (describing that community of practitioners).

[20] *See, e.g.,* CHRIS BRUMMER, SOFT LAW AND THE GLOBAL FINANCIAL SYSTEM 80–84 (2012).

[21] *See, e.g.,* Benedict Kingsbury et al., *The Emergence of Global Administrative Law*, 68 L. & CONTEMP. PROBS. 15, 23 (2005).

in future debates over a particular rule is dependent on how it is perceived by the actors reading it. Precedent is what Friedrich Kratochwil[22] and John Ruggie have described as an "institutional fact."[23] Like a "hit" or a "strike" in baseball, it is a fact only within the particular rules of a particular institution or community.[24] Just as a student of baseball and a student of cricket will see two very different sets of facts in a group of people with bats and ball on a field, so too will actors biased toward the authority of courts or the binding nature of precedent perceive the value of a tribunal decision differently than actors biased toward state consent, state prerogative, and pragmatism. Different international law regimes may involve different mixes of actors – advocates, political leaders, diplomats, military personnel, scientists, economists, international lawyers, and domestic lawyers. Each of these different actors will bring their own professional norms and biases to the debate, and different mixes of actors will agree on different norms and operating assumptions.[25] Understanding the relative weight different decisions by different bodies seem to carry in different contexts requires understanding the communities of actors who might perceive them that way.

The third part of this chapter thus attempts to outline the beginnings of an account of international precedent oriented around communities of practice and practitioners. Because most discussions of international precedent have focused instead on states, a complete account is a massive theoretical and empirical undertaking – more a research agenda than a specific project. This chapter can only set out an initial, tentative framework for such an account. Such an account focuses on the intertwined questions of audience and authority. Why might a particular decision carry authority and with whom? Or in reverse, who makes up the audience for various international decisions and arguments and which decisions or arguments will resonate with them? The goal is to explain when and why certain types of decisions, taking certain forms, will carry varying weight with different international actors. A sociological account that maps the varied professional, expert, and political communities of actors who practice within each regime and across them, can go a long way toward explaining patterns of both borrowing and rejection, when and why certain principles will spread from one institution to another, but not others.

---

22 FRIEDRICH KRATOCHWIL, RULES, NORMS AND DECISIONS 22–28 (1989).

23 John Ruggie, *Epistemology, Ontology, and Regimes, in* CONSTRUCTING THE WORLD POLITY 90–91 (1998) (discussing FRIEDRICH KRATOCHWIL, RULES, NORMS AND DECISIONS 22–28 (1989)).

24 *See* Ruggie, *supra* note 23, at 91 (quoting John Rawls, *Two Concepts of Justice,* 64 PHIL. REV. 3, 25 (1955)).

25 *See, e.g., generally* David Luban, *Military Necessity and the Cultures of Military Law,* 26 LEIDEN J. INT'L L. 315, 318 (2013).

As an initial sketch of how such an account might work, The fourth part of this chapter continues on to consider one group of actors, namely transnational lawyers, and the role they might play in the stickiness of precedent. It suggests a series of both normative reasons and sociological reasons why transnational lawyers may be attracted to precedent even in the absence of its formal authority. From a normative standpoint, it seeks to understand the role precedent plays in legal argumentation and describes precedent's role as an application of rule of law norms of consistency and coherence. From a sociological standpoint, it describes the political and social capital lawyers derive from legal-analogical reasoning.

THE PUZZLING PULL OF PRECEDENT

One of international law's dirty little secrets is that precedent matters – a lot. Traditionally, states have jealously guarded their authority to interpret international law.[26] As such, they have generally denied the more general authority of judicial decisions,[27] at best remaining coy whether international courts should follow even their own prior decisions.[28] And yet, arguments from precedent are pervasive; the decisions of the International Court of Justice, the WTO Appellate Body and WTO panels, international criminal courts, human rights courts and committees, and international investment arbitral panels are regularly invoked as authority in arguments over international law's requirements.[29] Courts and tribunals have, in turn, rewarded these arguments, citing these international decisions regularly.[30]

---

[26] *See* Harlan Grant Cohen, *International Law's* Erie *Moment*, 34 MICH. J. INT'L L. 249, 272–80 (2013).

[27] ICJ Statute, *supra* note 9, arts. 38(1)(d), 59 ("The decision of the Court has no binding force except between the parties and in respect of that particular case.").

[28] The ICJ Statute specifically denies ICJ judgments' stare decisis effect. *Id.* art. 59. Other treaties setting up courts or tribunals may be silent on the effect of those decisions (*see* Optional Protocol to the International Covenant on Civil and Political Rights, opened for signature Dec. 16, 1966, 999 U.N.T.S. 302 (silent as to the precedential effect of the Human Rights Committee's views)), or may use language that can be read either way (*see* Understanding on Rules and Procedures Governing the Settlement of Disputes art. 3.2, Apr. 15, 1994, Marrakesh Agreement Establishing the World Trade Organization, Annex 2, 1869 U.N.T.S. 401 ("The dispute settlement system of the WTO is a central element in providing security and predictability to the multilateral trading system.")). The Rome Statute establishing the International Criminal Court is a notable exception. Rome Statute of the International Criminal Court, art. 21.2, July 17, 1998, 2187 U.N.T.S. 90 ("The Court may apply principles and rules of law as interpreted in its previous decisions.").

[29] *See supra* notes 1–6 and accompanying text.

[30] *See supra* notes 1–7 and accompanying text.

This would be remarkable if courts and tribunals simply cited their own precedent – international law doctrine requires no such result. In fact, it even seems to discourage it, relegating judicial decisions to a mere "subsidiary source."[31] But courts and tribunals go much farther (following the lead of international advocates), citing positively or negatively even the decisions of other unrelated courts and tribunals emanating from different areas of international law, with different mandates. To give but one example of the pervasiveness of this pattern, take the landmark *Tadic* case before the International Criminal Tribunal for the Former Yugoslavia (ICTY).[32] The first case heard by the ICTY, *Tadic* produced a range of important decisions on the jurisdiction of the court, the interpretation of its statute, and the scope of international criminal liability.[33] Those decisions have, of course, been widely cited in other decisions of the ICTY.[34] Not too surprisingly, these decisions have been cited by other international criminal tribunals.[35] The test for state attribution adopted by the ICTY in that case, "overall control,"[36] was famously distinguished by the ICJ.[37] And the decisions have been cited in dozens of U.S. federal court opinions.[38] More surprisingly perhaps, *Tadic* has been cited by

[31] *See* ICJ Statute art. 38(d).
[32] Prosecutor v. Duško Tadic, International Tribunal for the Former Yugoslavia, Case IT-94–1-A (1999), 38(6) I.L.M. 1518 (Nov. 1999).
[33] *See, e.g.*, Prosecutor v. Dusko Tadic a/k/a 'Dule' Decision on the Defense Motion for Interlocutory Appeal on Jurisdiction, ICTY Appeals Chamber, Oct. 2, 1995 (considering jurisdiction, role of customary international law, and scope of liability under the statute); Prosecutor v. Tadic, Case No. IT-94–1-A, Judgment in the Appeals Chamber, ¶¶ 115–145 (July 15, 1999) (establishing test for state attribution); Prosecutor v. Dusko Tadic, Case No. IT-94-I-A-R77, Judgment on Allegations of Contempt against Prior Counsel (Jan. 31, 2000) (considering court's authority to issue contempt orders).
[34] *See, e.g.*, Prosecutor v. Milan Milutinovic, Nikola Sainovic, Dragoljub Ojdanic, Case No. IT-99–37-AR72.2 Decision of 8 June 2004; Prosecutor v. Dragan Nikolic, Case No.: IT-94–2-S, Judgment of 18 Dec. 2003. The citations are in the hundreds, as a Westlaw search of the "International Criminal Tribunal for the Former Yugoslavia – Combined (INT-ICTY-ALL)" database attests.
[35] *See, e.g.*, Prosecutor v. Andre Rwamakuba, Decision on Appropriate Remedy, ICTR-98–44C-T (Jan. 31, 2007); Prosecutor v. Edouard Karemera, Mathieu Ngirumpatse, Joseph Nzirorera, Decision on Renewed Motion to Dismiss for Lack of Jurisdiction: United Nations Charter, Chapter VII Powers Rule 73 of the Rules of Procedure and Evidence, ICTR-98–44-R73 (5 Aug. 2005). A Westlaw search of the "International Criminal Tribunal for Rwanda (INT-ICTR)" database yields over one hundred citations.
[36] Prosecutor v. Duško Tadic, International Tribunal for the Former Yugoslavia, Case IT-94–1-A (1999), 38(6) I.L.M. 1518, 1541, § 117 & 1546, § 145 (Nov. 1999).
[37] Application of the Convention on the Prevention and Punishment of the Crime of Genocide (*Bosn. & Herz. v. Serb. & Montenegro*), Judgment, 2007 ICJ 43, 406 (Feb. 26).
[38] Westlaw Search, ALLCASES, "Tadic."

ICSID arbitration panels.[39] It has even made a recent appearance in the U.S. Department of Justice White Paper on the legality of targeted killings.[40] Even this widespread pattern of citation by entities with no obligation to do so must vastly understate the *Tadic* precedent's impact. A search yields ten times as many briefs mentioning the decisions to U.S. Courts as decisions eventually citing them.[41] Less formal invocations of the decisions by NGOs and other actors are impossible (or at least implausible) to count. And as will be discussed later, precedent's true impact will likely be felt in arguments rather than decisions. Even citations in arguments cannot capture all the situations in which actors predict that precedents will carry weight with others and adjust their actions accordingly.

Given this disparity between doctrine and reality, it is remarkable how unremarked upon the prevalence of precedent remains. Although there is a growing literature on international courts and their decisions, most of that literature focuses either on why states create courts or tribunals, or when states will comply with their decisions. Precedent though is a distinct question. The question isn't why a state will abide by a tribunal's decision in a particular case, but instead, why a state will reference that decision in a new one. Some answers to the former can though suggest accounts of the latter.

Whether they focus directly on precedent or not, most existing accounts look at courts/tribunals and their decisions from either a positivist or rationalist point of view. Centered on states, they tend to treat the weight to be given to prior decisions as a deliberate choice of the states that design or maintain a particular regime. The most traditional accounts treat precedent as a design feature.[42] States decide at the outset how much force precedent should have based on their relative interests in either predictability or control.[43] These accounts look to the constitutive agreements setting up particular courts, tribunals, and other

---

[39] *See* ICSID Case No. ARB/09/1 (Decision on Jurisdiction and Separate Opinion of Arbitrator Kamal Hossain) Teinver S.A., Transportes de Cercanías S.A., Autobuses Urbanos del Sur S.A. (Claimants) v. Argentine Republic (Respondent); ICSID Case No. ARB/05/15 (Award and Dissenting Opinion) Waguih Elie George Siag, Clorinda Vecchi (Claimants) v. Arab Republic of Egypt (Respondent); *see also* Ad Hoc Arbitration (Final Award and Dissenting Opinion) Republic of Italy (Claimant) v. Republic of Cuba (Respondent).

[40] U.S. Dep't of Justice, Lawfulness of Lethal Operation Directed Against a U.S. Citizen Who Is a Senior Operational Leader of Al-Qa'ida or an Associated Force at 4, *available at* http://msnbcmedia.msn.com/i/msnbc/sections/news/020413_DOJ_White_Paper.pdf.

[41] Westlaw Search, ALLBRIEFS, "Tadic."

[42] *See, e.g.*, Bhala, *supra* note 4, at 863–68; Anthea Roberts, *Power and Persuasion in Investment Treaty Interpretation: The Dual Role of States*, 104 Am. J. Int'l L. 179, 188 (2010) (describing orthodox position).

[43] *See* Roberts, *supra* note 42, at 188.

interpretive bodies, and ask how much authority they explicitly or implicitly delegate to these bodies and their decisions.[44] While accounts based on explicit delegation look to a body's mandate, accounts based on implicit delegation look to functional considerations like the open-endedness of the treaty's language or whether the treaty seems to create third-party rights holders.[45] Given that most international legal regimes explicitly deny precedent force,[46] the former approach has a hard time explaining the reality of how we argue. The latter approach does a better job suggesting that some regimes might be designed with precedent in mind, but relies more on ex ante normative conclusions about precedent's desirability for a particular regime than on empirical reality.[47] Not surprisingly, its suggestions are highly contested.

Other rationalist approaches suggest that precedent might emerge simply because it is useful.[48] In some contexts states may disagree over a particular rule, each preferring a particular interpretation over others. Nonetheless, they may prefer a coordination point over continued disagreement.[49] To the extent third-party decision making can provide a mutually acceptable rule (i.e., one that provides sufficient benefits to each party), continuing to hew to that rule may be desirable.[50] This explanation treats precedent as epiphenomenal. A precedent's force derives solely from the desirability of the rule reflected in it. Neither its status as the opinion of some body nor its internal reasoning have any independent effect. Although such an account may explain the stickiness of some international precedents, these types of accounts have a hard time explaining precedent in non-coordination games like human rights, or why arguments from precedent would have any force when the underlying decision goes against state interests.[51]

---

[44] *See id.*

[45] *See id.* (discussing this difference in the investment tribunal context); Meredith Crowley & Robert Howse, *US–Stainless Steel (Mexico)*, 9 WORLD TRADE REV. 117 (2010) (describing textual and functional perspectives on stare decisis at the WTO).

[46] *See, e.g.*, Bhala, *supra* note 4, at 863–68; Roberts, *supra* note 42.

[47] For example, functionalist accounts often suggest that because human rights treaties are vague and designed to protect third parties, human rights bodies have implicit mandates to fill gaps. *See, e.g.*, Karen J. Alter, *Agents or Trustees? International Courts in Their Political Context*, 14 EUR. J. INT'L REL. 33, 38–39 (2008).

[48] *See, e.g., generally* Eric A. Posner & John C. Yoo, *Judicial Independence in International Tribunals*, 93 CAL. L. REV. 1 (2005).

[49] This account essentially posits a "battle of the sexes" game, in which coordination is a dominant strategy, providing obvious benefit over non-cooperation, but where there are multiple equilibria, each providing greater benefit to one party over others.

[50] *See* Posner & Yoo, *supra* note 48, at 18.

[51] *See, e.g., generally*, Laurence R. Helfer & Anne-Marie Slaughter, *Why States Create International Tribunals: A Response to Professors Posner and Yoo*, 93 CAL. L. REV. 899 (2005).

More sophisticated rationalist accounts treat precedent as soft law.[52] As these accounts explain, from an individual state's point of view, its legal obligations are defined by predictions of what others will consider lawful and unlawful, and precedents can be suggestive of that. States creating a regime can thus use a tribunal to create rules or adopt interpretations that they would not have been able to achieve by agreement. States reading the court's views will have to take into account the possibility that that decision will be treated as binding law by other states and adjust their calculus and actions accordingly. This account assumes that actors will treat court decisions as predictive of the obligations other states will hold them to.[53] What it doesn't explain is why.

Finally, still other accounts see the use of precedent as strategic. Arguing to a body from its own precedent may make it more favorably inclined to your position. This is true not only for advocates to courts or tribunals, but also for courts or tribunals seeking support of other courts, something empirical data regarding the European Court of Justice and European Court of Human Rights and national court precedent seems to bear out.[54] Such accounts bring us closer to understanding precedent's role as advocacy, but they too fail to capture why advocates regularly cite precedents from courts other than the ones they're trying to convince. Perhaps citing other bodies lends prestige,[55] but this only begs the question where such prestige would come from. Why would particular audiences view certain citations in decisions as carrying extra weight?

Each of these accounts seems to tell part of the story of precedent's emergence within international law, but even together they seem incapable of explaining the utter pervasiveness of precedent's attraction. One of the limitations of these accounts is that, with the exception of the last one, each focuses almost exclusively on states. The assumption is that states are both the principal designers of international regimes, capable of calibrating ex ante the authority particular interpretative bodies and their decisions will have, and the principal compliance agents, making the final decision ex post whether to follow what that body has said. Both of these assumptions are questionable: States may not always control a treaty's drafting and more importantly, other compliance agents, for example, national courts, may be increasingly key in

---

[52] *See generally* Andrew T. Guzman & Timothy L. Meyer, *International Common Law: The Soft Law of International Tribunals*, 9 CHI. J. INT'L L. 515 (2009).

[53] *See id.*

[54] *See, e.g.*, Laurence R. Helfer & Anne-Marie Slaughter, *Toward a Theory of Effective Transnational Adjudication*, 107 YALE L.J. 273 (1997).

[55] *See id.* at 325–26 (suggesting that the ECJ and ECHR enhance each other's prestige by citing each other's decisions).

the implementation of specific decisions.[56] But the broader problem is that these accounts, centered as they are on states, focus too much on law as a set of inputs and outputs. What is lost is the role law plays before, in between, and after those moments of ratification or compliance, the role law plays in constructing the possibilities for a regime, arguments over what that regime is meant to do, and how the products of that regime should be perceived. What is lost in the role of law as process, or really, as practice.

The last account does move away from this focus on states to focus more on courts. Why would courts, international or national, cite each other's decisions? This gets us much closer to an understanding of precedent's role within the practice of law and provides a number of powerful insights for constructing a fuller account of precedent that doesn't depend on explicit state decisions. Notably, however, this account still assumes that giving weight to precedent is an intentional, conscious decision, perhaps giving too little weight to the ways prior decisions might implicitly and automatically constrain legal argumentation. Much of the actual use of precedent in international law argumentation seems almost reflexive. This account only begins to suggest why. Moreover, this account, like some other rationalist ones, depends almost entirely on factors external to the decision being cited, for example, what court pronounced it or whether the rule adopted buttresses the citing body's own decision. The internal aspects of the decision, how well it is reasoned, how well the interpretation conforms to prior interpretations or the broader legal scheme, are given shorter shrift.[57]

In order to fully capture the influence of precedent, a different focus is required, one that looks at the actors who actually invoke or respond to precedents in their arguments. Why do precedents carry weight in the everyday practice of international law? Exploring that question requires a new focus of inquiry, a move from states to practitioners.

---

[56] *Cf.* Erik Voeten, *Does a Professional Judiciary Induce More Compliance?: Evidence from the European Court of Human Rights* *4–6 (Georgetown University – Edmund A. Walsh School of Foreign Service, Working Paper, last revised Mar. 29, 2012), *available at* http://papers.ssrn .com/sol3/papers.cfm?abstract_id=2029786 (suggesting that the role of national judges as compliance agents for ECHR decisions may explain empirical evidence that decisions by professional judges have a greater impact on compliance with the ECHR).

[57] Though it does mention that factors like strong reasoning, adherence, and coherence may be playing a role in the perceived legitimacy of specific decisions. *See* Helfer & Slaughter, *Effective Supranational Adjudication, supra* note 54, at 319–21. In fairness, Helfer and Slaughter were not examining the role of precedent per se, but instead the attributes of an effective supranational court. In all likelihood, had precedent been their focus, they likely would have ended up where this chapter suggests going.

COMMUNITIES OF PRACTICE

Existing accounts of international precedent focus almost entirely on two key moments: (1) design, when states decide how much authority to delegate to interpretive bodies, and (2) compliance, when states decide how much weight a certain decision or interpretation will have in their decision how to act. As previously discussed, focusing on these moments alone fails to capture law's distinctive nature as a "practice," a set of ongoing rules and processes for discussing and debating the meaning of existing rules and the possibilities for future ones. Between these design and compliance moments, a wide range of actors bandy over exactly what the rules that have been "made" mean. It is these debates and discussions that frame the decision before a particular interpretive body and the extent its eventual interpretation will conform to state expectations. It is also in these debates and discussions that the everyday use of precedent takes place. Understanding how precedent emerges and develops in international law thus requires a different focus, one on the range of actors, some who may represent states, many who may not, who argue with each other over these rules.

In a sense, the question of precedent requires us to re-center our focus, away from the states and courts who seek to control legal meaning, and toward what Robert Cover has described as the "jurisgenerative process" through which "communities do create law and do give meaning to law through their narratives and precepts."[58] Although this move may always be of value in capturing how law is actually practiced, both the general features of the international system and specific features of international precedent make it essential here.[59] Cover describes how in response to the law-creating or jurisgenerative forces of the broader community, courts must exercise a form of "jurispathy," essentially choosing one rule or interpretation over others.[60] By invoking their authority within the state (or "jurisdiction") and their ability to mobilize the state's monopoly on force, courts can kill off other meanings. International law though lacks the clear undisputed sites of jurispathy Cover described in domestic law.[61] Instead, international law exhibits multiple fora (both at

---

[58] Cover, *supra* note 12, at 40.

[59] Perhaps strangely, relatively few scholars have applied Cover's rich account to international law. Two important exceptions are Jeffrey L. Dunoff, *A New Approach to Regime Interaction*, *in* REGIME INTERACTION IN INTERNATIONAL LAW: FACING FRAGMENTATION 136 (Margaret A. Young ed., 2012), and Paul Schiff Berman, *A Pluralist Approach to International Law*, 32 YALE J. INT'L L. 301 (2007).

[60] Cover, *supra* note 12, at 40, 53.

[61] *See* Berman, *supra* note 59, at 328.

the international and domestic levels) with overlapping and/or conflicting jurisdiction all jockeying for the right to say what the law is, all fighting for jurispathic control. Moreover, usually denied stare decisis effect,[62] these fora must share authority with communities of actors who practice there. These fora must convince these actors to adopt their views and adapt their practices accordingly. In a sense, even with courts and tribunals, much of the authority to determine legal meaning remains with the community of practice rather than with a judicial or arbitral body.

It is thus to these communities and the range of actors acting within them that we must turn our gaze. A helpful conceptualization of this group of actors, emerging from constructivist international relations literature, is Emanuel Adler's "communities of practice."[63] As Adler explains, "[c]ommunities of practice 'consist of people who are informally as well as contextually bound by a shared interest in learning and applying a common practice.'"[64] Such a common practice, "in turn, [is] sustained by a *repertoire of communal resources*, such as routines, words, tools, ways of doing things, stories, symbols, and discourse."[65] Community members do not need to agree on everything – members may disagree sharply on substance and desired outcomes; instead, members need only accept a set of common ground-rules for negotiation and contestation. Communities of practice can come in various shapes and sizes; their boundaries "are determined by people's knowledge and identity and the discourse associated with a specific practice."[66] Some communities will be tightly organized, with small groups of practitioners who know each other well and engage with each other regularly on a defined set of issues.[67] Others will be much more diffuse, with members who never meet and are connected only by their shared practices – practices they apply to a broad range of activities.[68] Members may also have different relations to these communities. Some may

---

[62] *See supra* notes 8–11 and accompanying text.

[63] Emanuel Adler, Communitarian International Relations: The Epistemic Foundations of International Relations (2005). This discussion is adapted from Cohen, *supra* note 14, at 1065–67.

[64] Adler, *supra* note 63, at 15 (quoting William M. Snyder, *Communities of Practice: Combining Organizational Learning and Strategy Insights to Create a Bridge to the 21st Century*, Community Intelligence Labs (Aug. 1997), http://www.co-i-l.com/coil/knowledge-garden/cop/cols.shtml). Adler himself borrows the idea of communities of practice from the work of Jean Lave and Etienne Wenger on education and learning theory. Adler, *supra* note 63, at 15 n.116.

[65] *Id.* at 15. *See also* Cover, *supra* note 12, at 39–40 ("In the workings of a committed community with common symbols and discourse, common narratives and interpretation, the law undeniably grew.").

[66] Adler, *supra* note 63, at 24.

[67] Adler gives the example of U.N. weapons inspectors. *Id.* at 25.

[68] Here, Adler uses the collective security community as an example. *Id.* at 24–25.

be core members who actively work to develop its rules and norms, whereas others, further from the core of the community of practice, may simply adopt, accept, or apply the results of that work.[69]

Law and legal discourse seem like particularly good examples of Adler's "common practice," and legal communities like particularly good examples of communities of practice.[70] Law provides a medium for debate and agreement, requiring actors to engage with each other in very specific fora, using very specific language and procedures. The legal community, in turn, is constituted by its members' shared acceptance of certain ground rules and their shared expectations about good and bad arguments. As Adler observes, "[i]t is as members of communities of practice that people exercise one of the highest forms of power: determining the meanings and discourses that produce social practices."[71] The proposed structure of communities of practice, with concentric circles of core experts/practitioners and more peripheral adopters, helps conceptualize the relationship in a legal community between the expert lawyers who practice the law and the broader community of stakeholders whose influence and involvement are weaker, but whose broad acquiescence is still necessary.

Applied at the international level, such insights can begin to explain international actors, and in turn, the practice of international law. "The closer we get to the level of practice, in fact, the more we can take the international system as a collection of communities of practice; for example communities

---

[69] "Communities of practice may be viewed as being composed of three concentric circles." *Id.* at 24. As Adler explains:

> Practices are brought into existence in the first or inner circle. For example, a look at cooperative security and the role of the Conference on Security and Cooperation in Europe (CSCE) in the evolution of this practice shows that the Helsinki Final Act and subsequent normative injunctions and practices, such as CBMs, were developed in the inner circle of CSCE practitioners. In an intermediate circle we find people, who, due to expertise or normative commitment, help diffuse the practice. This would include CSCE experts, the Helsinki Human Rights groups, and European political leaders, who assimilated cooperative practices, diffused them more widely, and brought them to their respective domestic systems. The outer circle is made up of those experts, practitioners, and activists who adopt and help implement such practices beyond their original functional or geographic boundaries. In our case, that includes people from the North Atlantic Treaty Organization (NATO), the Association of Southeast Asian Nations (ASEAN), and the Euro-Mediterranean Partnership (EMP) or Barcelona Process.

> *Id.* at 24–25.

[70] *Cf.* Jutta Brunnée & Stephen J. Toope, Legitimacy and Legality in International Law: An Interactional Account 13–16, 28 (2010).

[71] Adler, *supra* note 63, at 25; *cf.* Kenneth Anderson, *The Rise of International Criminal Law: Intended and Unintended Consequences*, 20 Eur. J. Int'l L. 331, 349 (2009) (discussing "communities of interpretation and authority").

of diplomats, of traders, of environmentalists, and of human-rights activists."[72] Different areas of international law – international human rights law, international humanitarian law, international investment law, international criminal law – might each be conceptualized as a community of practice, in which a diverse, but specific group of actors engage with each other over the rules of that field,[73] developing amongst themselves norms of proper argumentation and authority.[74] Elsewhere, I have argued that this conceptualization can help explain some of the doctrinal, methodological, and philosophical differences emerging between these areas of law.[75] Each involves different mixes of actors, with different assumptions and training – caricatured, international humanitarian law may be dominated by military professionals, international criminal law by domestic criminal lawyers, international arbitration by the elite litigation bar[76] – and we should not be surprised when these different groups coalesce around different norms of argumentation.[77]

PRECEDENT AS PRACTICE

This conceptualization can help to unlock the mystery of international precedent. It is important here to think more clearly about what precedents are and what precedents do. Precedent might best be understood as the burden prior decisions about a particular rule put on future arguments about the content or meaning of the rule.[78] In its weakest form, precedent simply supplies an argument that one must respond to; one cannot make an argument about the rule's meaning without some reference to why the prior decision is right, wrong, or distinguishable.[79] In its strongest form, precedent creates a strong

---

[72] ADLER, *supra* note 63, at 15.

[73] This conceptualization of areas of international law as communities of practice echoes Pierre Bourdieu's conceptualization of law as a "field." Pierre Bourdieu, *The Force of Law: Toward a Sociology of the Juridical Field*, 38 HASTINGS L. J. 805 (1987). *See also generally* DEZALAY & GARTH, DEALING IN VIRTUE, *supra* note 19 (applying Bourdieu's insights and describing the "field" of international commercial arbitration). *See also infra*, "Precedent as Practice," applying the insights of Bourdieu's sociological school to help explain the attraction of lawyers to precedent.

[74] Dunoff draws similar insights from the work of Robert Cover. *See* Dunoff, *supra* note 59, at 150–56.

[75] *See generally* Cohen, *Finding International Law, Part II*, supra note 14.

[76] *See* DEZALAY & GARTH, DEALING IN VIRTUE, *supra* note 19.

[77] *See* Cover, *supra* note 12, at 42 (recognizing "that different interpretative communities will almost certainly exist and will generate distinctive responses to any normative problem of substantial complexity.").

[78] *See* Marc Jacob, *Precedents: Lawmaking Through International Adjudication*, 12 GERMAN L.J. 1005, 1019 (2011).

[79] *Id.* at 1019 (suggesting that "deliberately ignoring relevant prior decisions is so arbitrary and artificial a suggestion as to verge on farce").

presumption that the prior interpretation of the rule is in fact the rule.[80] The question we need to answer is not why actors follow or don't follow precedent, but instead why it places these burdens on arguments about the rule.

A particular interpretation of a legal rule does not carry any weight or place such a burden in-and-of-itself. The weight it carries, as previously described, is a contingent or "institutional" fact.[81] Whether a precedent is binding, or weighty, or irrelevant is completely contingent on the rules and norms of a particular group. Some of those norms will be found in positive law sources, for example, an interpretive body's constitutive treaty, but others will be part of the implicit operating code of a particular community of practice. How much weight a precedent should be given must be in some sense a function of how much weight a particular community of actors will expect that it be given.

Studying the diverse range of actors that make up different areas of international practice can help decipher that area's operating code and precedent's role within it. Such a focus might help explain why the decisions of the ICJ or European Court of Human Rights or the Human Rights Committee or national constitutional courts carry certain weight within the field of human rights but different weight in international humanitarian law. On the flipside, it might help explain why actual state practices in wartime carry more precedential weight in international humanitarian law than within human rights.[82]

An account of international precedent focused on the communities of practice in which it is used would thus start by trying to identify (1) the range of particular audiences for a particular decision and (2) the range of reasons that a particular decision might carry weight. Audiences might be identified by their training and background – for example, lawyers, activists, diplomats, military professionals, economists, scientists, etc. – or they might be

---

[80] While undoubtedly, any focus on precedent (rightly) opens this chapter to accusation of an Anglo-American bias, this definition should make clear that this understanding of precedent is broader and more generalizable than a common law conceptualization of precedent as binding or even as itself a source of law. *Cf.* James Parker Hall, *The Force of Precedents in International Law*, 26 INT'L J. ETHICS 149, 152 (1916) ("On the continent of Europe no such effect is theoretically attributed to judicial decisions, but in recent years the greatly increasing citation of former decisions by the courts with a visible reluctance to depart from them has made the difference in practice between the Continental and the Anglo-American systems one of degree only. Similarly, judicial precedents in international law have great weight as authorities, especially where rendered by nationally impartial tribunals composed of recognized experts in the subject.").

[81] *See* Ruggie, *supra* note 23.

[82] For an example of a disagreement of this sort, over how much relative weight ICJ judgments or state practice should get in establishing the proper interpretation of a rule, see the discussion of self-defense against non-state actors and the "unwilling or unable standard" in Part II.B.3 of Cohen, *International Law's* Erie *Moment*, *supra* note 26.

identified by their institutional role in developing, advocating, interpreting, or complying with international law rules – political leaders, state department lawyers, military leaders, domestic judges, commercial litigators, domestic defense attorneys, academics, NGO activists. Reasons for a decision's weight or "authority" would include reasons both (1) external and (2) internal to the particular decision. External reasons might include the perceived mandate of the body (has the body been given the authority in its constitutive agreements to definitively interpret a treaty?[83]); the identity of the interpreters (are they professional judges, political actors, or experts in a particular field;[84] are they dependent arbitrators or independent judges?[85]); or the usefulness of the rule embodied in the decision (does it solve a coordination problem, increase predictability or monitoring, or make compliance less costly?). Internal reasons might look to the power of the interpretation's reasoning and its relationship to both prior interpretations and the broader rules of the regime. The overall goal would be a matrix that could line up various sources of authority with specific audiences. Combined with a sociological account of professional, expert, and political communities of actors who practice within each regime and across them, such a matrix should go a long way toward explaining when and why certain precedents will carry weight and with whom.

Developing this account is a massive project, more a research agenda than a chapter. Peeling off and studying one potential audience group, lawyers, can demonstrate some of the potential of the broader endeavor.

LAWYERS AND PRECEDENT

Initial Sketch

As previously discussed, precedent's force is in many ways a function of how it is invoked or used in legal argumentation. Lawyers play a key role in such arguments (though as discussed later, the amount may differ depending on the regime), and it thus makes sense to look at how as a group, lawyers might contribute to precedent's weight. There are both (1) normative and

---

[83] For example, is it more like the WTO Dispute Settlement Body or more like the Human Rights Committee?

[84] *See* Voeten, *supra* note 56.

[85] *See* Posner & Yoo, *supra* note 48 (suggesting circumstances in which dependent arbitrators are more effective); Helfer & Slaughter, *Why States Create International Tribunals, supra* note 51 (suggesting circumstances in which independent judges are more effective).

(2) sociological reasons to think that lawyers may be particularly attracted to arguments based on precedent.

From a normative standpoint, lawyers may be attracted to precedent because of precedent's relationship to rule of law principles in which they have been trained. There is a common intuition, reflected in many theories of law, which is that one of the core principles or qualities of law is that it treats like situations alike. Lon Fuller describes consistency as part of the internal morality of law,[86] Ronald Dworkin's law as integrity denies the legitimacy of checkerboard laws that treat like cases differently,[87] and Tom Franck describes coherence and adherence as a key factors in the perceived legitimacy of laws.[88] From this standpoint, precedent's pull can be seen as a direct articulation of rule of law norms. If like cases must be treated alike, future decisions must at least make reference to prior ones.[89] To ignore a prior decision entirely might violate basic tenets of legal professional ethics.[90]

Some international tribunals have come close to saying something like this. In explicating the force of precedent within the World Trade Organization (WTO), the WTO Appellate Body explained:

> It is well settled that Appellate Body reports are not binding. . . . This, however, does not mean that subsequent panels are free to disregard the legal interpretations and the ratio decidendi contained in previous Appellate Body reports that have been adopted by the DSB. . . . Ensuring "security and predictability" in the dispute settlement system, as contemplated in Article 3.2 of the DSU, implies that, absent cogent reasons, an adjudicatory body will resolve the same legal question in the same way in a subsequent case.[91]

The connection to rule-of-law principles gives lawyers strong normative reasons to give prior precedents at least some weight. This is true even if we remain agnostic whether these principles are, in Fuller's terms, part of an internal morality of the law.[92] Nor must we think that lawyers are particularly ethical and pulled toward precedent because they have internalized rule

---

[86] Lon L. Fuller, The Morality of Law 41 (1964).

[87] Ronald Dworkin, Law's Empire 176–224 (1986).

[88] Thomas M. Franck, *Legitimacy in the International System*, 82 Am. J. Int'l L. 705 (1988).

[89] *See* Helfer & Slaughter, *Effective Supranational Adjudication*, *supra* note 54, at 319–20 ("In a social or legal culture that venerates tradition for its own sake, consistency with earlier decisions provides an autonomous bulwark of legitimacy.").

[90] *See* Jacob, *supra* note 78, at 1019 (suggesting that "deliberately ignoring relevant prior decisions is so arbitrary and artificial a suggestion as to verge on farce").

[91] Appellate Body Report, *United States – Final Anti-Dumping Measures on Stainless Steel from Mexico*, ¶¶ 158, 159–162, and n.309 (WT/DS344/AB/R 2008) (Apr. 30, 2008) (*adopted* May 20, 2008).

[92] *See generally* Fuller, *supra* note 86.

of law norms. These rule-of-law principles have been deeply embedded into the mythology of law, are reinforced in the training of lawyers, and are codified in both implicit and explicit codes of professional ethics. Lawyers may hew toward precedent simply as a matter of self-interest, a fear of professional consequences. Internalized professional ethics and fear of professional consequences are not mutually exclusive explanations; on the contrary, we should expect them to reinforce one another.

Sociological explanations reinforce these normative ones. Lawyers as a professional group have specific sources of political and social capital that they can use to maintain their importance and relevance in relation to other societal actors.[93] Among these sources of social and political capital is lawyers' purported expertise in interpreting and applying certain legal sources. This expertise includes, among other things, stylized forms of analogical reasoning. Lawyers, seeking to maximize their own power and authority vis-à-vis other international actors, will want to emphasize the value of precedents and their unique ability to understand them.

In other words, lawyers at the U.S. State Department or Defense Department may argue that precedents need to be followed (1) because they believe that rule of law requires it, (2) because they fear formal or informal professional or group sanction (i.e., shunning) if they fail to adhere to it, or (3) because arguing for precedent reinforces their authority within decision-making circles.[94] We do not need to choose between these reasons; they reinforce one another.

These normative and sociological explanations suggest that at least some decisions will carry a certain amount of weight among lawyers. Although they are too abstract to suggest exactly which ones, they may hint at some of the factors that might give some precedents greater pull than others.

Precedents may matter to traditional (nonlawyer) state actors but in specific ways. For traditional state actors, precedent places a burden on action to the extent it predicts how other states will react in the future. It is a prediction about state actions rather than about court or expert reasoning.[95] A coherent system of law is not nearly as important as a coherent account of state actions or preferences. This means, in turn, that the precedents that have authority that carry weight will be the ones that can best channel and articulate state preferences.[96]

---

[93] *See* DEZALAY & GARTH, *supra* note 19.

[94] *Cf.* Rebecca Ingber, *Interpretation Catalysts and Executive Branch Legal Decisionmaking*, 38 YALE. J. INT'L L. 360 (2013).

[95] *See generally* Guzman & Meyer, *supra* note 52; Posner & Yoo, *supra* note 48.

[96] This arguably tracks current debates over the relative weight that should be given to state practice vs. reasoned elaboration. *See* Cohen, *International Law's* Erie *Moment, supra* note 26, at 280–91.

An account of precedent as an outgrowth of legal professional reasoning suggests different sources of authority. If the weight of precedent results from a legal norm of consistent treatment, then those interpreters who can wield the strongest legal reasoning, who are most able to fit their decisions into a greater, more coherent picture of the law, will place more of a burden on future arguments than others whose decisions may be less reasoned or which may look like legal orphans, distinct from the broader legal corpus.

This is suggested by the literature of the effectiveness of judicial decision making. Larry Helfer and Anne-Marie Slaughter, for example, have suggested that some of the success of the ECHR and ECJ is attributable to their own tactical use and citation of precedent, both their own and that of other courts.[97] Even more suggestively, in a recent study of compliance with ECHR decisions, Erik Voeten found that decisions rendered by ECHR panels made up of majority professional judges were more likely to be complied with than decisions made by panels whose majority hailed from other areas, for example, diplomats or politicians.[98] Voeten suggests that this disparity might be explained by the relative importance of national judges as an audience for ECHR decisions and as compliance agents in enforcing those decisions at home. The hypothesis is that national judges are more likely to be swayed by decisions that read like reasoned court opinions and that professional judges on the ECHR are more likely to write decisions that read that way.[99] This is suggestive of the argument so far, that decisions that look more like judicial decisions, (1) better match legal professional norms and (2) better mobilize a legal audience's political and social capital, elevating legal sources and legal reasoning over other considerations.

This relationship between audience and authority is important because it suggests that judicialization and professionalization reinforce one another. The more courts, tribunals, and expert bodies we have in international law, the more legal specialists we will need to respond to them; the more lawyers in the practice of international law, the more force the decisions of courts, tribunals, and expert bodies will have.

Areas for Further Study

So far, lawyers have been considered as a single monolithic group, separate from other potential actors. In reality, lawyers wear many different hats,

---

[97] Helfer & Slaughter, *Effective Supranational Adjudication*, *supra* note 54, at 319–20.

[98] Erik Voeten, *Does a Professional Judiciary Induce More Compliance?: Evidence from the European Court of Human Rights*, *4–6 (Georgetown University – Edmund A. Walsh School of Foreign Service, Working Paper, last revised Mar. 29, 2012), *available at* http://papers.ssrn.com/sol3/papers.cfm?abstract_id=2029786.

[99] *Id.*

and legal professional norms will only be one demand on them. Their membership in other communities of actors may carry other obligations. International lawyers, for example, act on behalf of the state in foreign ministries, in defense ministries, and in the military. Moreover, different groups of lawyers – domestic criminal prosecutors and defense attorneys, commercial litigators, or JAGs – will have different operating norms. Building on the work of Pierre Bourdieu,[100] a series of scholars including Bryant Garth, Yves Dezalay, and Mikael Rask Madsen, have begun to study the sociology of specific groups of lawyers operating in different fields and in different countries, examining their training, their culture, and the social and political capital they wield in particular political system.[101] International law scholars have barely begun to plumb this work, let alone embark on it themselves. Lawyers are only one type of actor within communities of practice. The specific norms that lawyers as a group bring to the table must be studied as one piece in a larger mosaic.

Understanding the role of lawyers as lawyers can suggest a range of exciting studies. We might, for example, look at how lawyers interact with others actors in specific communities of practice to develop the norms of authority in each – human rights, criminal law, trade, investment. The different mix of actors, and the prevalence of lawyers as a group (including whether the principle legal actors are lawyer-statesmen like Elihu Root or broad cadres of professional lawyers) within each community, should make a difference, should change the mix of factors that will be considered in assessing the law.

We might also want to explore what happens when pre-existing communities overlap, bringing different community norms into dialogue or conflict. Some have argued that this is currently taking place in international investment arbitration where the professional biases of commercial arbitration lawyers, international lawyers, and domestic constitutional lawyers seem to be pulling in different directions.[102] A similar phenomenon may explain debates over rules regarding the use of force against non-state actors: Human rights lawyers with a bias toward judicial opinions and teleological interpretations are

---

[100] *See generally* Bourdieu, *supra* note 73.

[101] *See generally* DEZALAY & GARTH, *supra* note 19; *see also* Yves Dezalay & Mikael Rask Madsen, *The Force of Law and Lawyers: Pierre Bourdieu and the Reflexive Sociology of Law*, 8 ANN. REV. L. & SOC. SCI. 433 (2012); YVES DEZALAY & BRYANT G. GARTH, ASIAN LEGAL REVIVALS (2010); YVES DEZALAY & BRYANT G. GARTH, THE INTERNATIONALIZATION OF PALACE WARS: LAWYERS, ECONOMISTS, AND THE CONTEST TO TRANSFORM LATIN AMERICAN STATES (2002); YVES DEZALAY & BRYANT G. GARTH, GLOBAL PRESCRIPTIONS: THE PRODUCTION, EXPORTATION, AND IMPORTATION OF A NEW LEGAL ORTHODOXY (2002).

[102] *See generally* Anthea Roberts, *Clash of Paradigms: Actors and Analogies Shaping the Investment Treaty System*, 107 AM. J. INT'L LAW 45 (2013).

increasingly in conflict with traditional state and military actors who continue to look to state practice as a primary interpretive guide.[103]

Finally, we can explore how lawyers, as citizens of multiple communities of practice may act as conduits for normativity between them, bringing precedents from human rights to bear on investment arbitration or the law of war. In these pictures, the lawyer is key as both a state and non-state actor, maneuvering between the demands of citizenship in a professional community, communities of practice, and states.[104]

CONCLUSION

States traditionally chose not to imbue courts with the power to create precedents in an effort to retain greater control over the meaning and content of international law.[105] States may have wanted to create mechanisms for resolving individual disputes, but they generally did not mean to cede total authority over legal meaning.[106] Denying courts the power to create precedential interpretations guaranteed that states would be able to continue to debate and negotiate international law's meaning, even as they followed (or failed to follow) individual tribunal judgments. To again put it in Robert Cover's terms, states chose to deny international courts and tribunals the power of jurispathy.[107]

And yet, practices of citing precedent nonetheless emerge. This may be a conscious choice. States may not want total control of future interpretation; although flexibility may be desirable, so are predictability and stability. Recognizing the normative and sociological force of precedent, states may choose to leave the status of tribunal decisions ambiguous, denying their formal precedential effect while simultaneously arguing for their persuasive authority. But it may also be that, in Cover's terms, international law's communities of practice inhabit a nomos, a normative universe, and must constantly construct narratives that can integrate the legal materials within it, including

---

[103] *See* Cohen, *International Law's* Erie *Moment, supra* note 26, at 288–90

[104] As Oscar Schachter writes, "Individuals who move from one role to another are unlikely to remain uninfluenced by the ideas and considerations which impinge on them in their different capacities. The mingling of the scholarly and the official affects both categories, and often creates tension as individuals move from one role to another or perceive themselves as acting in the dual capacity of objective scientist and government advocate." Oscar Schachter, *The Invisible College of International Lawyers*, 72 Nw. U. L. Rev. 217, 217 (1977).

[105] Cohen, *International Law's* Erie *Moment, supra* note 26, at 272–80.

[106] *Id.*

[107] *See supra* notes 58–62 and accompanying text.

tribunal decisions.[108] Through interaction and argumentation the community must establish shared meanings. States (or rather, their proxies) have a say in developing this narrative, but ironically, in the absence of authoritative state controlled fora of jurispathy (i.e., state-controlled international courts with strong stare decisis authority), states cannot fully control it. Other actors too, lawyers included, must deal with the meaning and weight of tribunal interpretations. It is within the community of practice that the precedential weight of decisions must constantly be hashed out.

---

[108] *See* Cover, *supra* note 12, at 4–11.

PART III

Negotiating State Law and Religious/Indigenous Law

8

Religion, Family Law, and Competing Norms

Joel A. Nichols[1]

Today's headlines about marriage concern what *forms* of marriage should be recognized by the state – sometimes over the objection of religious groups and sometimes at their insistence: straight versus same sex marriage, contract versus covenant marriage, monogamous versus polygamous marriage, and more. But an emerging battle concerns not the forms of marriage, but the *forums* in which marriage and family cases are adjudicated. Specifically, the new battle centers on the place of faith-based family laws and religious tribunals in our democratic system of government – especially ancient and sophisticated religious legal systems based on Jewish *halakha*, Christian canon law, and Muslim Sharia, among others that quietly govern a good number of the family law questions of religious believers.[2] The question of the legitimacy and authority of these faith-based family law systems is lurking just over the horizon of American family law. Muslim laws in particular have already become a newly controversial issue at state constitutional law. Controversies over the jurisdiction of these religious legal systems will become sharper in the years ahead as various religious individuals and groups – often dismayed by the marital fragility, family breakdown, and sexual liberality of modern society – press for greater freedom to make judgments about sex, marriage, and family life based on their own religious beliefs.

---

[1] Associate Dean for Academic Affairs and Professor of Law, University of St. Thomas School of Law (Minnesota), and Senior Fellow, Emory University Center for the Study of Law and Religion. Portions of this article were previously published in *Who Governs the Family? Marriage as a New Test Case of Overlapping Jurisdictions*, 4 FAULKNER L. REV. 321 (2013) (with John Witte, Jr.).

[2] *See* MARRIAGE AND DIVORCE IN A MULTICULTURAL CONTEXT: RECONSIDERING THE BOUNDARIES OF CIVIL LAW AND RELIGION (Joel A. Nichols ed., 2012).

RELIGION, MARRIAGE, AND THE STATE

For many religious people today – and for many nonreligious people, too – marriage is "more than a mere contract."[3] It is not merely a private contract between two individuals but also an important familial, communal, and even spiritual event. It is not merely an avenue by which the state confers status benefits and burdens on a couple, but also a unique marker of fundamental change in a person's identity and responsibility within his or her community. For many people, the proper formation of a marriage thus requires more than compliance with state procedural forms of adequate notice, consent, licensing, and registration. It also requires a religious ceremony before a qualified officiant who solemnizes and consecrates the union, with witnesses and a celebrating community looking on and promising to help the new couple in their life together and in their (hoped-for) roles as parents. For many people, these communal and ceremonial dimensions of marriage are more important as a religious matter than a civil matter. Similarly for them, a marital dissolution is not valid unless and until granted by competent religious authorities on adequate grounds, proven through appropriate procedures that are recognized and validated within their community. For such people, a statement by the state – of either marriage or divorce – is simply not morally weighty or conclusive enough to have a binding effect.[4]

This is partly because, as Professor Abdullahi Ahmed An-Na'im and others have argued, individuals exercise complex citizenships as members of multiple communities.[5] They frequently possess strong citizenship affiliations to a religious group while also possessing a citizenship affiliation to the civil state. If those two communities lack alignment on a critical matter such as marriage or divorce, individuals may feel competing normative pulls. It is not a given that the normative stance of state law will control.[6] Sometimes the "unofficial

---

3   *See* John Witte, Jr. & Joel A. Nichols, *More Than a Mere Contract? Marriage as Contract and Covenant in Law and Theology*, 5 U. St. Thomas L.J. 595, 603–06 (2008).

4   See examples in Sex, Marriage, & Family in World Religions (Don S. Browning, M. Christian Green & John Witte, Jr. eds., 2009).

5   Abdullahi Ahmed An-Na'im, What is an American Muslim? Embracing Faith and Citizenship (2014). *See also* Ayelet Shachar, Multicultural Jurisdictions: Cultural Differences and Women's Rights (2001); Ayelet Shachar, *Faith in Law? Diffusing Tensions Between Diversity and Equality*, 36 Phil. & Social Criticism 395 (2010).

6   In the United States, for example, 70% of Muslims "with a high level of religious commitment... consider themselves to be Muslims first.... But among those with a low religious commitment, just 28% see themselves this way while a 47% plurality identifies first as American and 12% say they consider themselves equally Muslim and American." Pew Research Ctr., Muslim Americans: Middle Class and Mostly Mainstream 31 (May 22, 2007), *available at* http://pewresearch.org/assets/pdf/muslim-americans.pdf. This is

law" of the religious or cultural community has a stronger hold on individuals than does the sanctioned official civil law of the secular polity.[7]

Protestant Dilemmas

For many conservative Christians today, among other cultural conservatives, the norms of sex, marriage, and family in liberal society stand increasingly unaligned with traditional Christian norms. Until recently, American family law generally reflected Christian norms, especially Protestant norms of sex, marriage, and family life.[8] Marriage was limited to one man and one woman with the freedom, fitness, and capacity to marry each other. The parties had to be of marriageable age and without prohibited degrees of consanguinity or affinity. A priest or pastor was vested with the authority to preside over the wedding on behalf of both the church and the state. Divorce was available only for proven hard fault, with ongoing obligations of care and support for the innocent spouse and dependent children.

This congruence between state law and marital theology corresponded to basic Protestant beliefs that the state's law itself had a constructive teaching function for society (concerning the ideals and goods of marriage) as well as a restrictive boundary function for its members (concerning who may or may not marry or divorce).[9] American Protestants historically did *not* maintain church courts to govern their marriage disputes – unlike minority Jewish and Catholic communities who maintained their *beth din* and consistory courts with the gradual acquiescence of the states in some ways.[10] Instead, majority

not a uniquely Islamic notion, as a significant portion of American Christians also identify with their religion first before identifying with their country. Richard Wike & Greg Smith, Pew Research Religion & Public Life Project, *Little Support for Terrorism Among Muslim Americans* (Pew Research Ctr., Dec. 17, 2009), http://pewresearch.org/pubs/1445/little-support-for-terrorism-among-muslim-americans.

[7] Ann Laquer Estin, *Unofficial Family Law*, 94 Iowa L. Rev. 449, 456 (2009); *cf.* Sarah Beresford, *Seeking Secularism: Resisting Religiosity in Marriage and Divorce – A Comparative Study of England and America*, 3 Web J. Current Legal Issues (2011), *available at* http://www.bailii.org/uk/other/journals/WebJCLI/2011/issue3/beresford3.html (advocating for a secular marriage law and assuming that non-recognition by the state would lead to compliance and adherence to civil law norms).

[8] *See, e.g.*, John Witte, Jr., From Sacrament to Contract: Marriage, Religion, and Law in the Western Tradition 287–88 (2d ed. 2012).

[9] *See* John Witte, Jr., God's Joust, God's Justice: Law and Religion in the Western Tradition 263–94 (2006) (discussing uses of the law).

[10] Joel A. Nichols, *Louisiana's Covenant Marriage Law: A First Step Toward a More Robust Pluralism in Marriage and Divorce Law?*, 47 Emory L.J. 929, 986–87 (1998); Joel A. Nichols, *Multi-Tiered Marriage: Reconsidering the Boundaries of Civil Law and Religion, in* Marriage and Divorce in a Multicultural Context, *supra* note 2, at 11, 15–32.

Protestant groups were content to put jurisdiction over marriage and divorce in the hands of elected government officials who were presumed to be Christians or, at least, would maintain Christian standards of morality.

This system of church–state cooperation in the governance of marriage worked well enough for most American Protestants until the 1950s. But with the sexual revolution of the culture and the constitution, and the corresponding decline of Protestant political and judicial clout, state marriage and divorce laws were rapidly liberalized in the later 1960s and thereafter. Protestants and other conservative Christians saw a growing dissonance between their traditional marital teachings and the new state family law. The differences were not just about same sex marriage – the hot topic today – but about a host of family issues, including contraception, abortion, and privacy rights in general. Many things have combined to contribute to a cultural conflict for conservative Christians, including the onset of no-fault divorce (and the lack of any "grandfathering" provisions for those married under other regimes), the adverse effects of divorce on weaker parties (especially women and children), the sheer number of divorced individuals over the ensuing years, the increased judicial solicitude toward cohabitation and nonmarital procreation, and the attendant creation of alternative legal norms for the same.[11]

The looming question for conservative American Protestants and Evangelicals today is whether it is time to acknowledge that they are rapidly becoming religious and political minorities in the United States who lack the clout to bend state policy to their moral visions for sex, marriage, and family life. This is so despite the continued efforts of groups like Focus on the Family and their local equivalents today, despite the ample new interreligious Marriage Movement with conservative Christians at the lead, and despite the earlier successes of the Moral Majority to change state and national policies. Those days are numbered, if not over.

Protestants faced a comparable crisis in the education field a century ago when they slowly lost their control of the public schools, especially after the Supreme Court got involved after 1948.[12] Although some have continued to fight to keep religion in the public schools, the response of many conservative Protestants has been to set up more of their own private Protestant schools to educate their children in the faith. Perhaps conservative Protestants are reaching a comparable crossroads in the marriage and family field. Perhaps

---

[11] *See, e.g.*, Philip Jenkins, *Living Through a Revolution*, PATHEOS (May 9, 2014), http://www .patheos.com/blogs/anxiousbench/2014/05/living-through-a-revolution/.
[12] JOHN WITTE, JR. & JOEL A. NICHOLS, RELIGION AND THE AMERICAN CONSTITUTIONAL EXPERIMENT ch. 8 (3d ed. 2010).

it is time for them to develop sophisticated new forms of religious mediation and arbitration,[13] perhaps even an independent church court system to handle some of the marriage and family law issues of their voluntary faithful.[14] This would take massive new political thinking among Protestants about the relationships of church, state, and family. But there are historical prototypes in place in the historical Protestant world,[15] and there are contemporary analogies at hand among American Jews, Catholics, Muslims, and other religious minorities who have lacked either the inclination or clout to shape state laws on marriage and family life and have thus quietly operated their own religious legal systems.

Islamic Plights and Anti-Sharia Laws

Ironically, Protestants are now beginning to contemplate this brave new world of church, state, and family just at the time when religious tribunals and matters of internal religious decision making are becoming ever more visible and controversial in the United States. The power of Jewish *beth din* over marriage and divorce within Orthodox Judaism has always raised a few constitutional eyebrows, but there has been no sustained campaign to eradicate them.[16] The power of Fundamentalist Mormon communities to maintain polygamous families in open defiance of state criminal laws has triggered stronger political reaction, and a growing number of court cases of late are challenging the legitimacy of their religious leadership and legal structures. The recent scandals in American Catholic circles concerning pedophilia and clerical cover-ups have raised even stronger cultural and legal reactions and a relentless stream of litigation that has cost the Catholic Church hundreds of millions of dollars in damage awards and out-of-court settlements.[17]

---

[13] *See generally* Amanda M. Baker, *A Higher Authority: Judicial Review of Religious Arbitration*, 37 VT. L. REV. 157 (2012); Michael A. Helfand, *Religious Arbitration and the New Multiculturalism: Negotiating Conflicting Legal Orders*, 86 N.Y.U. L. REV. 1231 (2011).

[14] For an overview of existing religious dispute resolution models, see David Masci & Elizabeth Lawton, Pew Research Religion & Public Life Project, *Applying God's Law: Religious Courts and Mediation in the U.S.* (Pew Research Ctr., Apr. 8, 2013), http://www.pewforum.org/2013/04/08/applying-gods-law-religious-courts-and-mediation-in-the-us/.

[15] *See* JOHN WITTE, JR. & ROBERT M. KINGDON, SEX, MARRIAGE, AND FAMILY LIFE IN JOHN CALVIN'S GENEVA: COURTSHIP, ENGAGEMENT, AND MARRIAGE (2005).

[16] *See* Michael J. Broyde, *New York's Regulation of Jewish Marriage, Covenant, Contract, or Statute?*, *in* MARRIAGE AND DIVORCE IN A MULTICULTURAL CONTEXT, *supra* note 2, at 138.

[17] *See, e.g.*, Doe v. Holy See, 557 F.3d 1066, 1069–71 (9th Cir. 2009); Moe v. Trustees of Stigmatine Fathers, Inc., No. 05-0059, 2008 Mass. Super. LEXIS 157, 24 Mass. L. Rep. 125 (Mass. Super. Ct. June 4, 2008); *Redwing v. Catholic Bishop for Diocese of Memphis*, 363 S.W.3d 436, 467 (Tenn. 2012).

But the concerns about the operation of such "overlapping jurisdictions" pale by comparison to the growing antipathy against American Muslims and their sophisticated legal system called Sharia.[18] Muslims now "represent the second largest religion in Europe and the third in North America."[19] But Muslims are also on the receiving end of a great deal of cultural antipathy, allegedly because of their religion. This backlash has had a substantial uptick the past decade – after the tragic events of 9/11, followed by London's 7/7, Fort Hood, the bloody and unpopular wars in Afghanistan and Iraq, and the inhuman and ruthless acts of the so-called Islamic State.[20]

The public rebuke of Islam in the United States in the past decade has come from various quarters. For example, television commentator Bill O'Reilly compared the Qur'an, Islam's holy book, to Adolf Hitler's *Mein Kampf*.[21] Talk radio host Michael Savage told his listeners that lawmakers should institute an "outright ban on Muslim immigration" in order to "save the United States"; he also recommended making "the construction of mosques illegal in America."[22] An enormous public outcry in 2010 delayed construction of a mosque near the site of the World Trade Center attacks.[23] Republican 2012 presidential hopeful and one-time frontrunner Herman Cain stated that he would not hire

---

[18]　*See* ABDULLAHI AHMED AN-NA'IM, ISLAM AND THE SECULAR STATE: NEGOTIATING THE FUTURE OF SHARI'A 267–93 (2008) (proposing a future course for Shari'a law in western culture). *See also* KHALED ABOU EL FADL, REASONING WITH GOD: RECLAIMING SHARI'AH IN THE MODERN AGE (2014) (describing Islamic law, and also proposing a path for Shari'a in the twenty-first century).

[19]　John L. Esposito, *Foreword, in* MUSLIMS' PLACE IN THE AMERICAN PUBLIC SQUARE xi (Zahid H. Bukhari et al. eds., 2004). Islam is the fastest growing religion in America, and some scholars assert that it will be the second largest religion in America by the mid-twenty-first century. *See generally* KAREN ARMSTRONG, ISLAM: A SHORT HISTORY (2000); JANE I. SMITH, ISLAM IN AMERICA (1999); Lee Ann Bambach, *United States Law, Muslims and,* OXFORD ISLAMIC STUDIES ONLINE, http://www.oxfordislamicstudies.com/article/opr/t343/e0098.

[20]　*See, e.g.,* LORI PEEK, BEHIND THE BACKLASH: MUSLIM AMERICANS AFTER 9/11, at 16 (2011) ("In the aftermath of the terrorist attacks, Muslims experienced a dramatic increase in the frequency and intensity of these hostile encounters.").

[21]　Deborah Amos, *Students Discuss Koran Book after Battle,* ABC NIGHTLINE (Aug. 25, 2002), http://abcnews.go.com/Nightline/story?id=128548&page=1.

[22]　Ryan Chiachiere, *Savage: To "Save the United States," Lawmakers Should Institute "Outright Ban on Muslim Immigration" and on "the Construction of Mosques,"* MEDIA MATTERS FOR AMERICA (Nov. 29, 2006), http://mediamatters.org/mmtv/200611290005.

[23]　*See, e.g.,* Laurie Goodstein, *Across Nation, Mosque Projects Meet Opposition,* N.Y. TIMES, Aug. 8, 2010, at A1. For part of the vision of Islamic law from the imam primarily behind the mosque, see Imam Feisal Abdul Rauf, *A Cordoba Initiative Project Justification and Theory of Sharia Law: How The American Declaration of Independence, Bill of Rights and Constitution are Consistent with Islamic Jurisprudence,* 7 U. ST. THOMAS L.J. 452 (2011). For a discussion on whether states can regulate religious land use, see Heather Greenfield, Comment, *International Law, Religious Limitations, and Cultural Sensitivity: The Park51 Mosque at Ground Zero,* 25 EMORY INT'L L. REV. 1317 (2011).

Muslims as part of his administration; he also firmly opposed the construction of mosques, wrongly justifying his stance on First Amendment grounds.[24] Indeed, as Professors Greg Sisk and Michael Heise have said, "We are all living in the shadow of 9/11 – but that shadow appears to be longer and darker for Muslim Americans."[25] To be sure, there have also been calls for accommodation, toleration, and better incorporation of Muslims' beliefs into liberal democracies via dialogue and greater respect for multiculturalism. But even these conversations and actions have tragically given rise to extreme violence at times, as witnessed, for example, in Norway when Andres Breivik slaughtered dozens of people, ostensibly because they supported the Muslim population in Norway.[26]

To date, many of the political controversies in the United States regarding Islam have not centered directly on family law matters, but the tide may be changing. Controversies focused instead on the building of mosques or on generic charges of the imposition of Sharia. But a number of states over the past four years have debated new laws that ban the application of Sharia in their state legislatures and courts, and the most recent versions of these laws specifically target family law. Oklahoma was the first state to pass such an anti-Sharia law in November 2010, with its popularly ratified "Save Our State" Amendment to the Oklahoma Constitution. That amendment was promptly enjoined by a federal court and eventually struck down as unconstitutional.[27] But several other states have stepped into the fray. Nine states have passed variations on anti-Sharia statutes and proponents continue to push them in a few more (although bills have been introduced and defeated in many U.S. states).[28] Recent additions include North Carolina, where a new law addresses

---

[24] *See, e.g., Your World Cavuto: Herman Cain Defends Controversial "Muslim" Comments* (Fox News television broadcast Mar. 28, 2011), *available at* http://www.foxnews.com/on-air/your-world-cavuto/transcript/herman-cain-defends-controversial-muslim-comments; Gabriella Schwarz, *Cain: Opposing Mosque Construction Is not Discrimination*, CNN POLITICAL TICKER BLOG (July 17, 2011, 3:22 PM), http://politicalticker.blogs.cnn.com/2011/07/17/cain-opposing-mosque-construction-is-not-discrimination/.

[25] Gregory C. Sisk & Michael Heise, *Muslims and Religious Liberty in the Era of Post 9/11: Empirical Evidence from the Federal Courts*, 98 IOWA L. REV. 231, 291 (2012) (showing that Muslims face a "distinct and substantial disadvantage" when asserting U.S. constitutional free exercise or religious accommodation claims – in addition to the cultural challenges mentioned above).

[26] Miguel Marquez, *Norway Shooting Suspect Anders Breivik: Attacks Were "Price of Their Treason,"* ABC WORLD NEWS (July 25, 2011), http://abcnews.go.com/Blotter/anders-breivik-hearing-closed-pulpit-alleged-shooter/story?id=14152129.

[27] *See* Awad v. Ziriax, 670 F.3d 1111, 1119 (10th Cir. 2012), *aff'g* 754 F. Supp. 2d 1298 (W.D. Okla. 2010).

[28] Alabama, Arizona, Kansas, Florida, Louisiana, North Carolina, Oklahoma, South Dakota, and Tennessee have all passed such laws. See citations at Pew Research Religion & Public

only family law concerns in its 2013 anti-Sharia statute called the "Family,
Faith, and Freedom Protection Act,"[29] and Florida, which also targets family
law matters in a 2014 law.[30] Alabama also passed an anti-Sharia law by referendum in November 2014, and at least nine other states had anti-Sharia bills
under consideration in 2014.[31]

Simply put, the anti-Sharia campaign is "a solution in search of a
problem."[32] The purportedly authoritative resource for supporters of anti-
Sharia laws is a binder of assembled cases titled *Shariah Law and American
State Courts: An Assessment of State Appellate Court Cases* [SLASC][33] – and
it fails to show any real problem that must be addressed. The SLASC trolls
through forty years of cases, spanning the appellate courts in all fifty states,
in search of Sharia cases that "conflict with the Constitution or state public

Life Project, *State Legislation Restricting Use of Foreign or Religious Law* (Pew Research Ctr.,
Apr. 8, 2013), http://features.pewforum.org/sharia-law-map/. *See also* 2013 N.C. Sess. Laws
2013-416/House Bill 522 (2013) and Florida Senate Bill 386 (2014). For regular updates and
compilations, see Bill Raftery, *Bans on Court Use of Sharia/International Law: Active in GA,
FL, MO Only; Dead in MS*, GAVEL TO GAVEL (Mar. 5, 2014), http://gaveltogavel.us/2014/03/
05/bans-on-court-use-of-shariainternational-law-active-in-ga-fl-mo-but-dead-in-ms/. *See also*
Symeon C. Symeonides, *Choice of Law in the American Courts in 2012: Twenty-Sixth Annual
Survey*, 61 AM J. COMP. L. 217, 293–95 (2013). Washington is arguably another state with such
a statute, as there was a phrase added to a bill otherwise encouraging specialty courts (like
drug courts and family courts). Washington Senate Bill 5797 (2013), as amended by the House
(ch. 257, Laws of 2013, effective Aug. 1, 2013).

29 North Carolina General Assembly House Bill 695 (2013).

30 Florida Senate Bill 386 (passed by the Florida House after House Bill 903 was tabled) (2014).

31 Alabama Const. Act 2013-269 appeared on the Nov. 4, 2014, ballot and was passed by the
    Alabama voters. Greg Garrison, *Amendment Banning "Foreign Law" in Alabama Courts Passes;
    Will Be Added to Alabama Constitution* (Nov. 4, 2014), http://www.al.com/news/index.ssf/
    2014/11/amendment_banning_foreign_law.html. Other states considering bills include Geor-
    gia, Iowa, Kentucky, Missouri, South Carolina, Mississippi, Vermont, West Virginia, and
    Washington.

32 Matthew J. Franck, *A Solution in Search of a Problem*, Bench Memos, NAT'L REV. ONLINE
    (June 15, 2012), http://www.nationalreview.com/benchmemos/303028/solution-search-problem-
    matthew-j-franck; *see also* Matthew Schmitz, *Anti-Sharia Laws are Magic*, The Corner, NAT'L
    REVIEW ONLINE (June 18, 2012, 12:23PM), http://www.nationalreview.com/corner/303135/
    anti-sharia-laws-are-magic-matthew-schmitz (calling the SLASC a "flimsy document"), and
    Bob Pitt, *Islamophobia Watch: Panel Debunks Shari'a Myths*, ISLAMOPHOBIA WATCH (Nov.
    2, 2012), http://islamophobiawatch.co.uk/university-of-chicago-panel-debunks-sharia-myths
    (describing three panelists at an event at the University of Chicago Divinity School event who
    criticized anti-Shari'a laws).

33 *Sharia Law and American State Courts: An Assessment of State Appellate Court Cases*,
    Center for Security Policy, (version 1.3, May 20, 2011), http://shariahinamericancourts.com/
    wp-content/uploads/2011/06/Sharia_Law_And_American_State_Courts_1.4_06212011.pdf [here-
    inafter SLASC].

policy."[34] That it finds only twenty-nine "highly relevant" cases in this vast sea of cases already says a lot; that none of these cases actually reflect a legitimate problem says even more: namely, that the anti-Sharia campaign in the American states is transparently discriminatory in its effort to single out Muslims and their laws for special restrictions.[35] Courts have long had a boundary of "public policy" when faced with enforcing a contract or other matter that runs afoul of accepted civil norms, and many of the examples adduced in SLASC involve the navigation of that boundary. Even more, the Supremacy Clause of the United States Constitution, which renders the Constitution as the supreme law of the land and supersedes any other law in conflict, operates as a clear backstop for the wrongful imposition of foreign or religious law. The anti-Sharia legislation in place in the states today is unnecessary, harmful, and most often unconstitutional.

Comparative Examples

Although Islamic family law issues are only recently growing into a flashpoint in the United States (outside their application in these anti-Sharia matters more generally), they have seen greater attention in Canada and the United Kingdom. In both places, the focus has been whether to permit Muslims to adjudicate family law disputes according to religious principles through religious arbitration. In both places, opposition has centered, in part, on political opposition to the principles of Sharia and the fear of its possible "imposition" of Sharia upon citizens of those countries. And in both places, Islamic religious arbitration of family law disputes has continued, despite opposition.

In Canada, Christians, Jews, and Muslims had been submitting their personal disputes to religious arbitration for years (using marital contracts that designate a specific dispute resolution forum). But when news broke in the province of Ontario in 2003 that an outspoken imam was publicly advocating a more formal procedure to promote the application of Sharia to Canadian Muslims in family law matters, citizens and citizen groups complained loudly to the government. The government commissioned former Attorney General Marion Boyd to consider the matter. She undertook a thorough investigation that culminated in a lengthy report about the use of alternative

---

[34] *Id.* at 9.

[35] See much more detailed criticism of SLASC and the specific cases adduced there (and criticism of an earlier Missouri bill) in Witte & Nichols, *Who Governs the Family, supra* note 1.

dispute resolution in family law, including the use of religious norms (e.g., Sharia) as a choice of law in family law arbitration.[36] Attorney General Boyd recommended that Ontario should continue to *allow* religious arbitrations – on the condition that certain safeguards be implemented and followed to ensure proper consent and fairness.[37] Contrary to this recommendation, in 2005 political leaders removed the legal option of applying any religious principles and insisted that there would be "one law for all Ontarians."[38]

In the United Kingdom, Archbishop Rowan Williams gave an important speech on the intersection of civil and religious law in February 2008. In that speech, he suggested that some sort of "accommodation" of Sharia by British common law was "unavoidable."[39] For both pragmatic and substantive reasons, he advocated a sort of "plural jurisdiction," according to which Muslims could resolve family law disputes (and some other civil matters) either in British courts or in religious arbitration tribunals.[40] His remarks gave rise to a flurry of articles, the vast majority denouncing the idea – in part because it would "license polygamy."[41] Despite the cries of many critics, however, the Archbishop was not advocating a wholesale abdication of the state's marriage and divorce law, but rather calling for a constructive conversation about the complex citizenships exercised by Muslim believers. Rather than engage in productive dialogue about this difficult issue, many in the popular press instead merely aired unrealistic concerns about the wholesale takeover of British law for everyone (or at least for some British citizens) by Sharia.[42]

---

[36] *See* Marion Boyd, Office of Canadian Attorney General, Dispute Resolution in Family Law: Protecting Choice, Promoting Inclusion (Dec. 2004), *available at* http://www.attorneygeneral.jus.gov.on.ca/english/about/pubs/boyd/fullreport.pdf.

[37] *Id.* at 133.

[38] *See* Prithi Yelaga & Robert Benzie, *McGuinty: No Sharia Law*, The Toronto Star, Sept. 12, 2005, at A1.

[39] Archbishop's Lecture – Civil and Religious Law in England: A Religious Perspective, Dr Rowan Williams, 104th Archbishop of Canterbury (Feb. 7, 2008), *reprinted in* Shari'a in the West (Rex Ahdar & Nicholas Aroney eds., 2010).

[40] *Id.* at 302.

[41] *See, e.g.*, Catherine Bennett, *It's One Sharia Law for Men and Quite Another for Women*, The Observer (The Guardian (U.K.)), Feb. 10, 2008 ("licensed polygamy").

[42] Meanwhile, the Law Society of England and Wales recently published "Practice Notes" for its members on how to draft a "shari'a compliant" will, recognizing that clients may wish to avail themselves of such laws. *See* Law Society, *Sharia Succession Rules*, Mar. 13, 2014, http://www.lawsociety.org.uk/advice/practice-notes/sharia-succession-rules/#sharia3. Some banks actively seek business from clients seeking to comport with Shari'a law also. For example, Lloyd's Bank offers an "Islamic Account" that guarantees compliance with Islamic banking principles. *See* http://www.lloydsbank.com/assets/media/pdfs/islamic_account_welcome_pack.pdf.

The facts on the ground in Canada and the United Kingdom underscore the impossibility of the civil law claiming full allegiance and commitment from religiously devout citizens, including Muslims. In Canada, although Ontario provincial law is uniform and courts will not enforce family arbitrations that purport to apply religious law, this does not mean that religious arbitrations have ceased. Rather, Attorney General Boyd has reported that Muslim arbitrations have "merely becom[e] invisible to official law without ceasing operations."[43] And in the United Kingdom, one of the main reasons behind Archbishop Williams's speech was the reality that a very high percentage of Muslims already lack alignment between their civil and religious marriages. For example, one study indicated that 27% of all Muslim marriages in the United Kingdom are not official marriages under English law.[44] This mirrors the experience of many Orthodox Jews in New York who also marry and divorce only under religious law, and not according to the civil law.[45]

In Search of a Middle Way

The potential legal brinkmanship on both sides is unhelpful – whether that is the effort by anti-Sharia critics in Oklahoma and elsewhere to pass state constitutional amendments against Sharia, on the one hand, or, on the other, the constitutional rights arguments pressed by some advocates to allow for voluntary use of Sharia on grounds of religious freedom, nondiscrimination, and self-determination. Surely adults have a fundamental right to be married and divorced, and religious parties have a fundamental right to religious freedom and equal treatment. But this need not mean that religious tribunals have the fundamental right to govern all marriage and family questions of their voluntary faithful, nor that religious parties have an unalterable free exercise right to

---

[43] Prakash Shah, *A Reflection on the* Shari'a *Debate in Britain*, 13 Studia z Prawa Wyznaniowego (Studies of Ecclesiastical Law) 71 (2010), *available at* http://papers.ssrn.com/sol3/papers.cfm?abstract_id=1733529 (citing Marion Boyd, "The Past, Present and Future of Arbitration in Religious Contexts: Reflections on Ontario Law in a Comparative Context," (lecture given at the Institute of Advanced Studies, London, July 10, 2009)).

[44] Sonia Nûrîn Shah-Kazemi, Untying the Knot: Muslim Women, Divorce and the Shariah 31 (2001). For further background, see generally Gillian Douglas et al., Social Cohesion and Civil Law: Marriage, Divorce and Religious Courts (2011); Farrah Ahmed & Jane Calderwood Norton, *Religious Tribunals, Religious Freedom, and Concern for Vulnerable Women*, *in* Child and Family Law Quarterly 363 (2012) (describing the "current legal position in the United Kingdom"); John R. Bowen, *How Could English Courts Recognize Shariah?* 7 U. St. Thomas L.J. 411 (2010) (describing interactions between Muslim arbitration tribunals and the English legal system).

[45] *See* Broyde, *supra* note 16, at 161.

choose which family law governs them: the state's or that of their own religious community. The state cannot simply cede jurisdiction over an institution as fundamental as marriage, which is deeply woven into sundry other public, private, penal, and procedural laws. But the state can and should share marital jurisdiction with religious officials by allowing religious officials to preside at weddings, testify in divorce cases, assist in the adoption of a child, facilitate the rescue of a distressed family member, preside in mediation and arbitration proceedings, and perhaps more.

American parties should take a longer historical and developmental view of this new jurisdictional contest over marriage and family life. Marriage has long been both a spiritual and temporal institution in the history of the West, and changes in religious and political jurisdiction over marriage have always taken time, patience, negotiation, and experimentation. In American history, this has occurred by what Professor Steven Smith has aptly called "soft constitutional" developments, which depend heavily upon gradual and skillful cultural negotiation outside of the formal instruments of state law and beyond the purview of constitutional law.[46] American Catholics and Jews have, for two centuries and more, used this technique to balance the marital jurisdictional claims of their own religious communities with those of their state sovereigns. And they now have sophisticated tribunals that govern some of the hard family law questions of their voluntary members. American Protestants, Evangelicals, and Muslims are now slowly learning to do the same. Each religious group can learn from the other in developing these necessary skills of cultural and legal navigation.[47] They can also learn from the examples of earlier American jurisdictional struggles over education that slowly gave rise to the shared public and private school system we have in place today.

To be sure, anti-Sharia laws are wrong because of their targeted discrimination, their duplication of other laws and decisional norms, their potential conflict with the Federal Arbitration Act, and more. The first generation of anti-Sharia laws (like Oklahoma's) were patently unconstitutional for wrongly singling out "Shari'a" for special restrictions.[48] That violates elementary First Amendment prohibitions on religious discrimination under both the Free

---

[46] *See generally* Steven D. Smith, *Nonestablishment, Standing, and the Soft Constitution*, 85 ST. JOHN'S L. REV. 407 (2011).

[47] Jean-Francois Gaudreault-DesBiens, *Religious Courts, Personal Federalism, and Legal Transplants, in* SHARI'A IN THE WEST, *supra* note 39, at 160.

[48] Awad v. Ziriax, 670 F.3d 1111 (10th Cir. 2012), *aff'g* 754 F. Supp. 2d 1298 (W.D. Okla. 2010). *See also* Jeremy Grunert, *How Do You Solve a Problem Like Sharia? Awad v. Ziriax and the Question of Sharia Law in America*, 40 PEPPERDINE L. REV. 695 (2013).

Exercise and Establishment clauses.[49] The second generation of anti-Sharia laws are more nuanced; they do not mention "Shari'a" at all, but rather seek to preempt use of any "foreign" or other law. Such laws are redundant, however, of the Supremacy Clause of the United States Constitution. They are also discriminatory in their efforts to single out Muslim Sharia even while allowing Jews, Christians, and other religious communities to retain their "foreign" laws.[50] So even if these second generation statutes are constitutional, they are still problematic from a civil society perspective because they alienate, if not target, Muslims for no real gain.[51]

But hard questions persist that cannot be easily swept away with the assertion that religious groups should enjoy autonomy over the marriage and family affairs of their voluntary faithful: What *are* the appropriate lines between the civil state and religions with respect to marriage? Can there be a place for "new legal pluralism in the domain of intimacy"?[52] Civil marriage and divorce are perhaps a least common denominator for all citizens, but can there be variations once base-level protections for women, children, and other vulnerable members of the household are in place?[53] What exactly would such base-level protections be? How can the state best protect vulnerable members and also

[49] That is clear discriminatory intent in violation of *Church of Lukumi Babalu Aye v. City of Hialeah*, 508 U.S. 520 (1993). *See also* Asma T. Uddin & Dave Pantzer, *A First Amendment Analysis of Anti-Sharia Statutes*, 10 First Amend. L. Rev. 363 (2012). There are other problems that are too numerous to mention, including that the statute seemingly even outlaws the mention of Blackstone, if one follows its explicit statutory text.

[50] *See* Abed Awad, *The True Story of Sharia in American Courts*, The Nation, June 13, 2012 (describing Kansas's new second-generation anti-Shari'a law and its discriminatory intent, and quoting a state senator who said, "This [bill] doesn't say 'Sharia law'... but that's how it was marketed back in January and all session long – and I have all the emails to prove it."). A recent case relied upon the Kansas statute in refusing to enforce an Islamic *mahr* contract. Soleimani v. Soleimani, Case No. 11CV4668, (Aug. 28, 2012 Dist. Ct. Johnson Cty., Kan., Civ. Ct. Dep't) (final divorce decree), *available at* http://www.volokh.com/wp-content/uploads/2012/09/soleimani.pdf.

[51] Robert K. Vischer, *The Dangers of Anti-Sharia Laws*, First Things (Mar. 2012), http://www.firstthings.com/article/2012/02/the-dangers-of-anti-sharia-laws. *Cf.* Eun-Jung Katherine Kim, *Islamic Law in American Courts: Good, Bad, and Unsustainable Uses*, 28 Notre Dame J.L. Ethics & Pub. Pol'y 287 (2014).

[52] Jean L. Cohen, *The Politics and Risks of the New Legal Pluralism in the Domain of Intimacy*, 10 Int'l J. Const. 380, 382 (2012) (arguing against "introducing any version of religious status-based legal pluralism" based on gender equality concerns). *See also* Marie Ashe & Anissa Hélie, *Realities of Religio-Legalism: Religious Courts and Women's Rights in Canada, the United Kingdom, and the United States*, 20 U.C. Davis J. Int'l L. & Pol'y 139 (2014) (same).

[53] Linda C. McClain, *Marriage Pluralism in the United States: On Civil and Religious Jurisdiction and the Demands of Equal Citizenship, in* Marriage and Divorce in a Multicultural Context, *supra* note 2, at 309–40; Robin F. Wilson, *The Perils of Privatized Marriage, in* Marriage and Divorce in a Multicultural Context, *supra* note 2, at 253–83.

advance its liberal ends? Which "citizenship" will affected individuals follow when jurisdictions overlap – religious or civil? The debate about the propriety of Sharia should not distract us from the actual complications of growing marital and legal pluralism in the United States.

POSSIBLE PATHS AHEAD

Professor Brian Tamanaha recently wrote: "The longstanding image of a uniform and monopolistic law that governs a society is plainly obsolete."[54] If this is a true description of our modern legal condition, what does it mean for American family law? Will we find ways to recognize and accommodate believers with differing understandings of marriage and divorce? Given the dissonance internal to family law for many religious believers, including (increasingly) for Muslims in the United States, what are the possible avenues for interaction between civil law and religion in the United States?[55] Four possibilities suggest themselves.[56]

First, and perhaps the most extreme, is to "take the state out of the business of deciding what is a marriage and leave that question to the churches" and other religious groups.[57] This approach would attempt to divide conclusively the notions of "civil marriage" and "religious marriage," which lie at the heart of many of the debates about marriage. It would disentangle the state from the religious aspects of marriage and emphasize the state's higher priority of equality. It would accomplish this, presumably, by enacting civil unions.

---

[54] Brian Z. Tamanaha, *A Framework for Pluralistic Socio-Legal Systems*, in CULTURAL DIVERSITY AND THE LAW: STATE RESPONSES FROM AROUND THE WORLD 381, 400 (Marie-Claire Foblets et al. eds., 2009).

[55] Critics might broadly contend that the First Amendment of the U.S. Constitution completely prohibits direct involvement of religion in matters of family law. Such an assertion is both an overreading of Supreme Court precedent and a misunderstanding of the principle of separation of church and state in the United States. For further discussion, see John Witte, Jr. & Joel A. Nichols, *The Frontiers of Marital Pluralism*, in MARRIAGE AND DIVORCE IN A MULTICULTURAL CONTEXT, *supra* note 2, at 357–78.

[56] Of course, there may be more than four, or a different grouping of possibilities. *Cf., e.g.*, Brian H. Bix, *Pluralism and Decentralization in Marriage Regulation*, in MARRIAGE AND DIVORCE IN A MULTICULTURAL CONTEXT, *supra* note 2, at 60 (providing an alternate listing of ways the regulation of marriage could become more decentralized). *See also* Shahar Lifshitz, *The Pluralistic Vision of Marriage*, in MARRIAGE AT THE CROSSROADS: LAW, POLICY AND THE BRAVE NEW WORLD OF TWENTY-FIRST-CENTURY FAMILIES (Marsha Garrison & Elizabeth S. Scott eds., 2012).

[57] Stephen B. Presser, *Marriage and the Law: Time for a Divorce?*, in MARRIAGE AND DIVORCE IN A MULTICULTURAL CONTEXT, *supra* note 2, at 78, 81. *Cf.* Julia Halloran McLaughlin, *Taking Religion Out of Civil Divorce*, 65 RUTGERS L. REV. 395 (2013).

Proposals of this sort have been floated by those on both the left and the right of the political spectrum.[58] Whatever its merits, this proposal seems like a nonstarter. A similar proposal was debated in Canada (which is often more liberal on family law matters than most American states), but gained very little political traction even there.[59]

Second, a quite different approach is that the state remain involved in regulating marriage – but do so according to a majority's particular religious, moral, or political views. This used to be the avenue of choice for Protestant Christians, but it increasingly has led to conflict as society has become more liberal in its laws governing both entrance to and exit from marriage, and conservative Christian groups have felt alienated. This alienation has been substantially exacerbated by the same sex marriage debates over the past decades, and it has reignited the culture wars. There have been Defense of Marriage Acts (DOMAs), state level mini-DOMAs, state court decisions in favor of same sex marriage, sometimes (as in California) democratic reversal of such decisions, and, occasionally (as in New York), democratic instatement of the possibility of same sex marriage. Perhaps these winner-take-all political battles will continue to be the norm. But at present, they show little promise of resolving the tension and conflict even if the cases trend in one direction.[60]

Third, a variation on the option of instantiating one set of religious values into a single and exclusive governing law for marriage and divorce would be to offer different models and regimes of marriage that are animated by different religious beliefs, and let the parties choose one. Louisiana's "covenant marriage laws" are an example of this: couples choose either a regular contract marriage with easy entrance and no-fault divorce, or a covenant marriage,

---

[58] *See, e.g.,* Martha Albertson Fineman, *The Meaning of Marriage, in* MARRIAGE PROPOSALS: QUESTIONING A LEGAL STATUS 29–69 (Anita Bernstein ed., 2006); Martha C. Nussbaum, *A Right to Marry?*, 98 CAL. L. REV. 667 (2010); Edward A. Zelinsky, *Deregulating Marriage: The Pro-Marriage Case for Abolishing Civil Marriage*, 27 CARDOZO L. REV. 1161 (2006).

[59] Law Commission of Canada, *Beyond Conjugality: Recognizing and Supporting Close Personal Adult Relationships* (2001), *available at* http://www.samesexmarriage.ca/docs/beyond_conjugality.pdf (last visited Jan 6, 2013). Anita Bernstein, *Subverting the Marriage-Amendment Crusade with Law and Policy Reform*, 24 WASH. U. J.L. & POL'Y 79, 83 (2007) (noting that the Canadian Parliament tabled Beyond Conjugality in 2002).

[60] As another proposed way forward, especially regarding same sex marriage, some have proposed choice of law proposals across state lines whereby couples in one state could "choose" the marriage law of another state to govern them. *See, e.g.,* Adam Candeub & Mae Kuykendall, *Modernizing Marriage*, 44 U. MICH. J.L. REFORM 735 (2011). *See also* Mae Kuykendall & Adam Candeub, *Symposium Overview: Perspectives on Innovative Marriage Procedure*, MICH. ST. L. REV. 1 (2011) (summarizing symposium papers).

which requires premarital counseling and other entrance requirements with correspondingly higher exit requirements. Or a state might offer a blend of civil and religious marriage/divorce norms and procedures for its citizens. New York's *get* statutes are an example of this model. These statutes aim to prevent Orthodox Jewish couples from divorcing at state law unless and until they are divorced at Jewish law, and they thereby implement an "invisible dance" between the civil and religious courts.[61] But neither covenant marriage statutes nor legislatively enacted *get* statutes seem promising practically. Only three states have enacted covenant marriage statutes (and none since 2001), and only a few couples in those states have availed themselves of the covenant marriage option. Moreover, no state besides New York has passed a *get* statute despite other attempts in the past twenty years.[62]

A final option is for the state to show more solicitude for the private choices of dispute resolution set out by marital couples in their pre- and post-marital agreements.[63] Currently, marital parties may agree in advance to arbitrate any marital disputes rather than litigate them. That choice of forum provision in a prenuptial agreement is typically enforceable. But, as can be seen in Ontario and the United Kingdom, the growing presence of arbitration done by religious authorities is making these agreements more controversial. Even more controversial would be the parties' agreement to choose the law that governs within that chosen forum – state law or religious laws. Having such a choice of law within the arbitration tribunal would make it easier for parties to align their commitments as both religious and political citizens. But such religious arbitration, especially on choice of law matters, would itself likely be contested by the state, especially if the religious laws used displace the state's norms and aspirations for gender equality or the best interest of the child.[64] Religious

---

[61] *See* Broyde, *supra* note 16, at 159.

[62] *See* STEVEN L. NOCK, LAURA ANN SANCHEZ & JAMES D. WRIGHT, COVENANT MARRIAGE: THE MOVEMENT TO RECLAIM TRADITION IN AMERICA 3 (2008) (describing how only 2 percent of couples entered covenant marriages during the first five years of law's enactment (1998–2001)). This has been attributed to a lack of interest by couples, a lack of knowledge of the law (partly due to the failure of clerks to inform engaged couples), and the failure of institutionalized religion to encourage or mandate covenant marriages. There is also a *get* statute in the United Kingdom. Matrimonial Causes Act 1973, 1973, c. 18, § 10A (inserted by Divorce (Religious Marriages Act), 2002, c. 27).

[63] *See* Brian H. Bix, *The ALI Principles and Agreements: Seeking a Balance Between Status and Contract, in* RECONCEIVING THE FAMILY: CRITICAL REFLECTIONS ON THE AMERICAN LAW INSTITUTE'S PRINCIPLES OF THE LAW OF FAMILY DISSOLUTION 372 (Robin Fretwell Wilson ed., 2006). For a comparative perspective, see the chapters in MARITAL AGREEMENTS AND PRIVATE AUTONOMY IN COMPARATIVE PERSPECTIVE (Jens Scherpe ed., 2012).

[64] *See, e.g.*, Aleem v. Aleem, 947 A.2d 489 (Md. 2008) (disapproving an Islamic religious marital dissolution on public policy grounds).

arbitration is attracting more scholarly attention of late,[65] and the topic will likely yield more articles and court opinions as American society becomes ever more mobile and multicultural. Whether American courts will treat religious arbitrations of family law matters the same as they treat arbitrations of other matters is still an open question,[66] although the new Uniform Premarital and Marital Agreement Act is one more step in this direction.[67] Some of the concerns about arbitration in general are magnified when applied to a family law context and suggest the need for caution: these include its general lack of a public process, its lack of a court record or precedent, and its nearly irreversible decisions on appeal. But other concerns with arbitration seem less pressing, especially concerning the potential deference given to "repeat players" in arbitration.

One avenue that is *not* viable, however, is to presume that Professor Tamanaha is incorrect and that, in family law matters, there can be one "uniform and monopolistic law"[68] enforced throughout the land. We would be better served to recognize, as Professor Werner Menski has said, that "perhaps we must all be conscious pluralists, whether we like it or not."[69] This means that we must realize that "unofficial law" will operate regardless of what the civil law says. That is, some individuals are going to feel themselves bound by their communal (religious) norms regardless of what the civil law prescribes. And some individuals are going to seek religious adjudication of their disputes, even if the civil law refuses to enforce those arbitral judgments. This is already happening in Ontario and the United Kingdom, as previously mentioned.[70] There is a growing literature observing this and beginning to discuss religious family arbitration in the United States, especially

---

[65] *See, e.g.*, Lee Ann Bambach, "That Ye Judge With Justice": Faith-Based Arbitration by Muslims in an American Context (2014) (unpublished PhD dissertation, Emory University) (on file with author); Baker, *supra* note 13, Helfand, *supra* note 13; Nicholas Walter, *Religious Arbitration in the United States and Canada*, 52 Santa Clara L. Rev. 501 (2012). *See also* Farrah Ahmed & Senwung Luk, *How Religious Arbitration Could Enhance Personal Autonomy*, 1 Oxford J. Law & Rel. 1 (2012).

[66] *See* Robert L. McFarland, *Are Religious Arbitration Panels Incompatible with Law? Examining "Overlapping Jurisdictions" in Private Law*, 4 Faulkner L. Rev. 321 (2013) (contending that courts should recognize faith-based arbitral decisions pertaining to the family).

[67] Uniform Premarital and Marital Agreements Act § 2(5) and cmt. (2012) (providing a narrower definition of premarital agreement in order to avoid, among other considerations, undermining the enforceability of Islamic *mahr* contracts).

[68] Tamanaha, *supra* note 54, at 400.

[69] Werner Menski, *Ancient and Modern Boundary Crossings Between Personal Laws and Civil Law in Composite India, in* Marriage and Divorce in a Multicultural Context, *supra* note 2, at 219, 222.

[70] Samia Bano, Muslim Women and Shari'ah Councils: Transcending the Boundaries of Community and Law 3 (2012) (analyzing "the experience of South Asian British Muslim

concerning Muslim marriages and divorces.[71] Failing to understand the complicated interplay of official law with unofficial law (or of civil law with religious law, if one likes) means that a liberal state may protect vulnerable parties the *least* when the state claims and seeks to exercise hegemonic control over marriage and divorce and when it passes anti-Sharia statutes. Instead, it may be that *only* through recognizing and respecting alternate norm systems may the state have more of an avenue to influence change and protect vulnerable parties.[72]

women using Shari'ah councils as unofficial dispute resolution mechanisms to resolve matrimonial disputes in England"). *See also* MANAGING FAMILY JUSTICE IN DIVERSE SOCIETIES (Mavis Maclean & John Eekelaar eds., 2013) (discussing the interplay of family law and diverse norms more generally).

[71] *See, e.g.*, JULIE MACFARLANE, ISLAMIC DIVORCE IN NORTH AMERICA: A SHARI'A PATH IN A SECULAR SOCIETY (2012).

[72] Any conversation about joint governance (to use Ayelet Shachar's term) with the state raises very serious concerns *from a religious perspective*, however, because it suggests less than full respect for religious liberty and separation of church and state. It runs a very serious risk of the state co-opting religion and shaping/molding that religion. Indeed, that would be one aim of the state, presumably – and would be exactly the kind of thing many religious people would want to avoid. *See, e.g.*, F.C. DeCoste, *Caesar's Faith: Limited Government and Freedom of Religion in* Bruker v. Marcovitz, 32 DALHOUSIE L.J. 153, 175 (2009) ("[O]nly if faith and family are secure from state management and predation is a state a constitutional state."); Abdullahi Ahmed An-Naim, *Religious Norms and Family Law: Is it Legal or Normative Pluralism?*, 25 EMORY INT'L L. REV. 785, 786 (2011) (stating that religious believers should eschew coercive state enforcement of religious norms).

9

The Resolution of Disputes in State and Tribal Law in the South of Iraq

Toward a Cooperative Model of Pluralism[1]

Haider Ala Hamoudi,[*] Wasfi H. Al-Sharaa,[†] and Aqeel Al-Dahhan[‡]

Do we wish to have more disputes enter the official system and proceed further toward definitive resolution? Is the utopia of access to justice a condition in which all disputes are fully adjudicated? Do we want a world in which there is perfect penetration of norms downward through the pyramid so that all disputes are resolved by application of the authoritative norms propounded by the courts? We know enough about the work of courts to suspect that such a condition would be monstrous in its own way.

– Marc Galanter[2]

If every working matter comes to the law, believe me, neither the Iraqi courts nor the religious authorities could handle it . . . There are a lot of things the state doesn't know, and we solve it among ourselves mutually. . . . What, every suit, every working matter is going to go to court?

– Shaykh Mazen Falih Muhammad Al-'Araiby[3]

If we adopt a conventional, but by no means unchallenged, definition of legal pluralism as the existence of two or more legal systems operating within the same social field,[4] is it necessarily the case that these legal orders are

[*] Associate Professor of Law, University of Pittsburgh School of Law.

[†] Assistant Professor of Law, University of Basra College of Law.

[‡] Assistant Professor of Law, University of Basra College of Law.

[1] The authors would like to thank Mohammad Fadel, Michael Helfand, Barak Richman, Jessie Allen, Kilian Bälz, and all of the participants at the Toronto Faculty of Law Workshop of October 23–24, 2014, for their generous comments and support. All errors are the authors' responsibility alone.

[2] Marc Galanter, *Justice in Many Rooms: Courts, Private Ordering and Indigenous Law*, 19 J. LEGAL PLURALISM 1, 3–4 (1981).

[3] Interview with Shaykh Mazen (Apr. 25, 2013).

[4] John Griffiths, *What Is Legal Pluralism?* 24 J. LEGAL PLURALISM 1, 38 (1986); Sally Engle Merry, *Legal Pluralism*, 22 L. & SOC'Y REV. 869, 870 (1988). Respecting debate over the contours of

in perduring and well-nigh irresolvable conflict? Based on our own work among Iraq's Shi'i tribes, we answer the question emphatically in the negative, and assert that more attention needs to be paid to the possibilities of some form of cooperation between seemingly inconsistent legal systems. Although these have been discussed before, all too often the study of the relationship between state and non-state law presumes a high level of competition that may well be accurate in some contexts, but is fundamentally misplaced in others. Our work in Iraq has demonstrated that far from resenting state law, or regarding its rules as ineffective, alien or inferior, Iraq's Shi'i tribes often embrace Iraq's state law, and quite often regard the tribal law as being in broad cooperation with it in the maintaining of order within their respective social field.

To demonstrate this thesis, this chapter proceeds in six parts. The first part is a highly general and necessarily far from comprehensive survey of what we might call the "conflict paradigm" in legal pluralist literature. This part seeks to demonstrate the existence of a predominant (but by no means exclusive) narrative in the context of the descriptions of the interaction of state law to indigenous, customary or religious forms of non-state law that presumes a significant level of conflict and competition. This part also demonstrates, in connection with the burgeoning "private ordering" literature in the American legal academy, that such competition and conflict among systems may not be as prevalent as is often believed. The next part turns to Iraq itself, to outline the rules of order within the tribe and to demonstrate their obvious divergence from principles of state law.

Inconsistency, however, does not necessitate conflict, as inconsistent legal systems may just as readily *cooperate* with one another using their disparate rules to maintain order as they might be in conflict over which rules to apply. The third part of the chapter therefore explains the modalities of cooperation generally in Iraq as between tribe and state as we have found it. This part also provides a fuller definition of the "thin" version of cooperation between tribe and state, which we claim is present in Iraq, to be distinguished from a "thicker" conception, which would involve more sustained interaction between state and non-state authorities. The fourth part offers some limitations on the thesis, in particular on the manner in which even a cooperative paradigm does not preclude the existence of some level of conflict between the inconsistent legal systems. The fifth part offers an application of the same principles in the

the concept of legal pluralism, see generally Gordon R. Woodman, *Ideological Combat and Social Observations: Recent Debate about Legal Pluralism*, 42 J. LEGAL PLURALISM 1 (1998). Suffice it to say, it is not the intention of the authors to offer a radically new conception of such a vast and varied field of law given how much attention has been dedicated to that subject over the past several decades, hence our use of a conventional definition.

context of a case that we had an opportunity to follow closely. The case is of the type that Llewellyn and Hoebel might describe as a "trouble case,"[5] one that threatened some level of disruption if left unresolved. It demonstrates the use of both state and non-state law to effect resolution. Finally, in the sixth part, we try to draw some broader lessons from the exercise on the manner in which the divide between state and non-state law might be understood and mediated.

LEGAL PLURALISM AND LEGAL COMPETITION

In offering a different, potential approach to understanding the interaction of state and non-state law in particular contexts, we do not contend that we are the first ever to have considered the possibility that the two forms of law cooperate with one another. To the contrary, the matter has received modest attention. In the first case, there are, of course, many instances of "state law pluralism," wherein the state explicitly defers to a foreign body of law in one or more areas. In such cases, some broad level of cooperation must have at least been presumed by the drafters.[6] To the extent that one regards federalism – or a clause in a constitution forbidding legislation that is repugnant to Islam or the *sharia* – to even be a form of pluralism, then instances of cooperative pluralism abound.[7]

Yet even when considering "strong" forms of pluralism, where state law does not itself formally sanction the operation of plural legal systems in the same social field, instances of cooperation between legal orders unmistakably appear in the literature. Sarah Ben Nefissa has written of "implicit delegation" on the part of the state to Arab tribes as concerns the administration of justice in the context of blood feuds.[8] The context in that case was not entirely dissimilar to that which we engage here. In an entirely different context, and many years

---

[5]   Karl N. Llewellyn & E. Adamson Hoebel, The Cheyenne Way 61–62 (1941).

[6]   Woodman, *supra* note 4, at 34.

[7]   For his part, Griffiths dismisses this sort of formal legal delegation as a "weak" form of legal pluralism that is more the study of legal doctrine than the descriptive assessment of how plural legal orders apply in any given social field. It does little to dispel the legal centralist "myth" that all legal order arises from the state, in that the alternative order is presumed only to have force because the state chooses to recognize it. Griffiths, *supra* note 4, at 8. The categorical nature of this distinction as between state law pluralism and other forms of legal pluralism has been criticized by others. Woodman, *supra* note 4, at 35–37. We take no view on the subject, noting only that our work in these pages deals exclusively with a "strong" form of legal pluralism, as there is no express constitutional delegation of authority to the tribe in Iraq's state law system, as discussed in greater detail herein.

[8]   Sarah Ben Nefissa, *The Haqq al-'Arab: Conflict Resolution and Distinctive Features of Legal Pluralism in Contemporary Egypt, in* Legal Pluralism in the Arab World 154 (Baudouin Dupret, Maurits Berger & Laila al-Zwaini eds., 1999) (quoting Bernard Botiveau).

earlier, Stuart Henry described the manner in which housing communes, while proclaiming their opposition to prevailing state structures of capitalism, in fact at times benefitted from the very laws they opposed and sought to use those laws to enforce their own forms of communal justice.[9] Perhaps most pertinently, the legal anthropologist Larry Rosen has done extensive work in Morocco to demonstrate that within the specific Moroccan, cultural context, legal pluralism exists in abundance, and among Moroccans there is "a very diminished sense of contradiction among identifiably distinct legal orders."[10] Brian Tamanaha is therefore surely correct, and certainly in keeping with legal pluralist literature, in indicating that the mere fact that legal systems within a particular social field are *inconsistent* does not mean that they will necessarily *clash.*[11]

At the same time, it is difficult to read legal pluralist literature without discerning a dominant narrative of conflict and competition between inconsistent legal orders, in particular in the context of the relationship between state law and indigenous, customary, or religious forms of ordering. In the words of Bernard Botiveau, a leading legal anthropologist who has studied the Arab world:

> While accepting that a single society contains a multitude of normative fields and that an individual may, at one time, be involved in several of those fields, we cannot hope to maintain that these fields coexist peacefully. In fact each of them is constantly vying with the others for greater legitimacy.... Competition is a reality.[12]

In a less absolutist fashion, Tamanaha indicates, as we do, that the coexistence of inconsistent legal orders does not necessarily result in perduring conflict among them. However, he devotes most of his attention to the subject of conflict. Tamanaha, that is, seems to suggest by his focus that harmony and cooperation among different legal orders is a sort of exception to an implicitly general modus operandi of conflict.[13] As Sally Engle Merry remarked in 1988 in a highly satisfying review of legal pluralist literature, "the theme . . . is the

---

[9] Stuart Henry, *Communal Justice, Capitalist Society, and Human Agency: The Dialectics of Collective Law in the Cooperative*, 19 L. & SOC'Y REV. 303, 311–14 (1985).

[10] Lawrence Rosen, *Legal Pluralism and Cultural Unity in Morocco, in* LEGAL PLURALISM IN THE ARAB WORLD, *supra* note 8, at 92–93.

[11] Brian Z. Tamanaha, *Understanding Legal Pluralism: Past to Present, Local to Global*, 30 SYDNEY L. REV. 375, 405 (2008).

[12] Bernard Botiveau, *Palestinian Law: Social Segmentation Versus Centralization, in* LEGAL PLURALISM IN THE ARAB WORLD, *supra* note 8, at 76.

[13] Tamanaha, *supra* note 11, at 405.

penetration and domination of state law, and its subversion at the margins."[14] This is no less true today.

Within the American legal academy, one of the most significant early contributions to the ways of non-state law is located firmly in a context where conflict with state law was almost sure to predominate. Llewellyn and Hoebel's *The Cheyenne Way* maintains that the Cheyenne had an elaborate and carefully constructed legal system and seeks to examine that system through the Cheyenne administration of "trouble cases."[15] In its efforts, it presages much of the work of the legal pluralists in the decades following its publication in 1941. As with the later legal pluralists, its authors insist that there is more to "law" than that issued by the political state.[16] They maintain that even in the political state, there are plural bodies of law that constrain conduct, not all of which are recognized in a court of law (or in Llewellyn's words, constitute "Class A Law-stuff").[17] And perhaps most importantly, in keeping with what would become the obsession of legal pluralists for a period of decades,[18] they insist both that there must be a distinction between "law" and "norms" and then seek to find a satisfactory definition for law that does not depend on state promulgation.[19]

Equally importantly, the absolute incompatibility of the Cheyenne ways with those of the white man is not so much stated as presumed. Given the nature of the political disputes between the United States and the Native

---

[14] Merry, *supra* note 4, at 886.

[15] LLEWELLYN & HOEBEL, *supra* note 5, at 61–62.

[16] *Id.* at 52–53.

[17] *Id.* at 52.

[18] The central problem with which legal pluralists have grappled is the method by which one determines precisely what "law" is once it is determined that it is independent of the law of the state. Tamanaha, *supra* note 11, at 391. Merry's indication in 1988 that "the literature in this field has not yet clearly demarcated a boundary between normative orders that can and cannot be called law" remains true to this day. Merry, *supra* note 4, at 878–79. Some have argued that even attempting such a distinction is impossible. Joel-Noël Ferrié, *Norms, Law and Practices: The Practical Obstacles That Make It Impossible to Separate Them, in* LEGAL PLURALISM IN THE ARAB WORLD, *supra* note 8, at 21. Tamanaha offers a definition wherein law is that which is socially recognized as such. Tamanaha, *supra* note 11, at 396. In an interesting article on legal pluralism as it operates in Egypt, Baudouin Dupret elaborates on (and to some extent criticizes) Tamanaha's rather straightforward idea by giving more robust recognition to the practical and temporal context in which social actors may choose to deploy the term "law" to refer to a particular normative system. Baudouin Dupret, *What Is Plural in the Law: A Praxiological Answer,* 7 EGYPTE/MONDE ARABE 160–61 (2004). Given our approach herein, we are obviously sympathetic to the realist and praxiological claims that underlie the analyses of Tamanaha and Dupret, respectively. However, a conclusive answer to the question of what type of non-state normative systems may be termed "law" is far beyond the scope of this chapter.

[19] LLEWELLYN & HOEBEL, *supra* note 5, at 24–25.

American tribes, there is some sense to this. It is almost unimaginable that the two systems could in fact work in any sort of harmony.[20] The arrival of American law and order, Llewellyn and Hoebel make clear in the memorable passage at the end of the book, necessitates the end of the Cheyenne ways: "while the buffalo vanish, and the white man moves exorably in. Cheyenne law leaped to glory as it set."[21]

The context of a colonial power imposing imperial law in a developing society is different, and the role of the Western-inspired legal transplant in a postcolonial society more different still. Dupret is correct respecting a regrettable tendency in legal pluralist literature toward a certain cultural essentialism that somehow regards every influence deemed to have arisen outside the "native" culture as unwelcome and inauthentic.[22] "Authenticity" then seems to be found, Dupret notes, in some sort of pristine "indigenous" law that hardly seems to exist outside of the mind of the scholar describing it.[23] The reality is that legal transplants are not foreign systems with which local populations are unfamiliar. In the Arab world, the primary, transplanted civil and criminal codes are drafted by local authorities, rendered binding law by local legislatures, taught by local law professors to local students and interpreted by local scholars and judges.[24] The Iraqi Civil Code, to take the simplest example, was drafted by the greatest Arab jurist of the twentieth century, Abdul Razzaq al-Sanhuri, enacted in 1951, decades after Iraq was recognized as an independent state, and has been in effect ever since, through Arabist revolution and Islamist revival alike.[25] The Civil Code self-evidently adopts a number of principles from Continental Law, including the all-important general theory of obligation.[26] It would be a mistake to take from this any sort of principle of legal centralism – where courts interpreting the Iraqi Civil Code

---

[20] There is also the point, of course, that the Cheyenne "law ways" and United States law are, to use a phrase developed by Kilian Bälz in a different context, "radically autonomous." Kilian Bälz, *Shari'a and Qanun in Egyptian Law: A Systems Theory Approach to Legal Pluralism*, 2 Y.B. ISLAMIC & MIDDLE EAST L. 37, 39 (1995). Any attempt to formally integrate one into the other would result in its effective displacement and reimagining in the context of the surviving system, similar to what Bälz claims occurs whenever a secular national court attempts to interpret *shari'a*. Bälz, *supra* at 47.

[21] LLEWELLYN & HOEBEL, *supra* note 5, at 340.

[22] Dupret, *supra* note 18, at 158.

[23] *Id.*

[24] On the general centrality of the transplant in much of the Muslim world in establishing the state's legal order, and the insistence of all too many scholars to deem it less authentic and worthy of study than the far less applicable *shari'a*, see Lama Abu Odeh, *The Politics of (Mis)recognition: Islamic Law Pedagogy in American Academia*, 52 AM. J. COMP. L. 789, 790–92 (2004).

[25] Civil Code No. 40 of 1951 (Iraq).

[26] Haider Ala Hamoudi, *The Death of Islamic Law*, 38 GA. J. INT'L & COMP. L. 293, 310–11 (2010).

determine the outcome of any tort related dispute that might arise as between private parties, for example. Yet it would be equally a mistake to veer toward what Eric Feldman aptly calls "norm centralism," where somehow the state's law was almost by necessity an inefficient, bumbling, and hostilely regarded interloper and the "true" manner of dispute resolution something deemed more "authentic" and "local."[27]

There are of course very serious problems relating to state legitimacy in Iraq, and consequently the legitimacy of state law. This is particularly so in light of the rise of the Islamic State of Iraq and Syria (ISIS) in 2014 and its assumption of control of large swaths of Iraqi territory, including the major urban center of Mosul. This phenomenon is orthogonal to the themes of this chapter, however, for two reasons. First, and most importantly, our work here relates to Shi'i tribes and Shi'i resolution processes, and the problem of state illegitimacy is not one that is prevalent in the majority Shi'i community. Thus, the broadly revered Shi'i cleric Grand Ayatollah al-Sistani reacted to the ISIS threat by urging Iraqis to join state institutions for the express purpose of reversing the ISIS gains.[28] The call was, to say the least, well received within the Shi'i community, demonstrating a significant level of commitment on the part of Iraq's Shi'a to the state in at least some contexts.[29]

Secondly, to the extent that the minority communities are less than enthused with the operation of the Iraqi state, their demands relate to a better functioning state, or perhaps in the Kurdish case a different state exercising effective political control, and not the withdrawal of state authority entirely.[30] Thus, the existing cleavages within Iraqi society that threaten its very existence do not

---

[27] Eric A. Feldman, *The Tuna Court: Law and Norms in the World's Premier Fish Market*, 94 Cal. L. Rev. 313, 316 n.8 (2006).

[28] Thomas Erdbrink, *Challenges to Shiite Establishment Further Threaten the Future of Iraq*, N.Y.Times, June 24, 2014, at A11 (noting Sistani's position and contrasting it with that of a more junior cleric, Muqtada al-Sadr).

[29] *Id.* It bears mentioning that Sistani has also promulgated rules respecting marriage that derogate quite significantly from the law of the state. *See, e.g.,* 3 Ali al-Sistani, Minhaj al-Saliheen 16 (2008) (deeming a "temporary" marriage to be permissible, in a fashion that it is decidedly not in Iraqi law). This demonstrates in a separate context from that discussed in this chapter the means by which prominent Iraqi actors embrace state authority for particular purposes (for example, national security) while at the same time eschewing it for others (for example, marriage).

[30] Thus, there is some dispute in the academic literature respecting whether or not the Sunni community in its political demands wishes to see some greater level of local, state-based autonomy, or it seeks a more inclusive national state. *Compare* Haider Ala Hamoudi, Negotiating in Civil Conflict: Constitutional Construction and Imperfect Bargaining in Iraq 179–82 (2014) (taking the position that the Sunni demands were for a strong, central state that included them) *with* Feisal Amin Rasoul al-Istrabadi, *A City of Two Tales*, 68 Middle East J. 333, 335–36 (2014) (arguing that Sunni protestors seek greater separation from Baghdad). The dispute, however, relates to the *form* of state authority rather than to its *existence*. No scholar

arise because of a conflict between two conceptions of authority, one vested in the state and the other in the tribe, but rather in two disparate conceptions of statehood, one presuming a strong central authority and the other presuming more localized control. Hence, when trying to understand the relationship of state to non-state law in a nation like Iraq, reference to colonial era efforts is not useful.

More useful analogies, we submit, are offered in the substantial amount of "private ordering" literature that has arisen in the American legal academy to describe rulemaking and application in various, discrete "semi-autonomous social fields"[31] as they exist in the United States. The domestic law in Iraq, in other words, is likely to be regarded by its population less like a colonial imposition and more like any state law would to private actors operating in a semiautonomous social field in a developed nation such as the United States.

The two leading, seminal works on "private ordering" demonstrate the importance of cooperation of disparate legal systems quite well, even if they had a primary purpose that was different. The first, Lisa Bernstein's well-known article concerning diamond sellers in New York City, describes how individuals involved in the diamond industry have developed their own rules pursuant to which they adjudicate disputes. The manner in which they manage this is through rules of membership in the all-important diamond exchange, the New York Diamond Dealers Club. Members are obligated to submit their disputes, whether they concern the sale of rough diamonds or polished stones, to an arbitration board in the Club pursuant to the Club's rules. The board then adjudicates according to the bylaws of the Club as well as trade customs and usages. Failing to abide by the contractual, arbitral agreement and proceeding to court is against the Club's rules and can result in expulsion from the Club.[32] Though disputes with nonmembers do not have to be submitted to the Club, often they are, for a variety of reasons, including minimizing transactional and reputational costs.[33]

---

of note to our knowledge takes the position that any minority community wishes to see state authority replaced with a pure tribal system as opposed to a differently oriented state system.

[31] The phrase "semi-autonomous social field" was coined by Sally Falk Moore in a highly influential 1972 article wherein she maintained that the appropriate subject of study of the interaction of law and other normative ordering was a "semi-autonomous social field," which was capable of making its own rules, but also set in a larger social matrix which affects it. Sally Falk Moore, *Law and Social Change: The Semi-Autonomous Social Field as an Appropriate Subject of Study*, 7 L. & Soc'y Rev. 719, 720 (1972).

[32] Lisa Bernstein, *Opting Out of the Legal System: Extralegal Contractual Relations in the Diamond Industry*, 21 J. Legal Stud. 115, 119–20 (1992).

[33] *Id.* at 126.

In terms of decision making, the arbitration board never publishes its rulings or its basis for them.[34] However, failure to comply with a ruling comes with the stiff reputational penalty of broad publicity of such failure to comply, which seriously hinders the ability of the reluctant party to continue to do business.[35] Apparently, it is this extralegal reputational sanction that tends to influence compliance the most, rather than any sort of threat of legal action.[36] Bernstein points out that this organizational system bears a striking resemblance to Jewish law, which strictly forbids a Jew in quite strident terms from seeking redress in gentile courts to resolve commercial disputes, and subjects a person to ridicule and shame if the prohibition is ignored.[37]

The other seminal work on private ordering, a book by Robert Ellickson, describes in some detail the conduct of farmers and ranchers in Shasta County, California. Ellickson's extensive research indicates that these actors in their semi-autonomous social field very rarely litigate their disputes, at least to the extent that such disputes relate to damage caused by trespassing animals and responsibility for building and repairing fences.[38] In fact, most of the time, they do not even know the underlying law particularly well.[39] Rather, the community has developed its own norms and has developed its own forms of policing, which involve shaming and a variety of other self-help mechanisms, used incrementally and with restraint so as to avoid feuding.[40] Although the community does not invariably ignore state legal rules (motor vehicle accidents, for example, are routinely referred to law), they seem to do so in their "workaday" affairs in a manner that derogates considerably from the state law rules.[41]

It is important when considering such valuable work to keep in mind Moore's famous phrase describing the social field as *semi*autonomous. As with Moore before them, Bernstein and Ellickson have identified social fields that are capable of generating their own rules, and yet, as Moore has properly indicated, the social field is affected by its location within a larger social matrix, which certainly includes the state, the state's law, and those officers and agents responsible for its promulgation and enforcement.[42]

---

[34] *Id.* at 124.

[35] *Id.* at 128.

[36] *Id.* at 152.

[37] *Id.* at 141.

[38] ROBERT C. ELLICKSON, ORDER WITHOUT LAW: NOW NEIGHBORS SETTLE DISPUTES 52–53, 69 (1991).

[39] *Id.* at 49–50, 70.

[40] *Id.* at 57–59.

[41] *Id.* at 94–95, 174.

[42] *See supra* note 31.

Put more concretely, it simply is not true that the farmers and ranchers of Shasta County have managed a form of "order without law." Law, in fact, is everywhere in this social matrix. It merely has been internalized by the social actors and therefore is out of view. Shasta County does not have its own rules on murder, for example. These come from the state of California. The same is true of arson. Hence, when the ornery villain in Ellickson's absorbing narrative, Frank Ellis, continues to permit his cattle to maraud his neighbors' property and proves impervious to the reputational sanctions the community seeks to impose upon him, nobody in Shasta County seems particularly inclined to shoot him, or to burn his house down. It is highly likely that their conscious motivations for doing so involve considerations beyond violations of state law. It is also highly likely, or at least perfectly plausible, that in the absence of such "exogenous" rules, to use Ellickson's preferred economic phrasing of the matter, Shasta County might not exist as Ellickson describes it.[43] The remedy of murder, arson, or something equally felonious might be used, at least at times, leading to a rise in blood feuds. Alternatively, and perhaps more plausibly given the structure of contemporary American society, the entire two industries of ranching and farming would be taken over by organized criminal syndicates who would not shy away from deploying methods that the current citizens would not consider. The normative order of Shasta County *cooperates* with a state law paradigm that its residents broadly regard as legitimate to prevent more serious disputes. That the state's law against theft, for example, is by Ellickson's own reckoning viewed overwhelmingly positively by the residents of Shasta County demonstrates this more than anything.[44]

At the same time, the state law might well be understood to be cooperating with the normative order as well. It is true that in a narrow, formal sense, some of the self-help remedies to which Ellickson's social actors frequently resort are illegal. A rancher may not, we may fairly assume, legally castrate a person's bull because it has repeatedly caused damage to his property, nor may a landowner legally shoot trespassing cattle. These are both examples offered by Ellickson as examples of self-help deployed when reputational sanctions do not seem to work.[45]

---

[43] Ellickson, *supra* note 38, at 174–75. Given Ellickson's reference to the need for such exogenous rules, and his certain knowledge that these come from state law in this instance, we do not believe we are asserting anything he might necessarily disagree with, so much as elaborating on a point that he may not have felt required the same emphasis we do for our purposes. We do, however, have a quibble with the title of his work – "Order Without Law" – for the reasons explored in the main text.

[44] *Id.* at 175.

[45] *Id.* at 58.

Yet even the example of the castrated bull, quite intriguing by Ellickson's reckoning and ours, points to a some level of cooperation in the management of disputes using both state law (to limit the possibilities of feuding) and non-state law (to administer the disputes once the background, exogenous rules are set). For although the rancher in the case of the trespassing, castrated bull may fairly be credited with some restraint, turning to that remedy only when others failed him, and the owner of the castrated bull can be credited with similar restraint for not retaliating, the involvement of state officials was also quite notable. For the rancher in that case did not merely decide to castrate the bull without notice. Before doing so, *he informed a law enforcement official of his intent to do so, and the law enforcement official indicated he would "turn a blind eye" were that to occur.*[46]

The rancher, that is, sought state sanction before deploying his remedy – he wanted to make sure that he did not exceed the bounds that the state's officers permitted him in administering his workaday affairs and negotiating his relations with his fellow Shasta County residents. This restraint on the rancher's part was coupled with restraint on the part of the state officer as well. Here, the state officer chose to leave the matter for the residents to resolve without state interference, at least for so long as the matter related only to castrated bulls, even if he could have deployed state law to force a different resolution.

The decision to defer was almost surely not due to any sort of hostility to the state on the part of the state officer. We may fairly assume that the law enforcement official in question took the role of state officer seriously, and did not join the police force to undermine it. The officer, again we may assume, would not have "turned a blind eye" if the rancher had threatened to kill or burn down the home of the offending bull owner. Instead, the officer was choosing to grant some space to the rancher to maintain order, an "implicit delegation" of sorts. Far from a model wherein each normative order is competing for respective supremacy, here each is pulling back to avoid interference – seeking to work together in maintaining order in the social fields. The cooperation is "thin" in that it involves limited, ad hoc interactions between the inconsistent legal systems rather than a sustained and highly systematized means of engagement across them. Nevertheless, it is very much a form of cooperation, in that each of the two systems is managing itself in a manner that minimizes difficulties with the other system.

If this is the case with respect to Shasta County, it is doubly so in the case of New York's diamond sellers. In fact, one might take issue with describing

---

[46] *Id.*

the contracts in which the parties engage as "extralegal" at all. There are no violations of law involved in the negotiation, administration and enforcement of these contracts. Quite the opposite is true. Not only might a member who ignores her agreement to arbitrate be suspended or expelled from the New York Diamond Dealers Club, but also under formal, state law, *the court will stay her state court suit because of the binding arbitration agreement that exists pursuant to Club rules.*[47] If a member fails to comply with the arbitral ruling, not only will he be exposed to the reputational sanction of being publicly described as one who failed to comply, but the ruling can be confirmed in a state court, which will not look to the substantive basis of the arbitral decision in upholding the ruling.[48] Bernstein's point is well taken that it is not the state law's rules that in fact induce compliance given how infrequently the state law's apparatus are used, even when they can be.[49] Our only elaboration here is to demonstrate that the state is not competing with the normative order for greater influence, but rather voluntarily restraining itself in order to create the space for the normative order to proceed as it has.

Similar to the farmers and ranchers, we must assume that the non-state agents of the normative order are doing the same, using prudence and restraint in deploying their own rules in order to avoid conflict and competition with the state. Although the similarities of the diamond sellers to Jewish law are certainly striking as Bernstein notes, what appear to be the dissimilarities are also quite notable. The authority cited by Bernstein respecting Jewish law does not merely indicate that a Jew should not go to a gentile court to resolve a *commercial dispute*, but rather that to seek redress in a gentile court *at all* was to be "deemed to have reviled and blasphemed and rebelled against the Torah."[50] Such a broad and strident rule, laid down at a time when Jewish courts were struggling to maintain their autonomy,[51] hardly seems the basis upon which the New York Diamond Dealers Club operates, whatever its applicability in other contexts.[52] Although we do not know, it is hard to believe that the

---

[47] Bernstein recognizes this, of course. Bernstein, *supra* note 32, at 120.

[48] *Id.* at 125.

[49] *Id.* at 152.

[50] MENACHEM ELON, I JEWISH LAW: HISTORY, SOURCES, PRINCIPLES 13–14 (Bernard Auberbach & Melvin Sykes trans., 1994). ("Resort to a non-Jewish court was compared to the denial of the existence of God and his Torah. . . . "). We pretend no mastery of Jewish law, and merely rely on the authority cited by Bernstein herself.

[51] *Id.*

[52] The press has reported on the presence of some religious Jewish communities who shun members of their community who report crimes as serious as child abuse to state authorities. Sharon Otterman & Ray Rivera, *Ultra-Orthodox Shun Their Own For Reporting Child Abuse*, N.Y. TIMES, May 9, 2012. We claim no expertise in Jewish law, and so we have no comment

New York Diamond Dealers Club would have a rule expelling a member who sued another member whom he accused of burning down his house, or that they would in fact expel such a member for seeking redress for such an injury from a state court. The semiautonomous social field appears to have internalized a great deal of state law in setting the rules of the game.

To be clear, these are not criticisms of the laudable work of Bernstein and Ellickson, nor are they remarks with which they would necessarily disagree. Our purpose in describing and elaborating on the idea of private ordering as it has been laid out in leading scholarly accounts in the American legal academy is not to attack it, but to make a more modest point. Even in such accounts, where the role of a normative order – a non-state law – is emphasized, the existence of a thin, but real, form of cooperation between state and non-state law in maintaining the broader order in the social field should not be minimized.

In the commercial context, this is an easy fact to overlook because the state's role can be buried deeply in the background, though other leading scholarly accounts point to situations where it is not, in particular in developing societies.[53] Once the state's laws against murder, theft, arson and the like are not only presumed, but also deeply internalized by social actors, they can be swiftly forgotten, and the state's role might then be understood to be more minimal in ensuring the continuation of the order than is appropriate. It takes a different social field to notice the cooperation at work more clearly, one where

on the extent or prevalence of such practices. Our point is only that it is highly unlikely in our estimation that the New York Diamond Dealers Club would operate on this basis.

[53] In particular, in studying the phenomenon of private ordering in the context of societies where the state courts are to some extent dysfunctional, McMillan and Woodruff point out the possibility of criminal violence in the context of private ordering in the absence of public law. They indicate, in a statement with which we wholeheartedly agree, that as a result of problems such as this, "private order can usefully supplement public law, but cannot replace it." We only seek to emphasize herein the means by which such supplementing, which we describe as a thin version of cooperation, takes place in one social field we have had the opportunity to study. *See* John McMillan & Christopher Woodruff, *Private Order Under Dysfunctional Public Order*, 98 MICH. L. REV. 2421, 2423 (2000).

It should be noted in addition that the importance of state law and its potential to cooperate with informal norms has been discussed in the literature as well. Most notably, Eric Feldman has written an illuminating work on the tuna court that exists in Tokyo's Tsukiji Fish Market. Feldman points to an interesting circumstance where informal normative ordering mechanisms and formal state law machinery is combined to create a widely used hybrid formal/informal adjudicative tribunal responsible for administering disputes over the quality of tuna. Feldman, *supra* note 27, at 352–59. The form of cooperation in Feldman's account is admittedly thicker than that which prevails in Iraq, where the interactions between state and tribe are far less formal and sustained than would exist in a hybrid tribunal.

the state plays a role in maintaining order, but is simply not as effective as the police of Shasta County and New York City in limiting violence. One where non-state application of violence would quite plainly exist, and yet tribal feuds might be limited in form and extent by virtue of an imperfect, only partially functioning state system that cooperates with the tribes in maintaining order. Such is the case of Iraq, as the balance of this chapter shall demonstrate.

DISPUTE RESOLUTION UNDER THE LAW OF THE TRIBE

The Role of the Tribe in Iraqi Society

The importance of tribes in maintaining order in the territory currently known as Iraq precedes the actual Iraqi state by centuries. While the Ottoman Empire nominally came to be in control of Iraq in the sixteenth century, the territory lay at its eastern periphery near the Persian Empire with whom the Ottomans were frequently at war.[54] As such, the Ottomans tended to neglect Iraq, and left the tribes to operate in whatever manner they saw fit.[55] Some of this changed in the latter part of the nineteenth century, in particular with the enactment of the Tanzimat reforms and the efforts of the Ottoman governor of Baghdad, Midhat Pasha.[56] Nevertheless, the tribes remained a central force in maintaining order in Iraq's earliest years, an important player in the semiautonomous social fields in which they tended to operate. Marr reports that as late as 1933, Iraqi tribes possessed roughly six times as many guns as the entire government.[57]

Much has changed since 1933, the year after Iraq obtained independence. Iraq's police and military forces now number nearly one million.[58] Iraq's state institutions, from courts to law schools to its government ministries and independent agencies, are far greater in size and influence after a massive expansion in the middle of the twentieth century.[59] Still, Iraq's 150 existing tribes continue to provide an important source of order throughout much of

---

[54] YITZHAK NAKASH, THE SHI'IS OF IRAQ 14 (2003).

[55] *Id.*

[56] *Id.* at 32–33; PHEBE MARR, MODERN HISTORY OF IRAQ 7 (3d ed. 2011) (describing reforms of Midhat Pasha).

[57] Marr, *supra* note 56, at 19.

[58] Iraq's military and nonmilitary security forces aggregate to approximately 800,000 people. Robert Perito & Madeline Kristoff, *Iraq's Interior Ministry: The Key to Police Reform*, UNITED STATES INSTITUTE OF PEACE, July 2009, *available at* http://www.usip.org/sites/default/files/iraq_interior_ministry_perito_kristoff.pdf.

[59] *See, e.g.*, PETER SLUGLETT & MARION FAROUK-SLUGLETT, IRAQ SINCE 1958: FROM REVOLUTION TO DICTATORSHIP 248–50 (3d ed. 2001) (describing vast increase in government bureaucracy in the early 1970s).

Iraq.[60] Indeed, every Iraqi belongs to a tribe, and we personally know of no Iraqi who is entirely unaware to what tribe he belongs.[61]

That said, this does not mean that every Iraqi relies exclusively, or even extensively, on tribal resolution procedures. Importantly, there is a significant level of geographic variation in the influence of the tribes. At one extreme, urban elites often dismiss their tribal affiliation as irrelevant, and view tribal order with some level of contempt. Beyond the urban elite, tribal affiliation carries at least some significance, and among rural populations, it bears particular importance.

To add further complication, according to the tribal leaders with whom we spoke, there is temporal variation in the extent to which tribes exercise meaningful authority in Iraq relative to the state. When the state is in a position of relative strength, the state tends to adjudicate more disputes. When it is not, tribal authority increases accordingly. The precise ebb and flow of tribal authority relative to the state over the course of Iraq's history is a matter we do not explore in detail here, though it is worthy of further study that we hope to undertake in the future.

Because every Iraqi belongs to a tribe, there are tribes among all segments of Iraq's population, and some of the larger tribes span the Sunni–Shia divide.[62] Among the larger and historically more influential tribes among the Arabs are the Shammar, the Dulaym, the Jibur, the Rubai'e and the Zubaydis, each of which has at least several hundred thousand members.[63] The largest and influential Kurdish tribes are the Jaf and the Barazan. Many Iraqis are affiliated with tribes that are smaller in population than these extremely large tribes.[64] Even these larger tribes are divided into smaller subtribes, or clans, where it seems that more meaningful authority was effectively exercised.

---

[60] HUSSEIN D. HASSAN, CONG. RESEARCH SERV., RS22626, IRAQ: TRIBAL STRUCTURE, SOCIAL AND POLITICAL ACTIVITIES 1 (Apr. 7, 2008).

[61] *Cf.* Neil MacFarquhar, *Unpredictable Force Awaits U.S. in Iraq: Storied Tribes in the Middle East, Devout, Armed and Nationalistic*, INT'L HERALD TRIB., Jan. 7, 2003, at 2 (describing three quarters of Iraq's population as belonging to tribes). It is possible that MacFarquhar's errant number comes because the estimation is of those who affiliate closely or moderately closely with their tribe, thereby excluding casual members whose sole affiliation is symbolic or nominal.

[62] HASSAN, *supra* note 60, at 2.

[63] *Id.* at 3. Obviously, dispute resolution cannot in each instance demand the full attention of leaders of hundreds of thousands of people. Tribes are thus divided into subunits such as clans, which tend to address most ordinary affairs. Because we treat the tribe as a discrete unit, as described below, we do not address herein the internal organization of the tribe in any depth. Suffice it to say, a local or regional tribal leader has the authority to manage disputes of the type discussed in this chapter on behalf of his tribe with counterparts in other tribes.

[64] *Id.* at 1.

According to the tribal authorities with whom we spoke, tribal affiliation is passed exclusively along the male line. This means that the tribes are not opposed to, and indeed often welcome, intertribal marriages as a means to cement a reconciliation process. The woman in such a marriage would retain her original tribal identity, and her children would obviously be nephews of men of a different tribe, making conflict less likely. However, whatever (maternal) *family* connections might exist, as a *tribal* matter children would be regarded as belonging to the tribe of their father.

Our field research was conducted solely among the Shi'i tribes in Iraq's south, whose reach extended through to the heavily Shi'i areas of Baghdad, such as Sadr City, which is in effect an immense squalid neighborhood filled with recent migrants from Iraq's south. All of the tribal leaders we interviewed told us that the system of resolution they described that related to their tribes did not differ significantly from that used by tribes firmly located in Iraq's center, such as Baghdad, nor was it very different from the practices of the predominantly Sunni tribes of the west, except as specifically indicated herein. We have not sought to ascertain this directly, however.

Methodology

We conducted a series of interviews with eight tribal leaders who led entire tribes or at least significant branches of them and therefore managed disputes on a regular basis on behalf of the tribe, or branch thereof. Our early interviews were highly general and designed primarily to grasp the basics of the dispute resolution processes deployed by Iraqi tribes. We used later interviews to seek clarification, to discuss actual examples of the principles described, and to elicit answers to more pointed questions in regard to the relationship of particular tribal procedures to state law. Finally, we had the opportunity to attend a single large dispute resolution ceremony. All this field research was conducted during the spring of 2013, beginning in April and ending before the middle of June. Unless otherwise indicated, our knowledge of contemporary tribal practices derives from these experiences.

Although we strongly believe that our methods have yielded broadly accurate and interesting findings, it is important to note their limitations. There are two in particular that stand out. First, we did not conduct interviews with state law officers and personnel to elicit their views on the manner and extent to which the state deferred as a matter of practice to tribal processes in particular circumstances. We did attempt this as a preliminary matter, but received largely formal and highly practiced answers to the effect that the state uses its investigative powers thoroughly to pursue every possible crime and will not relinquish a case until it has been satisfactorily resolved. As Iraqi law does not recognize the tribal resolution procedures at all, these officials insisted, there was no deference on their part to the tribes, or any other non-state actors, at any time or in any place. Not only was that plainly not true in the particular context of Iraq, it is not true in any jurisdiction of which we are aware. To conduct useful interviews, we found that we would need more time than we had to gain the trust of judges and other state law officers so they would speak more candidly with us.

That said, direct interviews with state officers, although they would be quite helpful, are probably less important than they are in the tribal instance simply because the state keeps ample records of its activities while the tribe's records are comparatively scant. Of course, there is value in understanding when a police officer might turn a blind eye to particular activity without filing a report. It would also be useful to know when a police officer might arrest and detain a person, followed by a release ordered by an authority in a police station before a file is prepared and after tribal intervention. A more complete description of the interaction between state and tribe would require that such important fieldwork be undertaken.

Nevertheless, we can glean much of the state's passive, "thin" cooperation with the tribes from court records. Hence, in addition to the interviews described, we spent days in the summer of 2013 researching court files in Baghdad's Rusafa criminal court, as well as criminal courts in Basra and 'Amara, a smaller city in Iraq's south. Records from police files are not as accessible, and are hardly as important as they might be in the United States. This is because under Iraq's inquisitorial system, the police must record any information respecting a potential crime and immediately transfer the case to the investigative courts, where an investigatory judge is then responsible for gathering facts and evidence to make a preliminary determination of whether further criminal proceedings are warranted.[65]

Secondly, with the one exception of the tribal settlement we witnessed, we derived our findings not from our own direct observations of the tribal processes at work, but rather accounts of those processes from the actors operating in the social field. Ideally, given sufficient time, we would directly follow a series of disputes as they wound through tribal and state law processes to determine

---

[65] Criminal Procedure Code No. 23 of 1971, art. 49(a) (Iraq) ("It is incumbent on any responsible authority in the police station upon the reaching to him of any news of the commission of a felony or a misdemeanor that he record immediately the statements of the informant, obtain [the informant's] signature thereon, and send a report of that to an investigative judge or an investigator . . .") (translation by authors).

their ultimate outcomes. Although it is possible to discover active cases in court files, connecting them to the tribal resolution processes that appear to have transpired alongside those active cases would take considerable work to unearth and explore. We have been unable to do this in the time we have devoted to the matter to date.

Addressing these two limitations in future work would, we strongly believe, unearth further findings that might prove more interesting, and we hope to do this in the months and years to come. However, we stress that it would be extremely unlikely to change our conclusions so much as develop them further.

The Tribe as Corporate Unit

On its surface, it may appear incongruous to relate the dispute resolution processes between Iraqi tribes to those that arise in much of the private ordering literature in the American academy. Yet the similarities are in fact quite remarkable. To see how this is so, it is important to note at the outset that we focus on the tribes as discrete, self-contained units, interacting with other, similar units much like individuals. A rough analogue would be the manner in which modern company law invests various types of companies, most particularly corporations, with legal personality and treats them as individuals though they are, like tribes, not natural persons.

This approach greatly simplifies our examination of the resolution procedures, though it does leave unexplored important areas of Iraqi tribal law that certainly deserve greater study. Most glaringly, by treating the tribe as a single corporate person, we do not address issues of tribal governance in any level of detail. Hence, the relationship of the branches of the major tribes to the larger tribe, both fiscally and administratively, is a matter we do not touch upon. Nor do we discuss the manner in which the tribe might choose to address disputes within the tribe, or across branches of it, as opposed to disputes arising between members of two distinct tribes. Finally, there may be important issues relating to how to handle claims of compensation within the tribe due to an injury caused by an outsider that resulted in harm to several victims. We leave all of this to a subsequent and more extensive study.

The advantage of our more focussed approach, however, is that it makes much clearer the relationship of tribal ordering and private ordering. As with actors in the private ordering literature, the tribes are certainly "close-knit" and interact with each other frequently. Tribes are not all of precisely the same size and influence, but informal power is about as evenly distributed among them as it is among private, commercial actors in many private ordering settings.

Information certainly circulates among the tribes extremely fluidly as it does among actors in private ordering accounts.[66]

Finally, and most importantly, the tribes are "repeat players" in their dealings with one another, and they are perfectly aware of this. They have frequent disputes, and they can expect such disputes to continue over the near-to-medium term. One of our interviewees, Shaykh Chamil of the tribe of Abu Muhammad, summarized the situation using a popular tribal adage: "today you have means, and we complain to you of misfortune, but tomorrow, in your home, you shall find need to complain to others." This is important. Richman notes that it is a "mainstay" of private ordering literature that "prospects for future transactions induc[e] compliance with current contractual obligations."[67] This expectation of repeat interaction is entirely true of the Iraqi tribes, the only difference being that the obligations to which compliance is induced are not only, or even primarily, contractual, but rather delictual.

The Mechanisms Deployed to Resolve Intertribal Disputes

Given the similarities in structure between the Iraqi tribes on the one hand and individuals in the literature of private ordering on the other, the means by which they resolve disputes tend to be quite similar. Iraqi tribes tend to rely on reputational sanctions in their early phases. They then resort to escalating self-help remedies that are used with some level of restraint to avoid the negative consequences and threats to public order that can attend as remedies grow more severe. They turn to the more extreme remedies only in the rare case.

Notification

In keeping with the desire to rely on reputation and avoid remedies that could escalate out of control and thereby garner the attention of the state, the tribal disputes begin with what is known as a *tanbih*, or notification. Effectively, an injured party from one tribe sends notice to the perpetrator from the second tribe that an injury is claimed, and that recompense is demanded. Importantly, in particular for smaller injuries (anything from a stolen car to an unpaid debt) this does not need to involve significant tribal elders. The notice is sent through a *sayyid*, meaning a direct descendant of the Prophet Muhammad (such figures being universally respected throughout Iraq, and within the Shi'i

---

[66] *See, e.g.*, Ellickson, *supra* note 38, at 179.
[67] Barak D. Richman, *Firms, Courts, and Reputation Mechanisms: Towards A Positive Theory of Private Ordering*, 104 COLUM. L. REV. 2328, 2339 (2004).

community in particular). If it is responded to, an accommodation might be reached quickly and with minimal reputational damage to the offending party. The notification, in other words, is an opportunity to resolve the matter in a sort of mediation, without resort to the more elaborate tribal processes.

In more serious cases, the notification process might be forgone, though it need not be. As an example that was given to us, two young men from opposing tribes were in a drag race, and due to the negligence of one of the drivers, the second was killed, before a number of witnesses. The first youth never informed his tribe of the death of the second and instead hoped, as adolescents always do, that the problem would somehow resolve itself. In such fatal cases, it is the male members of the immediate family of the victim who are expected to raise the matter with their own tribe in order to initiate formal dispute resolution procedures. This would be the father if he is living, but if not, it would be the closest male relatives, which could be brothers, uncles, or even sons depending on the age of the victim.

However, in this particular case, rather than escalate the dispute formally, the broader family of the victim sent a notification to prominent family members of the perpetrator, believing (accurately) that it was impossible that the offending tribe was ignoring a death and that instead the matter was not being reported to the family and the tribe. Promptly after the notification, the matter was resolved among the immediate families, without broader tribal involvement.

The Confrontation

If the notification does not lead to a fruitful result, the next self-help mechanism is known as the *guama*, perhaps best translated as the confrontation. It is here where reputational sanctions begin to have their bite. The injured party invokes tribal processes, and the tribal *shaykh*, presuming that he accepts the legitimacy of the complaint, authorizes a sizable delegation to go to the home of the perpetrator in full view of the neighborhood. The delegation will be composed of those who are, to use the words of one tribal *shaykh*, "severe personalities" [*nas al jalda*]. They will be accompanied by a third party to act as witness as to the occurrence of the confrontation. They will, in strict fashion, note the injury, demand recompense, and insist on a visit from the perpetrator's tribe to the victims within a set period.

The confrontation is intended to be nonviolent, and violence does not generally result from it. It serves the dual purpose of warning the perpetrator of further consequences and initiating reputational sanctions against the perpetrator and by extension, his tribe.

The Striking

It is important to note that the vast majority of disputes are addressed in a mutually beneficial fashion before this next, more serious dispute resolution stage arises. As noted, the tribes are "repeat players"; they are well aware that although there may be a claim against them one day, they will be making a claim on the next. It is therefore in their interest to avoid reputational sanctions, and to cooperate with those who make claims against them for the benefit of the easier settlement future claims they might make. By and large, they do this.

Nevertheless, if following a confrontation, the offending tribe does not pay a visit to the injured tribe, the first actual use of violence ensues. The injured tribe sends armed men to the home of the perpetrator and sprays it with some number of bullets in a process known as the *degga*, or the striking. The striking can be repeated one or more times, in each case involving more bullets and more damage to the home. The visits might be in the middle of the night, or during the day, and although the risk of personal injury is obviously present, the clear intention is not to harm any person.

Though it is a clear use of violence, and the threat of harm is obvious, in fact the striking has very much the same dual purpose as the confrontation, but in escalated form. It is not only a threat; it is also a serious reputational sanction to the individual and to the tribe. The entire community is aware when a striking occurs, and news travels relatively fast within Iraq. It is unwise for a tribe to earn a reputation for having to endure a striking before it is willing to compensate for an injury that one of their own may have caused.

Kidnapping

In the rarest of cases, members of the injured tribe kidnap members of the offending tribe and hold them until the offending tribe agrees to pay the requisite compensation. Although the measure is permissible under the tribal law in extreme circumstances, when other measures have been exhausted, it is rarely employed. If it is used, it is considered a matter of considerable honor to treat the kidnapped members of the tribe well. A failure to do so would lead to severe reputational sanctions. An analogy to Shasta County is notable, though in the cases reported by Ellickson, the matter involved the abduction and holding of cattle, not human beings.[68] The reason for the difference, of course, lies in the relative role of the state in maintaining order, which is

---

[68] Ellickson, *supra* note 38, at 63.

discussed in the next section. One presumes that the state of California would not turn a blind eye to the kidnapping of human beings. Neither does Iraq, as we shall see, though its ability to police the matter is considerably more limited.

Arbitration

It is important to note that until this point, we have proceeded under the assumption that there is some clarity as to who the responsible party happens to be for any given injury. This is often true in cases ranging from assaults to theft to intentional and unintentional killing. Of course, it need not be. If it is not, then prior to escalation and upon notification or confrontation, the allegedly offending tribe may demand an informal arbitration to be handled by a single, well-respected senior figure selected by the parties known as a *faridha*. (In practice, there are only a handful of such figures to whom tribes turn, making the selection process relatively straightforward.) The arbitrator is authorized to hear evidence, to take witness statements from those who have been endorsed as reliable by their own tribal leaders and to render rulings on the basis of those statements in a process that is quite informal and relatively swift, usually taking no more than a day or two in the most. Naturally, no self-help remedies may be used pending the outcome of the tribal arbitration.

The only relatively unique aspect of the arbitration that bears mentioning is the role and form of oath taking. At times, there is no evidence in favor of a claim on the part of an injured party, nor against it. Neither witnesses, nor pictures, nor documentation appears, and of course the tribe lacks capacity to engage in any sort of extensive forensic analysis. In such cases, what is resorted to is known as taking an oath of the tomb of Abbas. In Shi'a lore, Abbas is the half brother of the Prophet Muhammad's grandson, the Imam Hussein, who is himself deemed the third righteous leader of the Muslim community following the Prophet's death.[69] Imam Hussein's killing in an area of southern Iraq known as Kerbala by the then Sunni caliph is regarded by the Shi'a as a cataclysmic event, commemorated with excessive lamentations to this day. Abbas, who died with Imam Hussein in Kerbala, was regarded as one of Imam Hussein's most fearsome warriors, one who continued to fight even as his right hand, and then his left, was severed by the caliph's forces. Both he and his half brother are buried in Kerbala.[70]

---

[69] Moojan Momen, An Introduction to Shi'i Islam: The History and Doctrines of Twelver Shi'ism 30–31 (1987).

[70] *Id.* at 31–33.

So as to ensure the veracity of a particular party claiming injury where no evidence exists in either direction,[71] a victim can be taken to Kerbala at the insistence of the offending party and be made to swear on the tomb of Shi'a Islam's mightiest warrior that what he or she claims is true.[72] Once undertaken, a party's honor, referred to among the tribes using the colloquial term *bakht*, is invoked, and to involve one's *bakht* is a serious matter.[73] Were the party later deemed not to be telling the truth, then the person will be committing a grievous sin, a matter that cannot be readily ignored among a deeply pious people. Moreover, high levels of communal shaming would result. They would no longer be deemed to be honorable members of the community, their testimony would be deemed worthless, they would not be lent money, and other similar social consequences would follow.[74] As a result of this combination of divine and human sanction, we are told that it is not unusual for an injured party to insist that a particular injury arose from a particular person to demur once the other party insists on an oath at the Abbas tomb.

The Respite

Whether the result of an adverse arbitrary ruling or self-help remedies directed against it, when an offending tribe relents, it must then seek a respite,[75] or *atwa,*

[71] Importantly, the process is used as a substitute for evidence when no conclusive evidence exists. It does not supplant evidence should there be enough for the arbitrator to make a ruling in the absence of an oath. Nor would it be wise for any person to seek to make an oath in the face of considerable contrary evidence, given the severe reputational sanctions that can attach.

[72] While we do not doubt that there is some form of oath taking that takes place among Sunni tribes, it almost surely does not involve travel to the tomb of Abbas, a person of no particularly important stature within Sunni Islam. As our work did not involve the investigation of Sunni tribes, however, this is entirely a matter of speculation.

[73] It is not strictly necessary to take one to the tomb of Abbas in order to invoke their *bakht*. An arbitrator could simply require a swearing on the Qur'an, or even ask them "on their *bakht*" if a particular matter was true. At the insistence of the allegedly offending tribe, however, a matter of sufficient importance is taken to the shrine of Abbas.

[74] Reliance on social sanctions to induce compliance with rules is by no means unique to Iraq's tribes, even if the particular religious manifestations of it are more unusual. As McMillan and Woodruff report, circumstances where spontaneous cooperation thrive tend to be those where groups "lack the ability to implement formal sanctions . . . although they may, and generally do, rely on social sanctions as an enforcement mechanism. These social sanctions usually operate through ostracizing or excluding members from the group." McMillan & Woodruff, *supra* note 53, at 2434.

[75] Interestingly enough, one of the tribal leaders we interviewed, attempting to justify all of these various processes as being in accordance with the *shari'a,* insisted that the origins of the respite are from the Prophet's ceasefire with the non-Muslim tribes in Mecca. The analogy is strained and difficult to support. The Prophet's ceasefire was between warring parties who saw mutual advantage in a break from fighting that both intended to continue at a later time, after the

from the injured tribe. The respite is designed to give the offending tribe an opportunity to gather its members and others for the large resolution that will take place. It is effectively an admission of guilt, however, and an agreement to pay whatever compensation the injured tribe demands. In return, the offending tribe is prohibited from pursuing any self-help remedies during the period of the respite. The length of the respite varies depending on the circumstances, but usually runs from a month to two months.

The *Fasl*

The final step in the process is what is known as the *fasl*, the best-known part of the tribal proceedings throughout Iraq, and the most difficult to translate. The term encompasses both the convening of the tribes to effect a final resolution, and the resolution arising therefrom. Because a phrase like "convening and resolution," although accurate, is awkward and cumbersome, we will in this case adhere to the Arabic term *fasl*.

To hold the *fasl*, the offending tribe pays a visit to the injured tribe – either at the home of the injured party, or, if they demur because they do not wish to permit the perpetrator in their home, then in the home of the injured party's *shaykh*. They invariably bring a *sayyid* with them to memorialize the ceremony. Formally, there is no negotiation during the *fasl*. The injured tribe indicates its demands, and the offending party does not challenge them.

As a matter of practice, this is not what occurs. Instead, the injured tribe demands compensation that is many multiples of the amount that they ultimately seek. They then reduce it based on those who happen to be present – the *sayyid*, notables from the other tribe, and others. Ultimately, as the injured tribe reaches a compensatory demand that is closer to that which might be expected, members of the offending tribe urge some level of restraint on any basis that might seem reasonable under the circumstances. In the end, the injured tribe settles on a reduced amount.[76]

At this point, the parties engage in a formalization ceremony to memorialize the deal. The offending tribe representative ties a cloth to a wooden stake that

ceasefire ended. The respite in this context is one that effectively acknowledges a surrender of sorts. The difference can be demonstrated by the period of time set for the ceasefire alone. The Prophet's ceasefire was ten years long, unthinkable in the context of an injured tribe offering a respite for a rival offending tribe prior to final resolution. This is not the only tendentious reference to Islamic history to support the almost unsustainable claim that the tribal compensation system is based largely on *shari'a*. Unfortunately, the very important matter of the relationship between tribal law and Islamic law is beyond the scope of this chapter.

[76] We were told that this system was different among the urban tribes of Baghdad, such as the Rabi'a, and in the Euphrates Valley, among the Sunni tribes. There, the amounts demanded for compensation were firmly set by custom, and not subject to variation during the *fasl*.

the *sayyid* declares to be the Banner of Abbas – the flag that Abbas held to represent the warring party of Imam Hussein in Kerbala.[77] The injured party then attaches a similar cloth, and the deal is thereby formalized, on the staff carried by Shi'a Islam's noblest warrior in the most important battle in Shi'a Muslim history. The *sayyid* then has the discretion to reduce the compensation, and frequently does so, by half typically, though more or less is always possible. As a matter of practice, the *sayyid* has cleared the reduction amount in advance with the injured tribe, but formally the sealing of the staff of Abbas ends any discretionary power on the part of either party. They have done the equivalent of take an oath on the tomb of Abbas, and no retraction is possible without severe reputational sanctions regardless of what reduction the *sayyid* orders.

Generally, the compensation demanded and received is money. In that event, the perpetrator is usually responsible for one-third of the payment, with the tribe supplying the other two-thirds.[78] Payment can be immediate or delayed, depending on the amount. On the receiving end, the injured party is entitled to two-thirds, with the tribe entitled to the final third. Tribal leaders hold the tribal share in a fund pending future disputes, thereby demonstrating their full awareness that the tribe is effectively a repeat player in this semiautonomous social field.

The *fasl* may also involve matters beyond the mere payment of money, including, for example, a requirement that a party leave their home and move to a location farther away from the home of the victim or other members of his tribe. That may be accompanied by a written guarantee that the perpetrator will not return again to the same city, neighborhood, or village. If he is then seen in the place where he had promised not to appear any longer, then, to use the tribal phrasing, "his blood could be shed with impunity."

Although more uncommon than it was in the past, the use of women as compensation for injury remains possible among Iraqi tribes. Hence, for example, a tribe that has suffered the death of a young man may still in some cases insist on compensation in the form of both money and women. In these cases, the expectation is that the women will be married to the immediate male relatives of the victim so as to heal the rift by making the families relatives of

---

77 It is almost surely the case that the resolution is not formalized among Sunni tribes on anything like the banner of Abbas, given the marginal importance of Abbas within Sunni Islam. Precisely how a resolution is formalized among such tribes is, unfortunately, beyond the scope of this chapter.

78 An exception exists when an injury arises from the commission of a *sauda*, or "black," crime. Injuries caused by drunk driving constitute a central example of this given the Islamic prohibition against the consumption of alcohol. In such a case, the offending party must pay the entire compensation without contribution from the tribe.

one another. This is unheard of in the cities and practiced in only more remote areas, and even then, we are told, with steadily decreasing frequency.

The more common instance where women are part of the bargain is when they are offered to an injured party if he fails to recover from his injury. The idea here is that the injury will prejudice his ability to marry. However, even when this condition comes to fruition, the normal course is to then offer monetary compensation in the place of a woman, and the custom has developed to accept it. In effect, the woman serves as a placeholder of sorts, so that if the victim does not recover as expected, the tribe is able to demand more money for the injury suffered.

The Treatment of Honor Crimes

No discussion of tribal resolutions can be complete without mention of honor crimes, and in particular the treatment of situations where a young male from one tribe seeks a relationship with a young woman from another tribe[79] without obtaining permission from their respective male kin. In such situations, the easiest result, and the one that the tribal leaders encourage and facilitate in many instances, involves a hasty marriage between the two to avoid any reputational repercussions. The previous relationship between the parties in such cases is left a secret. This, we are told, occurs nearly all of the time. If, however, despite the urging of tribal leaders, immediate male family members of either of the two parties (usually, the father) object to the marriage strenuously, as does occur from time to time, only one solution is possible under the tribal law. Both of the romantically involved parties are killed, and the father or nearest male relative of the young woman has a right to compensation from the father of the young man on the belief, we presume, that it was the young woman who was seduced and therefore her death was the responsibility of her paramour.

Intratribal Discipline

The focus of this chapter is on the tribes as self-contained units. Largely, so long as the acts of an individual are attributed to the tribe, as they certainly are under the tribal law, this works well. Nevertheless, the question may well be asked, what constrains a tribal member from ignoring the dictates of his

---

[79] Although this chapter treats tribes as self-contained units and therefore is concerned only with intertribal disputes, it bears mentioning that tribes treat honor crimes similarly whether committed within the tribe or beyond it. In fact, while we are aware of no studies on the subject, the majority of illicit unions are probably intratribal, simply because exposure of young men and young women from different tribes to one another is rather limited.

tribe and thereby repeatedly entangling the tribe in difficulties that need to be resolved through this system? The perpetrator is required to pay one-third of the damages in a *fasl*, but this may not act as sufficient deterrent.

Overwhelmingly, given that an individual's reputation is derived largely from dealings within the tribe, informal reputational sanctions, bolstered by negative gossip respecting "shameful," or '*aib*, activity, work remarkably well to constrain individual behavior. This does not seem entirely dissimilar from relations in other societies with significant levels of legal dysfunction, among them merchants in pre-communist South Vietnam.[80] In these close-knit contexts, the instances of derogation from the norm of compliance with tribal dictate are rare indeed.

Still, they do exist, and the tribe has mechanisms to deal with them. In the first instance, it can agree to a *fasl* that includes a sentence of individual exile from a particular village, neighborhood, or city, accompanied by a written indication that if the perpetrator is found again in that prohibited area, his blood may be shed with impunity. The perpetrator then knows his tribe will not protect him if he ignores the mandate.

If this is insufficient, or inapplicable in a given circumstance (perhaps because the injured tribe had no interest in exile), then the tribe may escalate the matter to what is known as an internal, conditional expulsion. They inform the perpetrator that although they will represent him in a subsequent resolution should one arise, he will be responsible for all damages. The tribe thus does not, for its own internal purposes, regard him as one of their own. This will certainly have a severe impact on the perpetrator's social status, and will make it difficult for him to marry or carry out commercial activity. Even if he wishes to direct such activity solely beyond the tribe, nobody within the tribe will be willing to vouch for him (even if they do not formally disown him), and his social and commercial prospects will be limited.

If even this is not enough, and there exist exceptional times when it is not, then the next step is a formal expulsion announced through a document known as the *sanad*, or certification, that is sent to all the tribes. The certification informs the tribe that a particular member of the tribe has been expelled, and that any activity he undertakes from that point on is on his own account, and not the responsibility of the tribe. (The certification is applicable only for activity undertaken after its issuance; a tribe cannot issue a certification after one of their own commits a particularly grave offense and before a *fasl* in order to avoid responsibility for harm arising from the offense). In our discussions with them, tribal leaders strongly resisted our suggestion that this renders the object of the *sanad* liable to be killed upon its issuance. After all, whatever

---

[80] McMillan & Woodruff, *supra* note 53, at 2434.

the person had done in the past had already been settled through a *fasl*, and one could not simply kill a human being because a document was issued. The point is well taken, but from the sole perspective of the tribal law, the issuance of the *sanad* is the same as declaring the person's blood liable to be shed, because no tribal action is possible to defend him if violence were directed against him. The state law, however, may prove applicable in such instances, as further explored in the next section.

THE COOPERATIVE PARADIGM

The inconsistencies with state law should be perfectly obvious, once two facts are borne in mind. The first is that there is no formal recognition of tribal resolution procedures within state law for the most part. The Iraq Constitution does indicate that the state will "strive to restore the Iraqi tribes and clans, and to take heed of their affairs to the extent they accord with religion and law, and to strengthen their noble human values."[81] The same provision also says that the state will prohibit tribal customs that violate human rights. To date, this provision has not been understood to require the state to recognize tribal dispute resolution procedures as a form of legally binding arbitration, though that is certainly a plausible reading of it. In any event, absent a radical change in the approach of the courts, and in particular the Federal Supreme Court, toward of the dispute resolution procedures of the Iraqi tribes, Iraqi law takes no formal heed of them.

The second fact to bear in mind is that Iraq generally derives its Penal Code and its Criminal Procedure Code from continental law.[82] It is clearly illegal to spray homes with bullets.[83] It is an even more serious crime to kidnap members of a rival tribe, as kidnapping is now a capital offense in Iraq in response to the rise of criminal gangs that engage in the practice routinely.[84] Iraq does not permit the marriage of women without their consent.[85] It certainly does not countenance the privately ordered killing of people for any reason, including those relating to honor.

---

[81] Article 45, Section 2, Doustour Joumhouriat al-Iraq [The Constitution of the Republic of Iraq] of 2005 (translation by authors).

[82] Dan E. Stigall, *Comparative Law and State-Building: The "Organic Minimalist" Approach To Legal Reconstruction*, 29 Loy. L.A. Int'l & Comp. L. Rev. 1, 27 (2007) (also noting, correctly, the failure of the Ba'ath regime to adhere to these rules in practice).

[83] The Penal Code of Iraq, No. 111 of 1969, as amended [hereinafter Penal Code] Art. 430 (prohibiting a threat to commit a felony against a person, which spraying bullets against a home certainly is).

[84] *Id.* at art. 421.

[85] The Personal Status Code, No. 188 of 1959, art. 9(1) (Iraq).

Moreover, in a manner strikingly similar to that of Ellickson's actors in Shasta County,[86] Iraqi tribal leaders have fundamental misapprehensions of law. In the Iraqi tribal context, however, these misapprehensions are of the sort that those within Western societies, even those who reside in a social field that has very little interaction with the state law, would find difficult to fathom. Some tribal leaders seemed to think, for example, that the state could not initiate legal proceedings for a killing in the absence of a complaint by a living person. That the presence of a dead body self-evidently killed by another automatically opened an investigation came as some surprise to them. They seemed to believe that a written undertaking that a tribal member's blood was subject to being shed with impunity as a binding legal commitment that a state court investigating a murder would take seriously. While conceding that the state could vindicate the public's right to order, they seemed to conceive of such a public right in narrow terms. They failed to see, for example, why it would be that an ordinary theft would involve the state at all if the parties to each side, victim and perpetrator alike, could settle the matter between them. That there was a public interest in seeing a car thief put into prison did not meet their conception of public right. By comparison, New York diamond sellers and Shasta County ranchers are surely aware that the police will investigate a dead body irrespective of whether anyone has come forward to register a complaint and irrespective of whether the family declared the victim's blood for the taking. This demonstrates that American laws of murder are deeply internalized among nearly all actors in the United States in a manner that Iraqi laws are not among many Iraqis.

Still, to speak of *competition* in providing broader security in the state, in the manner that organized crime competes with state law to provide security to local businesses,[87] is to miss the point. In reality, the tribes do not seek to compete with the actual operation of state law, but to cooperate with it in maintaining order in the social field. To be clear, we refer to "cooperation" in a thin sense of the word. Thus, the tribes and the state do not cooperate with state officials in criminal investigations in the same manner that, for example, state and federal authorities in a jurisdiction like the United States might cooperate. They do not share information, second officials from one office to another, or coordinate intelligence gathering. Nevertheless, the tribes and the state do engage in a thin form of cooperation. Specifically, the tribes adopt a series of maxims when deploying tribal rules to avoid conflict with the state.

---

[86] Ellickson, *supra* note 38, at 48–50.
[87] Curtis J. Milhaupt & Mark D. West, *The Dark Side of Private Ordering: An Institutional and Empirical Analysis of Organized Crime*, 67 U. CHI. L. REV. 41 (2000).

In turn, the state does something of the same, declining to enforce its own formal rules in areas where the public interest might be slighter and the tribal interests in enforcing their own order comparatively stronger. Each side, that is, does not seek *maximum influence*, but rather *shows notable restraint* when conflict seems to arise. It is in this sense that they can be understood to be cooperating with one another. To demonstrate this, we lay out the maxims, and explain each one in turn.

Maxim #1: *The Tribe Purports to Prefer State Law Where It Works*

Though listed first, this is the one that might be discounted to some degree because it relies to a large extent on a counterfactual. Tribal leaders insist that much of the reason that they resort to their procedures so extensively is because they have no real choice. The state has proven self-evidently ineffectual in addressing claims for recompense arising from car accidents, thefts or other disputes, and the tribes therefore handle these lower level matters on their own. When the state was even less effectual, immediately after the American invasion, the tribes assumed even greater responsibility, handling on their own virtually any disturbance to the public order that arose – including, for example, deterrence against acts of terrorism. They then happily ceded back much of this authority when the state regained its footing, and they would cede back even more were the state to become more functional.

This is not to suggest that the tribes are legal centralists who think proper order always lies with the state. That would surely be preposterous given the elaborate nature of their normative system. They do thus insist with some vigor that the tribe must handle certain matters on its own – among them slander of one of their own, or addressing issues relating to stains on honor. They further insist that Iraq is not a society where every dispute can be settled in the courts. (Naturally, a legal pluralist would maintain this was equally true of any society, but tribal leaders appropriately focused their remarks on the society they knew best.) Yet they did insist, repeatedly and often without solicitation, that they were ready to cede more duties to state courts if only they functioned better.

This seems rather consistent with much private ordering in societies where the legal system is in some level of dysfunction. McMillan and Woodruff examined the conduct of merchant communities from places like precommunist Vietnam, where there was little faith in the courts, to those of Eastern Europe and the former Soviet Union, where confidence in the court was somewhat higher though not as much as it might be in developed societies. They found that merchants use "social networks and reputation" as the bases for contract enforcement most often when the merchants could not rely on the courts.[88] Tribes are among the most significant social networks that exist in Iraq, particularly beyond the urban elite, and it would therefore make sense that part of the reason for the reliance on them to resolve disputes is not because the tribes particularly relish that role, but because there is no viable state alternative in many instances.

Nevertheless, as noted, there is something of a counterfactual inherent in this. Iraq's formal justice system is highly imperfect to put the matter charitably, and the tribes are not so much making a real concession as expressing an abstract sentiment that binds them to little. That the tribal leaders were speaking to three *law* professors and might have felt some desire to earn our endorsement of their activities may well have played a role as well.[89] Still, the tribal sentiment was noteworthy for two reasons. First, the mere expression of the sentiment disposes of any argument that the tribes regarded Iraqi law as some sort of postcolonial construct imposed on them against their will, which they were dedicated to resisting. Surely, Llewellyn's Cheyenne would not have expressed any desire for American law to somehow supplement their tribal ways, even if they were speaking to an American law professor. At the very least, the mere expression of this sentiment on the part of the tribal leaders revealed a broader conception of cooperation that we found to be of fundamental importance.

Second, the matter was not entirely an abstraction. One leader provided us with a remarkable, concrete example where tribal law now supplants state law, and where the tribe indicated a strong desire to return to the past. Prior to the fall of the Ba'ath, Iraq had a national insurance scheme that dealt with car accidents. Pursuant to the scheme, the National Insurance Company was required to offer a rather generous payout upon injury or death in a car accident – slightly less than double what a *fasl* would be likely to yield – irrespective of fault.[90] Tribal leaders thus were in the practice of permitting a party to choose among the two different options available – payment through the National Insurance Company pursuant to state law, or whatever emerged from the *fasl*. Overwhelmingly, the state law process was chosen and one of the major forms of tribal dispute – injuries arising as a result of automobile accidents – was thereby transferred to the state realm, with the consent, it

---

[88] McMillan & Woodruff, *supra* note 53, at 2453.

[89] There is no doubt in our mind that the tribal leaders were in no way intimidated by us – in reality they were far more powerful than we were as academics, and they surely knew it. Yet the desire to be approved and deemed meritorious in one's activities is a natural one, and we would not discount its effect here.

[90] Law for the Mandatory Insurance for Car Accidents No. 52 of 1980 (Iraq), as amended, art. 2.

must be stressed, of the tribal actors. It was only the fall of the regime and the resulting dysfunction[91] of the formal national insurance scheme that caused the tribes to assume the role of adjudicating disputes arising out of automobile accidents once again.

It is not difficult to see what made the state insurance scheme superior in this instance. Iraq is largely a rentier economy heavily reliant on oil exports to fund itself and provide social and economic benefits to its citizens. The National Insurance Company was a form of government largesse that the state provided. To accept the state system was effectively to accept free money, and it would have made little sense for any tribal member to turn that down, particularly when the alternative would be to make a claim against another tribe and thereby risk poorer relations with it. As others have pointed out, where a community that has developed its own semiautonomous rules of order is capable of "externalizing" costs onto a third party, it will do so, precisely so as to minimize the costs falling on the community itself.[92]

Others have described what circumstances must exist for private ordering to be effective enough to supplant state law ordering.[93] We do not intend to undertake such an exploration in this largely descriptive account of how order is maintained in the semi-autonomous field of the south of Iraq. We note only that the tribes seem to hold to the principle, at least at times, that where the state's resolution mechanisms work better for them, however that might be measured, they will not seek to challenge them.

Maxim #2: The Principle of "Complementarity"

The principle of complementarity is best known in the context of the Rome Statute, where the International Criminal Court is not permitted to pursue claims of violations of international criminal law except to the extent that the relevant domestic legal system is unwilling or unable to do so.[94] Iraqi tribes adopt something of the same. When they feel that they are capable of handling a matter on their own, they do so. It is only when they cannot or one tribe is unwilling that the state system becomes an acceptable venue.

---

[91] Formally, the national insurance scheme remains in effect but as a matter of practice, it does not exist. The payments made under its aegis dwindled during the hyperinflation of the 1990s brought about by United Nations sanctions. Eventually the relevant offices and institutions were shuttered, rendering the law even before the U.S. invasion one of many Iraqi laws whose existence extended no further than the paper it was printed on.

[92] Ellickson, *supra* note 38, at 258.

[93] *See generally* Richman, *supra* note 67; Ellickson, *supra* note 38, at 94–95.

[94] Rome Statute of the International Criminal Court, 37 I.L.M. 1002 (entered into force July 1, 2002), art. 17(1)(a).

Hence, for example, tribes feel that they are perfectly capable of addressing an ordinary, garden-variety theft that arises when a member of one tribe steals something from a member of another tribe. They see no particular need to involve the state and are almost always willing to use the tribal processes to solve it. *Importantly, this by no means precludes the injured tribe from initiating a case in the courts.* Often it will, as another means of pressuring the offending tribe to seek a settlement – in addition to the "striking" previously discussed. The injured tribe will even pursue the state law claim for as long as is necessary to induce resolution. However, once there has been a *fasl*, the victims stop pursuing the case. In other words, pursuant to the principle of complementarity, it would only proceed to judgment under the state system if the offending tribe refused to adhere to the tribal procedures.

Moreover, the state broadly *cooperates* in the scheme in the thin sense of the word. It does not pursue claims of garden-variety theft unless the victims are actively pursuing the case. For example, if alleged victims file a claim and then, after pursuing it for some period of time, seem to abandon it, the case sits on the record books, formally active but in reality unpursued by the state authorities. In other words, the tribe does not need to find a reason to drop charges, nor does the state need to find a reason to close the file. It is left to wither and die.

We have been able to confirm this on our own primarily through extensive examination of court files, where numerous examples of ordinary crimes appear, complete with ample witness statements and photographic evidence. Although some of these cases have moved to resolution, many more appear to be lingering for years. The case is not exactly closed, but little more appears in it than an annual scribbled notation by some sort of judicial officer indicating that the investigation is ongoing. It is hard to believe that the court will ever take action to investigate these ordinary crimes, ranging from arson to theft to slander many years after they allegedly occurred. The state seems to be engaging in purposeful delay because, it seems, the matter has been addressed elsewhere.

The tribe, similarly, cooperates by limiting its use of self-help remedies that might very well induce a state law response for these types of cases. There is no reason, for example, for a tribe to kidnap a rival tribe member to ensure that the offending tribe agrees to tribal resolution of a garden-variety theft claim. The state might respond to a kidnapping with more vigor than it would to a theft given the extremely strong punishment for kidnapping and the increased interest of the state to prevent it. Moreover, the state law processes for prosecuting theft, if actively pursued by the victims, provide sufficient inducement to the offending tribe to negotiate. After all, if the victims file the case and allow the state process to go forward, and the perpetrator is found guilty as a result, he will be imprisoned. This is far more likely to influence a tribe to negotiate a tribal settlement than a temporary kidnapping of one of its members will be.

The situation is obviously different for murder than it is for theft. The state does not neglect corpses found on the street, even if its ability to limit murder through effective crime management seems quite limited. Hence, there are unsolved murders in the case files we examined that bear some resemblance to those of ordinary crimes, with little more than a notation roughly annually that the matter remains under investigation. The file, however, never appears to have any sort of evidence in it, and it thus appears to be not so much an example of state acquiescence to murder as a general incapacity to deal with such crimes in an adequate fashion. When evidence does appear, the murder case either seems to proceed to fruition, or it is dismissed for lack of sufficient proof to convict (at times under mysterious circumstances, as we shall describe).

Therefore, it is unlikely that the tribe could keep the state away from a murder entirely once information of the perpetrator reaches the police. Nor is it clear that they would want to, given that the tribe can only demand compensation. It has no means of punishing the perpetrator for murder other than by engaging in more killing, thereby garnering even more state attention. Hence the tribe cooperates by not seeking punitive measures, *indeed by allowing the state to undertake whatever punitive measures the injured tribe seeks.*

In other words, where a punishment is merited, *the tribal system relies upon the state to carry it out.* To achieve this, quite often in the case of murder, an injured tribe will insist not only that a sum of money is paid to recompense a killing, but also that *the perpetrator turn himself into the authorities.* The state can then mete out whatever punishment it seems appropriate, and each tribe can argue to the court what it will respecting the appropriate punishment. In this highly symbiotic method of interaction, the state gets its perpetrator, and the injured tribe gets its compensation.[95]

Maxim #3: The Tribe Avoids Deploying Formal Traditional Mechanisms
to Which the State Objects

As noted, the state is not likely to neglect dead bodies that it finds in the street. As a result, though the tribes often do issue a note promising that a particular person will not appear in a particular area again for a period of years, or for

---

[95] There would be, of course, no ready means to confirm that this transpires from state records. All that would appear in the file is a guilty person confessing to a crime, which happens a great deal in Iraq whether or not a tribe is involved in the disposition of the case.

life, and declaring that his blood can be shed with impunity if it is, in practice, they do not effect this remedy very often. Instead, if the perpetrator is found in the prohibited area, rather than kill him, they initiate another tribal resolution process and demand compensation. Part of this is because money is preferable to blood, at least if the person exiled poses no serious threat to the community. Part of this, however, is a clear effort on the part of the tribes to operate in a fashion that does not involve such an open and notorious violation of state law as intentional killing is. Even if tribal leaders are not always aware of the precise contours of the state law, they are aware enough to know it is best to avoid killing where possible.

A similar result attaches with respect to the traditional involvement of women as part of the compensation for an injury. Although in the past the practice was common, almost customary in cases of death, the use of women as objects of exchange has been reduced drastically everywhere, and to virtual extinction in urban areas. Where it is used in the cities, the matter is a formality and broadly not implemented. The woman is offered as compensation if an injury does not heal. If it does heal, then nothing is due. If it does not, the method effectively permits the injured party to demand more monetary compensation, with the woman acting as placeholder. The system is more efficient than fixing a sum in the case of the failure of an injury to heal, given the uncertainty attending to the level of evaluating the cost of future injuries.

To be clear, these remarks are not meant to suggest that we condone this offensive practice of using human beings as placeholders, nor do we deny the obvious negative social repercussions that arise when women are treated as objects for trade, even symbolically. Indeed, we condemn it in the strongest possible terms. We only seek to highlight the fact that even as the tribal practices show remarkable resilience, certain aspects of them, those most likely to result in conflict with the state, are noticeably declining in practice if not in form, thereby demonstrating a thin form of cooperation between the non-state legal system and that of the state.

REMAINING AREAS OF CONFLICT

Though we have highlighted and emphasized the areas of cooperation between the state and the tribe, we of course acknowledge that there is conflict and tension between the tribe and the state at times. There is no reason to replace the "conflict" centralism that dominates the literature with a form of "cooperation" centralism. We group the inevitable conflicts that arise by virtue of the inconsistencies in the normative systems into three categories to be discussed in turn.

The Resilient Remnants

One breakdown in the system arises from the stubborn resilience of some tribal practices to which the state plainly takes exception, but which the state and other social forces are not powerful enough to eradicate. The trading of women as compensation in a *fasl* is declining, but very much present, particularly in more remote areas where the presence of the state is less keenly felt. The same might be said respecting the use of killing to avenge death, rather than the compensation/state imprisonment scheme that has largely been adopted by the tribes over the past two decades. In a more remote area, where no one would think to report a tribal killing, the tribe may feel confident that a police investigation will likely not result in any conviction of one of their own because of the lack of evidence. Hence, almost certainly, some of the unsolved murders that appear in the court files we have examined, particularly in 'Amara, where the numbers of such cases seem comparatively high, are the result of a tribal blood feud, though it is impossible to know how many.

The use of killing as a form of self-help, when combined with tribal notions of collective responsibility that are broadly unrecognized in modern criminal law, can lead to disturbances in the public order that can be serious. In 2010, for example, a dispute between Bani Malik and the Frayjat tribe that had clearly spun out of control resulted in roadblocks in Basra, an individual being dragged from his car whose sole crime appears to have been belonging to the wrong tribe, followed by his killing and the burning of his corpse, a matter that is a violation of both state and tribal law. The state intervened at that point, and such outbreaks as between tribes are not common. However, they occur frequently enough to demonstrate that the system does not always work in perfect harmony, and resorting to forms of self-help of long pedigree among the tribes is not impossible, even if it is less common nowadays.

Settlement of Disputes of Public Interest

A more frequent, though less spectacular, area of conflict lies in something of the opposite direction – when the tribe seeks to deploy *restraint* as to matters in which the state would naturally claim an interest. For example, where a theft occurs that is only witnessed by members of two tribes – the offending and the injured – the state's mechanisms are often not invoked, and once invoked, are readily abandoned. But if a third-party witness reports the incident, or a police officer apprehends the suspect, the state's ability to drop the matter is compromised significantly, despite the tribal preference for the matter to be handled swiftly and beyond the state's purview. If this is the case with theft, it is even more so with murder, as to those cases where the injured tribe has no interest in seeing the perpetrator punished. Where it is easy to rely on the state to *carry out* punishments for serious crimes for which there is a valid confession, it is hard to expect the state to simply abandon a case involving a serious crime for no formally valid reason when its agents have witnessed it merely out of informal deference to tribal rules.

Here the tools deployed by the tribe clearly involve the manipulation of the state processes in a manner that confounds and frustrates those responsible state officials seemingly intent to try to extend their jurisdiction. If no case file has been opened at all, and nobody has died (such that there is no death certificate that mandates an investigation), the matter is easy to dispose of. A jail officer can be convinced, or bribed, to let one in custody go free without any case file report ever being written.

If there is an active case file, or an official death certificate, the matter is more complex, because it is harder to close an open case file than it is not to open one in the first place.[96] A reason must exist. Yet the tribes have ways to find one in some cases. Third-party witnesses who report crimes to state courts are subject to receiving a "confrontation" on the ground that this was not their business and therefore there was no cause for them to interfere. (This shows the rather narrow grounds on which tribal leaders construe conceptions of public interest.) Leaders of injured tribes tell us that they direct their members to lie in court as to murder case files that have been opened – perhaps opened by the injured party itself, prior to a *fasl* – so as to let the perpetrator go free, if that is the outcome decided upon in the *fasl*. If all else fails, court officials can be persuaded to close open case files at times, though this usually requires a high-level tribal intervention. The case files seem to reflect this, through examples of unexplained recanted testimony and, even more telling, cryptic references to a file being closed for lack of evidence without elaboration despite what appears to be a plethora of evidence in the file itself concerning the identity of the perpetrator. That this appeared more often in 'Amara, where the tribal role in maintaining order is more pronounced, than it did in Baghdad or Basra, is further evidence that some sort of manipulation of state judicial process was involved.

---

[96] This appears to be the case in Egypt as well, to little surprise. Sarah Ben Nefissa gives an example of a blood feud that resulted in the arrest of thirty detainees. The police agreed to release all of them after a protracted negotiation except for the three against whom the police had already opened case files. Ben Nefissa, *supra* note 8, at 146.

In our opinion, these examples of corruption and manipulation differ markedly from a state officer exercising restraint in deference to a genuine conviction that a matter is best handled privately and informally. One involves an honest and sincere attempt to fulfill a duty using discretion, and the other is a failure to do so through fraud, perjury and manipulation of records, often in anticipation of private gain. The latter is less an example of legal systems cooperating as it is a demonstration of the weaknesses of the state legal system in this particular context.

The Honor Crimes

A third, important area of conflict involves honor crimes, no doubt because it is where state law norms differ from those of the tribe most markedly. Where the tribes, the state, and Iraqi society converge is in a general belief that it is not the function of the state to engage in broad morals policing.[97] Nobody particularly thinks of it as a the job of the police to arrest a consenting, unmarried couple for engaging in sexual activity, a fact reflected in the lack of any reference to a crime of fornication in the Penal Code.[98]

Yet where the state would then deem such conduct legally permissible, neither the tribes, nor Iraqi society, regard fornication as socially acceptable. Although much of Iraqi society might regard (quite severe) reputational sanctions as sufficient, the tribes would take matters considerably further. In fact, they would regard illicit relations between the unmarried as being a crime under the tribal law to be punished with death.

In keeping with the maxim that it is best to avoid contravening central state law principles when possible, tribal leaders seek to resolve the matter without killing, notably through a swift and secret marriage. To the extent that the woman's closest male relative (usually her father) still wants the man to be modestly punished notwithstanding the marriage, a false crime can be concocted (perhaps that of slander, carrying a lighter sentence) and reported to state authorities, and to the tribes, thereby avoiding the need to pursue the honor crime. Tribal leaders indicated that they had arranged this on more than one occasion, though it is impossible to confirm this through a reading

---

[97] Haider Ala Hamoudi, *Brandon Davies, Iraq and the Privatization of Islamic Law*, Muslim Law Prof (Mar. 25, 2011), http://muslimlawprof.org/2011/03/brandon-davies-iraq-and-the-privatization-of-islamic-law/

[98] Adultery is a crime under the Penal Code, though it is one that can only be initiated by the wronged spouse as a matter of law. Penal Law No. 11 of 1969(Iraq), art. 378(1). The state has no authority in the absence of a spousal complaint to initiate an investigation or prosecute an offender.

of court files, which would reflect nothing more than a confession for, and a conviction on the basis of, slander.

However, because there is no crime for fornication per se, and because the right of the father of the woman to demand the death of the parties is unconditional in the tribal law, then an obvious conflict arises when the woman's father insists on his right. The only way that the tribes can conceivably carry out their sentence is through the privately orchestrated killing of both parties. They do this generally with impunity, particularly beyond the larger cities, because of the unwillingness of witnesses to report the matter. The victims are then among the countless numbers of other unsolved murders that appear in Iraqi court files.

Still, it would be wrong to describe this as something that the state tolerates. In 2007, male relatives of a teenage girl of the Yazidi faith publicly stoned her to death for falling in love with a Muslim, with the police watching. There was a large public outcry in protest, and the state at least professed to take measures to prevent such things from happening again given the broad public expressions of disgust.[99] This surely would not have been the case if two tribes settled a dispute over a stolen automobile among themselves and the police did not pursue the matter. Yet even if stoning is not tolerated, the state is sufficiently weak, and the tribal values sufficiently strong, that broad violations are frequent enough. Thus, the conflict between the values that the state seeks to vindicate and those of the tribe are particularly stark when honor crimes are involved.

THE CASE OF THE REPEAT ARSONIST: FROM NOTIFICATION TO RESOLUTION

The foregoing describes the Iraqi tribal system generally, and the manner in which Iraqi tribes tend to broadly cooperate with state authorities in maintaining order, even if serious conflicts do continually arise as well. This section attempts to develop some of these themes in a case we observed, that of the repeat arsonist. In the interests of privacy, we will not use his real name, but refer to him herein as Issa.

The story began when a dispute erupted between Issa, from the tribe of Bani Uqba, known also as the Uqbis, and a young member of the tribe of Abu Muhammad, otherwise known as the Muhammadawis. In the initial dispute, Issa was stabbed, and a tribal resolution process initiated that resulted in an

---

[99] Natalie Clark, *The Girl Who Was Stoned to Death for Falling in Love*, DAILY MAIL, May 17, 2007.

award to Issa and the Bani Uqba tribe of 8 million dinars (roughly equivalent to $7200) and a woman, should he fail to recover from the stab wounds. The Uqbis did not file a claim in state court, and Issa did recover.

Unfortunately, Issa had a reputation for being what the tribes describe as *ma'tuh* – wild, uncontrollable, or, to put the matter in terms more familiar in the private ordering literature, not easily swayed by reputational sanctions. He was also known as a drunkard and a drug addict. Accordingly, he ignored the resolution, bought a canister of gasoline, and used it to set fire to the door of the stabber's home, threatening even more damage before being restrained. The amount of property damage was minimal, but according to the Muhammadawis, the injured family feared his return and had difficulty sleeping as a result. Moreover, and quite significantly, Issa had broken the pact signed on the banner of Abbas, pursuant to which the Muhammadawis had paid 8 million dinars to settle the claim fully and finally. This breach was quite serious given the reliance on the banner to formalize the *fasl*. Without respect for the sanctity of the banner, there was no reliable way to end a feud.

Given the gravity of the situation, two actions were taken, one by each tribe. The Muhammadawis, for their part, took the case to court, filing a complaint against Issa for his activity. The Uqbis, equally aware of the ramifications of a violation of the pact formalized by the banner, visited the Muhammadawis and asked for, and received, a respite. It seemed as if the matter might yet be resolved.

During the respite, Issa initiated another arson, causing nominal property damage once again. The Muhammadawis filed a second case, and the Uqbis immediately sought, and received, a second respite. To this point, interestingly, the Muhammadawis refrained from initiating a striking, or engaging in any other tribal form of self-help. The sole means by which they sought to apply pressure was another lawsuit, which they were willing to drop if they were paid money. The effort to use the tribal mechanisms in a way that harmonized with the state law is quite notable.

As for why they demonstrated such restraint, the reasons seemed clear enough. The Uqbis had immediately recognized their own fault in the matter, had conveyed to the Muhammadawis their own distress over the conduct of one of their own, and had assured the Muhammadawis that they would address the matter. Given that there are surely "wild" youth among the Muhammadawis who are difficult to control, and given the likelihood that the Uqbis would be before the Muhammadawis in the future making their own claims for compensation, restraint seemed the proper course.

When Issa attempted arson a third time during the respite, this time causing slightly more damage to the home, the Muhammadawis felt that they had to respond using different means. More restraint, in their view, would be a sign of weakness, so they undertook a striking, *in addition to* filing yet another complaint about Issa in the criminal courts. The Uqbis asked for a respite, received a short one, and the resolution was planned for April 2013, in the home of one of the tribal leaders of the Muhammadawis.

The resolution took place out of doors, under a tarp that was perhaps half the length of a football field, with long rows of plastic chairs lined up facing each other along the two sides. The elder tribesmen from the injured tribe, the Muhammadawis, sat at one end and along one side as they waited for the offending tribe and the *sayyid* to appear. The rest of the tribe was seated along the same side, generally in rough order of their station within the tribe, such that elders and notables were closest to the leaders (and most likely to speak during the resolution) and those who had barely emerged from adolescence were furthest away. In all, perhaps several dozen members of the Muhammadawis were present, not including the young men from the tribe who were shuttling back and forth bringing tea, setting up tea tables, and obeying orders barked at them from their elders.

When the Uqbis made their appearance, led by the *sayyid*, instantly recognizable by his black cloak and turban, the entire group stood, and a long ceremony transpired where each of the several dozen visitors greeted each of the several dozen hosts. The process was not entirely different from a wedding's "greeting line" though many more people were being greeted on each side, thereby causing small talk to be kept to a minimum.

When the parties were finally seated, and tea had been swiftly served by the Muhammadawi boys, the process began. It did not take long for voices to rise, with leaders of the Muhammadawis wanting to know why a particular notable was not present. The Uqbis pointed out that other, even more senior notables had appeared, and this should suffice, but the Muhammadawis did not seem mollified. They raised another complaint – that of security. It had become apparent, they told the leaders of the Uqbis, that they could not control this wild member Issa in their midst, who was a drunkard and a drug addict and who listened neither to his tribe, nor to his family *nor to the law*. What use was the resolution if he will simply do this again? While taking some exception to indications respecting what they could and could not control, the Uqbis showed remarkable restraint in the uncharacteristically sharp attack on one of their own. They seemed nearly as tired of Issa's antics as the Muhammadawis. They simply asked what it was the Muhammadawis wanted, as they had the right to ask, instead of piling attack after attack on the renowned tribe of the Bani Uqba. There appeared to be no method in the gathering once it was fully underway, no order by which people spoke, and at times they attempted to speak over one another. To one unaccustomed to the practice, the idea that violence might break out at the *fasl* seemed somewhat plausible, but for the dignified presence of the *sayyid*, respected by both parties and hardly a person either side would wish to see stuck in the middle of a knife fight. The reputational consequences would be severe.

But there was no real threat of violence. As tensions rose, cooler heads caused them to dissipate. Usually this was done through quoting the Prophet Muhammad, or one of the Imams of Shi'a Islam to one effect or another. As everyone naturally agreed on the wisdom of the words spoken (even if they might disagree vigorously on their application in the given circumstance), this served to defuse tension, and to bring the parties together in a common language.

After perhaps twenty minutes of introductory complaints and objections, the Muhammadawis began their demands. First, the initial *fasl* for the stab wound to Issa was revoked and all sums theretofore paid were to be returned immediately. The Uqbis accepted this immediately, it would be unimaginable otherwise. Second, the young man was to leave the relevant quarter of Sadr City where the offenses took place and he was not to be found within its confines again, or his blood could be shed. This caused some hesitation among the Uqbis, for they felt the need to speak to Issa's father. Issa was unmarried, and Iraqi children live with their parents until they marry and often after that if they do not have means. Issa had no means to support himself, and hence an order of exile for him effectively required his father to sell his house and move with Issa somewhere else.

Issa's father was called forward. He was present throughout, though far from where the negotiations were taking place. This is common, to avoid the emotional consequences of involving perpetrators, victims, and their immediate family directly in the negotiations. Passions then could fly out of hand. The Uqbi leaders negotiated with him, perhaps agreed to help him financially with a move (we can only surmise, as the discussions were done quietly enough that bystanders could not hear), and the father agreed. The guarantee document was signed. All that was left in the *fasl* was to discuss compensation for the arson.

The price began at 150 million dinars, or roughly $135,000 – an extraordinary sum for an arson that resulted only in a burned door. Silence followed. Then the Muhammadawi leaders continued. However, they indicated, the *sayyid* had honored them with his presence, and out of respect for him, they would reduce the sum by 20 million dinars. Other notables were mentioned, for whom a reduction of 5 million dinars per notable was given. There was a tribal leader from the Dulaym, a predominantly Sunni tribe, who was present.

The Muhammadawis wished to express their open mindedness and their lack of sectarian sentiment. (As with racism in the United States, sectarianism is publicly denounced regularly by all in Iraq. This is different from saying that it does not exist.) For the presence of the Dulaymi, then, the reduction was to be 10 million dinars, twice that of the others. Ultimately, the price lowered to 20 million dinars, and the Muhammadawi leaders announced there was no space for further reduction.

It is here where the Uqbis for the first time began to implore for greater restraint in demands. They were content for what seemed like good reasons to us to sit in silence and watch the Muhammadawis steadily reduce their own figures, but when the number seemed stuck, they spoke. They pointed out the hardship that would befall the father who now had to move to another location. They indicated that the matter could not happen again as Issa would no longer be near them. And they reminded them that restraint has its virtues in the afterlife (and, of course, in repeat dealings in this life). Eventually, the price settled on 10 million dinars. Each side tied its ribbon to the banner of Abbas (which was represented in this case by a crutch carried by the *sayyid*), and the *sayyid* formalized the deal and used his discretion to cut the sum by half, resulting in a total payment of 5 million dinars, or roughly $4,500.

The sum was paid immediately given that it was not of the amount that would be difficult to raise. As for the legal case, it was never mentioned in the proceedings, because there was no need to. For our own scholarly purposes, we asked after the *fasl* what would become of the suit. The case would not be pursued by the Muhammadawis, and the state would know not to pursue it further either. Effectively, legal proceedings ended once the *fasl* had come to an end.

BROADER LESSONS

We have intended a descriptive account of a cooperative method of achieving order as between a state and non-state system in the context of a developing state where state processes are functioning, but ineffective and weak. We do not seek to advance any particular normative case in favor of nor in opposition to the model heretofore described, other than to say that in the context of Iraq, to call for the eradication of either of the two systems of law described herein is to engage in an exercise of hopeless utopianism given how deep rooted they are. Nevertheless, there is some sense to addressing in this concluding section the substantial literature on the advantages and disadvantages of the use of state law and non-state legal systems in resolving disputes.

The flaws in the state system are more readily apparent to some legal pluralists. The state legal system, it is often said, is almost always more costly and cumbersome than informal resolutions.[100] Because it is designed to apply to all actors in the political state, it is less responsive to their individualized particular needs.[101] Law is also more easily subject to manipulation by equally distant interest groups and requires the use of professionals to make it understandable.[102] In many states, court orders are simply not as reliable a means to ensure compliance with a norm as informal determinations may be.[103]

On the other hand, wiser commentators are quick to note that it is a mistake to discount the problems that non-state law produces. Non-state legal systems tend to be hierarchical and closed. It is difficult to penetrate them, and those who are not participants are almost always at a disadvantage.[104] If there are going to be rules preventing gender and race discrimination, for example, they are less likely to come from a homogenous merchant group that has set its own rules than they are from the state.[105] External costs are often shunted onto the broader public through private ordering in a manner that can be brutally destructive of the public interest.[106] Finally, if non-state law achieves superior compliance, this is all too often because of "harsh and indiscriminate" coercion.[107]

All these considerations apply to Iraq. Iraqi courts are notoriously slow and cumbersome, and court orders can be difficult to enforce. It would be a mistake to lump all developing countries into a single "dysfunctional" basket; Iraqi courts are not akin to those reported in other nations such as Afghanistan, where rulings seem almost entirely irrelevant.[108] At the same time, it would not be to our mind controversial to state that a tribe has an easier time ensuring compliance with a *fasl* sworn on the banner of Abbas than the state does ensuring compliance with a court order. Moreover, the rules of the Civil Code

---

[100] *See* McMillan & Woodruff, *supra* note 53, at 2421 (pointing out tendency to favor private ordering in states where court systems are particularly dysfunctional); *cf.* Richman, *supra* note 67, at 2366 (discounting role of administrative costs in determining when private ordering takes place).

[101] Ellickson, *supra* note 38, at 250.

[102] *Id.* at 252.

[103] *See* Richman, *supra* note 67, at 2366 (emphasizing importance of the ability of the state to enforce agreements when determining when private ordering will arise).

[104] Galanter, *supra* note 2, at 25; Ellickson, *supra* note 38, at 250.

[105] McMillan & Woodruff, *supra* note 53, at 2423.

[106] Ellickson, *supra* note 38, at 249 (pointing out how whaling norms result in overfishing).

[107] Galanter, *supra* note 2, at 25.

[108] Jennifer Kristen Lee, *Legal Reform to Advance the Rights of Women in Afghanistan Within the Framework of Islam*, 49 SANTA CLARA L. REV. 531, 544 (2009).

are completely incomprehensible to the tribes, require the intermediation of lawyers and certainly from the tribe's perspective are readily subject to manipulation and corruption in their application. By contrast, tribal resolutions are swift, understandable, and compliance with them is broadly achieved.

The disadvantages are equally clear. The idea of women participating meaningfully in tribal resolution is impossible to consider. Not only are they completely excluded, they are treated as objects of exchange in a broader compensation system, even if for the most part the matter is symbolic. External costs do exist when blood feuds erupt, as they have from time to time. And woe is the Kurd, the urban professional, or the non-Iraqi Arab who finds himself in a car accident and called to a *fasl* in Sadr City, unable to turn to anyone to represent his interests in this closed and insular system. Finally, nobody who has seen an honor killing take place, either directly or on television, could possibly describe the sanction being deployed as anything but harsh and indiscriminate in the extreme.

What we have sought to demonstrate in this chapter is not that one system is "superior" to the other in any normative sense, but rather that in seeking to integrate the legal with the nonlegal, as we must to make the social field intelligible, it is not necessary to think of one value, or the other, triumphing in any given context. Rather than imagining the integrated system as a war, with separate battles being fought and won either by state law in some cases, or the non-state law in others, it might be more fruitful to consider the systems engaged in a thin form of cooperative interaction.

Hence, when the state makes its abhorrence of forced marriages, kidnappings and killings clear, the tribe works to steer clear of them, internalizing to some extent the state values within its system so as to remain in broad harmony with it. Similarly, as to disputes where the tribes appear able to handle the matter and the public interest is comparatively lower, the state seems content to defer to the tribe and acknowledge its limitations, though it never does so formally.

Conflict is present in some contexts, to be sure. If Iraq is to be rid of the scourge of honor crimes, then forceful state action and imposition would be necessary in the near term, as the tribes seem nowhere near internalizing broader state values on the point. However, these circumstances should be the exception, not the rule. Iraqi tribes are, after all, part of Iraqi society, and it would seem incongruous that the laws of the society would be at such stark odds with tribal values as a universal matter, any more than they would, or should, be in the United States. We have a hard time believing that however insular the actors of Shasta County are, they somehow have failed to internalize not only values as against murder or theft, but also as against racism or sexism.

They do live in the same country that went through the civil rights movement and women's rights movement, and they do, presumably, watch the same television, listen to the same radio and read the same newspapers as the rest of the country. Surely inasmuch as the law reflects American social values, it reflects the values of the people of Shasta County as well.

Thus, we need not view tribes either as an enemy of the broader social good, nor as its faithful defender. Nor do we need to assume that state law changes will result in resistance and conflict. Something quite the opposite might occur – the tribe might well find a way to cooperate with the state, and in so doing, incorporate and internalize some of its values. The state might do something of the same. And through the interaction of the two, along with some level of deliberate, limited, and careful design, perhaps better justice might be done.

10

Is There Such a Thing as Non-State Law?
Lessons from Kiryas Joel

*Nomi Maya Stolzenberg**

PUTTING THE QUESTION

Is there such a thing as non-state law? The premise of this volume – borrowed from legal pluralism – is that non-state law exists. Indeed, legal pluralism has been animated from its very beginnings by the desire to overcome the commonplace equation of law with the law of the state, its core project being to recognize the existence of non-state legal regimes.[1] Within this discourse, questions about whether non-state systems of regulation are properly denominated as "law" have largely been treated as issues of terminology with emphasis placed on the genuinely legal nature of "fields of reglementation" found outside the state and on the genuinely autonomous nature of such semiautonomous legal systems.[2] The prevailing attitude in the legal pluralist community seems to be that we shouldn't get bogged down in questions of semantics. Accordingly, the fundamental jurisprudential question of what law is has been pushed into the background in favor of relying on common sense

---

* Nathan and Lilly Shapell Chair in Law, USC Gould School of Law.

[1] *See* Marc Galanter, *Justice in Many Rooms: Courts, Private Ordering, and Indigenous Law*, 19 J. LEGAL PLURALISM 1 (1981), John Griffiths, *What Is Legal Pluralism?*, 24 J. LEGAL PLURALISM & UNOFFICIAL L. 1 (1986), Sally Engle Merry, *Legal Pluralism*, 22 L. & SOC. REV. 869 (1988), Brian Z. Tamanaha, *Understanding Legal Pluralism: Past to Present, Local to Global*, 30 SYDNEY L. REV. 375 (2008), PAUL SCHIFF BERMAN, GLOBAL LEGAL PLURALISM: A JURISPRUDENCE OF LAW BEYOND BORDERS (2012).

[2] "Reglementation" is a coinage of Sally Falk Moore's adopted with the aim of avoiding begging the question of what law is. Unlike some of the later work in legal anthropology, which puts the theoretical questions raised in this chapter to the side, Moore's pioneering work squarely confronted them and proposed the ideas of "semi-autonomy" and "reglementation" as a response. *See* Sally Falk Moore, *Law and Social Change: The Semi-Autonomous Field as an Appropriate Subject of Study*, 7 L. & SOC'Y REV. 719 (1973). *See also* SALLY FALK MOORE, LAW AS PROCESS: AN ANTHROPOLOGICAL APPROACH 18–21 (1978).

261

to identify the non-state social formations that are sufficiently law-like to merit the designation "non-state law."

Indeed, it is hard to question that intuition when applied to religious law and international law – the two phenomena that are the subject of this symposium. International law is, by definition, law that is not the law of any sovereign state, but rather a body of law to which all states are (theoretically) subject. Religious law presents a somewhat different, more variable relationship to "the state." In theory – and in some places, in practice – religious law could be incorporated into the positive law of the state. States defined as Islamic Republics are an example of this type of arrangement. In such states, religious law is precisely *not* autonomous and separate from state law. More to the point, state law in these regimes is not autonomous and separate from religion.[3] Far from being examples of non-state law, these are legal regimes more accurately characterized as state law *and* religious law, producing the compound offensive to modern ears but historically commonplace: religious state law.

But this only sharpens the contrast perceived to exist between such religious state law regimes and non-state religious law. The latter seems more aptly to describe the situation of religious law in modern secular societies. Deprived of the powers of law enforcement that have been monopolized by the modern secular state, separated from the sovereign state, relegated to the private sphere of individual faith and voluntary associations, religious law (when it is not incorporated into the state as it is in the case of Islamic Republics and other religious polities) is seen to be at once a species of law and a species of law that exists outside the state. Even when religious law is established by the state, its existence is understood to be prior and separate from it. The perception of religious law as a form of non-state law is accordingly nearly irresistible. And if this perception rests more on a "we know it when we see it" intuitive approach to defining non-state law than upon a fully theorized definition of what makes something "non-state" as opposed to state "law," who would be so pedantic as to deny that religious law is law – and to deny that it exists outside the state?

This chapter challenges our easy reliance on such an intuitive approach. It undertakes to begin (or rather, restart) the process of developing a theoretical account of what we mean by non-state law. If I were to put the challenge in its strongest, most tendentious form, I might assert, á la Stanley Fish, that non-state law simply doesn't exist.[4] For reasons hinted at in this chapter, I'm increasingly inclined to endorse this Fish-y proposition about the nonexistence

---

3 Ran Hirschl, *The Theocratic Challenge to Constitution Drafting in Post-Conflict States*, 49 WM. & MARY L. REV. 1179, 1186–99 (2008), and RAN HIRSCHL, CONSTITUTIONAL THEOCRACY (2010).

4 *Cf.* STANLEY FISH, THERE'S NO SUCH THING AS FREE SPEECH, AND IT'S A GOOD THING, TOO (1994).

of non-state law, both as a conceptual and as an empirical matter. But I'm not going to go so far as to make that assertion here. Instead, I'm going to reframe the assertion that there is no such thing as non-state law as a question and a challenge. Is there such a thing as non-state law? Confronting the claim that there is no such thing has the salutary effect of provoking us to think more deeply and rigorously about what we mean by the words we casually throw around in these conversations. It requires us to sharpen our definitions and deepen our understanding of the relationship between state and law as a conceptual matter. This in turn requires disaggregating the constituent concepts and thinking hard about what we mean by "state," what we mean by "non-state," and also (that hoary old question of jurisprudence) what we mean by law. Whatever our ultimate conclusion is (and I repeat, I reach no ultimate conclusion in this chapter), we have to interrogate the meaning of our terms before we can either defend, or refute, the claim of non-state law's existence.

I want to force us to confront these questions of definition, because I believe that they are not "merely" semantic. Semantic they are, to be sure, but to label the debate over terminology as "mere" semantics is to duck important and necessary questions. This includes questions about the relationship of so-called non-state law to the state, which rest in turn on fundamental questions about the relationship between the state and law, *tout court*. It is perhaps a natural division of labor to let those in the legal pluralist camp focus on the empirical dimensions of non-state law, leaving the definitional questions to the philosophers. Conversely, philosophical inquiries into the concept of law typically proceed in an analytic vein, with no (or perhaps worse, very little) empirical material used to support, illustrate, or challenge the philosophical conceptions under discussion.[5] This chapter is animated by the belief that much is to be gained by overcoming this division between empirical and analytic legal studies.

In this spirit, I propose to use the example of the Village of Kiryas Joel – a legal municipality in the suburbs of New York City established by the "Satmar" branch of Hasidic Jewry – as an empirical case study from which to draw some analytical lessons about the meaning and existence of non-state law. Indeed, I want to suggest that the Village of Kiryas Joel can serve as a test case for the very possibility of non-state law. To put it slightly differently, Kiryas Joel is a kind of natural experiment in the feasibility of implementing a truly non-state system of law. By providing an example of a community that espouses a particularly rigorous ideal of non-state law and that has furthermore succeeded

---

[5] For a prime example of the style of legal philosophy that uses just a little empirical material, see H.L.A. Hart, on "the minimum concept of natural law." H.L.A. HART, THE CONCEPT OF LAW 193–200 (1961).

in realizing its ideal to a remarkable degree, the Village of Kiryas Joel illustrates the obstacles that confront even the most successful and committed legal separatists.

This chapter documents the various ways in which the Satmars have fallen short of their own ideal, *notwithstanding the remarkable degree of success they have had in establishing their own autonomous political enclave, separated from the jurisdiction of "gentile law" and secular society, and governed largely by Jewish law, Jewish courts and Jewish legal institutions.* The italicized portion of the last sentence bears emphasis. The Satmars have in fact established their own separate municipality, where members are largely insulated from exposure to the outside world and protected from the interference of outsiders, enabling them to live in accord with the "Holy way of the Rebbe," their spiritual leader whose authority governs every aspect of Satmar life. As such, the story of the Satmars is neither a story of failure, nor of unqualified success. Rather, it is a story of failure *within* success. More specifically, it is a story of a very specific form of failure – the failure to maintain a separation from state law – within success at that very venture. It is thus a paradoxical story. And the paradoxes that it illustrates, in which the Satmars rely on American law to enforce their separatist religious law project, raise serious questions about whether a separatist community governed by non-state law is an ideal that is capable of implementation.

This chapter proceeds in three parts. The first gives an overview of how the Village of Kiryas Joel was created and how its legal and political institutions operate. It describes the vision of law that animated the creation of the Village, emphasizing the separatist and quietist nature of the Satmars' "political theology," which demands as complete as possible a separation of their community from secular society and a total separation of Jewish law from the law of the state. This first part also traces the remarkable extent to which the Satmars have succeeded in turning this theological vision into a reality.

If one were to stop reading this chapter after this first part, one might come away with a picture of law in the Satmar community that confirms the intuitive picture of religious law as non-state law. It presents a picture of a community that is guided by a spiritual leader, the "Rebbe," whose interpretations of *halakha* (Jewish law) are regarded as the ultimate authority on all matters of Satmar life. It shows how, within the community, religious law is viewed as not only comprehensive and independent of state law, but also, in important regards, as antagonistic to the law of the state inasmuch as it rejects the values of modern society embodied in state law in favor of traditional, illiberal norms. It is precisely because of the antagonism between the values of the two legal systems (Jewish and secular) that the Satmars seek to withdraw from the jurisdiction of secular society and to form a separate society within which they can live according to their own law.

This is not to say that the Satmars are antagonistic toward America. To the contrary, the United States is venerated in Satmar culture as a *malkhus shel hesed*, a virtuous and fair-minded regime. But precisely what makes the United States a *malkhus shel hesed* in the Satmars' eyes is the wide berth it creates for subcommunities like theirs with radically different values. This is a view of America that fits the standard picture of a liberal society as one in which the law of the state protects but does not interfere with private action, leaving people free to form and run private communities as they see fit. In this standard picture, American law is playing a purely facilitative, subordinate role in Kiryas Joel – subordinate, that is, to Jewish law, as it is expounded by the Satmar Rebbe.

The irony is that the Satmars have been able to fulfill their ideal of living under Jewish law, of submitting to religious authority, and of repudiating the individualism of modern American society, by exercising the individual rights and liberties protected by American law. In theory, such rights are consistent with the claim that the "private" institutions formed by their exercise are not connected to state institutions. The mere fact that the Village of Kiryas Joel was literally built out of private property and other individual rights conferred by American law does not by itself show that the religious and political institutions formed in Kiryas Joel are in any sense extensions of the state. Nor does it prove that the law those institutions enforce is a kind of state law or that they are wielding political power. To the contrary, the conventional liberal bifurcation between the private domain of individual action and the public legal domain supports viewing the religious legal institutions in Kiryas Joel as private, and viewing the "law" those private religious institutions apply as non-state law. So long as it is produced by private actors exercising their individual rights, religious regulation is seen as a form of private government and, therefore, as neither state action nor the law of the state.

The second part of this chapter deconstructs this standard picture by uncovering the roles played by American law in Kiryas Joel that go beyond the mere facilitation of private, voluntary action. In the spirit of a true deconstruction, the goal is not to demonstrate the falsity of the picture generated in the first part of the chapter, but rather, to show that Jewish law in Kiryas Joel is "both/and" – both autonomous from the secular state and dependent upon it, both different from and enmeshed in American law, both antagonistic to and actively enabled, authorized, and enforced by the law of the state. The second part of this chapter shows that American law penetrates deeply into the life – and law – of the Satmar community. More specifically, it catalogues multiple regimes of American law that penetrate into Kiryas Joel and intertwine with Jewish law in ways that make it difficult to maintain the practical, institutional and conceptual separations necessary for religious law to be truly separate and autonomous.

As this synopsis suggests, this second part is primarily descriptive. The idea is to describe and demonstrate the sheer amount of American law that enters into the ostensibly closed society of Kiryas Joel, and in so doing, to challenge the assumption that the Satmar community can and does forego the law of the state. But of course no empirical state of affairs can definitely disprove the possibility of a conceptual alternative. Even if it is true that the Satmars have fallen short of their own ideals by resorting to American law (a proposition which itself is open to dispute), that does not mean that the ideal is incapable of being realized. The final section of this chapter addresses some of the obvious objections to concluding that non-state law does not exist (in Kiryas Joel or as a general matter). It then seeks to meet those objections by analyzing the causes of the Satmars' resort to, and reliance upon, state law.

What could have induced a community as zealously committed to separating from the state as the Satmars to go to the law of the state? Was there in fact a choice? What are the factors that have led to such extensive dependence on the law of the state? And what, precisely, do the Satmars rely upon the state to do? The third part of this chapter tries to answer these questions. Recognizing the difficulty inherent in seeking to draw conclusions about what *can* exist from empirical observations about what *does* (or doesn't) exist (a variant of the well-known empirical fallacy), it not only tries to identify the factors that have led the Satmars to the law of the state; it also considers whether these factors are avoidable. The fact that the Satmars have not fully lived up to their own ideal of separating themselves and their law from state law is, of course, susceptible to more than one explanation. It is only natural that there be a gap between the rigorously quietist ideals of Satmar theology and the actual lived experience of Satmar political life. The question is whether this merely shows that (some) Satmars have fallen short of their own ideals or, rather, that the ideal is itself incapable of realization. The conclusion tentatively advanced in the third part of this chapter is that the factors that have led to the Satmars' (extensive) reliance on state law are universal, necessary, unavoidable conditions of all human societies.

In this way, the empirical analysis of Kiryas Joel leads us back to an ancient philosophical – and theological – debate. One side of that debate took the position that there are universal features, shared by all societies, which lead to the existence of commonalities between all systems of law. This is the point of view associated with the philosophy of natural law. Although today we tend to think of natural law as opposed to legal positivism, historically, natural law

theology grew out of the recognition of the need for a human political institution capable of enforcing law (i.e., a state) as a basic universal condition
of all societies. Further, natural law theology recognized the inevitability of a
gap between the law of God and the law that would be instituted by human
legal authorities, but rationalized it by making the case that God accommodated to human imperfection by authorizing the institution of such inherently
defective (i.e., secular) legal systems.[6]

Opposing this political theological position was not legal positivism, but
rather, quietist theology, which refused to accept the accommodation to the
imperfections of human rule and human law inherent in this natural law
theology (which actually accepts imperfect positive state law as a necessity).
The Hasidic movement in Judaism, of which the Satmar community is a part,
was heir to this quietist, radically separatist theological tradition. Kiryas Joel
thus embodies a theological position that repudiates the accommodationist
philosophy associated with natural law inasmuch as it insists upon a total
separation between religious and state law that can be achieved only by a
complete withdrawal from society and the jurisdiction of the state.

That describes the Satmars' aspirations. What, then, to make of the gap
between those separatist aspirations and the actual lived experience of Kiryas
Joel? The third part of this chapter offers an analysis of the conditions that
have prevented the Satmars from fully implementing their quietist theology.
What emerges out of that analysis is an argument that essentially recapitulates
the old case for natural law. The gap between Kiryas Joel's separatist ideals and
how the implementation of those ideals has actually unfolded points up the
conditions that historically led to the triumph of the "accommodationist" view
associated with natural law over quietist theology. Today, that once-triumphant
theology of natural law is widely rejected, not only by religious separatists like
the Satmars, who have always subscribed to the opposing quietist theology,
but also by legal pluralists and others who subscribe to modern-day secularist
views. Outside certain conservative circles and a narrow band of analytic legal
philosophy, natural law has no champions. Indeed, it has become something of
an intellectual embarrassment. Nonetheless, the empirical analysis of Kiryas

---

[6] On the natural law tradition in Judaism, see DAVID NOVAK, NATURAL LAW IN JUDAISM (2008).
On the logic of accommodation embedded in this tradition, see Aaron Kirschenbaum & Jon
Trafimow, *The Sovereign Power of the State: A Proposed Theory of Accommodation in Jewish
Law*, 12 CARDOZO L. REV. 925 (1991); Perry Dane, *The Maps of Sovereignty: A Meditation*, 12
CARDOZO L. REV. 959 (1991); Suzanne Last Stone, *Sinaitic and Noahide Law*, 12 CARDOZO
L. REV. 1157 (1991); Arnold Enker, *Aspects of Interaction Between the Torah Law, the King's
Law and the Noahide Law in Jewish Criminal Law*, 12 CARDOZO L. REV. 1137 (1991); and J.
David Bleich, *Jewish Law and the State's Authority to Punish Crime*, 12 CARDOZO L. REV. 829
(1991).

Joel offered here illuminates the combination of material conditions and theological precepts that historically led mainstream Christian and Jewish thinkers to reject religious separatism and to embrace the necessity of a secular state as a principle of natural law. Recovering this natural law argument in, as it were, its natural habitat, may help to illuminate not only the legal culture of the Satmars but also our own confused philosophical conceptions of law.

CONSTRUCTING KIRYAS JOEL

The ideological origins of the Satmar community of Kiryas Joel are deeply embedded in these old political theological debates. Satmar is a branch of the Hasidic movement in Judaism, which, Jewish historian David Myers explains, "was a Jewish pietist movement that took rise in Eastern Europe in the late eighteenth century."[7] Hasidism developed in opposition to the prevailing culture of rabbinic Judaism and a fundamental part of its opposition to this culture was the presentation of "a new theological system."[8] This "new theological system" had a number of different facets that differentiated it from the traditional rabbinic approach, two of which are particularly pertinent for understanding the present-day (and historic) relation of Jewish law to state law in Satmar society.

First, in opposition to "the elitist culture of Torah study that was the pride of Eastern European (and more broadly, Ashkenazic) Jewry for centuries," and made the sacred vocation "accessible only to a few," Hasidism maintained that the most profound access to God could be established by any pious Jew, regardless of life station or status, in any domain of activity or life.[9] This vision of Hasidism was promoted by "Rebbes," charismatic rabbis who communicated to their followers that God could be found through ecstatic song and dance, through mystical practices, but also through participation in the most mundane activities of everyday life. In its insistence that God could be found everywhere, not just in the houses of Torah study and worship, Hasidism both enfranchised "the common people" and broke down the traditional distinction between spiritual and material realms upheld by the normative rabbinic tradition.

The second point of theological opposition between Hasidism and normative rabbinic Judaism is related to this vision of God as everywhere. If every

---

7 David N. Myers, *"Commanded War": Three Chapters in the "Military" History of Satmar Hasidism*, 81 J. Am. Acad. Religion 311, 311 (2013).

8 *Id.* at 312.

9 *Id.*

aspect of life is subject to God's jurisdiction, as the religious enthusiasts of Hasidism maintained, then the question that arises for the pious is how to avoid being sullied by social norms and codes of law that demand acting in ways that violate God's law. This is a question that has been faced by every religious group confronted with a system of state law at odds with its beliefs about religious law. But the question has been particularly acute for Jews because the condition of Exile definitively rules out the possibility of having the law of the state reflect Jewish law. Broadly speaking, there are three possible solutions to the problem of reconciling religious and state law, the first of which is to make the law of the state conform to religious law. Loosely speaking, one might think of this as the theocratic approach: Make God's law the law of the state.[10] This response was not available to diaspora Jews because, even if the state were to try to incorporate religious law into the positive law of the state, it was bound to reflect the vision of God's law espoused by the Christian or Muslim majority, not the version of religious law recognized by the Jews.

The traditional Jewish response to the dilemma of being forced to submit to "gentile" law was to elaborate a strategy – and a theology – of accommodation. On this view, the exercise of legal and political authority by gentile states was authorized *by Jewish law*. In essence, Jewish law authorized its own suspension, a self-suspension that was justified on a variety of theological grounds, making room for the jurisdiction of gentile (which is, by Jewish lights, secular) state law.[11] At the same time, the principle of accommodation also served to limit the jurisdiction of the law of the state and mark out a domain of Jewish legal autonomy, which, until the rise of the modern nation-state, was "considerable."[12] This accommodationist position represents the second possible solution to the problem of reconciling religious and state law.

For obvious reasons related to the Jews' political powerlessness, accommodationism became a prominent if not dominant theme in medieval rabbinic political thought, where it was enshrined in such doctrines as *dina de-malkhuta dina*

---

[10] As Suzanne Stone says, "[w]e can quibble over the term theocracy, rather than 'divine nomocracy' or 'sacred anarchy,'" but the key idea here, in contradistinction to the two other solutions, is that of a religious polity the law of which is God's law, or what is believed to be God's law. Suzanne Last Stone, *Religion and State: Models of Separation from Within Jewish Law*, 6 Int'l J. Const. L. 631, 635 (2008).

[11] *Id.* at 643–60. Gil Graff, Separation of Church and State: Dina de-Malkhuta Dina in Jewish Law, 1750–1848 (1985).

[12] *See* Stone, *Religion and State, supra* note 10, at, 637 ("Because the imperial corporatist models in which [Jews were] situated cooperated . . . [c]ontrary to what Salo Baro labeled the 'lachrymose' view of Jewish history, the legal and political autonomy Judaism enjoyed under Roman rule, feudal Europe, and the Ottoman Empire was considerable.").

("The law of the kingdom is the law").[13] But while rabbinic authorities grav-
itated to the accommodationist point of view, they by no means held a
monopoly on it. (Nor was it the only political theology that they espoused).
To the contrary, although theoretically Christians had the option that Jews
living in exile lacked, of making the law of the state reflect their understanding
of God's law, Christian theologians also arrived at the view that this was not
a course of action that could or should be implemented. This conclusion
grew out of their perception of an inevitable gap between what human beings
believed to be the requirements of God's law and its actual requirements, a gap
they saw as resulting from the inherent limitations of human cognition that
cloud human understanding. This view of an inevitable gap between human
and divine law led to the development of a Christian political theology that
had more in common with the Jewish philosophy of political accommodation
than with more strictly theocratic visions of instituting God's law. Underlying
this shared Christian and Jewish repudiation of a theocratic approach was the
basic belief that even a state that tried to follow and enforce God's law was
doomed by the conditions of human frailty to fail in that endeavor. Mired
in the material world, enmeshed in power relations, driven by base appetites,
prone to cognitive error, human rulers could never succeed in instituting
God's law on earth.[14]

This basic antitheocratic belief in fact led in two opposite directions. On
the one hand, there were those who accepted the inevitability of the profanity
of law and politics, but sought and found theological reasons to accept it as
divinely ordained. The primary theological explanation for God's authorization of imperfect human legal and political institutions was that it reflected
God's "divine accommodation" to human imperfection. This formed the basis
of the theology of political accommodation described above, which squarely
accepted the nonreligious character of the state and its law and the "dirty
hands" that necessarily accompanied its implementation.[15]

---

[13] On the doctrine of *dina de-malkhuta dina*, see the contributions to the Cardozo Law Review
Symposium on Religious Law and Legal Pluralism cited *supra* note 6. In addition to the
doctrine of *dina de-malkhuta dina*, Stone sees the Noahide commandment to establish systems
of law as another doctrinal site where an accommodationist theory of law and politics was
developed. *See* Stone, *Sinaitic and Noahide Law*, *supra* note 6, at 1208–12.

[14] Nomi M. Stolzenberg, *The Profanity of Law*, *in* LAW AND THE SACRED 29-70 (Austin Sarat,
Lawrence Douglas & Martha Umphrey eds., 2007).

[15] Although on my analysis, the recognition of the problem of dirty hands is rooted in the
theological tradition of political theory that derives from the doctrine of divine accommodation,
(i.e., the tradition of accommodationism), the conventional historical view is that the "dirty
hands tradition traces back to Machiavelli," who is commonly viewed as effecting a break
with religious thought. *The Problem of Dirty Hands*, *in* Stanford Encyclopedia of Philosophy

On the other hand, there were those who concluded that the only acceptable solution to the inherently corrupt nature of politics was to withdraw from the world of material and political relations. Like the opposing accommodationist philosophy, this philosophy found adherents among both Christians and Jews. Unlike the accommodationist position, in both faith traditions, the quietist tradition has always been a minority position, no doubt because of its radical rejection of the terms of normal society. On its view, all systems of human law and politics are hopelessly corrupt and corrupting, spiritually polluted and incapable of being redeemed or accommodated. There can be no justification for the dirty hands made inevitable by participating in statecraft, politics, and the exercise of power either as a subject or, worse, as a ruler. The only correct mode of conduct is to withdraw from society and cultivate a life of spiritual purity within a walled-off ostensibly apolitical community. This is the radical separatist impulse of political quietism.

Of course, these three political theologies – theocratic,[16] accommodationist, and quietist – are just ideal types. In theory, they are mutually exclusive positions. In real life, proponents of one or another vision of religion and government often blended elements from each. In Christian thought, in particular, it was possible to combine accommodationist political principles with more "theocratic" aspirations of establishing Christianity as the state religion (the kind of aspiration that was not available to Jews except as a messianic vision linked to the restoration of Jewish political sovereignty in the land of Israel).[17] The line between the theocratic conception of the state as the

---

(Apr. 29, 2009; rev. Jan. 27, 2014), *available at* http://plato.stanford.edu/entries/dirty-hands/. The most influential contemporary revival of that tradition is Michael Walzer's *Political Action: The Problem of Dirty Hands*, 2 PHIL. & PUB. AFF. 160 (1973).

[16] I use the term "theocratically" advisedly for lack of a better word. Only in relatively rare circumstances have religious polities denied the need for secular authority. Most polities (and most theoretical models of polities) that undertake to legislate or institute religious law recognize the gap between human implementation and God's actual law and the concomitant need for secular as well as religious legal institutions. They therefore typically articulate complex institutional structures that in one way or another separate religious from secular authority, creating systems of government that are not strictly speaking theocracies either in deed or in aspiration. The European model of the King and the Church is a classic example. The blend of kingly and religious authority was not conceived of as a theocracy. To the contrary, the jurisdictions of the law of the King and the law of the Church were carefully circumscribed so that each respected the separate sphere of the other. Too often the term "theocracy" is used loosely, more as a term of opprobrium than as a term possessed of exact propositional content, to refer to any state that "adopts" religious law or provides an institutional role for clerics. On these issues and the general problem of defining "theocracy," see RAN HIRSCHL, CONSTITUTIONAL THEOCRACY (2010).

[17] Stone, *Religion and State, supra* note 10.

institution of Christianity and the more secularist conception of the state implicit in Christian accommodationist theology often blurred.

Less blurry was the basic opposition between the acceptance of the state's political authority common to the theocratic and accommodationist visions and the antipolitical theology of religious quietism. But even here, what in theory are mutually exclusive alternatives can end up being implemented in ways that confound the distinction between them, as the contemporary example of Hasidism illustrates. Both quietist and nonquietist philosophies depend upon some notion of separation between religion and the state, but their respective notions of how to implement the principle differ dramatically. The accommodationist strategy goes hand in hand with the assertion of a subject matter distinction between a realm of life that is subject to the jurisdiction of state law and a separate realm of life subject to religious law. Many Christian theologians, from Augustine to Acquinas, espoused one or another version of the principle "render unto Caesar what is Caesar's," which posited such a distinction between spiritual and material matters and called for a corresponding institutional separation between the jurisdiction of religion and the jurisdiction of the state. Even the most "theocratic" (and therefore not truly theocratic) versions of Christian political theology recognized such a distinction between the jurisdiction of the Church and the jurisdiction of the state, and to that extent they incorporated elements of the accommodationist philosophy of accepting and accommodating to religiously imperfect (i.e., secular) rule.[18] In the Jewish case, the accommodationist principle of separation between political and spiritual spheres served to protect a core of ritual life from the incursion of gentile law (at least in theory if not always in practice) at the same time that submission to gentile authorities with respect to "nonspiritual" matters was justified in *halakhic* terms.[19] The distinction drawn between spiritual and material realms thereby upheld the authority of Jewish law and, simultaneously, fostered the drawing of the status-based distinction

---

[18] My view of the centrality of accommodationist thought to the theological conception of the separation of church and state is elaborated in Nomi Maya Stolzenberg, *Political Theology with a Difference*, 4 U.C. IRVINE L. REV. 407 (2014). For other accounts of the theological origins of the principle of separation of church and state, which, unlike my account, do not privilege the principle of accommodation, see John Witte, *That Serpentine Wall of Separation*, 101 MICH. L. REV. 1869 (2003), STEVEN D. SMITH, THE DISENCHANTMENT OF SECULAR DISCOURSE (2010); Steven Douglas, *Recovering (From) Enlightenment?*, 41 SAN DIEGO L. REV. 1263, 1276–77 (2004), Steven D. Smith, *Separation and the "Secular": Reconstructing the Disestablishment Decision*, 67 TEX. L. REV. 955, 958–59 (1989).

[19] *See* GRAFF, *supra* note 11. *See also* Stone, *Religion and State*, *supra* note 10, and MENACHEM LORBERBAUM, POLITICS AND THE LIMITS OF LAW: SECULARIZING THE POLITICAL IN MEDIEVAL JEWISH POLITICAL THOUGHT (2001).

between those with a sacred vocation (i.e., participation in ritual and the study of Jewish law) and the rest of the Jewish populace.

It was precisely this traditional recipe for protecting religion by separating it from everyday life against which Hasidism would eventually revolt and propose its radically different "system of theology." Traditional rabbinic Judaism had achieved a separation of religion from the jurisdiction of the state essentially by narrowing the domain (and definition) of sacred activity, thereby leaving space for a realm of everyday life that could be subject to secular state jurisdiction without that encroaching on the jurisdiction of Jewish law. Hasidism, by contrast, because of its insistence that religion was everywhere, left no room in Jewish life for state law. On the hypothesis that *everything* was a site for the sacred, Hasidism adopted the theology of political quietism. On this view, worldly affairs, such as the activities of the state, are inherently corrupt and corrupting, incapable of being conducted in conformity with the requirements of religious law. Accommodation to the imperfect state law had to be resisted to the greatest extent possible. To achieve this, quietism proposed a strategy of separation very different from the version of separation embodied in the accommodationist doctrines of "render unto Caesar what is Caesar's" and the corollary Jewish doctrine of *dina de-malkhuta dina*. Instead of drawing a distinction between everyday worldly affairs (rightfully subject to the jurisdiction of the state) and spiritual affairs (subject to the separate jurisdiction of religion), the quietist solution was to withdraw into a separate walled-off society within which no distinction between religious and material matters would be observed. The world outside the community was by definition secular and therefore under the jurisdiction of secular state law. In this way, not only was a version of the principle of separating religion from the realm of secular law upheld. So too was the principle of accommodation, which was interpreted by Hasidic Rebbes as "demand[ing] passive submission to gentile hosts until the advent of the messianic age."[20] Both principles are observed in the Hasidic scheme of things by, in effect, jettisoning them into the outside world so that within the community, neither one need be observed.

Proponents of Jewish political quietism recognized of course that, as a practical matter, there would be limits to the extent to which such a state of perfect separation could be achieved. The success of religious separatism would always be dependent upon being left in peace by the powers that be, a condition that proponents of quietism were savvy enough to recognize

---

[20] Myers attributes this view to the Satmar Rebbe in particular, noting that he endorsed it with a zeal that distinguished him from some other, more accommodationist, Hassidic Rebbes. Myers, *supra* note 7, at 315.

could never be guaranteed. But it was precisely this recognition of the nature of political power and its susceptibility to abuse that led proponents of theological quietism to counsel withdrawal from "worldly society." The encroachment of worldly society had to be resisted to the greatest extent possible even if some submission to the demands of the gentile state was recognized to be a practical necessity.

This basic worldview animated a variety of religious separatist movements, both Christian and Jewish. Most well known are the Christian Anabaptists, including the Amish and the Mennonites, who settled in America in the early eighteenth century. It is for good reason, then, that Hasidic Jews are frequently referred to as the "Jewish Amish." Notwithstanding the religious and cultural differences between them, both are heirs to a similar quietist political tradition. What the Amish and the Hasidim have in common most fundamentally is the total renunciation of politics as a realm of spiritual pollution and impurity.

Perhaps the most notable expression of this sweeping repudiation of politics is the attitude that Satmars and other Hasidic and ultra-Orthodox Jewish groups hold toward Zionism. When Zionism arose as a political ideology in the late nineteenth century, Hasidic Jews were amongst its most vociferous critics, not just because it was secularist in its orientation, but also, more fundamentally, because to exercise political power is to violate the fundamental tenet of theological quietism, regardless of whether the people commanding the reigns of the state view their reign as religious or secular in nature. From this point of view, for Jews to establish a religious state is just as bad as establishing a secular state – indeed, worse. For Jews to exercise political power and assume command of a state in any circumstances is anathema to the Hasidic tradition of political quietism. But to establish a Jewish state in Israel is the ultimate sin because it entails arrogating the power to restore Jewish sovereignty over Israel, a messianic action that belongs to God alone.

Over time, some Hasidic groups softened their original opposition to Zionism. Not so for the Satmars, who continue to regard Zionism as the single greatest evil in the world.[21] Indeed, the Satmar community has been repeatedly singled out for the intensity (some might say extremity) with which it holds positions that other Hasidic groups share but hold with less intensity. Perhaps this is because Satmar was a relative latecomer to the Hasidic scene. Most Hasidic groups were founded over the course of the late eighteenth to early nineteenth centuries, inspired by the founder of the Hasidic movement, known as the Ba'al Shem Tov, who lived from 1700–1760. His immediate disciples were rabbis who "established dynastic 'courts' throughout the East and

---

[21]   Myers, *supra* note 7, at 315.

East Central Europe... each of which contained its own distinctive teachings, ritual variations, music, sartorial norms, and lore."[22] The Satmar court, which gathered around the charismatic figure of Rabbi Joel Teitelbaum, did not begin to form until 1910, when "Reb Yoilish," as he was known familiarly, assumed his first post as chief rabbi of a small Hungarian Jewish community sixty miles from the town of Szatmar, whence the Satmar community takes its name.[23] It was not until the 1920s that Rabbi Teitelbaum began to solidify the community around him that would come to be known as the Satmars. He did not become the chief rabbi of Szatmar (now renamed Satu Mare) until 1934, and within a decade, this newly formed "court" was almost completely annihilated, along with ninety percent of the rest of the country's Jewish population, when the Nazis occupied Hungary.

Ironically, the rescue of the Satmar Rebbe was engineered by a leader of the Zionist movement he so reviled.[24] Few other members of the Satmar community survived the Holocaust. Those who did regrouped with the Satmar Rebbe in New York following the end of the Second World War. At the time of their arrival to America in 1946, they numbered just a few. But the community swiftly grew. Survivors of other Jewish European communities were flooding into the Williamsburg neighborhood of Brooklyn where the Satmars had settled. Disoriented, lost, and searching for community and replacements for their own Rebbes, who had perished in the Holocaust, many were drawn to Reb Yoilish's magnetic personality. In this time period, the Satmar Rebbe focused his followers on rebuilding, concentrating first and foremost on establishing a synagogue and heeding the biblical injunction to be fruitful and multiply. Satmar families, eschewing birth control, typically had (and still have) eight to ten children and, not infrequently, more. And so it was not long before the Satmar community had swelled in size, quickly coming to dominate the burgeoning ultra-Orthodox community in the Williamsburg neighborhood of Brooklyn.[25]

All the while that the Satmar Rebbe was dedicating himself to building up his community in Brooklyn, he nursed the idea of establishing an outpost of "four pure cubits" outside the city where his dream of a truly separatist community could be fulfilled. Reb Yoilish had always been known for his extreme pietism and stringent standards of religious purity. In Europe, he had

---

[22] *Id.* at 312.

[23] *Id.* at 330.

[24] Yehuda Bauer, Jews for Sale? Jewish Negotiations 1933–45 (1994); Anna Porter, Kasztner's Train: The True Story of an Unknown Hero of the Holocaust (2009).

[25] According to historian Israel Rubin, by 1961, the community numbered 4,500 people. Israel Rubin, Satmar: An Island in the City 27 (1972).

engaged in numerous attempts to purge the Jewish community of any and all elements of impurity, a label he applied equally to "'modernizers,' who were attempting to introduce innovations into Judaism through a mix of religious reform, secular education, and assimilation to Gentile culture" and Zionists as well as non-Jews.[26] In America, his dreams of religious purity grew even more ambitious as he imagined the possibility of creating an enclave outside the city, populated solely by his followers, completely separated from the rest of the world. Beginning in the 1970s, plans to implement this longstanding dream were set in motion as agents of the community were sent out to scope for undeveloped land where a satellite group could set down roots. After a few false starts, the Satmars succeeded in purchasing an undeveloped tract in the Township of Monroe, in Orange County, New York, about an hour's ride outside New York City.

The early years of settling Monroe were a case study in the process of suburbanization then spreading across America. In some respects, the Satmars' move from city to suburb partook of the dynamics of white flight common to that era. The typical pattern of white flight involved relatively affluent whites reacting to desegregation and the increased presence of blacks by leaving the city for the rapidly developing suburbs. There, the barriers between the suburbs and the city were fortified by the practice of "exclusionary zoning" in which land-use regulations, such as single-family zoning, served to prevent affordable housing from being built, and thereby excluded minorities and others who could not afford to purchase housing that satisfied the suburbs' pricy land-use requirements.[27] Inasmuch as part of what motivated the Satmars' exodus from the city was the desire to escape growing tensions with their black and Latino neighbors in Williamsburg,[28] they could be seen as exemplars

---

[26] Myers, *supra* note 7, at 313.

[27] On the concept of exclusionary zoning that lawyers developed in the 1970s, see, for example, Robert J. Hartman, Village of Belle Terre v. Boaraas: *Belle Terre Is a Nice Place to Visit – But Only "Families" May Live There*, 8 URBAN L. ANN. 193 (1974); Thaddeus Marciniak, *Up the Down-Sliding Scale*: Boraas v. Village of Belle Terre *and Equal Protection Assault on Restrictive Definitions of the "Family" in Zoning Ordinances*, 49 NOTRE DAME L. REV. 428 (1973–74).

[28] Competition for public housing has been the site of intense and prolonged conflict between the Hasidim in Williamsburg and their Black and Latino neighbors. Housing discrimination litigation arising out of this conflict commenced in the late 1960s (*see* JEROME R. MINTZ, HASIDIC PEOPLE: A PLACE IN THE NEW WORLD 251–57 (1992)), and has continued up until the, with settlements reached in the litigation still in force and subject to ongoing challenges. *See* Williamsburg Fair Hous. Comm. v. N.Y. City Hous. Auth., 73 F.R.D. 381 (S.D.N.Y. 1976); 493 F. Supp. 1225 (S.D.N.Y. 1980); 599 F. Supp. 509 (S.D.N.Y. 1984); 2005 WL 736146 (S.D.N.Y. Mar. 31, 2005); 2005 WL 2175998 (S.D.N.Y. Sept. 9, 2005); 2007 WL 486610 (S.D.N.Y. Feb. 14, 2007). This litigation is entirely separate from the 1976 zoning conflict involving the Satmars who moved to Monroe.

of white flight. Once arrived in the Town of Monroe, however, the Satmars found themselves more victims of exclusionary zoning than perpetrators, at least initially. Indeed, even before they arrived in Monroe, the Satmars had to defend themselves from the suspicions and prejudices held against them by the town's residents, who by and large fit the mode of the prototypical suburb, although the population there was more "light blue-collar" (civil servants, policemen and firemen) than the proverbial wealthy suburb. In order to combat the town residents' suspicion of them as an alien minority, the Satmars went so far as to use a purchasing agent who did not look like a Hasid in order to disguise their intention of creating a settlement for Hasidic Jews. (Previous experience had taught them that suburbs would otherwise organize to try to exclude Hasidic Jews by preventing them from buying and developing property.) Having circumvented this initial obstacle with the clever subterfuge of a purchasing agent with none of the telltale sartorial marks or hairstyle of a Hasid, the Satmars succeeded in purchasing the real estate they had set their sights on, and they quickly set about building a residential development to accommodate the Satmar families who elected to move from Williamsburg to the suburbs. But before the development was even completed, disputes over the builders' compliance with Monroe's zoning laws began to arise. In some respects, these disputes followed the classic pattern of exclusionary zoning, with the Satmars occupying the position of the poor minority potentially "zoned out" of the suburb by its exclusion of high-density affordable housing. Indeed, the typical Satmar family was poor. (The Satmar community of Kiryas Joel is, by official measures, among the poorest communities in the nation, a measurement that owes something to the very large size of the typical Satmar family and even more to the fact that the community shuns higher education while exalting the vocation of lifelong Torah study (for males), which results in depressed of employment and relatively low average salaries among those who are employed.[29]) All this created a demand for exactly the sort of high-density, multi-unit housing that was anathema to the architects of suburban land-use planning and the typical object of exclusion through low-density zoning. The

---

[29] Decades after the establishment of Kiryas Joel, the official measurement of Kiryas Joel as "the poorest community in America" grabbed public attention after the release of the latest census data. *See* Sam Roberts, *A Village With the Numbers, Not the Image, of the Poorest Place*, N.Y. TIMES, Apr. 21, 2011, at A1 (noting that "[a]bout 70 percent of the village's 21,000 residents lives in households whose income falls below the federal poverty threshold, according to the Census Bureau," that "[m]edian family income ($17,929) and per capita income ($4,494) rank lower than any other comparable place in the country" and "[n]early half of the village's households reported less than $15,000 in annual income." The unit of comparison is "the nation's 3,700 villages, towns or cities with more than 10,000 people.").

inability of the Satmars to comply with the Town of Monroe's single-family ordinance and other zoning requirements was further exacerbated by the building of second kitchens (to accommodate their religious dietary practices) and attempts to house "shitbls" (small, informal worship congregations) and even some small businesses in the basements and lower levels of some of the new homes.

To say that none of this went over well with the good citizens of Monroe would be an understatement. Tensions flared as the two sides traded accusations, and the result was the rapid-fire secession of the Satmars from the Township of Monroe and the simultaneous creation of a separate municipality, formally incorporated in 1977 as the Village of Kiryas Joel.[30] Although creating a legally incorporated municipality had never been the intention of the Satmar Rebbe or of his faithful lieutenants who were assiduously working to carry out his vision of a Torah-true society, the expedient devised by town leaders trying to deal with the zoning crisis presented the Satmars with an unparalleled opportunity to perfect the condition of political autonomy that they sought. All that was required to carry out the plan to secede and form a separate local government were the votes of five hundred voting residents in the area.[31] The implementation of this plan to separate the Satmars from the Town of Monroe was greeted by both sides with palpable relief, the residents of Monroe being as happy to be rid of the Satmars as the Satmars were happy to be rid of them. Indeed, when the boundaries around the newly formed Village of Kiryas Joel were originally proposed, following the procedures for establishing new local governments laid down by New York state law, it was the hapless few non-Satmars whose homes were initially contained within the boundary line of the new Village who demanded that it be redrawn so as to exclude them. The result was an officially incorporated local government with a perfectly homogenous population made up exclusively of Satmar Jews.[32]

The early years of the Village following its incorporation were focused on institution-building. Notwithstanding the death of the Rebbe just two years after the Village's incorporation, an event which cast a pall over the entire Satmar community and set in motion political grudges and grievances that would eventually divide it, Satmar leaders in Kiryas Joel were focused on constructing more housing, building a new grand synagogue, establishing the "bais midrash" (the traditional "house of learning," where adult male Torah

---

[30] One of the immediate precipitants of the secession was the filing of a lawsuit against the Satmars by the town's building inspector. Matter of Barone, 89 Misc. 2d 1009 (N.Y. Sup. Ct. 1976) (upholding the right of the building inspector to inspect the Satmars' buildings).

[31] N.Y. Village, art. 2. § 2-200.

[32] Bd. of Educ. of Kiryas Joel Vill. Sch. Dist. v. Grumet, 512 U.S. 687, 699 (1994).

study would take place), and creating the other key institutions of Satmar life: private religious schools for girls and boys; mikvahs (the traditional ritual baths); and all the necessary commercial institutions, such as the much-used wedding hall and shops where members of the community could purchase the special food and clothing that they needed to comply with the strict requirements of their all-encompassing Jewish law.

At the same time that they were developing these "private" institutions (private, that is, from the standpoint of American law), the leaders of Kiryas Joel were also busy developing its local government institutions. A mayor and members of the Village Board of Trustees (its town council) were elected, new Satmar-friendly zoning laws were enacted, and municipal services were established, all under the protocols established by New York's local government laws. In addition, although the vast majority of the Village's burgeoning population of children attended the Satmars' religious schools (a traditional "yeshiva" for boys and a separate religious school for girls), in 1989, just twelve years after the Village was formed, a public school district was established in Kiryas Joel. The intent behind the formation of the school district, which was authorized by the enactment of special legislation by the New York State legislature,[33] was to provide a setting in which Satmar children with special needs could receive the state-funded special educational services to which they were entitled without offending the Establishment Clause's prohibition on providing government aid to religious schools.[34] Just as the creation of a separate Village was an expedient that had been improvised in response to the political conflict between the Satmars and the Town of Monroe, not an idea that Satmars themselves initiated or pursued by themselves, so too, the creation of a separate school district was a political solution devised to deal with the problems that resulted when Satmar children with special needs were sent to the Monroe regional school.[35] In neither case did the idea of creating a separate local government entity originate with the Satmars. But once presented, the Satmars not only welcomed the idea, but quickly mastered the political arts of running of their own (secular) public institutions in ways that would maximize both government benefits and the political clout from which these benefits derived.

The upshot of all this activity was the creation of a separate Satmar society with unprecedented levels of homogeneity, religious stringency, and political

---

[33] 1989 N.Y. Laws, ch. 748.

[34] Governor's Approval Memorandum, ch. 748, *reprinted in* 1989 N.Y. Legis. Ann.

[35] Satmars alleged that children who were sent to the public school district that served their region suffered "pain and trauma" as a result of being exposed to a different culture that was insensitive to the children's cultural and linguistic differences. *Grumet*, 512 U.S. at 692.

autonomy. Save for a similar village created by another Hasidic sect in nearby "New Square,"[36] never before had a traditional Jewish community had its own separate municipality and local government institutions. Certainly no such political entities were found in Europe, whence the community originated. Notwithstanding the romantic notion that Kiryas Joel was a recreation of the proverbial prewar European *shtetl* (a notion cultivated by Reb Yoilish himself), the real shtetl had been a place where Jews had lived side by side with non-Jews and where different forms of Judaism (and, over time, secular movements as well) flourished and vied with each other for the hearts and minds of the local Jewish community. By contrast, Kiryas Joel was a place run by Satmars, ruled by Satmars, and populated by Satmars alone. Freed from the interference of hostile or uncomprehending town members bent on enforcing inimical zoning laws, sheltered from all people with different values and lifestyles, and largely insulated from the imposition of secular law, the Satmars of Kiryas Joel were authorized to use the powers of local government in ways that would be supportive of their distinctive religious way of life. In exercising its power to enact local ordinances, the Village itself did not enforce Jewish law or deny non-Satmars the right to live within its boundaries. It didn't have to. Those jobs were safely left to the domain of "private action," to the community's private developers who oversaw the selling and leasing of residential units to Satmar families; to the rabbis who staffed the "beit din," the rabbinic courts to which the adjudication of internal disputes was entrusted, and the schools, where boys and men studied Jewish law and girls and young women were prepared for their religious duties as wives and mothers; and ultimately, to the Rebbe himself, the spiritual leader of the Satmar community whose religious authority extended to every single member and every single aspect of Satmar life.

In the face of such awesome, all-encompassing power, selecting a successor for the Rebbe would be no easy matter. Indeed, controversy over the matter of succession arose immediately upon his Reb Yoilish's death and, more than thirty-five years later, it still has not ceased. But that controversy has not prevented the community of Kiryas Joel from growing and thriving. From a population of a few hundred families at the time of the Village's incorporation in 1977, the population has grown to 22,000 by the last census count. (The population of the Satmar community in Williamsburg is estimated to be from 65,000 to 75,000 and the worldwide Satmar population worldwide stands at somewhere between 100,000 and 150,000). Far from weakening, the levels of

---

[36] For a discussion of New Square, see Nomi Maya Stolzenberg, *Return of the Repressed: Illiberal Groups in a Liberal State*, 12 J. CONTEMP. LEGAL ISSUES 897, 902 (2001).

commitment and stringency in the Satmars' observance of Jewish law have, if anything, grown stronger. Although some aspects of modern culture have filtered into Satmar society, most notably the Internet and other forms of modern media and technology, even more notable is the strength of their ongoing resistance to assimilation into the norms of modern society, particularly in regard to matters of sexuality, gender and family life. Traditional sex-role differentiation has been maintained and in some respects even intensified. In the years after the Rebbe's death, there has been movement in two directions as real and perceived increases in laxity have engendered the fear that more constraint is necessary, fuelling a perpetual cycle of increasing levels of stringency in the articulation and enforcement of traditional gender roles in response to real and perceived behavioral deviations. Women in the Satmar community, always expected to dedicate themselves to having babies and taking care of their families and traditionally excluded from the practices of Jewish learning and ritual observance reserved for males, are now also subject to prohibitions on driving and redoubled commitment to enforcing the community's stringent interpretations of the traditional rules of modesty. According to these rules, a man must not be in the presence of females unrelated to him, must not hear a woman sing, nor see a woman's hair or flesh. Changing styles of women's head-coverings and self-appointed "modesty committees" attest to the extent to which these strict interpretations of Jewish law have been internalized throughout the community.

To be sure, there are some defectors and, among those who remain in the community, varying levels of observance and adaptation to the surrounding culture, particularly in the areas of technology and women's fashion, can be observed. But by any account, the Satmars' attempt to create a separate enclave, sheltered from outside cultural influences and dedicated to following "the holy way of the Rebbe" and strict adherence to Jewish law, has been a stunning success. The question, though, is whether that success has been accomplished with, or without, American law.

DECONSTRUCTING KIRYAS JOEL

Where is American law in all of this? Jewish law, of course, is everywhere in the community, in the yeshivas and the "beis midrash" where it is studied, in the rabbinic courts where it is applied to the adjudication of disputes, in the synagogue, in the mikvah, in the performance of daily prayers on the commuter buses that shepherd residents of Kiryas Joel to and from the city in gender-segregated seating, in the butcher shops and pizza restaurants, in the shops selling hats and the separate shops selling wigs, in the wedding halls and maternity convalescence home, in the streets, in the homes, in the marital beds (twin, not double), and in the hearts and minds of every member of the community, as evidenced by the ubiquitous self-appointed modesty patrols.

The presence of American law is more elusive. Of course, some American law has to be present. But the mere fact that the Satmars rely upon, make use of, or have acted under American law (what else could they have done?) does not by itself deprive the religious law that they live by of its private, non-state character. The question is whether a distinction between private and state action in Kiryas Joel is maintained.

On the face of things, institutions would seem to be carefully arranged in such a way that the distinctions between public and private institutions necessary to keep American and Jewish legal institutions separate are maintained. In keeping with this formal distinction between public and private law, the legal construction of Kiryas Joel might be pictured metaphorically as something like an astrodome, with private action conducted in conformity with private law having paved the ground, and the formal incorporation of the Village having erected a thin layer of secular government arching above that foundation. In this view of things, the Village is a separate entity from the people who populate it. The public entity of the Village (technically an arm of the state) is separated from the private action on the ground. Religious activity takes place on the ground level and is thereby institutionally separated from the activity of the local government, which is both formally and functionally secular in nature.

Seen this way, the same structure that serves to maintain a separation between the secular/public institutions and the religious/private institutions within the Village also serves to separate the Village from the outside world. The thin layer of municipal law that constitutes the Village forms a sort of carapace, arching over the community, protecting it from outside interference while freeing its residents to establish private legal institutions by exercising their individual rights. Such private action takes place far below the local government structure under which it is sheltered. Apart from this thin layer of municipal government (which is obliged to conform to a variety of public law regimes and which itself produces public law), public as opposed to private American law hardly enters into the community. What public law does enter the community is captured and contained in the membrane of the Village government that rises above life on the ground. Underneath that outer shell of public law, life is largely freed from state regulation, governed instead by non-state (Jewish) law.

American law, in this view of things, is not absent, but its role is strictly facilitative, enabling the Satmars to organize themselves in such a way that outside interference is kept to a minimum and the regulatory authority of their own autonomous religious legal institutions is brought to a maximum. When it comes to action on the ground, so-called private conduct, it is American "private law," not public law, that plays the dominant role. The result is what I have elsewhere referred to as "communitarianism from the bottom up."[37] It was private law that provided individual members of the Satmar community with the rights to acquire and develop private property in the territory that is now Kiryas Joel before it was separately incorporated. That same body of private law continues to govern property transactions, enabling private property owners to control who will occupy the property units that Satmar developers have built. Outside the field of real estate law, other bodies of private law facilitate the creation and maintenance of the Satmar's separatist religious community by protecting the basic individual rights of freedom of religion, freedom of association, and the freedom of parents to determine their children's religious upbringing, subject to only minimal regulation. Public law enhances these private powers by granting residents the right to vote on local government boundaries and the right to vote for local officials once those boundaries have been formed, enabling them to form more responsive local democratic institutions. But, although the two work in tandem to enable the Satmars to achieve their goals of separating from society and instituting religious law, the public and private entities (and the regimes of public and private law that govern them) are functionally and formally separate. According to the conventional view, private law itself is not regulatory or restrictive but rather facilitative and permissive in nature. And the public institutions of the community that are subject to and themselves produce public law are not themselves responsible for the work of exclusion of non-members and internal discipline of members that is performed by private actors, which is governed (i.e., enabled) by private law. So long as public law institutions are produced through the local democratic process, they too are viewed as emanating from the bottom up, i.e., as expressions of popular choice, not as lines of division imposed by the government on the basis of some invidious

---

[37] Nomi Maya Stolzenberg, *The Culture of Property*, 129 DAEDALUS 169, 186 (2000) ("In lieu of the sort of top-down approaches to separating groups and endowing them with their own territory and jurisdiction found in nondemocratic societies (like the former Soviet Union or the Ottoman Empire) or in consociational democracies (like Switzerland), the coordinated exercise of the rights of private property can similarly serve to separate and endow subgroups from the bottom up.").

group-based classification. To put it otherwise, the lines of division are viewed as the product of private choice (the desire of individuals to "live with their own kind") rather than state action.[38]

This is the basic picture of the situation that the Supreme Court adopted in the one case where the developments in Kiryas Joel were brought to its attention. That was a case, brought in 1990 and decided in 1994, in which the law creating the Kiryas Joel Public School District was challenged as a violation of the principle of separation between church and state.[39] The challenger claimed that the state had effectively delegated the powers of local government exercised by public school districts to a religious community, thereby constituting a fusion of religious and political authority forbidden by the Establishment Clause of the federal Constitution.[40] Although the Supreme Court technically agreed with the challenger, striking down the state law under which the Kiryas Joel School District had been created, it did so on narrow grounds, making it clear that there was nothing wrong, in principle, with a religiously homogenous community having its own local government institutions or exercising political power.[41] The basis for this reasoning was precisely the distinction asserted between Kiryas Joel's municipal institutions

---

[38] *Accord* Richard Ford, *The Boundaries of Race: Political Geography in Legal Analysis*, 107 HARV. L. REV. 1841, 1847–52 (1994).

[39] *Grumet*, 512 U.S. 687.

[40] *Id.* at 687, 699, 702.

[41] "Clear" is perhaps the wrong word since the welter of opinions produced by the Justices, each offering a different theory about what was wrong with the law, produced little clarity about the nature of the constitutional defect or the governing principles. That said, with the sole exception of Justice Stevens, both the Justices in the majority and those in dissent concurred in the proposition that there is nothing unconstitutional about a law which permits religiously homogeneous populations to form their own separate local government entities – so long as the laws are not passed with the specific intention of granting that privilege to a particular religious group (and not to other groups). Justice O'Connor, in her concurring opinion, provided the clearest formulation of this apparent point of agreement. *See* Grumet, 512 U.S. at 717 (O'Connor, J., concurring) ("There is nothing improper about a legislative intention to accommodate a religious group, so long as it is implemented through generally applicable legislation. New York may, for instance, allow all villages to operate their own school districts. If it does not want to act so broadly, *it may set forth neutral criteria that a village must meet to have a school district of its own;* these criteria can then be applied by a state agency, and the decision would then be reviewable by the judiciary. A district created under a generally applicable scheme would be acceptable even though it coincides with a village which was consciously created by its voters as an enclave for their religious group. I do not think the court's opinion holds the contrary.") For further explication of the opinions, see Nomi Maya Stolzenberg, Board of Education of Kiryas Joel Village School District v. Grumet: *A Religious Group's Quest for Its Own Public School, in* LAW AND RELIGION: CASES IN CONTEXT (Leslie C. Griffin ed., 2010).

and its private institutions. Accepting the view that religious law was not being enforced by the Village's public institutions and that the school district itself was run as a secular institution, the Supreme Court heavily implied that the exclusion of non-Satmars from the school district (and the Village itself) was acceptable so long as it resulted from private choices rather than being legally imposed. So too, by this logic, was it acceptable for private "choices" to be guided by (or made in submission to) religious authority, so long as such submission was not commanded by the school district or the Village's elected officials. In short, the formal legal distinction between the Satmars' governmental institutions and their formally private social institutions served to alibi the public school district. More broadly, it served to defend the Satmars against accusations that they use their powers of local government to exclude outsiders and legislate religious law.

Boiled down to its essence, this reasoning amounts to distinguishing de facto from de jure segregation. Put otherwise, it assumes that Jewish law in Kiryas Joel is non-state law. But is it? Certainly it is true that both the school district and the village confine themselves to secular functions. The school district in particular is scrupulously professional. It is staffed and run by administrators and educators from outside the Satmar community and the therapeutic and educational services that it provides to boys and girls (taught together) are completely secular in nature. The Village similarly confines itself to secular functions, though there is a much more intimate relationship between the office-holders of the Village and the Chief Rabbi and the religious leaders who follow his direction. But in order to see exactly where power lies in Kiryas Joel, and what the relationship between public and private, secular and religious, American and Jewish law is, it is necessary to look at the law in Kiryas Joel in its totality. Instead of focusing exclusively on public law (the body of American law that regulates governmental entities and other public institutions), as the Supreme Court and most previous legal analyses of Kiryas Joel have done, we need to look at both public law and private law (the body of American law that governs "private relations," such as real estate transactions, for-profit and nonprofit corporations and family relations) *and the way that private and public law interact.* Only by looking at their interaction is it possible to see how private power in Kiryas Joel (expressed through the exercise of private rights) has been effectively converted into public power through the combined legal mechanisms of property holding and voting in local elections. It then becomes possible to see that the result of this conversion of private into public power is that Kiryas Joel's local government, rather than merely facilitating local democracy, becomes a tool for maintaining the political authority of the established religious leaders and suppressing political dissent.[42] At the same time, so-called private law, rather than being simply facilitative of private choices, becomes a tool for enforcing religious law and communal norms, disciplining dissidents and nonconforming members of the community, and keeping people who are not members of the community out. In short, the public–private distinction, which plays an essential role in maintaining the perception of Jewish law as non-state law, is shown to blur if not altogether collapse in Kiryas Joel. Rather than operating separately in independent domains, public and private institutions work *together* to play an active and essential role in discouraging exit, adjudicating conflicts, and enforcing *halakhic* norms.

At the same time, the conditions that erode the boundary between public and private *within* Kiryas also have the effect of blurring the boundary that separates Kiryas Joel from the outside world. Although that boundary is very real and very effective in minimizing the exposure of Satmars to non-Satmar culture, it turns out to be less a hard shell (or "impregnable wall"[43]) than a permeable membrane through which elements of American law and culture selectively flow. Indeed, on inspection, Kiryas Joel is seen to be suffused with American law.

A simple catalog of the many forms of American law that flow into Kiryas Joel shows just how much American law there is in the supposedly closed society of the Satmars. Although many different types of state law regimes penetrate into the Village, and penetrate into it in different ways, there are two broad categories that warrant being distinguished: law as it is enforced by courts in the context of litigation and law that filters into the community "in the shadow of litigation," not through lawsuits, but rather, through private activity conducted under the framework of transactional law and other facilitative legal regimes. The operation of state law is always more visible in litigation than it is in structuring private transactions. In the case of Kiryas Joel, litigation is especially arresting because one of the most fundamental tenets of Jewish law that the Satmars purport to uphold is a strict prohibition against bringing disputes before gentile courts. Under this traditional Jewish law doctrine, it is permissible for disputes between Jews and gentiles to be adjudicated in gentile courts. But Jews are commanded to bring their disputes with other Jews to

---

[42] *Accord* Ford, *supra* note 38, at 1847–52.

[43] The image of the "impregnable wall" of separation comes from the Supreme Court. See Everson v. Bd. of Educ. of Twp. of Ewing, 330 U.S. 1, 18 (quoting Thomas Jefferson for the proposition that "the clause against establishment of religion by law was intended to erect a 'wall of separation between church and State'" (*id.* at 16) and stating "[t]hat wall must be kept high and impregnable" (*id.* at 18), while holding that a program providing publicly funded bus transportation to parochial schools does not breach that wall).

the rabbinic courts.[44] And in many cases, that is exactly what Satmars do, the robust system of rabbinic courts being one of the more interesting features of Satmar life that conforms to the standard legal pluralist picture.

Yet, despite this taboo, Satmars have been involved in an astounding number of lawsuits. Some of this litigation has been thrust upon them by outsiders. The *Grumet* case, challenging the constitutionality of the public school district, is of this type. The checkered career of that litigation, which stretched out for over ten years with losses and triumphs for both sides, reflects the unresolved tension within American law between pluralist values, which empower separatist groups to form their own political enclaves, and competing values, which cut against separatist aspirations. The *Grumet* litigation also highlights the fact that American courts, applying American law, are the ultimate arbiters of the boundaries of permissible separatism. Indeed, the school district litigation is not the only legal challenge that has been brought by outsiders against the Village's municipal leaders and institutions over the years. In the *Grumet* case itself, the Supreme Court's decision striking down the law passed to authorize the school district in 1994 was followed by another six years of legal challenges, during which the New York State Legislature responded to the Supreme Court (and to the entreaties of the Satmars' political operators) by passing a series of new authorizing statutes designed to meet the Court's stated concerns about singling out one religious community for special favors. Each time the state legislature passed another law reauthorizing the school district, the plaintiff, Grumet, went back to court to challenge its constitutionality until finally, on the state legislature's fourth try, the last piece of authorizing legislation was left to stand.[45]

[44] *See* J. David Bleich, *Litigation and Arbitration Before Non-Jews*, 34 TRADITION 58, 62–63 (2000); Simcha Krauss, *Litigation in Secular Courts*, 2 J. HALACHA & CONTEMP. SOC'Y 35 (1982); *see also* Michael A. Helfand, *Religious Arbitration and the New Multiculturalism: Negotiating Conflicting Legal Orders*, 86 N.Y.U. L. REV. 1231, 1247–49 (2011).

[45] In the first case that Grumet brought against the first statute enacted by the state legislature to authorize the creation of a school district in Kiryas Joel, the trial court granted summary judgment in favor of the plaintiff, holding that the statute violated the Establishment Clause. Grumet v. N.Y. State Educ. Dep't, 579 N.Y.S.2d 1004 (N.Y. Sup. Ct. 1992). Both the state appellate court and the United States Supreme Court affirmed. Grumet v. Bd. of Educ. of Kiryas Joel Vill. Sch. Dist. 592 N.Y.S. 2d 123 (N.Y. App. Div. 1992); Bd. of Educ. of Kiryas Joel Vill. Sch. Dist. v. Grumet, 512 U.S. 687 (1994). Following the Supreme Court's decision (indeed a mere eleven days later), the New York legislature produced a new piece of legislation reauthorizing the school district. 1994 N.Y. Laws 2744, ch. 241. When Grumet challenged the constitutionality of that statute, the trial court held that it was constitutional and did not violate the Establishment Clause or state constitutional provisions. Grumet v. Cuomo, 625 N.Y.S. 2d 1000 (N.Y. Sup. Ct. 1995). The appellate court reversed, 647 N.Y.S. 2d 565 (N.Y. App. Div. 1996), and that judgment was affirmed by New York state's highest court, 681 N.E.2d 340 (N.Y. 1997), sending the state legislature back to the drawing board. A third authorizing

The Village of Kiryas Joel has been the subject of other lawsuits brought by outsiders as well. Most recently, state and local government officials have been suing the Village over its plans to expand its water district, raising questions about the extent to which the powers of local government can be exercised to the detriment of the interests of neighboring communities.[46] Like the school district litigation, the water district litigation pits the Village of Kiryas Joel against outsiders. More precisely, they are lawsuits in which outsiders pit themselves against the Satmars. Although these lawsuits challenge the Satmars' ability to separate themselves from the law and society of the outside world, they do not run afoul of the *halakhic* prohibition, which requires that only *internal* disputes be adjudicated by rabbinic, rather than gentile, courts. Criminal lawsuits and child abuse proceedings are more ambiguous in this regard. In cases where Satmars are alleged to have committed crimes not against other members of the community, but rather, against outsiders, they clearly fall outside the *halakhic* prohibition on internal disputes. But when crimes are committed against fellow-members, then serious questions arise about the *halakhic* propriety of reporting crimes to the police and bringing charges. The intervention of outside authorities in domestic violence and sexual abuse cases has proven to be a particularly thorny issue.[47]

statute produced by the legislature, 1997 N.Y. Laws 2495, ch. 390, also was challenged by Grumet in *Grumet v. Pataki*, 675 N.Y.S. 2d 662 (N.Y. App. Div. 1998). There, the trial court held that the law authorizing the school district had the impermissible effect of endorsing a religion and hence was unconstitutional, a decision upheld by the appellate court. *Grumet v. Pataki*, 720 N.E.2d 66 (N.Y. 1999). A petition for certiori to the Supreme Court in this case was denied. *Pataki v. Grumet*, 528 U.S. 946 (1999). Finally, a fourth authorizing statute was passed by the New York legislature, 1999 N.Y. Laws 2513, ch. 405. By this time, Louis Grumet, the man behind the challenges to all three previous statutes, had departed from his position as the head of the New York State School Board Association, where he had presided ex officio over bringing these cases. (In an early procedural ruling in the first case, Grumet was denied standing to bring a challenge in his capacity as director of the school board association, owing to a conflict of interest, but was permitted to continue litigating in his capacity as an individual taxpayer.) The only legal challenge to chapter 405, brought by "the dissidents" in Kiryas Joel, was based on the failure to meet the population requirements of the statute, not on constitutional grounds. When they failed to prevail in their claim, this fourth and final authorizing statute was left to stand. *Birnbaum v. Bd. of Educ. of Monroe-Woodbury Cent. Sch. Dist.*, No. 7306-99, 2001 WL 36241683 (N.Y. Sup. Ct. Feb. 14, 2001).

[46] *Cnty. of Orange v. Vill. of Kiryas Joel*, 815 N.Y.S. 2d 494 (N.Y. Sup. Ct. 2005); 844 N.Y.S. 2d 57 (N.Y. App. Div. 2007).

[47] Whether or not it is permissible to go to the police and bring charges against a fellow-member of the community in cases of grave offenses is hotly debated. A recent New Yorker article describes the arguments on both sides of the issue and exposes the opprobrium attached to whistleblowers in a high profile case of alleged sexual abuse of young boys. *See* Rachel Aviv, *The Outcast*, THE NEW YORKER, Nov. 10, 2014.

The recent sexual abuse scandals in the Satmar community have drawn a good deal of media attention to this issue. But for all the controversy that has arisen within the community over the propriety of going to the authorities in criminal and domestic violence cases, there are even more striking, though less publicized, departures from the prohibition on bringing internal disputes to gentile courts. Two types of cases in particular have propelled Satmar on Satmar disputes into America's civil courts in substantial numbers. One is the growing number of custody disputes, which call upon New York's family courts to decide whether a parent whose religious standards are more lax – or who decides to leave the community altogether – can be required to raise her child in accordance with the strict standards of religious observance upheld by her former spouse or lose custody to observant ex-spouse. Like legal disputes with outsiders, these are cases where the Satmars have no choice but to submit their disputes to the law of the state because the state asserts its jurisdiction over custody and divorce. In the typical divorce and custody situation in the Satmar community, though the parties go first to the rabbinic court, often accompanied by legal advocates, who need not be, but not uncommonly are, the lawyers who will later represent them in civil court.[48] There, rabbis decide whether to grant a Jewish divorce in accord with Jewish law and, in cases where a divorce is granted, also often issue rulings pertaining to custody. Following the obtaining of the *get* (the Jewish divorce), the parties are required to file for a civil divorce under state law in order to make their divorce legal. Although the submission of the dispute to the jurisdiction of the state courts is accepted in principle and as a practical necessity, the rabbinic courts have been quite aggressive and creative – and successful – in finding ways to prevent the jurisdiction of the state courts from undermining their own jurisdiction.

These family law cases, which still await systematic study, reveal the important role that is being played by state law in enforcing *halakhic* norms of childrearing and marital conflict resolution, as interpreted by the Satmar rabbinic authorities. Because divorce and custody cases are generally settled, not litigated, and because the records in these cases are sealed, it is exceedingly difficult to gather information about how the courts are actually deciding these cases, or even how many such cases there are. Confidentiality obligations raise further barriers to collecting and presenting evidence. But even in the face of these obstacles to gathering information, there is evidence that in at least some number of cases, family court judges are incorporating rabbinic decrees into

---

[48] Interview with divorce attorney Martin Johnson.

civil law settlements including detailed regulations about the kind of people the noncustodial parent can permit the child be in contact with, the kind of clothes the children are permitted to wear, and the kind of food the defecting noncustodial parent must serve. Anecdotal evidence also suggests that parents who leave the community are at risk of losing custody to the parent who stays.

In the absence of data, it is impossible to know how common such decisions are or the extent to which they reflect a bias against parents who seek to raise their children without abiding by the community's stringent religious norms. Because these rulings are based on private settlements, it is possible to defend family court decrees that incorporate rabbinic decrees as doing no more than enforcing private agreements. However, the social dynamics underlying these cases give rise to concerns about how consensual these settlements truly are. Whether it is well-founded or not, there is no denying the perception that exists among those who have left the Satmar and other Hasidic communities that New York's family law courts have obliged the ultra-Orthodox by essentially incorporating the rulings of the rabbinic courts into their own "secular" decrees. In response to the concern that family courts may be biased against them, "formerly ultra-Orthodox people" have begun to mobilize, forming an organization called Footsteps, which provides a variety of services to people leaving or considering leaving the ultra-Orthodox community, including a legal services program devoted to helping people who leave the community to navigate the family court system.[49] A "Family Issues Handbook" produced by Footsteps cautions that "[j]udges are elected by the public in the location where they serve" and "[i]n some areas with high concentrations of ultra-Orthodox Jews, there is a concern that some judges rule far more favorably for the ultra-Orthodox side."[50] The handbook provides people seeking to leave the community with advice about how to avoid losing custody of their children, as is alleged to have occurred in a number of cases involving parents who defect.

Indeed, there is good reason to believe that the threat of losing custody serves as one of the most powerful deterrents to leaving the Satmar community. To the extent that is true, family law courts, and family law more generally, constitute a crucial site of legal discipline *within* the community, which defies any bright-line distinction between state and religious law.

The second category of Satmar versus Satmar disputes that have made their way into state court does not have the same obligatory nature. These

---

[49] *See* footstepsorg.org. A recent New York Times article on the group says that its other programs include "classes in math and evolution, lessons in how to flirt, workshops on preparing a resume, camping trips, Thanksgiving dinners, art exhibits." Samuel Freedman, *Stepping Off the Path and Redefining Faith*, N.Y. TIMES, Oct. 17, 2014.

[50] The Footsteps Family Issues Handbook can be found online at footstepsorg.org.

are cases where no one is requiring the Satmars to submit their disputes to the adjudication of state courts. (Indeed, in most of these cases, the judges visibly and vigorously struggle to get out of having to adjudicate the conflict).[51] These cases thus fall squarely under the *halakhic* prohibition against bringing internal disputes to gentile courts – a religious prohibition that is increasingly being honored in the breach.

Virtually all of the cases that have this character arise out of the long-running political conflicts that have been roiling the community since the death of the original Rebbe and founder of the Satmars, Rabbi Joel Teitelbaum, after whom the Village of Kiryas Joel is named. In these cases, members of the community who have been branded as "dissidents" use American law and American courts to challenge the leadership of those who have succeeded in grasping the reigns of power. Who gets labeled as a "dissident" varies depending on where the dispute is taking place. In Kiryas Joel, where "Reb Aron," one of the founding Rebbe's great-nephews, is the Chief Rabbi, his opponents are the ones labeled as dissidents. But in Williamsburg, the Brooklyn neighborhood where the Satmars first settled after World War II, it is Reb Aron's followers who are labeled dissidents by the followers of his brother and arch-rival, Reb Zalman. The "Aronis" and "Zalis" have been battling over who is the rightful heir to the rebbe's throne for over two decades now, and neither faction has shrunk from initiating lawsuits against the other when and where it has found itself on

---

[51] Matter of Congregation Yetev Lev D'Satmar, Inc. v. Kahan, 5 Misc. 3d 1023(A), 9 (N.Y. Sup. Ct. 2004) ("[I]n every aspect of anything Satmar, the final arbiter is the Grand Rebbe himself. His word is supreme from which there is no appeal. His decision is *binding upon every member* . . . this Court declines to make any determinations in regard to declaring valid or voiding either side's election. (emphasis in original)); Frankel v. Congregation Yetev Lev D'Satmar, 17 Misc. 3d 1114(A), 2–3 (N.Y. Sup. Ct. 2007) ("Justice Barasch, after a lengthy analysis of why secular courts are reluctant to interfere with the internal affairs of religious organizations declined 'to make any determinations as to which faction's claims were valid or not.' Justice Barasch's observations could equally apply to the pending litigation."); Frankel v. Congregation Yetev Lev D'Satmar, 20 Misc. 3d 1137(A), 5 (N.Y. Sup. Ct. 2008) (invoking Justice Barasch's determination that "'dispute over the rightful board of the Congregation . . . cannot be decided by application of neutral principal [sic] of law,'" to support holding that "claims raised in the injunction are non-justiciable."); Congregation Yetev Lev D'Satmar, Inc. v. Kahana, 879 N.E.2d 1282, 1282 (N.Y. 2007) ("The central issue in this appeal is whether resolution of an election controversy between two rival factions of a religious congregation can be achieved through the application of neutral principles of law without judicial intrusion into matters of religious doctrine. Like the trial court and Appellate Division, we conclude that it cannot."); Congregation Yetev Lev D'Satmar of Kiryas Joel, Inc. v. Congregation Yetev Lev D'Satmar, Inc., 820 N.Y.S. 2d 69, 71 (N.Y. Sup. Ct. 2006) ("The record reveals the existence of numerous questions of fact regarding the circumstances surrounding the authorization of the transfer of an interest in the property and the execution of the 2001 deed that preclude summary judgment on the issue of its validity, which questions cannot be answered because they involve ecclesiastical issues that are beyond the competence of the courts.").

the losing side of the battle. The cases that have been brought pursuing this battle through a variety of legal means and (sometimes means of questionable legality) now number over a dozen.[52]

The fight between the Aronis and the Zalis is the deepest cleavage within the Satmar community, so great that it has essentially torn the community in two. But it is not the only internal political conflict in Kiryas Joel or in the Satmar community at large. Other sources of political dissension also have emerged, creating a complex tangle of political alliances and divisions – and still more lawsuits and resorts to state courts.

The most direct challenge to the picture of a sharp separation between state and private action in Kiryas Joel has come from a group of Satmar residents, discontented with both Reb Aron and the Village officials. An assortment of grievances stemming from the mid-eighties, including frustrations with the yeshiva and conflicts with the Kiryas Joel zoning board, congealed into a block of critics who charge that the Village is controlled by the Chief Rabbi of Kiryas Joel, Reb Aron. Branded as "dissidents" by both the Village leaders and the religious leadership of Kiryas Joel, the so-called dissidents return the favor by claiming that the religious and municipal leaders together have abused the powers of the local government. This group has gone to court multiple times

---

[52] In Williamsburg, it is Reb Zalman who is in the position of power and the followers of his brother, Reb Aron, who are dubbed "dissidents." Cases initiated by followers of Reb Aron against the followers of Reb Zalman include *Frankel v. Congregation Yetev Lev D'Satmar; Congregation Yetev Lev D'Satmar Inc. v. Kahan; Congregation Yetev Lev D'Satmar of Kiryas Joel v. Congregation Yetev Lev D'Satmar, Inc.; Congregation Yetev Lev D'Satmar v. Kahana; Sher v. Congregation Yetev Lev D'Satmar.* All of these cases grow out of an election dispute that arose when each of the rival factions held separate elections to determine who would be the new president of the board of the synagogue in Williamsburg. Cases initiated by Reb Aron's opponents include *Congregation Yetev Lev D'Satmar v. Friedman,* which likewise grows out of the Williamsburg election dispute, as well as the cases enumerated in notes 53 and 54 below. A particularly interesting line of litigation, which originated as a garden-variety court-supervised property transfer proceeding, *Brach,* decades later became repurposed as a site for litigating the political conflict that *preceded* the current fight between the two brothers when their father, Moshe Teitelbaum, first succeeded the original Rebbe. Upon the original Rebbe's death, his nephew, Moshe, was selected to replace him, but the widow of Reb Joel and her supporters did not accept the legitimacy of Moshe's succession. This gave rise to the first political fissures in the community. It is difficult to map that earlier feud and the not inconsiderable amount of litigation that it spawned onto the current feud and litigation between the "Zalis" and the "Aronis," but it appears that over time, Moshe's opponents joined forces with Aron's opponents, thereby becoming aligned with the Zali camp. Much of the litigation that grew out of this "ur-feud" centered around ownership of a valuable piece of property, which included the original Rebbe's house in Williamsburg, but which was mortgaged to obtain a building loan for construction in Kiryas Joel. The lawsuits emanating out of this protracted conflict include *Congregation Yetev Lev D'Satmar, Inc. v. 26 Adar N.B. Corp.* and *Brach v. Congregation Yetev Lev D'Satmar, Inc.*

in an attempt to prevent the Village leadership from acting in ways that thwart their own attempts to set up an alternate set of religious institutions (a separate break-away yeshiva and a separate synagogue). In their first cause of action, the so-called dissidents alleged that the Village engaged in discriminatory practices against them.[53] In later cases, they have sought the dissolution of the entire Village, claiming that its very existence violates the principle of separation of church and state.[54]

In some ways, this claim echoes the argument made by Grumet against the law creating Kiryas Joel's school district, and indeed, the so-called dissidents did their level best to lend support to Grumet's legal action, although they were not formally parties to that case. But the dissidents' challenge to the Village is more far-reaching than Grumet's challenge to the constitutionality of the school district in several regards. Grumet only challenged the creation of the public school district, not the Village itself. Furthermore, his challenge was focused on the action taken by the New York legislature in authorizing the creation of a public school district in Kiryas Joel; it was the state's actions, not the action or existence of the public school district by itself, that was the object of concern. But the argument of the dissidents is that the Village's very existence violates the principle of separation between religion and state. In their view, the Village's leadership (the Mayor, the town clerk, the zoning board, the Village board of Trustees) is effectively controlled by the religious leadership (Reb Aron and his henchmen), rendering the distinction between the "secular" government and the "private" religious authorities a hollow formality.

Not once in their many attempts to sue the Village and bring about its dissolution have the dissidents succeeded. Their failure to succeed has made it easy for Village leaders to dismiss them as a bunch of disgruntled malcontents, rather than a serious political force. The failure of their legal claim might also seem to support the view that secular political authority and religious authority in Kiryas Joel are separate and distinct. As in the Grumet litigation, the court

---

[53] Khal Charidim v. Vill. of Kiryas Joel, 935 F. Supp. 450 (S.D.N.Y. 1996); 1997 WL 543091 (S.D.N.Y.); 1998 WL 601077 (S.D.N.Y.); 39 F. Supp. 2d 370 (S.D.N.Y. 1999) Waldman v. Vill. of Kiryas Joel, No. 97 Civ. 74 (S.D.N.Y. Apr. 9, 1997) ("Waldman I,") (dismissed with prejudice as part of settlement of Khal Charidim in March 1997, Rakoff, J., presiding).

[54] Waldman v. Vill. of Kiryas Joel, 39 F. Supp. 2d 370 (S.D.N.Y. 1999); 207 F.3d 105 (2d Cir. 2000) ("Waldman II"); Kiryas Joel Alliance v. Vill. of Kiryas Joel, 495 F. App'x 183 (2d Cir. 2012) ("Waldman III"). All of the cases enumerated here and in note 53 have been heard by Judge Jed Rakoff, the United States District Judge for the Southern District of New York best known for his decisions refusing to approve the settlements reached between the U.S. Securities and Exchange Commission and Citibank and the Bank of America. Michael Rothfeld, *No More Mr. Nice Guy – Just Ask Wall Street*, WALL ST. J., Nov. 9, 2011.

ultimately sided with the position that the distinction between public and private authority in Kiryas Joel is properly maintained.

That said, it is interesting to note how the dissidents' constitutional theory of church–state separation echoes the conception of separation between religion and state embedded in the theological tradition of political quietism. Conversely, the contrary view of the requirements of American constitutional law taken by the secular and religious leaders of Kiryas Joel in defense of the constitutionality (and secularity) of the Village comes much closer to the accommodationist position that theological quietists and separatists like the Satmars are supposed to reject. Although the dissidents articulate their objections to the Village in the terms of American constitutional law, what really animates their opposition to the existence of the Village (beyond their specific personal grievances) is the belief that incorporating as a local government constitutes precisely the kind of assumption of political power that theological quietism forbids. Of course, they also are animated by their own economic interests and their desire to overcome their political marginalization and the frustration of their alternative vision of how the Village should be run. Coexisting with these material motives, however, is a theory of law and religion and state that knits together their interpretation of the Rebbe's vision of a separatist community with their preferred interpretation of American constitutional law. In their eyes, the creation of a local government has not perfected the autonomy of Jewish law so much as corrupted it. They see the way that the Village has wielded its power (against them) as a fulfilment of the quietist belief that political power corrupts. But by their lights, the Village would be an abomination regardless of whether it was exercising its power in illegal ways. To remain truly pure, on their view, the religious community must keep itself apart from government. And on their stringent view of "keeping apart," it is not enough for there to be a formal separation between the local government institutions and the religious institutions. There must be no government in Kiryas Joel. No Satmar mayor, no Satmar office-holders, no Satmar-run security force, no Satmar tax collectors, no Satmar-run public school. Nothing less than a total evacuation of positions of government and political power will satisfy their vision of what both the constitution and Satmar theology demand.

In their demand for a complete separation from secular government and worldly politics, the dissidents give voice to the kind of stringent ideal of religious purity that historically motivated theological quietism, continually driving it to ever greater extremes. This is exactly the sort of drive for purity that Reb Yoilish exemplified, laying claim to the inheritance of theological quietism. In this regard, it is not difficult to see why the dissidents see themselves as the ones who are keeping faithful to the original Rebbe's vision and why they see the cooperative relationship between the Village leaders and Reb Aron – and the very existence of a Satmar municipality – as a betrayal of the Rebbe's separatist, quietist ideals. From their standpoint, the fact that they have not succeeded in court is less a mark of failure than of their faithfulness to a theological vision that is completely dissonant with the dominant American understanding of church–state separation, which they see the Village leadership as embodying.

Yet, at the same time that the anti-Aron dissidents advance this purist view of how *Satmars* should rule their community (without resort to the instrumentalities of government) – a view which rejects a separation between religious and secular authority *within* the Satmar world – they have articulated a theory of separation between church and state as a principle of *American* constitutional law, on the basis of which they have claimed (repeatedly and unsuccessfully) that the court must intervene in order to protect them from the unconstitutional (and unholy) fusion of political and religious authority in Kiryas Joel. On this view, the distinction between the public ("secular") and private (religious) leaders in Kiryas Joel is illusory, existing only in form but not in fact; in reality, they claim, the municipal office-holders do the bidding of the religious leaders. As a matter of American constitutional law, they argue that this fusion of religious and political authority in the municipal government of Kiryas Joel violates the Establishment Clause, which prohibits government "establishments" of religion. Conversely, they maintain that the establishment of secular political institutions controlled by the Satmars' religious leaders violates the Rebbe's vision of Jewish law.

An almost perfect mirror image of these arguments is presented in the fight that has been unfolding between the Zalis and Aronis over control over the community in Williamsburg since 2000. Here, the so-called dissidents are the Aronis, who have defended their resort to state law in their fight against the Zalis by arguing that there is a principle of separation between secular and religious authority *within* the Satmar community. On this basis, they have argued (again, for the most part unsuccessfully) that the secular courts can intervene in the dispute between the two factions regarding control over the board of the synagogue without intervening in religious matters. On their view, the Rebbe's authority extends only to spiritual matters, while the synagogue board is a "secular" body subject to the authority of the lay leaders of the community. The dispute over governance of the synagogue board can therefore be adjudicated by courts applying "neutral principles" of American

law without the courts being required to decide religious matters.[55] Whereas
the Kiryas Joel dissidents' theory of strict separation between religion and state
(as a principle of American constitutional law) serves to uphold their vision of
Jewish law within the "kingdom of Satmar" as undivided and comprehensive,
admitting no separation between secular and religious spheres, the dissidents
in the Williamsburg election controversy argue that the Satmars themselves
observe a distinction between religion and state within their own "polity." Each
side thus illustrates how theocratic, quietist, and accommodationist positions
can shade into each other, despite their apparent opposition.

The content of these arguments points to the difficulty of maintaining clear
lines between these positions and the concomitant difficulty of maintaining
a clear line of separation between the law of the Satmars (i.e., *halakhic* law
as it is expounded by the Satmar Rebbe, or rebbes) and the law of the state.
Even apart from the content of the claims (which is exceedingly difficult to
parse), the sheer volume of litigation emanating out of the Satmar community
is staggering and in itself a challenge to the claim that the authority of the
religious leaders and institutions in the Satmar community is exercised independently of secular law.[56] Particularly in light of the *halakhic* prohibition
on litigating in secular courts, the frequent resort to state law poses a serious
challenge to the picture of Jewish law in Kiryas Joel as standing *apart* from state
law. To be sure, some of this litigation can be reconciled with the *halakhic*

---

[55] *See* Brief for Petitioners-Appellants at 1, 5–7, 36–42, Congregation Yetev Lev D'Satmar, Inc. v.
  Kahan, 9 N.Y.3d 282 (2007). The Petitioners-Appellants in this case represent the Aroni faction
  in the synagogue board election controversy. The opposite position – that there is no division
  between temporal and spiritual spheres of authority in the Satmar community and therefore
  judicial intervention cannot be justified under the neutral principles doctrine – is articulated
  in the Brief of Respondents at 1, 2–4, 24–26, 33–43.

[56] In addition to all the cases enumerated above, the list would have to also include other cases
  brought by the leader of the Kiryas Joel dissident faction, Joseph Waldman, such as Waldman
  v. United Talmudical Acad, 147 Misc.2d 529 (1990) (challenging expulsion of his son from
  the Kiryas Joel yeshiva); Appeal of Chaim Hochhauser, Israel Weiss, Joseph Waldman, Jacob
  Landau, Jacob Samet and Ben Zion Friedman, Dec. No. 13,415 (1995) (challenging validity
  of Village referendum authorizing creation of Kiryas Joel school district and alleging that
  Waldman was illegally deprived of opportunity to run for a seat on the school board); cases
  emanating out of a fight between the two factions over control over the burial ground in
  Kiryas Joel, Friedman v. CYL Cemetery, 914 NYS2d 3015 (2011); Appeal of Friedman, 34
  Educ. Dep't Reps. Decision No. 12,882 (dismissed Jan. 29, 1993); Appeal of Friedman,
  34 Educ. Dep't Reps. Decision No. 12,927 (dismissed May 10, 1993); Appeal of Friedman,
  34 Educ. Dep't Reps. Decision No. 12,986 (denied Aug. 16, 1993); and litigation brought by
  the Zalman faction to establish guardianship over Reb Moshe in the waning days of his life
  in the midst of the synagogue board election controversy, In the Matter of the Application of
  Meisels for the Appointment of Co-Guardians, 10 Misc.3d 659, 807 N.Y.S.2d 268 (Sup. Ct.
  2005).

principle against submitting disputes to gentile courts, either because it does not involve internal disputes or, as in the case of family law disputes, the state demands that it be submitted to its jurisdiction and the Satmars respond to that demand by (a) justifying the submission of disputes to the state's jurisdiction on *halakhic* grounds and (b) finding ways to get the family law courts to enforce rabbinic decrees. But the extensive litigation involving internal political conflicts flatly contradicts the *halakhic* prohibition against submitting disputes to gentile courts. Both sets of cases challenge the assumption that Jewish law and rabbinic institutions operate autonomously without any connection (beyond being legally permitted) with state law.

That challenge is strengthened when we pay attention to the more pervasive (if less visible) role that American law plays outside the realm of litigation, in its transactional, facilitative mode. Transactional law is what enables real estate deals to be brokered and commercial and residential developments to be built. Without having been enabled by transactional law to acquire contiguous lots of property in the town of Monroe, the community of Kiryas Joel literally wouldn't exist. Similarly, family law structures family life and empowers religious authorities in often-invisible ways. The law of the state that governs family relations does not just determine how divorce and custody disputes will be settled. It also provides a framework, outside the realm of litigation, of private constitutionally protected rights, under which parents are granted authority to determine how their children will be raised and educated, including the power to insulate their children from exposure to the outside world.[57] Furthermore, as hinted at in the brief discussion of the "spiritual custody" cases, the knowledge of how cases are likely to be decided by the courts serves as a powerful deterrent to divorce and exit from the community. In this context as elsewhere, the American legal doctrine of family privacy creates a shield under which communal authorities are able to exercise

---

[57] Since 1925, it has been an established principle of constitutional law that parents have the right to control the upbringing of their children, including the right to determine their religious upbringing and to send their children, if they choose, to private religious schools instead of public schools. Pierce v. Soc'y of Sisters, 268 U.S. 510 (1925) (striking down a law aimed at eliminating parochial schools, which required all children between eight and sixteen to attend public schools). The right of religious parents to resist state education laws that interfere with their ability to transmit their religious values to their children was further affirmed in 1972. Yoder v. Wisconsin, 406 U.S. 205 (1972) (holding Amish parents were exempt from a state law which required that children to attend school after eighth grade). In theory there are limits to the ability of parents to control their children's upbringing and education, and the state has the authority "to compel attendance at some school and to make reasonable regulations for all schools," Meyer v. Nebraska, 262 U.S. 390 (1923). But in communities like Kiryas Joel, state education requirements are laxly enforced.

authority over actual and potential defectors and husbands are able to exercise traditional forms of patriarchal authority over their children and their wives.[58] These rights of family privacy reinforce, and are reinforced by, the private rights to freedom of association and freedom of religion, which likewise serve to uphold traditional structures of authority and dependency (e.g., unequal gender relations and far-reaching forms of parental authority) in the name of individual freedom.

At the same time that these various bodies of private law structure the community's social institutions, local government law enables the creation of a political infrastructure that provides for the basic secular needs of the community (like garbage collection, sewage and running water). Through the simple act of voting, an ostensibly individual right, a tight-knit group like the Satmars is able, by voting as a "bloc," to translate its collective power in the private realm into power in the public realm. Such public power takes multiple forms, including their own self-governing public institutions (i.e., the Village and the public school district) and, equally important, the ability to negotiate with regional, state, and federal governmental entities for various forms of government benefits and political influence.

In all of these different ways, American law empowers the members of the Satmar community not just to act, but also to govern and exercise authority over others, in accordance with their distinctive way of life. Litigation shines a spotlight on the use of state and federal courts by certain members of the Satmar community (against other members of the community). But it is the more pervasive, if less obvious, role played by transactional law, property law, family law, and state and local government law in the proverbial "shadow" of litigation that poses the most serious challenge to the autonomy (and "non-state-ness") of Kiryas Joel's religious law by demonstrating how easily private, supposedly consensual, forms of association and authority are converted into institutions of (local) government wielding political power. The question is whether the regimes of family law, property law and local government law are merely facilitative, simply allowing private individuals to do what they want, or whether they are playing a role – a critical role – in enabling Jewish law to be *enforced*.

More analysis is needed to arrive at a definitive answer to this question. But the same could be said of the opposite assumption, that state law is *not* involved

---

[58] The body of scholarship articulating the feminist critique of the doctrine of family privacy as a shield for patriarchal relations of authority includes, inter alia, CATHARINE A. MACKINNON, TOWARDS A FEMINIST THEORY OF THE STATE (1989); Carole Pateman, *Feminist Critiques of the Public/Private Distinction, in* PUBLIC AND PRIVATE IN SOCIAL LIFE 281 (S.I. Benn & G.F. Gaus eds., 1983); Frances Olsen, *The Myth of State Intervention in the Family*, 18 U. MICH. J.L. REFORM 835 (1985).

in the "internal" processes of enforcement. At the very least, it should not be just assumed that the authority of religious law and religious legal institutions in Kiryas Joel and the broader Satmar community exists independently of the state. That itself is a proposition that needs to be argued for and supported with evidence.

There is no doubt that a body of Jewish law, which is radically different from American law in its content, is being enforced in Kiryas Joel. But *how* is it being enforced? How, for example, is Jewish family law being enforced? How are the community's "internal" rules of governance – the rules that determine who is the Rebbe, who runs the synagogue board and who controls the religious community's considerable assets – determined and applied? If civil courts end up involved (often despite their best efforts not to be involved) in enforcing these rules and determining who has the authority to define them, that would seem to pose a real challenge to the claim that religious law in Kiryas Joel is autonomous. Again, there is room for debate about whether the state courts are playing such a role. They certainly have tried their level best to stay out of the fray.[59] But, as we all know, a decision not to decide is itself a decision,[60] one that effectively supports the party that has *de facto*, though not necessarily *de jure*, power. Deciding not to decide in effect converts *de facto* into *de jure* power, as the courts themselves have acknowledged in describing their decision not to decide as "leav[ing] intact the status quo."[61]

---

[59] Congregation Yetev Lev D'Satmar, Inc. v. Kahana, 9 N.Y.3d 282, 288 (N.Y. Sup. Ct. 2007) ("These particular issues must be resolved by the members of the Congregation, and cannot be determined by this Court."). *See also* Application of Congregation Yetev Lev D'Satmar, Inc. v. Kahan, 5 Misc. 3d 1023(A), 9 (N.Y. Sup. Ct. 2004) (concluding that "the final arbiter is the Grand Rebbe himself . . . this Court declines to make any determinations in regard to declaring valid or voiding either side's election"); Frankel v. Congregation Yetev Lev D'Satmar, Inc., 17 Misc. 3d 1114(A), 2–3 (N.Y. Sup. Ct. 2007) ("Justice Barasch, after a lengthy analysis of why secular courts are reluctant to interfere with the internal affairs of religious organizations . . . declined 'to make any determinations as to which faction's claims were valid or not'. . . . Justice Barasch's observations could equally apply to the pending litigation."); Frankel v. Congregation Yetev Lev D'Satmar, 20 Misc. 3d 1137(A), 2–16 (N.Y. Sup. Ct. 2008) (basing its decision on Justice Barasch's determination that 'the dispute over the rightful board of the Congregation cannot be decided by application of neutral principal [sic] of law,' and concluding that the "claims raised in the injunction are nonjusiticable").

[60] Robert Cover, *The Supreme Court, 1982 Term – Foreword: Nomos and Narrative*, 97 Harv. L. Rev. 4, 8 n.23 (1982) ("*Every* denial of jurisdiction on the part of a court is an assertion of the power to *determine* jurisdiction and thus to constitute a norm," and describing the "apologetic and "statist" effect of jurisdictional preferences of nonintervention and deference. *Id.* at 54.).

[61] Frankel v. Congregation Yetev Lev D'Satmar, Inc., 17 Misc. 3d 1114(A) 1, 2 (N.Y. Sup. Ct. 2007); 20 Misc. 3d 1137(A) 1, 4–6 (N.Y. Sup. Ct. 2008); 69 A.D. 3d 788, 789 (N.Y. App. Div. 2010). *See also* Application of Yetev Lev D'Satmar, Inc. v. Kahana, 820 N.Y.S. 2d 62 (N.Y. App. Div. 2006).

Seen as a totality, the various forms of American law that filter into Kiryas Joel sediment into so many layers, it is hard not to wonder if they entirely fill up the metaphorical space between the private "ground" and the public "dome," drawing the two together in a way that defies the formal distinction between state and private action (as the Kiryas Joel dissidents allege). Of course, these are just metaphors and metaphors alone are not enough to disprove the public–private distinction in Kiryas Joel. That said, it seems hard to deny the perception that the combined regimes of family law, property law, and local government law, buttressed by the constitutional principles of freedom of association and freedom of religion, confer upon the *authorities* within the community the ability to invoke the power of the state in order to uphold their authority. And without the ability to call upon the authority of the state to enforce their own authority, it is unclear in what sense, beyond the imaginary, the religious authorities in Kiryas Joel *have* authority and the ability to enforce Jewish law.

Of course the power of religious authorities to enlist the state in enforcing their vision of religious law is far from total. The simple fact that the community is riven in two, despite each side's best efforts to enforce its vision of religious authority, is evidence of the limits of the rabbis' power. But to make the case that religious law in Kiryas Joel is truly independent of state law, it needs to be shown that the surprisingly frequent resorts to state court by members of the community (against other members of the community) are not essential to upholding the authority of the putative religious leaders and enforcing the community's religious norms. It likewise needs to be demonstrated that the combined regimes of transactional law and local government are merely facilitative and do not confer upon Satmar religious authorities the power to enlist the state to help keep non-Satmars out and to maintain religious discipline within. Perhaps this case can be made, but I am dubious.

THE RETURN OF STATE (AND NATURAL?) LAW

Suppose we succeed in showing that the role of American law in Kiryas Joel goes beyond merely facilitating private action – that it actually plays an indispensable role in *enforcing* the community's religious law. Even so, what would that prove about the existence of religious law as non-state law, either in Kiryas Joel or in general? In the remainder of this chapter, I want to assume, for the sake of argument, that the role of American law in enforcing Kiryas Joel's religious regulations has been demonstrated, in order to focus on the theoretical question of whether such a demonstration defeats the non-state character of its Jewish legal institutions. In what sense does "going to law" (that is, to the law of the state) defeat the non-state character of Jewish law in Kiryas Joel and, assuming that it is defeated, was going to American law avoidable?

It may help to reverse the order of the questions. *Why* is there so much resorting to state law? The factors that have led Satmars to the secular courts are thoroughly unsurprising. When outsiders bring lawsuits, as in the ten-year litigation of *Kiryas Joel Public School District* v. *Grumet*, the Satmars have no choice but to submit to the power of the state that imposes its jurisdiction upon them. Submitting to the jurisdiction of the state in cases such as these is a simple matter of *realpolitik*. Perhaps more interesting are the cases in which Satmars *choose* to go to civil court, in defiance of the *halakhic* prohibition on "gentile" adjudication of internal disputes and in the face of the American courts' own resistance to taking such cases under their jurisdiction. The dissidents' actions against the Village of Kiryas Joel, the endless battle over the election of the synagogue president, property disputes involving control over the house inhabited by Reb Yoilish and access to the cemetery are all of this type. Here again, the forces that drive Satmars to go to the secular courts are entirely surprising, banal, even. Invariably, such litigation is initiated by whichever group has been labeled the "dissident" faction, reflecting its relative political weakness and the greater political strength of the faction it opposes. It is only because of the de facto power imbalance that exists when one group has succeeded in gaining control of the community's institutions and valuable assets that the other group is "dubbed" the dissident faction, a label conferred by the party with the upper hand, reflecting its position of superiority. In such conditions of unequal power, the only means that a weaker party has to vindicate its claims is to turn to outside authorities. Not surprisingly, courts try hard to resist getting drawn into adjudicating such claims, generally taking the position that the law requires a "hands-off" approach. Everyone understands that such refusals to adjudicate have the effect of preventing the "facts on the ground" from being upset and thereby upholding the status quo and denying the challengers' claims. Similarly, custody settlements frequently result in maintaining the pre-existing status quo and some family court judges actually make a preference for maintaining the status quo a principle.

Reflecting the judicial bias in favor of upholding the status quo (a bias that results in good measure from the desire to avoid intervening in religious disputes), most claims brought by dissidents end up in defeat. But not all of them. From time to time, the challengers of the status quo score a victory, and the mere possibility of this happening creates a threat of legal intervention. If this threat does not completely undermine the autonomy of the religious leadership and religious law in Kiryas Joel, it certainly complicates it.

Despite the Satmar community's high degree of cohesion, it was only a matter of time before disputes would emerge between different members of the Satmar community impelling the weaker party, and in response to the challenge to its authority, the stronger party as well to have recourse to a body capable of *enforcing* law. The need for effective mechanisms of law enforcement motivates the turn to the state. Indeed, as a theoretical matter, by the lights of the traditional theory of Jewish law to which quietists lay claim, a body capable of exercising the *power* to *enforce* "the law" is just what the state is. Holy law, by contrast, is, by definition, law that a holy people follow out of perfect piety and *not* out of coercion.

It is the aspiration to live according to this ancient purist ideal that theoretically separates the theology of religious separatists like the Satmars from the more mainstream forms of traditional Judaism that rejected that purist ideal and the extreme forms of separatism it necessarily entails in favor of a more accommodationist theology. Understanding such an ideal is rarely if ever capable of implementation, rabbis historically responded by elaborating "doctrines about the nature of divine law in society that explained practices departing from scriptural norms and vesting extralegal powers *in the political authority*."[62] This gave rise to a crystal-clear definition of what the state – and what state law – is. From the traditional rabbinic point of view, it matters less whether the political authority is composed of Jews or gentiles than that it is a *political* authority, meaning precisely, an *authority* that exercises *powers* that are not authorized by Jewish law and is *therefore* capable of providing the mechanisms of law enforcement that are necessary for effective dispute resolution. Understanding that the only way to avoid reliance on state law is to be perfectly holy – to be such a pious people that no one will engage in the kind of power struggles and fights over material resources that cannot be settled without the machinery of enforcement – the normative rabbinic tradition both defined state law (as, precisely, a law that is *enforced* through coercive mechanisms) and justified it as a necessary (and divinely ordained) accommodation to the weaknesses of human nature that make conflicts over political power and material resources viable.

Against the backdrop of this ancient theological debate between the accommodationist and quietist traditions of Jewish political thought, the banality of the factors that have led the Satmars to rely on state law assumes a greater significance. No one is surprised to learn about the development of internal political battles or of the resort to litigation by the party without de facto power in the face of such battles. Nor is there anything unexpected in the reliance

---

[62] Stone, *Religion and State, supra* note 10.

on state legal institutions to enforce claims to control over valuable material resources (or children) that are subject to contestation. Neither the contestation nor the reliance on the state's machinery of law enforcement is remotely surprising. The causes of the Satmars' resort to the state law are indeed utterly banal. But their very banality stands as a refutation of the quietist position to which the Satmars lay claim. What quietism requires – and promises – is precisely an escape from the banal, an escape from the ordinary condition of society in which people compete for power and scarce resources, thereby necessitating the resort to the machinery of effective dispute resolution and law enforcement which is, according to the traditional understanding, the hallmark of "gentile" or "state" law ("gentile" and "state" in this context being interchangeable terms for the same thing). What quietism requires is a state of exception, a holy state in which the people are so pious that no regime of power – no state, in the political sense of the term – is needed to enforce sacred law. In this holy vision, the law enforces itself without the apparatus of power; the law exists without being enforced; the law exists without a state.

This is the quietist ideal: law without power, law without state. Its secular phantom is the libertarian ideal of private law, of law without state. Both ideals depend for their "implementation" on the absence of political conflict. Once the identity of the spiritual leader is disputed, the need for enforcement appears and with it, by definition (from the quietist point of view), the apparatus of the state.

So to say that the causes of the resort to state law are banal is precisely to say that the conditions for the autonomy of religious law – its independence from the state – are not and *cannot* be present. When we say the factors that led to the invocation of the authority of the state are unsurprising, we are implicitly suggesting that those kinds of things (power struggles, contests for material resources) are inevitable, things that are bound to occur sooner or later in any human society. Another word for banality is inevitability. But when we say (as we implicitly do when we characterize things as banal) that that there are certain conditions that are universal, which no society can avoid – and that these are conditions that make the invocation of state law inevitable – we are engaging in a style of argument that is anathema to modern legal pluralists. Claims about universal, necessary characteristics of all societies are the stuff of natural law. And modern-day legal pluralism rejects natural law thinking. I happen to share that aversion to natural law and began my investigation of law in Kiryas Joel sharing the widespread premise that legal pluralism stands in opposition to natural law (and to the law of the state). But having undertaken that investigation, my observation is that if we follow the ethnography of legal pluralism faithfully where it leads, it leads us back to natural law – and to the law of the state. As a case study, Kiryas Joel illustrates the conditions that negate the ideal of non-state law. Thick description of how a community striving to implement non-state law actually works ends up recapitulating the terms of the old argument about why the state is a necessary element of all human systems of law. Accepting that argument does not imply the negation of legal pluralism. Nor does it mean that Kiryas Joel has failed to create a world governed by Jewish law. To the contrary, the argument that emerges out of this thick description is one that takes us back to an old theological tradition in which natural law, divine law, legal pluralism, and the law of the state converge.

If such a convergence of positive and natural law seems strange, that is only because we have lost touch with the old tradition of natural law, which was, in its origins, a theological tradition that recognized the need for positive (state, secular) law as the most fundamental tenet of natural law. This theological tradition is part of the shared heritage of Jewish and Christian thought. It is out of this tradition that modern political philosophy derived. And it is in reaction *against* this theological tradition that Hasidic Judaism, of which Satmar Hasidism is a part, was born. Hasidism was the heir to a very different tradition of theological thought, a quietist tradition that rejected the theological justification of positive law. It represents the aspiration for a society ruled by religious law without positive law, of law without state. American law has its own fantasies of law without state. In Kiryas Joel, the American fantasy of law without state ("private law") and the Satmars' theological fantasy of law without state ("religious law") converge.

That theological tradition, a part of the shared heritage of Judaism and Christianity, historically made the case for legal pluralism without rejecting what Robert Cover called the "jurispathic" or "imperial" state.[63] To the contrary, it was a (political) theological tradition that argued for the necessity of state law on the basis of its recognition of legal pluralism. The irony is that the Hasidic movement (out of which the Satmar community emerged) was born out of a rejection of this particular political theological tradition. Hasidic Judaism lays claim to a very different political theology, a quietist, antipolitical theology, which insists upon withdrawing from all forms of worldly power, especially the power of the state. The conditions that have prevented such perfect separation from being achieved in Kiryas Joel illustrate the conditions that led more mainstream Jewish and Christian philosophers to conclude that

---

[63] Cover, *Nomos and Narrative, supra* note 60.

state law was a necessity (of natural law) – the traditional theological position that Satmar Judaism, along with the rest of ultra-Orthodox, Hasidic Judaism, theoretically rejects, but practically reflects.

Cover himself is often mistakenly read as championing the "jurisgenerative" potential of law *against* its jurispathic face. By the same token, he is often viewed as a champion of "non-state law." Calling attention to the existence and to the value of the alternative visions and bodies of law possessed by subgroups outside the state, Cover has been mistakenly read as viewing the law of such subgroups as non-state law. But Cover was not calling for an end to the jurispathic function of the state. Nor did he describe subgroup law as non-state law. To the contrary, he carefully differentiated the *ideal* of non-state law from the *reality* of all legal systems as they are actually implemented, clearly stating that a "pure paideic normative order" (law without state) "exists only for an instant, and that instant is itself imaginary."[64] Far from recognizing non-state law, Cover was affirming that the existence of non-state law is an illusion – a powerful and valuable jurisgenerative ideal, to be sure (though also potentially dangerous), but powerful precisely *because* it is an ideal, not capable of implementation. Cover thus articulated a vision of *legal pluralism* that was not bound to the illusion that the law of groups outside the state is non-state law. Echoing ancient Jewish theological traditions and theories of law, he articulated a vision of legal pluralism not as a doctrine of *non-state* law, but rather, as a recognition of *multiple* law, of multiple sub-state and trans-state jurisdictions (including the courts when they depart from a positivist hermeneutics of jurisdiction) with their own visions and systems of law. Cover held that it is this very multiplicity and the "jurispotence" of the non-state *visions* of law that necessitates the jurispathic functions of the state and state law. He thus affirmed, as the story of Kiryas Joel also tends to confirm, that there is no actual law without state. Acknowledging the continuing force of the aspiration to free the law from the state, and pointedly recognizing the multiple sub-state and trans-state communities where this aspiration is nurtured, he stated very clearly that "law is that which holds our reality apart from our visions and rescues us from [...] eschatology.... "[65] He thus offered an alternative way of conceptualizing legal pluralism – an alternative that resists the urge to confuse the animating aspiration (of law without state) with the reality (of the need for enforcement mechanisms that, by definition, constitute state law). Like Cover, Kiryas Joel, insofar as it illustrates the thoroughly unsurprising

---

[64] *Id.*, at 15.
[65] *Id.*, at 10.

declension from the aspirational to the real, returns us to the fundamental tenet of natural law, inscribed in both rabbinic and Christian theological doctrines: that the conditions that drive this declension are completely unexceptional (i.e., universal) and that they necessitate the invocation of secular state law.

11

The Persistence of Sovereignty and the Rise of the Legal Subject

Michael A. Helfand[1]

In a November 2010 referendum, the Oklahoma electorate passed an amendment to its State Constitution prohibiting courts from "look[ing] to the legal precepts of other nations or culture," further specifying that "courts shall not consider international or Sharia Law."[2] Instead, the amendment instructed courts to "uphold and adhere to the law as provided in the United States Code, federal regulations promulgated pursuant thereto, established common law, the Oklahoma Statutes and rules promulgated pursuant thereto...."[3] Numerous other states followed suit by considering similar bills aimed at preventing courts from enforcing, considering, or relying on both religious and international law.[4]

Although reaction to this wave of state legislative initiatives has provoked significant commentary and criticism, much of it has focused either on the attack on Sharia law[5] or the rejection of international law.[6] But the simultaneous

---

[1] Associate Professor, Pepperdine University School of Law and Associate Director, Pepperdine University's Diane and Guilford Glazer Institute for Jewish Studies.

[2] H.R.J. Res. 1056, 52d Leg., 2d Reg. Sess. (Okla. 2010).

[3] *Id.* Oklahoma's amendment was subsequently struck down on constitutional grounds. Awad v. Ziriax, Case No. CIV-10-1186-M, 2013 U.S. Dist. LEXIS 115396 (W.D. Okla. Aug. 15, 2013).

[4] *See generally* Kimberly Railey, *More States Move to Ban Foreign Law in Courts*, USA TODAY, Aug. 4, 2013, http://www.usatoday.com/story/news/nation/2013/08/04/states-ban-foreign-law/2602511/, and FAIZA PATEL, MATTHEW DUSS & AMOS TOH, BRENNAN CTR. FOR JUSTICE, FOREIGN LAW BANS: LEGAL UNCERTAINTIES AND PRACTICAL PROBLEMS (May 2013), *available at* http://www.brennancenter.org/sites/default/files/publications/ForeignLawBans.pdf; *see also* Bill Cotterell, *Florida Legislature Forbids Use of Foreign Law in State Court*, REUTERS, Apr. 30, 2014, *available at* http://www.reuters.com/article/2014/04/30/us-usa-florida-sharialaw-idUS BREA3T14H20140430.

[5] *See, e.g.*, Michael A. Helfand, *Religious Arbitration and the New Multiculturalism: Negotiating Conflicting Legal Orders*, 86 N.Y.U. L. REV. 1231, 1233–34 (2011).

[6] *See* Martha F. Davis & Johanna Kalb, *Oklahoma State Question 755 and an Analysis of Anti-International Law Initiatives*, AM. CONST. SOC'Y FOR L. & POL'Y (Issue Brief, Jan. 2011), *available*

legislative pushback on both international and religious law is significant in and of itself. Such a two-pronged attack on non-state law reflects a concerted effort on the part of numerous states to consolidate legal authority by asserting the state as the only source of legitimate law. Indeed, at the core of this controversy stands an age-old philosophical dispute over the relationship between sovereignty and law: Does state sovereignty preclude the possibility of law both above the state – that is, international law – and below the state – that is, religious and customary law?

This tension between state and non-state law tracks a long-standing fissure within legal positivism – a bundle of philosophical views that conceptualize law as a social practice separate and apart from considerations of morality and ethics.[7] Many of the early positivists – most notably Thomas Hobbes and John Austin – contended that law was the exclusive province of the sovereign.[8] As a philosophical matter, such sovereignty precluded the existence of any competing legal system; thus, both Hobbes and Austin emphatically argued that customary law and international law were both philosophically incoherent concepts.

Such a perspective has fed continued skepticism of both international and religious *law* with critics dubious not only of their philosophical coherence, but also their political viability.[9] Indeed, the influence of such "legal centralism" – that is, the view that law remains the exclusive province of the nation-state[10] – persists, with the recent wave of legislation attacking both international and religious law serving as its most recent – and vivid – example.[11] And even

---

at http://www.acslaw.org/sites/default/files/davis_and_kalb_anti-international_law.pdf (noting that "[s]ome commentators couch their objections to courts' consideration of international or foreign material in the language of sovereignty.").

[7] *See, e.g.,* Leslie Green, *Legal Positivism, in* Stanford Encyclopedia of Philosophy (Edward N. Zalta ed. 2009) *available at* http://plato.stanford.edu/archives/fall2009/entries/legal-positivism/.

[8] *See infra* section, "The Persistence of Sovereignty."

[9] *See, e.g.,* Mehrdad Payandeh, *The Concept of International Law in the Jurisprudence of H.L.A. Hart,* 21 Eur. J. Int'l L. 967, 970 (2011) ("Nevertheless, doubts about the legal quality of international law may endorse and legitimize proponents of more restrictive approaches to the international legal order. Nevertheless, doubts about the legal quality of international law may endorse and legitimize proponents of more restrictive approaches to the international legal order.").

[10] John Griffiths, *What Is Legal Pluralism,* 24 J. Legal Pluralism & Unofficial L. 1, 3 (1986) (defining and critiquing "legal centralism").

[11] *See, e.g.,* Civil Rights, American Public Policy Alliance, at http://publicpolicyalliance .org/?page_id=195 ("Two major legal systems have emerged in America as threats to Constitutional protections and liberties: first, transnationalism, a particularly anti-Constitutional and extremist application of Customary International Law, in opposition to American sovereignty; and second, the Shariah legal doctrine, imposed as a separate legal system in America for Muslims (and eventually for non-Muslims.)").

with the success of legal pluralism within the academy,[12] legal centralism still drives questions regarding the status of non-state law.[13]

For many, this philosophical trend toward legal centralism reached a peak in the work of H.L.A. Hart. Indeed, conventional interpretations of Hart frequently conclude that law cannot exist in the absence of a complex legal system typified by the "secondary rules" that Hart made famous in his seminal work *The Concept of Law*.[14] On this reading, Hart's legal theory presupposed the existence of the nation-state and in particular the institutional infrastructure of legal officials that made the secondary rules possible. In turn, the concept of law is inextricably linked to the concept of a legal system. Thus, John Gardner has argued that "Hart showed that legal norms have no 'essence,' nothing that makes them distinctively legal, except that they are norms belonging to one legal system or another."[15] In this way, Hart has been understood as a critic of legal pluralism,[16] embracing instead a positivist brand of "legal centralism" that conceives of law as necessarily linked to the infrastructure of the nation-state.

---

[12] For some helpful discussion highlighting the growth of legal pluralism, see Sally Engle Merry, *Legal Pluralism*, 22 L. & Soc'y Rev. 869, 879 (1988); Paul Schiff Berman, *The New Legal Pluralism*, 5 Ann. Rev. L. & Soc. Sci. 226 (2009); Brian Z. Tamanaha, *Understanding Legal Pluralism: Past to Present, Local to Global*, 30 Sydney L. Rev. 375, 375 (2008).

[13] For example, this was the question addressed by a panel at the 2009 Conference of the American Society of International Law. *See generally* Antonia Chayes, Thomas Franck, Jose Alvarez & Sean D. Murphy, *In What Sense Is International Law Law?*, 103 Am. Soc'y Int'l L. Proc. 155 (2009).

[14] *See, e.g.*, Jules Coleman, *Incorporationism, Conventionality, and the Practical Difference Thesis*, in Hart's Postscript: Essays on the Postscript to the Concept of Law 99, 118 (2001) ("The possibility of their being law and purporting to govern as law, however, depends on a rule of recognition."); *see also id.* at 121 ("The rule of recognition makes law possible.").

[15] John Gardner, Law as a Leap of Faith: Essays on Law in General 179 (2012); *see also* Payandeh, *The Concept of International Law*, *supra* note 9, at 993 ("While his analysis of international law in Chapter X of *The Concept of Law* suggests an independent existence of the two concepts [law and legal system], parts of his general theory of law do not reflect this understanding, but rather imply a more intimate relationship between the two.").

[16] *See, e.g.*, Simon Roberts, *After Government? On Representing Law Without the State*, 68 Mod. L. Rev. 1, 10 (2005) (arguing that Hart's secondary rules "covertly recall" the "institutional shapes" in "which government and law are cemented securely together" and contending that "any claim that Hart encourages us to think about law as something other than the law of a centralised polity would be misleading."); Nicola Lacey, *Analytical Jurisprudence Versus Descriptive Sociology Revisited*, 84 Tex. L. Rev. 945, 959 (2006) (noting that legal pluralists have "long criticized" Hart for "giving . . . priority or distinctiveness to state law"); Nick Barber, *The Rechtsstaat and the Rule of Law*, 53 U. Toronto L.J. 443, 450–51 (2003) ("Pluralism presents a model of the legal universe in which legal systems and institutions can conflict and overlap. The classic model of the legal order, advanced by Hart and Kelsen, resembled a pyramid. At the top of the structure was the *Grundnorm*, or rule of recognition, which served to both legally validate and identify the remaining rules of the system. The pluralist view, in contrast, suggests that there can be several legal orders in a given territory, each of which asserts its supremacy over the others.").

But while some of Hart's text is susceptible to this view, there is much in *The Concept of Law* that indicates Hart had something very different in mind. Indeed, in his discussion of both customary law and international law, Hart appears to argue that law can exist in the absence of a legal system. Thus, contrary to many conventional interpretations, Hart provided an alternative conception of law that placed the legal subject – and not the legal authority – at the center of legal theory. By focusing on the legal subject, Hart predicated the existence of law not on the existence of a robust legal system, but on the legal subject's experience of legal obligation.

By shifting the concept of law, Hart denied that law was necessarily tied to the edicts of a sovereign or even a legal system. Thus, he argued that it would be a mistake to interpret the citizenry's recognition of non-state law as a threat to the nation-state's sovereignty. To the contrary, recognizing the existence of other forms of law – such as international or religious law – represents an understanding that the modern-day legal subject often participates in multiple social practices that entail a variety of expectations and a litany of obligations. And on this account, Hart's theory embraces a form of legal pluralism, willing to understand law as possible outside the confines of the nation-state's legal system.

Of course, Hart presents his theory as positivistic and therefore avoids providing any normative consequences stemming from the distinction between law and legal system. But emphasizing this distinction serves as a useful conceptual framework for exploring normative responses to conflicts between state and non-state law. If the nation-state is to successfully find ways to enable the legal subject to navigate the significant – and often conflicting – demands of alternative forms of law, it cannot simply ignore these other forms of law via legislative fiat. Instead, legislatures must openly encourage discussion and coordination of legal obligations so as to promote the evolution of a social practice that can address the unique dilemmas experienced by individuals who understand themselves as subject to the demands of multiple forms of law.

This chapter proceeds in three parts. The first part considers the work of two early positivists – Thomas Hobbes and John Austin – each of whom served as important interlocutors for Hart in *The Concept of Law*. In so doing, I consider how both Hobbes and Austin understood the concept of law as

To be sure, one could also be of the view that, on Hart's account, law lacked substance, but still argue that Hart's concept of law allows for legal pluralism. But for many of Hart's critics, these two claims are linked; law lacks any independent substance and therefore can only be understood as norms issued by a centralized legal system with exclusive authority over a particular geographic area.

inextricably linked to the notion of sovereignty. In the second part, I consider Hart's own legal theory, focusing on how Hart decoupled the link between law and sovereignty. In turn, I consider some of the primary features of Hart's own legal theory, including the internal point of view and the distinction between primary and secondary rules. In the third part, I argue that Hart believed law could exist even in the absence of a legal system, allowing for the possibility of a form of legal pluralism. I then further elaborate on this possibility of law without a legal system, emphasizing the importance of the distinction for understanding the dilemmas of the legal subject.

THE PERSISTENCE OF SOVEREIGNTY

Hart's argument in *The Concept of Law* served as a response to early legal positivists and their attempt to ground the concept of law in absolute sovereignty. On such early positivist accounts, law could be created only by the utterances of an unbounded authority. In turn, the very notion that a sovereign could submit to some sort of law of nations or that customary law could coexist within the jurisdiction of the sovereign was nothing short of incoherent. Although many early positivists converged on such a view, they differed in their philosophical justifications. Indeed, two of the most notable early positivists – Thomas Hobbes and John Austin – provided divergent accounts of why the concept of law was inextricably linked to a sovereign authority. And it was Hart's attempt to respond to these two divergent philosophical justifications that ultimately led to his decoupling the philosophical link between the concept of law and the concept of a legal system. In this way, understanding Hart requires that we first explore the theories of both Hobbes and Austin and the origins of their philosophical antipathy for non-state law.

The Concept of Law and Hobbes's Leviathan

Few philosophers have stressed the connection between law and sovereignty more than Thomas Hobbes in *Leviathan*. Hobbes approached the question of law through the prism of political origins, arguing that our political structure is created in response to the hazards of the state of nature. Thus, for Hobbes, the starting point for his legal theory was the state of nature – what he described as "a time of war where every man is enemy to every man"[17] – which Hobbes famously characterized as "nasty, brutish and short."[18]

---

[17] Thomas Hobbes, Leviathan 186 (C.B. MacPherson ed., 1968).
[18] *Id.*

On Hobbes's account, the only way to avoid the devastation of the state of nature is to establish a system of government that could control the natural passions of man. And Hobbes famously believed that the only way to inspire enough fear and awe sufficient to extract society from the state of nature was to establish a single authority to rule over society.[19] Hobbes described this all-encompassing authority as "that great LEVIATHAN" and "by this authority . . . he hath the use of so much power and strength conferred on him that, by terror thereof, he is enabled to form the wills of them all, to peace at home, and mutual aid against their enemies abroad."[20]

For the Leviathan to inspire sufficient fear and awe to bring society out of the state of nature, Hobbes believed his sovereignty needed to be uncompromised. Accordingly, Hobbes argued that the sovereign could be the subject of no entity save god,[21] and could not even be the subject of his own law.[22] Indeed, the sovereign could not submit to the law of another nation; such submission would terminate his status as a sovereign.[23] In this way, Hobbes divided society into rulers and ruled – sovereigns and subjects: "he that carryeth this person is called sovereign, and said to have sovereign power; and every one besides, his subject."[24] And it is the sovereign that serves as the exclusive source of law, using law as a tool to ensure that society does not slip back into a state of nature.[25]

Focusing on law from the perspective of the sovereign, Hobbes rejected the possibility of non-state law. Indeed, the very notion of customary law – that is, customary legal norms experienced by legal subjects – was philosophically incoherent. On Hobbes's account, no other law could exist within the sovereign's jurisdiction because there could be no source of law besides the sovereign: "When long use obtaineth the authority of a law, it is not the length of time that maketh the authority, but the will of the sovereign signified by his silence. . . ."[26] To allow for other sources of law would detract from the sovereign's exclusive authority thereby undermining his ability to deploy law as a tool to impose the fear and awe necessary to maintain social order.

---

[19] *Id.* at 227.

[20] *Id.* at 227–28.

[21] *Id.* at 265 ("[O]therwise than as he himself is the subject of God, and bound thereby to observe the laws of nature").

[22] *Id.* at 313 ("For having power to make and repeal laws, he may, when he pleaseth, free himself from that subjection by repealing those laws that trouble him, and making of new; and consequently he was free before.").

[23] *Id.* at 273.

[24] *Id.* at 228.

[25] *Id.* at 315.

[26] *Id.* at 313.

Accordingly Hobbes could not countenance pockets of law within the sovereign's nation-state – that is, pockets of law below the state.

The Concept of Law and Austinian Commands

The fact that John Austin's theory of sovereignty should be equally as unwilling as Hobbes's to allow for non-state law is, at least at first glance, somewhat surprising. As noted, Hobbes's conception of sovereignty was driven by his dismal characterization of humanity in the state of nature. According to Hobbes, the only way to ensure that people emerged from the nasty and brutish war of all-against all was to establish the all-powerful Leviathan as unlimited sovereign over the nation-state. However, notwithstanding his overall admiration of Hobbes,[27] Austin derided the notion of a state of nature.[28] But Austin's theory still rejected the possibility of non-state law because non-state law failed to satisfy the conditions of legality under Austin's command theory of law.

Austin's legal theory builds on his intuition that laws are a subset of commands. Commands, according to Austin, are "significations of desire,"[29] which are distinguished "by the power and the purpose of the party commanding to inflict an evil or pain in case the desire be disregarded."[30] In this way, Austin envisioned the subjects of commands being duty bound to the person issuing the command.[31] Laws, according to Austin, are simply commands that "oblige *generally* to acts or forebearances of a *class*."[32]

On Austin's account, the fact that laws are a subset of commands meant that laws could only "proceed from *superiors*, and to bind or oblige *inferiors*."[33] That laws can only be issued by superiors flows from Austin's definition of legal superiority: "the term superiority signifies *might*: the power of affecting others with evil or pain, and of forcing them, through fear of that evil, to fashion their conduct as one wishes."[34] Accordingly, Austin presented what he understood as a tautology: laws are commands backed by the threat of sanctions. In turn,

---

[27] JOHN AUSTIN, THE PROVINCE OF JURISPRUDENCE DETERMINED 231 n.22 (Wilfred E. Rumble ed., 1995) (writing of Hobbes "I know of no other writer (excepting our great contemporary Jeremy Bentham) who has uttered so many truths, at once new and important, concerning the necessary structure of supreme political government, and the larger of the necessary distinctions implied by positive law").

[28] *See id.* at 253–81.

[29] *Id.* at 21.

[30] *Id.*

[31] *Id.* at 22.

[32] *Id.* at 25.

[33] *Id.* at 29.

[34] *Id.* at 30.

laws – by definition – can only be issued by entities that have the ability to impose such sanctions – that is, by superiors.[35]

Positing that laws could be issued only by superiors required Austin to define who qualified as a superior. First, for an entity to qualify as a superior, he had to be "*certain* or *determinate*" such that he could formulate the intent required to issue a command.[36] Again, this condition was predicated on Austin's view that laws were a subset of commands; laws had to "flow from a determinate source" because each command, by definition, entails "a wish that another shall do or forebear."[37] And only "a determine source" could formulate an intent to "wish that another shall do or forebear."

Second, to qualify as a superior entailed two other related characteristics: "the *bulk* of the given society are in the *habit* of obedience or submission to a *determinate* or *common* superior" and that superior "is *not* in the habit of obedience to a determinate human superior."[38] This final condition of legality led Austin to divide political society into two distinct groups whose relation to each other could be expressed as "the *relation of sovereign and subject, or the relation of sovereignty and subjection.*"[39]

Given these conditions of legality, Austin's concept of law treated the very notion of customary law as a conceptual impossibility. Proponents of customary law, according to Austin, mistakenly conceived of such customary obligations as legal obligations "*because* the citizens or subjects have observed or kept them."[40] Austin found such arguments deeply misguided; customary obligations are established "by spontaneous adoption of the governed, and not by position or establishment on the part of political superiors."[41] Therefore, because the customary laws were not issued by a political superior, they cannot be considered law.[42] Accordingly, there could be no other forms of law circulating within the province of the nation-state. All such forms of law are promulgated by political inferiors and therefore fail to satisfy Austin's requirements to be considered law.

Similarly, Austin rejected the possibility of international law. To exist as an independent political society, the sovereign "must *not* be habitually obedient to a determinate human superior."[43] If a political society stood as subordinate

---

35 *Id.* at 31.
36 *Id.* at 118.
37 *Id.* at 117, 118.
38 *Id.* at 166.
39 *Id.*
40 *Id.* at 34.
41 *Id.*
42 *Id.* ("[C]ustomary laws, considered as positive law, are not commands. And, consequently, customary laws, considered as positive laws, are not laws or rules properly so called.").
43 *Id.* at 170.

to another, then it could not claim to have its own sovereign; instead, it was "merely a limb or member of a society political and independent."[44] Instead, Austin understood international law as a form of political morality merely "imposed upon nations of sovereigns by opinions current among nations."[45]

Thus by defining law as a command issued by a determinate political superior, Austin foreclosed the possibility of non-state law. Both international law and customary law represented misnomers to Austin, as each improperly adopted the moniker of law without being issued by a determinate political superior. Like Hobbes before him, Austin linked his conception of law to his understanding of sovereignty. Without a political sovereign, there could be no law.

SEVERING THE LINK BETWEEN LAW AND SOVEREIGNTY

As exemplified by Hobbes and Austin, legal positivism before Hart was hostile to the possibility of non-state law. Although Hobbes and Austin each began from different premises, both concluded that law could only be issued by the sovereign. Moreover, the sovereign could not be the subject of the law; such a possibility represented a conceptual mistake.

In fact, to claim the status of law within the jurisdiction of a nation-state was to attack the very foundations of that nation-state's authority. For both Hobbes and Austin, the sovereign could exist only to the extent he maintained exclusive authority within his borders. If law existed above the sovereign – in the form of, for example, international law – the sovereign would cease to retain his title, transforming him into a mere limb of the ultimate political superior. Similarly, to claim that law existed below the sovereign – in the form of, for example, customary or associational law – was to claim that such customs or associations were not, in reality, governed by the nation-state and thereby reject the sovereignty of the nation-state.

In this way, sovereignty and law were inextricably intertwined – each necessary conditions for the other. Accordingly, competing claims to the status of law constituted more than philosophical triflings. Such claims were outright attacks on state sovereignty – forms of political treason – because to claim law existed outside the state was to relocate sovereignty outside the state as well. One could not claim that international law existed above the nation-state without undermining the nation-state's sovereignty – or, to use Austin's phrase, turning the nation-state into the "mere limb" of another sovereign. And one could not claim to be following customary law without identifying a

---

[44] *Id.* at 171.
[45] *Id.* at 123.

competing sovereign, thereby undercutting the authority of the nation-state. By binding law and sovereignty so closely together, Hobbes and Austin turned the philosophical concept of law into a zero-sum game with the stakes no less than claim to ultimate political authority.

Many view Hart's legal theory as continuing in this positivist philosophical tradition by linking the concept of law to the nation-state's legal system. On this account, Hart understood a complex series of secondary rules – most notably, the rule of recognition – as necessary preconditions for the existence of law.[46] And by linking the concept of law to these secondary rules, Hart – for all intents and purposes – adopted a legal theory that understood law "as the law of a centralised polity,"[47] rejecting the possibility of non-state law coexisting alongside the nation-state.[48] In this way, law was simply defined by reference to a legal system with all of its attendant complexities and infrastructure.[49]

Although some of Hart's statements support such a view, much of the text in *The Concept of Law* provides the groundwork for a radically different approach to both legal pluralism and non-state law. Indeed, contrary to some of his critics, Hart predicated his legal theory on a distinction between the concept of law and the concept of a legal system, providing a radical alternative to earlier legal positivists. This distinction emerged from Hart's dual response to earlier positivist theories that mistakenly bound law and sovereignty in one inseparable bundle. By contrast, Hart's legal theory disaggregated the concepts of sovereignty and law, opening up the possibility of law outside the state. To do so, Hart adopted an alternative methodological approach to the questions of law, focusing not on the role of the sovereign in the creation of law, but on the experience of being a legal subject. In so doing, Hart conceived of law as

---

[46] Coleman, *Incorporationism, Conventionality, and the Practical Difference Thesis, supra* note 15, at 118 ("The possibility of their being law and purporting to govern as law, however, depends on a rule of recognition."); *see also id.* at 121 ("The rule of recognition makes law possible.").

[47] Simon Roberts, *After Government?, supra* note 16, at 10.

[48] Nick Barber, *The Rechtsstaat and the Rule of Law, supra* note 16, at 450–51 ("Pluralism presents a model of the legal universe in which legal systems and institutions can conflict and overlap. The classic model of the legal order, advanced by Hart and Kelsen, resembled a pyramid. At the top of the structure was the *Grundnorm*, or rule of recognition, which served to both legally validate and identify the remaining rules of the system. The pluralist view, in contrast, suggests that there can be several legal orders in a given territory, each of which asserts its supremacy over the others.").

[49] GARDNER, LAW AS A LEAP OF FAITH, *supra* note 15, at 179 ("Hart showed that legal norms have no 'essence', nothing that makes them distinctively legal, except that they are norms belonging to one legal system or another."); *see also* Mehrdad Payandeh, *The Concept of International Law, supra* note 9, at 993 ("While his analysis of international law in Chapter X of *The Concept of Law* suggests an independent existence of the two concepts [law and legal system], parts of his general theory of law do not reflect this understanding, but rather imply a more intimate relationship between the two.").

analytically distinct from the nation-state, providing important insight into the relationship between state and non-state law.

Legal Systems and Law's Persistence

Much of Hart's legal theory emerges from a critique of Austin's concept of law and the problematic link between law and sovereignty. In critiquing Austin's definition of law, Hart argued that Austin's theory failed to account for laws that were not simply commands back by threats. Most notably, Hart highlighted how rules that confer power failed to fit Austin's definition of law.[50] As noted, Austin had argued that sovereignty exists when "the *bulk* of the given society are in the *habit* of obedience or submission to a *determinate* of *common* superior."[51] Such circumstances identify the sovereign as the supreme legal authority able to enact and impose law on his legal subjects.

But such a view, Hart noted, failed to explain the persistence of a legal system.[52] Thus, the fact that citizens recognize the existence of rules governing legal succession indicates that legal authority is not simply a function of a widespread habit of obedience within a given society.[53] In Hart's example, the fact that a society may recognize that Rex II has the *right* to rule after his father, Rex I, dies cannot be explained by a definition of sovereignty that predicates the right to rule on a widespread habit of obedience.[54] A political society will typically recognize such a right to succession long before there exists any widespread habit of obedience to the new sovereign. In this way, Hart argued that some elements of law must precede legal authority.

Moreover, not only did Hart contend that law preceded legal authority, but it also persisted after the demise of a particular authority. Examples abound of instances where a law's legitimacy long-survived the life of the sovereign promulgating them. Thus, it seemed implausible to understand law's legitimacy as contingent on the obedience to the sovereign who issued the law.

To explain the continuity of legal systems, Hart sought to replace Austin's vision of habitual obedience to a certain and determined sovereign with a legal system that incorporates a set of not only "primary rules," but also "secondary rules." On Hart's account, primary rules describe a set of laws that require individuals "to do or abstain from certain actions, whether they wish to or not."[55] Secondary rules, on the other hand, "provide that human beings may

---

[50] H.L.A. Hart, The Concept of Law (2d. ed. 1997) (1961) 50–78.
[51] Austin, The Province of Jurisprudence Determined, *supra* note 27, at 166.
[52] Hart, The Concept of Law, *supra* note 50, at 51–66.
[53] *Id.* at 51–61.
[54] *Id.* at 53–54.
[55] *Id.* at 81.

by doing or saying certain things introduce new rules of the primary type, extinguish or modify old ones, or in various ways determine their incidence or control their operations."[56] Put succinctly, "rules of the first type impose duties; rules of the second type confer powers, public or private."[57]

Secondary rules, argued Hart, explained how legal systems persist even as the system's leadership changes. Without secondary rules, a legal system would lack methods to identify the content of its rules, choose to change its rules, and determine when one of its rules had, in fact, been broken.[58] Thus, Hart argued that a legal system required a "rule of recognition," which would provide the method for determining when a rule had become a legal rule of the group.[59] Such a rule would avoid rampant uncertainty regarding what were the mutually shared legal rules within the group.[60] In addition, Hart contended that a legal system required some sort of "rule of change," which provided for adapting the rules to new circumstances so as to ensure that group's legal rules did not become static.[61] And finally, Hart asserted that a legal system required "rules of adjudication," which enabled the group to determine when rules had been broken.[62]

Of these rules, Hart emphasized the centrality of the rule of recognition to the creation of a legal system. It is the rule of recognition, explained Hart, that facilitates discussion within the group regarding what the law is. Thus, "[t]o say that a given rule is valid is to recognize it as passing all the tests provided by the rule of recognition and so as a rule of the system."[63] In this way, the rule of recognition serves as not only the supreme rule of a legal system, but also as a necessary rule for the existence of a legal system. As Hart argued, the rule of recognition "is logically a necessary condition of our ability to speak of the existence of a single legal system" because without a mutually shared rule of recognition "the characteristic unity and continuity of a legal system would have disappeared."[64]

For a legal system to exist, there must be a shared standards regarding what constitutes legality so that both those applying the law and those adhering to the law are participating in a common social practice. Moreover, this rule

---

[56] *Id.*

[57] *Id.*

[58] *Id.* at 92.

[59] *Id.* at 94–95.

[60] *Id.*

[61] *Id.* at 95–96.

[62] *Id.* at 96–97.

[63] *Id.* at 103.

[64] *Id.* at 116.

of recognition must be shared by those applying the law from the internal point of view; it must serve as a "public, common standard of correct judicial decision."[65] If officials fail to share a rule of recognition, a legal system cannot hope to maintain consistency and continuity in its notions of legality as applied in legal proceedings; officials must be able to critique deviations from the standards of legality prescribed by the rule of recognition. Indeed, without such a rule of recognition, a legal system would devolve into chaos, failing to have coordinated standards for the application of the requisite social pressure necessary to maintain a legal system.[66]

For these reasons, Hart articulated two necessary and sufficient conditions for the existence of a legal system. First, "those rules of behaviour which are valid according to the system's ultimate criteria of validity must be generally obeyed."[67] Second, "its rules of recognition specifying the criteria of legal validity and its rule of change and adjudication must be effectively accepted as common public standards of official behaviour by its officials."[68] Where these conditions obtain, a legal system's continuity will not be threatened by transition from one sovereign to another. Instead, adherence to secondary rules that enable a set of officials to identify and interpret the law ensures that legal systems can continue even as the nation-state transitions from one particular sovereign to another.

Law and Legal Pluralism

While Hart's secondary rules explained the continuity often exhibited by legal systems, it has also served as the source of significant critique, especially from legal pluralists. Legal pluralism captures a wide range of anthropological, social science, and legal thinking, capturing "a situation in which two or more laws (or legal systems) coexist in (or are obeyed by) one social field (or a population or an individual)."[69] On this basis, "legal pluralism challenges a perceived monopoly of the state in making and administering law."[70]

According to his critics, Hart's emphasis on secondary rules forecloses the possibility of embracing legal pluralism. Hart is explicit that secondary rules of

---

[65] *Id.*

[66] *Id.*

[67] *Id.*

[68] *Id.*

[69] Ralf Michaels, *Global Legal Pluralism*, 5 ANN. REV. L. & SOC. SCI. 243, 245 (2009). For further discussion regarding the definition of legal pluralism, see Griffiths, *What Is Legal Pluralism*, *supra* note 10; *see also* SALLY FALK MOORE, LAW AS PROCESS: AN ANTHROPOLOGICAL APPROACH (1978).

[70] Michaels, *supra* note 69, at 245.

recognition, change, and adjudication are necessary and sufficient for the existence of a legal system.[71] Such secondary rules largely presuppose the existence of state government with its attendant officials and institutions. For example, Simon Roberts contends that Hart's secondary rules "covertly recall" the "institutional shapes" in "which government and law are cemented securely together."[72] "In this respect," claims Roberts, "any claim that Hart encourages us to think about law as something other than the law of a centralised polity would be misleading."[73] Others have echoed similar sentiments regarding what we might refer to as Hart's statist turn.[74]

There are passages in *The Concept of Law* that justify the criticisms leveled against Hart by legal pluralists. Hart notes that in complex legal systems, it is the officials of the legal system who must accept secondary rules as critical common standards of behavior. This is because in such complex legal systems it is the officials who adopt and adapt legal rules, thereby applying them to particular facts and circumstances. Accordingly, it is official behavior that must live up to the internally held standards embodied in the rules of recognition, change, and adjudication. The average citizen, explains Hart, might be "deplorably sheeplike" in simply following the commands of officials without adopting from an internal point of view the standards of validity within the legal system.[75] Thus for Hart, secondary rules are necessary for the existence of a legal system – but participation of the citizenry in the social practice of legal validity is not. In this way, Hart's conception of a legal system mimics the hard distinction between legal subject and legal sovereigns typical of Hobbes and Austin, once again raising the sovereign nation-state to the pinnacle of the legal system.

If true, then Hart's reformulation of the positivist project might be less ambitious than initially thought. Indeed, some have pursued this line of analysis, describing Hart as having merely "refined earlier notion of law as sovereign command," with state law continuing to serve as the paradigm for analyzing

---

[71] *Id.*

[72] Simon Roberts, *After Government?*, *supra* note 16, at 10.

[73] *Id.*

[74] *See, e.g.*, Lacey, *supra* note 16, at 959 (noting that legal pluralists have "long criticized" Hart for "giving . . . priority or distinctiveness to state law"); William Twining, *General Jurisprudence*, 15 U. Miami Int'l & Comp. L. Rev. 1 (2007) (describing Hart as an example of "[t]he great bulk of mainstream Western legal theory and legal scholarship in the twentieth century[, which] focused on the domestic law of municipal legal systems, sometimes extending to public international law in the narrow sense of law governing relations between states ('The Westphalian Duo')").

[75] Hart, The Concept of Law, *supra* note 50, at 117.

the concept of a legal system.[76] On such an account, Hart's emphasis on secondary rules constituted a missed opportunity to reconceptualize law beyond the state.

But this conclusion underestimates Hart's contribution to ongoing debates regarding legal pluralism. In fact, a close reading of Hart would appear to require a rethinking of his so-called statist turn. Indeed, to appreciate Hart's oft-ignored contribution to the legal pluralism literature requires recalling that his theory not only sought to explain the continuity of law, but also the experience of the legal subject. In meeting this twofold objective, Hart advanced a somewhat de-emphasized distinction between two fundamental but disparate concepts: the concept of law and the concept of a legal system.

For Hart, one of the key features distinguishing laws from mere habits of obedience was the "internal aspect" of such social rules. According to Hart, such an internal point of view is typified by a shared "critical reflective attitude to certain patterns of behaviour as a common standard."[77] This shared view "should display itself in criticism (including self-criticism), demands for conformity, and in acknowledgements that such criticism and demands are justified."[78] Hart noted that in this way his theory shared an important characteristic with Austin's theory: Both "started from the perfectly correct appreciation of the fact that where there is law, there human conduct is made in some sense non-optional or obligatory."[79]

Hart posited this internal point of view as a contrast to an external point of view, where the term legal obligation is entirely predictive; that is, an observer from an external point of view speaks of legal obligations simply in terms of the likelihood that individuals will comply with a stated rule. For Hart, to speak merely from an external point of view missed a core feature of how law functions. In one of his most oft-cited examples, Hart describes this distinction as follows:

---

[76] *See* H. Patrick Glenn, *A Transnational Concept of Law, in* THE OXFORD HANDBOOK OF LEGAL STUDIES 839, 842 (Peter Can & Mark Tushnet eds., 2003) ("In the common law Hart refined earlier notions of law as sovereign command and explained national legal systems as a combination of primary rules of obligation, directed to citizens, and secondary rules of recognition and change (of state primary rules) and adjudication. Hart was sufficiently confident of state law that he could present his analysis as simple description . . . and as general or universal in character.").

[77] HART, THE CONCEPT OF LAW, *supra* note 50, at 57.

[78] *Id.*

[79] *Id.* at 82.

> [The observer's] view will be like the view of one who, having observed the working of a traffic signal in a busy street for some time, limits himself to saying that when the light turns red there is a high probability that the traffic will stop. He treats the light merely as a natural *sign that* people will behave in certain ways.... In so doing he will miss out a whole dimension of the social life of those whom he is watching, since for them, the red light is not merely a sign that others will stop: they look upon it as a *signal for* them to stop, and so a reason for stopping in conformity to rules which make stopping when the light is red a standard of behaviour and an obligation.[80]

Accordingly, Hart's concept of law replaced the Hobbesian or Austinian sovereign with a shared commitment to a social practice, whereby individuals jointly commit to mutually held social rules. On such an account, law cannot simply be understood from an external point of view which defines legal obligation as a prediction of conforming conduct; instead, members of a social group experience law from the internal point of view, where legal obligation captures their experience of obligation to mutually shared rules. And deviation from such rules is understood by members of the social group to be sufficient reason for criticism and sanction.

The importance of this distinction to Hart's own legal theory cannot be overstated. Hart's legal theory conceives of law as a social practice where notions of legal obligation are premise upon "generally accepted" rules that are "supported by social criticism and pressure for conformity."[81] Such rules give rise to obligations "when the general demand for conformity is insistent and the social pressure brought to bear upon those who deviate is great."[82] In turn, Hart understands such obligations to rise to the level of legal obligations where the forms of pressure include the use of physical sanctions: "when physical sanctions are prominent or usual among the forms of pressure, even though these are neither closely defined nor closely administered by officials but are left to the community at large, we shall be inclined to classify the rules as a primitive or rudimentary form of law."[83] And here is the key point: Hart is explicit in his view that secondary rules as applied by legal officials are not necessary for the existence of *law* – even though, as noted above, they are necessary for the existence of a *legal system*.[84]

---

[80] *Id.* at 90.

[81] Hart, The Concept of Law, *supra* note 50, at 57.

[82] *Id.* at 86.

[83] *Id.*

[84] Payandeh rejects this possibility, in part, because Hart describes the introduction of secondary rules as "a step from the pre-legal world into the legal world." Payandeh, *The Concept of International Law, supra* note 9, at 94. But Hart is clear in that same discussion that in the

Of course, Hart's emphasis on the role of physical sanctions as a distinguishing characteristic of law poses a problem. Much of Hart's critique of Austin focused on the error of defining laws as commands backed by threats or sanctions. To do so, argued Hart, conceptualized law as merely a predictive enterprise where the existence of a legal obligation simply constituted a statement predicting that the legal subject, in light of the looming sanctions, was likely to comply. But if Hart himself understood law as intertwined with the existence of physical compulsion, his theory would appear at first glance to be subject to a similar critique.

Hart was keenly aware of this potential pitfall and his response emphasized the internal aspect of law: "The difference may seem slight between the analysis of a statement of obligation as a prediction, or assessment of the chances, of a hostile reaction or deviation, and our own contention that though this statement presupposes a background in which deviations from rules are generally met by hostile reactions, yet its characteristic use is not to predict this but to say that a person's case falls under such a rule."[85] The physical sanctions imposed by a social group for noncompliance do not serve as the source of the legal obligation. They simply indicate the degree of importance attached to the social rules by members of the group. In this way, physical sanctions serve to measure the *degree* to which members of the group experience – from the internal point of view – the importance of compliance with certain mutually shared obligations and the need for social criticism where members of the group fail their obligation to comply.

Here we begin to see how Hart's concept of law builds upon the internal point of view. The concept of law operates on the legal subject. The legal subject experiences, as a member of a social group, obligations. Failure to comply with these obligations is understood by members of the group to be sufficient reason for social criticism and in turn physical sanction. At the core of the concept of law is the experience of being a legal subject; the legal subject both experiences obligation and, as a member of a social group, opens himself up to the possibility of sanctions. Thus, the possibility of sanction is an experience inextricably intertwined with a self-understanding that includes membership in the social group.

---

absence of secondary rules, "the rules by which the group lives will not form *a system*, but will simply be a set of separate standards. . . ." Hart, The Concept of Law, *supra* note 50, at 92 (emphasis added). It seems clear, although not without some ambiguity, that Hart conceives of a social group governed by merely primary rules as having law, but not a legal system. He therefore describes such societies as "pre-legal" in the sense as they do not yet have a *legal system*.

[85] Hart, The Concept of Law, *supra* note 50, at 88.

Highlighting the internal experience of being a legal subject brings the contrast between the concept of law and the concept of a legal system into clearer focus. In Hart's view, the subject of the concept of law is the legal subject while the subject of the concept of a legal system is the legal official. Importantly, the legal subject can experience legal obligations even in the absence of officials who coordinates – through secondary rules – those legal obligations into an actual legal system. Thus one of Hart's key contributions to legal theory is the possibility of being a legal subject – with the potential for enduring physical sanction – in the absence of a system coordinating those obligations.[86]

This gap between law and legal system is most prominent in Hart's discussion of international law. From the outset of his discussion, Hart emphasizes the gap between law and legal system, indicating that international law might fit squarely between the two concepts: "[T]hough it would accord with usage to treat the existence of this characteristic union of [primary and secondary] rules as a sufficient condition for the application of the expression 'legal system,' we have not claimed that the word 'law' must be defined in its terms."[87] From there Hart moves on to reject arguments that refuse to accord international law the status of law on the grounds that it lacks an organized method to impose sanctions: "To argue that international law is not binding because of its lack of organized sanctions is tacitly to accept the analysis of obligation contained in the theory that law is essentially a matter of orders backed by threats."[88] On Hart's account, legal obligation remains viable even in the absence of organized sanctions. This is because law can exist even in the absence of secondary rules; a social group can simply maintain a series of legal obligations without an overarching legal system that coordinates legal validity, change and adjudication.

Hart next critiques those who argue that there can be no international law that is consistent with the sovereignty of nation-states. Such arguments, Hart notes, echo the claims of early positivists – such as Hobbes and Austin – who argued that to be sovereign meant to stand outside the scope of legal obligation; on such accounts, to be a sovereign state would preclude being

---

[86] On this account, it would be a mistake to characterize the rule of recognition as necessary to Hart's concept of law – just to his concept of a legal system. For a contrary claim, see Coleman, *Incorporationism, Conventionality, and the Practical Difference Thesis, supra* note 15, at 118 ("The possibility of their being law and purporting to govern as law, however, depends on a rule of recognition."); *see also Id.* at 121 ("The rule of recognition makes law possible.").

[87] Hart, The Concept of Law, *supra* note 50, at 213.

[88] *Id.* at 217.

subject to international law. Having already criticized both the Hobbesian and Austinian conceptions of sovereignty, Hart reiterates the incoherence of the argument as applied to international law. To predetermine that states cannot be subject to international law ignores the possibility that, as a matter of social fact, there exists a social practice among states to abide by a collection of rules – rules referred to as international law – and that failure to comply opens states to the possibility of criticism. As a matter of fact, Hart notes, "[w]hen the rules [of international law] are disregarded, it is not on the footing that they are not binding; instead efforts are made to conceal the facts."[89] Such behavior indicates the existence of a social practice where the participants, from an internal point of view, understand themselves to be legally obligated to conform to a body of rules described as international law.

Hart's reservations regarding international law stem from the lack of an institutional framework to determine legal validity and impose legal sanctions.[90] Indeed, Hart believed that this lack of framework was most apparent in the lack of a "basic rule providing general rules of validity for the rule of international law."[91] As a result, Hart argued that international law is best understood not as a "system but a set of rules."[92] Hart therefore compared international law to other primitive legal societies, where there exist primary rules without overarching secondary rules.[93]

But international law's status as *law* – as opposed to a *legal system* – was not, on Hart's account, a reason for belittling international law. To the contrary, Hart thought that attacks on the structure of international law as lacking a basic rule missed the possibility of legal obligation existing even in the absence of a legal system. Indeed, "if rules are in fact accepted as standards of conduct, and supported with appropriate forms of social pressure distinctive of obligatory rules, nothing more is required to show that they are binding rules. . . . "[94] Moreover, Hart believed that while international law constituted a set of independent legal obligations, the social practices between states were in the process of evolving whereby international law might soon become a legal system.[95] In this way, international law served as a paradigmatic example of law without a legal system. On Hart's account, the existence of law did

---

[89] *Id.* at 220.
[90] *Id.* at 232–37.
[91] *Id.* at 236.
[92] *Id.*
[93] *Id.* at 232.
[94] *Id.* at 234.
[95] *Id.* at 236–37.

not depend on the state and its institutional infrastructure; it emerged from
the legal subject's experience of shared obligation, criticism and physical
sanctions.

LEGAL SUBJECTS AND LEGAL PLURALISM

This all raises a final and ultimate question: why did Hart – and why should
we – care about the gap between the existence of law and a legal system. Put
differently, is this philosophical distinction merely a matter of semantics or
does it tell us something important about the interaction between state and
non-state law? My own view – which I believe tracks Hart's own intuitions – is
the latter. While Hart intended his legal theory to serve as a merely descriptive
project,[96] his concept of law provides a philosophical diagnosis that can enable
the nation-state to better address the challenges of non-state law. To understand
why requires appreciating how Hart's conceptual shift – focusing the concept
of law away from the legal sovereign and toward the legal subject – inverted
the way legal positivists related to the concept of non-state law.

First, Hart's embrace of law without the nation-state opens the door for legal
pluralism, recognizing the vulnerability inherent in the experience of the legal
subject. And once the nation-state recognizes this vulnerability, the obvious
failings of legislative initiatives – like the anti-Sharia initiatives in the United
States – come into sharper focus. Second, Hart's distinction also provides a
framework to appreciate the depth of conflicts between state and non-state
law – or, to use Hart's terms, between law and legal system. While conflicts
between legal systems entail tensions between symmetrical entities, conflicts
between law and legal system place law in a far more vulnerable position,
lacking the secondary rules that allow for coordination of efforts within a legal
system.

Embracing the Legal Subject and the Possibility of Legal Pluralism

As previously noted, Hart's discussion of customary and international law
emphasizes that such bodies of rules can, in fact, be considered law. In making
these claims, Hart adopted the perspective of the legal subject, highlighting
the internal point of view as experienced by members of the relevant legal
community. In this way, Hart's concept of law is premised on the vulnerability
of the legal subject to the distinctive forms of social pressure that typify uniquely

---

[96] *Id.* at 239–40 ("My account is descriptive in that it is morally neutral and has no justificatory
aims: it does not seek to justify or commend on moral or other grounds the forms and structures
which appear in my general account of law.").

legal obligations: "when physical sanctions are prominent or usual among the forms of pressure . . . we shall be inclined to classify the rules as primitive or rudimentary forms of law."[97] Indeed, in his discussion of the minimal content of natural law, Hart emphasizes the importance of human vulnerability and the fact of limited resources as underlying the human need for social practices such as law and morality.[98] Law exists where individuals experience an internal sense of obligation to comply with the rules of a social practice; moreover, they experience such obligations under conditions where the failure to comply with such rules is met not simply with criticism, but with physical sanctions. This twofold combination – the internal experience of obligation and the threat of physical sanction – highlights law's firm grasp on the individual legal subject.

Importantly for Hart, this sense of vulnerability and obligation can exist in the absence of an all-powerful sovereign. Thus, Hart's concept of law opens the door for a brand of legal pluralism where multiple social practices of law coexist in the same geographic area. As examples, religious law, customary law and international law all, on Hart's account, can exist simultaneously alongside the law of the nation-state. So long as the legal subject has an internal experience of pressure to conform to shared rules, then the legal subject can be said to be experiencing law.

Hart, of course, understood his legal theory as descriptive,[99] and therefore did not explicitly embrace a set of normative consequences. However, recognizing that the legal subject's experience stands at the heart of legality can still serve as first step in considering how the nation-state should treat various forms of non-state law. Indeed, on such an account, to identify various forms of non-state law – such as religious or customary law – is to identify instances where individual citizens face significant social pressure, criticism, and sanction for noncompliance with shared rules. In turn, members of communities with non-state law will often aim to organize their lives in such ways as to ensure compliance with these shared rules.

Inevitably, these various forms of non-state law will find their way into the courts of the nation-state. This may be because these shared rules will be incorporated into contracts between members – a party might contract, for example, to abide by certain shared rules regarding the financial obligations of marriage.[100] Parties might also incorporate this shared body of law into arbitration agreements, empowering a set of communal authorities to resolve

<hr>

[97] *Id.* at 86.
[98] *Id.* at 194–95, 196–97.
[99] *See supra* note 96.
[100] For examples of religious contracts, see Michael A. Helfand, *Litigating Religion*, 93 B.U. L. Rev. 493, 513–17 (2013).

their dispute in accordance with the shared body of law.[101] Or the conduct required by a particular body of non-state law might conflict with the legal requirements imposed by the nation-state.[102] In all such instances, the nation-state will have to determine how much space to create for non-state law within the law of the nation-state, employing a variety of techniques for resolving these tensions.

But when addressing such tensions, Hart's theory strongly discourages both courts and legislatures from seeing non-state law as somehow threatening the sovereignty of state law. On Hart's account, to recognize the existence of non-state law does not entail recognition of a competing sovereign within the border of the nation-state. It is simply a statement about the experience of the legal subject – and a realization that legal subjects often experience significant doses of social pressure, criticism and sanction to justify consideration within the courts of the nation-state. Thus, to reject non-state law – and banish non-state law from the courthouse – amounts to ignoring the experience of the legal subject on account of nonexistent claims of sovereignty.

This type of wholesale rejection of non-state law is best exemplified by the recent spate of anti-Sharia laws in the United States, which generally prohibit courts from considering religious or foreign law in their decisions.[103] In so doing, these legislative initiatives require courts to remove themselves from cases that touch upon the intersection of state and non-state law, unable to take the legal subject's complex set of commitments both to the nation-state and to his community into account when addressing legal conflicts. This is not to say that courts ought to bend state law to the demands of non-state law. But it would be a terrible mistake for legislatures to prohibit courts from considering non-state law for fear that such consideration undermines the sovereignty of U.S. law.

Indeed, to announce an inflexible rule of rejection prevents the nation-state from accounting for the vulnerable position of the legal subject who

---

[101] For the burgeoning literature on religious arbitration, see Helfand, *supra* note 5; Nicholas Walter, *The Status of Religious Arbitration in the United States and Canada*, 52 SANTA CLARA L. REV. 501 (2012); Farrah Ahmed & Senwung Luk, *How Religious Arbitration Could Enhance Personal Autonomy*, 1 OXFORD J.L. & RELIGION 424 (2012); Amanda M. Baker, *A Higher Authority: Judicial Review of Religious Arbitration*, 37 VERMONT L. REV. 157 (2012).

[102] Examples of such cases abound in debates over whether law should provide religious accommodations to practices that violate state law. Recent examples before the United State Supreme Court include *Employment v. Smith*, 494 U.S. 872 (1990), and *Church of Lukumi Babalu Aye v. City of Hialeah*, 508 U.S. 520 (1993).

[103] *See supra* notes 2–4 and accompanying text.

experiences the internal pull of two legal systems and the attendant criticism and sanctions for noncompliance with their conflicting demands. Where individual legal subjects experience two sets of legal obligations, the possibility for conflict is ever present. And where the potential for conflict exists, so does the possibility that the legal subject will find himself in a position where social criticism and physical sanction is inevitable – he may have to choose which set of legal obligations to comply with at the expense of the other. If the legal subject's experience of vulnerability stands at the heart of what it means to be law, then the nation-state's approach to non-state law should be sufficiently nuanced to consider that experience so as to consider the widest range of options when addressing conflicts between state and non-state law. At a minimum, phantom worries about sovereignty should not foreclose courts from accounting for the complex experience of the legal subject. By decoupling the link between law and sovereignty, Hart's theory reminds us that courts can consider non-state law by simply taking the experience of the legal subject seriously; judicial consideration of non-state law need not be seen as threatening the sovereignty of the nation-state.

Responding to Conflicts Between Law and Legal System

Hart's concept of law provides insight into the experience of the legal subject by decoupling the link between law and sovereignty. In so doing, his theory refuses to see judicial consideration of non-state law as a threat to the law of the nation-state. But his distinction between law and legal system also raises the stakes of the potential conflict experienced by a legal subject. By distinguishing between law and legal system, Hart draws attention to the unique precariousness of being a legal subject without a legal system.

At the core of Hart's concept of law is the severing of the link between law and sovereignty. As a result, law can exist in the absence of a sovereign. Having severed this link, Hart conceives of law as logically prior to and distinct from a legal system. Where law exists in the absence of a legal system, legal subjects experience the internal aspect of law and are vulnerable to social criticism and physical sanctions imposed by the group. But what makes the experience of the legal subject so precarious is that he experiences the internal aspect of law without the coordinating framework of a legal system. Thus, the possibility of critique and sanction occur in an environment typified by Hart's three worries about primitive law: uncertainty, static-ness, and inefficiency. Living under law – but not a legal system – requires the legal subject to contend with uncertainty regarding the content of his obligations, the absence of mechanisms to prevent the law from remaining static, and the inefficient use of social criticism to ensure conformity with social rules. And the legal subject must contend with criticism and sanction without some overarching method – typically embodied in secondary rules – to coordinate these obligations.

This challenge becomes only more fraught when we consider the possibility that such "primitive" forms of law can conflict with a robust legal system. On the standard legal pluralist account, legal systems conflict, but there remains the possibility of coordination – most likely, among officials – to address such conflicts. However, navigating conflicts between law and legal system is significantly more fraught for the legal subject *because* law exists in the absence of secondary rules.

Consider an individual who experiences legal obligations both as a citizen of a nation-state and a member of a religious community. Where the two come into conflict, the legal subject has little hope for a coordinated effort on the part religious law to modify its rules or alter its imposition of physical sanctions. The religious law might lack the body of secondary rules whereby religious officials might engage the host legal system in a process of coordination in order to enable the legal subject to comply with conflicting legal obligations. This lack of a legal system coordinating the religious law thereby handcuffs the legal subject in his attempt to comply with two sets of legal obligations.

In sum, it is Hart's identification of law without a legal system that helps us identify the depth of the challenges faced by the legal subject in a world of legal pluralism. It is precisely because such law can exist without the coordination of secondary rules that the legal subject faces immense challenges in navigating conflicts between non-state law and the state's legal system. Law, in the absence of a legal system, is uncertain, static, and inefficient, leaving it with limited resources to coordinate conflicts with a competing legal system. And it is the legal subject – who experiences legal obligations from both law and legal system – that is left in the unenviable position of facing such conflicts. It is this precarious experience of the legal subject that those who elide the distinction between law and legal system miss.

CONCLUSION

Hart himself claimed that his theory was merely descriptive. It is therefore an unlikely candidate for providing any programmatic approach to addressing such conflicts between law and legal system. Indeed, it is difficult to imagine much about how Hart would have us resolve such conflicts. That being said, Hart's diagnosis does, at a minimum, provide the philosophical resources to frame contemporary clashes between law and legal system. Most notably, it offers a powerful basis for critique of the contemporary trend among state legislatures in the United States to prohibit courts from considering or referencing religious or international law in their decisions.[104]

First, by decoupling the link between law and sovereignty, Hart's theory avoids the conclusion that mere recognition of another brand of law entails undermining the sovereignty of the nation-state. In this way, Hart's view stands in stark contrast with those of early positivists such as Hobbes and Austin who believed that recognition of other forms of law were incompatible with the sovereignty of the nation-state. Hart's concept of law, however, is not premised upon the authority of the sovereign, but instead the experience of the legal subject. Thus, for Hart, law exists where an individual experiences – from an internal point of view – obligations flowing from membership in a social group. Where failure to comply with such obligations opens the individual to both social criticism and physical sanction, the member of the social group can be said to experience something we call legal obligations.

Importantly, to say that an individual experiences law or legal obligations parallel to the legal obligations imposed by the nation-state is in no way contradictory. Hart's theory allows for the existence of multiples forms of law within the same geographic area – an endorsement of legal pluralism. As a result, for an individual to see himself as subject to multiple sets of legal obligations is merely to say that he participates in multiple social practices each of which comes with the potential for social criticism and sanction. But to recognize religious norms, for example, as imposing legal obligations in no way undermines the sovereignty of the nation-state. To recognize alternative forms of law is merely to recognize social fact and practice. For U.S. state legislatures to pass laws that conceptualize other forms of law as threats to the sovereignty of the United States is to resurrect the positivism of Hobbes and Austin – theories that simply wilt in the face of Hart's criticism.

Second, and relatedly, Hart's concept of law highlights the challenges faced by legal subjects when law and legal system collide. In such instances, individuals can be forced to navigate competing demands of two forms of law – the law of the group and the law of the state; however, navigating conflicts between law and legal system is significantly more fraught for the legal subject *because* law exists in the absence of secondary rules. Thus, in legal communities that lack a legal system, legal subjects must often address conflicts in the absence of secondary rules that help coordinate legal obligations. Without rules of recognition, change, and adjudication, law struggles to adapt, leaving legal subjects in a particularly precarious position when trying to resolve tensions between state and non-state law.

---

[104] *See supra* notes 2–6 and accompanying text.

Indeed, this added layer of complexity only further brings into question the tactic of instructing courts to ignore, for example, religious law. The strategy of marginalizing non-state law – and prohibiting such law from entering the court room – represents an attempt to bury social facts as opposed to engage them. For Hart, the existence of law – as opposed to the existence of a legal system – is premised upon the experience of the legal subject. The combination of internally experienced social norms – with the attendant possibility of social criticism and physical sanction – highlights the vulnerability of the legal subject as he hopes to comply with a form of law that, in the absence of secondary rules, is uncertain and static.

To address conflicts between other forms of law and the nation-state's legal system, legal actors will have to coordinate the validity and application of these conflicting legal obligations. Such coordination can evolve only through social dynamics between law and legal system – the interaction of criticism, sanction, and obligation. And the only way to foster the evolution of a new social practice addressing legal conflicts is by recognizing – and not ignoring – the existence of non-state law. Indeed, if Hart's concept of law tells us anything, it is that legal obligations arise from independent social practices that do not cease to exist merely because we close our eyes to them. We must be encouraging courts to think more about how to navigate conflicts instead of simply demanding that courts ignore them.

Index